UNTHINKABLE THOUGHTS

UNTHINKABLE THOUGHTS

ACADEMIC FREEDOM AND THE ONE-STATE MODEL FOR ISRAEL AND PALESTINE

Susan G. Drummond

UBCPress · Vancouver · Toronto

21 20 19 18 17 16 15 14 13 5 4 3 2 1

Printed in Canada on FSC-certified ancient-forest-free paper (100% post-consumer recycled) that is processed chlorine- and acid-free.

Library and Archives Canada Cataloguing in Publication

Drummond, Susan G. (Susan Gay), author
Unthinkable thoughts: academic freedom and the one-state model for Israel and Palestine / Susan G. Drummond.

Includes bibliographical references and index.
Issued in print and electronic formats.
ISBN 978-0-7748-2208-4 (bound). – ISBN 978-0-7748-2209-1 (pbk).
ISBN 978-0-7748-2210-7 (pdf). – ISBN 978-0-7748-2211-4 (epub).

1. Academic freedom – Canada – Case studies. 2. Arab-Israeli conflict – Peace – Case studies. 3. Israel/Palestine: Mapping Models of Statehood and Paths to Peace (2009: York University) – Case studies. I. Title.

LC72.5.C3D78 2013 378.1'2130971 C2013-904109-5
C2013-904110-9

Canadä

UBC Press gratefully acknowledges the financial support for our publishing program of the Government of Canada (through the Canada Book Fund), the Canada Council for the Arts, and the British Columbia Arts Council.

This book has been published with the help of a grant from the Canadian Federation for the Humanities and Social Sciences, through the Awards to Scholarly Publications Program, using funds provided by the Social Sciences and Humanities Research Council of Canada.

UBC Press
The University of British Columbia
2029 West Mall
Vancouver, BC V6T 1Z2
www.ubcpress.ca

For Noah

who, fluently bilingual, fluently binational,
embarks upon adulthood without a slingshot in his hand

For Jacob

who embarks upon childhood
endowed with a family name,
venerated and vulnerable,
that the tendrils and tentacles of history have already embraced

Contents

Preface

Mixed Marriages

As a Montreal anglophone, I went through Quebec's (and Canada's) FLQ crisis being pulled out of my elementary school several times due to bomb threats.[1] Driving in Montreal with my family as part of our regular routine in that period, I stared out the car window as we passed the army personnel carriers and Canadian soldiers in battle gear who were sent to the city as part of the War Measures Act. We drove stoically by, glancing at each other nervously but not speaking about what was going on all around us. I picked up on the hushed but omnipresent anxiety and tension of the adult world that surrounded me. We children were being kept safe in a watchful way that made my parents seem vulnerable. For a brief period of my childhood, at the intuitive and inchoate level at which children pick up on the world around them, I was aware that the safe enclave of my life was not secure.

Such episodes provide a foundation for the oft-repeated claims of critics of the one-state model for Israel/Palestine that there is no example of a successful binational state in the world, Canada being forever, in their estimation, on the verge of a return to this snapshot of my childhood (and my parents') experience.

Many Montreal anglophones – close to 400,000 – felt sufficiently unnerved by the crisis (and by the threatened loss of their place in the changing world of Quebec when the separatist Parti Québécois came to power in 1976) that they fled, creating a massive diaspora across the country and continent. An important part of Montreal's Jewish community – having more historically cultivated grounds for fear of the rise of any form of nationalism – also broke up and departed.

A significant number of anglophone families remained, however, my family included. For the most part, they remained in the safe and homogeneous English enclaves of the West Island, Westmount, Mount Royal, and, in my case, Montreal West. Despite the enduring homogeneity of these communities, they grew to adulthood with me, knowing that to continue to live in Quebec peacefully and fully meant to embrace the French fact willingly and with curiosity. I was one of the first generation of anglophones for whom a compulsory Grade 7 year was spent in a French immersion environment. It was clear to those of us who remained that it was no longer acceptable for a very privileged minority to shop and run workplaces and occupy the city as though the French majority around us were the ones who had to accommodate our linguistic handicaps, rather than the other way around.

I was surprised to read, as an adult, the opening passages of Sherry Simon's book *Translating Montreal: Episodes in the Life of a Divided City* and to find that Simon had had the same experience as I had as a young teenager, no doubt subtly cultivated by the stoic yet reformed ethos of the rump anglophone community that remained behind after the exodus. Both she and I used to hop onto the city bus as young girls, unbeknownst to our respective parents, and head out of the suffocating sameness of our enclaves in order, simply, to walk around in the French milieu of the east end of the city, drinking in both its and our otherness.[2] We were beginning to see and to know who we were more fully – something that was not robustly possible without a very pedestrian intermingling.

I was also a Montreal anglophone living in Quebec during another of Canada's most perilous periods of constitutional and existential uncertainty. I was a law student at McGill University from 1990 to 1995, a period that saw a referendum in which the country was almost hived into two or more parts. Ninety-four percent of the voting population cast votes in that referendum: 50.58 percent of the population voted not to separate from the rest of Canada; 49.42 percent voted in favour of that proposition.

It was not uncommon during the height of those tense weeks during which the country was precariously balancing on a high wire that relationships between anglophones and francophones that were otherwise mundane became circumspect and tense. For three weeks, my brother, who worked at one of Quebec's leading ad agencies, would pass by the staff room and find that conversations with his otherwise amicable French colleagues would cease abruptly or turn to something suspiciously anodyne. Marriages between anglophones and francophones became strained. In my own mixed marriage to my former husband, a Frenchman, I remember a heated argument in the extremely tense days before the poll with one of his friends, another Frenchman (a separatist) who had come to Quebec to serve his compulsory military service in a civilian capacity several years earlier and thereafter acquired citizenship. I railed against his assertion that he was part of the Québécois nation that was to make up the prospective nation-state of Quebec while I never would be, even though my family had lived in Quebec since 1814. While the taste of independence was intoxicating to a significant part of the Québécois, anglophones and allophones were deeply cynical about talk of a new "civic" nationalism. An outsider, taking away Montreal snapshots from these frenzied weeks, would be forgiven for thinking that it characterized perennial and intransigent irreconcilabilities.

Ironically, at this moment of acute national crisis, a group of thinkers (sometimes called "the Canadian school") emerged, many of whom were my teachers and mentors.[3] The focus of their intellectual work was on questions of nationalism, multiculturalism and binationalism, and the means of making a federal, binational model of governance and statehood both viable and just.

As a result of these formative experiences, I acquired a lifetime preoccupation with the concept of *mixité* – of the functions, merits, and limitations of intermingling and of the contextual and historical factors that facilitate or debilitate it. Having come to intellectual maturity at a time of acute national crisis, I have almost always focused my intellectual curiosity on the *bellum juridicum* of mixed jurisdictions and on the asymmetries of power embedded within *mixités.*

In retrospect, it seems natural that this intellectual preoccupation became the focus of my scholarly research, from the intermixing of Inuit and common-law criminal law sensibilities in northern Quebec;[4] to the intermingling of Gitano, Catholic, and Spanish family law;[5] and eventually to *mixité* within individual families from different family law systems in the mixed legal tradition of Israel/Palestine.[6] This latter research – which is not the subject of this book – was based on extensive periods of fieldwork in the region.

Divorced till Death Do Us Part

As an ethnographer in Israel/Palestine, I could foresee that my intellectual curiosity with the topic of *mixité* and binationalism would encounter the curiosity of those who questioned me about whether I saw possible ways out of the impasse that was the larger context for the detailed ethnographic interviews that I was conducting. My microproject might have been concerned with small-scale marriages and their petty animosities and pedestrian accommodations, but anybody who has been to Israel/Palestine knows how difficult it is to ignore the omnipresent macrocontext of the political impasse, even when trying resolutely to pretend that it does not impinge on one's thoughts or daily life. The very marriages that I was scrutinizing throughout Israel/Palestine were *intensely* inflected by those larger surrounding forces, their success or failure often locally contingent. Similarly, binationalism as an idea or a practice does not present an isolated and universal good of statehood but one that is context specific for its viability.

In the field, I quickly picked up a sense of how extraordinarily fraught even my curiosity with this topic was. On three separate occasions in the course of conducting the ethnographic component of my research, the topic of a binational state arose with Israeli Jews. When the topic came up among two of these people, one of whom was a colleague at the Faculty of Law of the Hebrew University, they immediately stood up and walked out of the room in the middle of otherwise civil exchanges as though an electrical jolt had just surged through their bodies. Both returned after spending several minutes composing themselves and attempted to explain why the very question was wrong-headed. The third person had asked me for my opinion on the politics in the region at a family Shabbat dinner in an Israeli suburb of Jerusalem. When I indicated that it was hard for me, as a Montreal anglophone, to dismiss *out of hand* a binational model for resolution of the impasse, the third interlocutor (as a child hidden from extermination in wartime Poland) immediately launched into a diatribe on his solution for the impasse: Israeli Jews are good at planting trees; they should establish a forest along the Euphrates and then transfer all of the Palestinians – from Israel, the West Bank, Gaza, and east of the Jordan River – to that forest. "What do you think of *that* solution to the problem?" he asked with aplomb. "I think it's utterly appalling," I replied with reciprocal aplomb. This man later approached me on the balcony shortly after our charged exchange and apologized for his outburst, indicating that his wife would be furious with him if she knew how he had talked to me.

From the field, I am familiar with how anxiety provoking for Jews is the idea that the safe haven of a state in which they form a majority might be imperilled by what appear to be idealistic – if not dangerously utopian – ideas of one-person-one-vote democracy and binational citizenship.

I noted a certain hypocrisy in finding the binational model worthy of contemplation. I myself had been in a mixed marriage in which the dynamics were so intractably hostile that I became intimately familiar with how naive are ideas that all disputes can be resolved with sufficient goodwill and good faith. I was able to extricate myself only by a physical separation that enabled both of us to move on to independent lives, each of which had greater integrity than the mismatched union had any prospect of generating for us together.

But Israel/Palestine does not seem to be fated to have any other than a Catholic indissolubility to it, no matter how much huddling occurs away from the eastern borders and around Tel Aviv, with gazes longingly directed out the window of the Mediterranean at the Western world,[7] and no matter the wall that splits the territorial home. As a result of a physical inability to sunder and separate, Israel/Palestine is caught in a "divorce till death do us part."

This sense of perpetually self-conscious separation is evident from a visit to Israel/Palestine. The curiosity about self and other that prompted a younger Sherry Simon and me separately and routinely to board a bus to the other side of Montreal is not just withered but in many cases has also become structurally all but impossible. On one of my many field trips to Israel/Palestine, I took my current husband and my then twelve-year-old son. Our foreignness to the land allowed us to wander a trajectory that is precluded to its inhabitants.

We spent Christmas in Bethlehem with a Christian family who has lived together in the West Bank for close to twenty years. The mother of the family is American and lives in fear that, on one of the trips that she has to make to Jordan every three to six months to renew her visa (the periods change according to Israeli demands), she will be prevented from re-entering and will have to have her children join her without their Palestinian father in the United States.[8] The father, a dedicated agitator for non-violent resolutions to the conflict, has not been permitted for years by Israel to visit Jerusalem, his birthplace, roughly a ten-minute car drive away (were the "security wall" and checkpoints not in place). In this he is like the masses of Palestinians in the West Bank and Gaza who are not permitted to visit the land of their ancestors.

We passed Hanukkah with my husband's family in Tel Aviv. They had not been to the Arab part of the Old City of Jerusalem in years, let alone the West Bank (forget about Gaza altogether), and indeed the option is not available even to Israelis who might feel stirrings of curiosity to intermingle (again) with their counterpart others. Ordinary Israelis are not permitted (by an Israeli military order) to travel to Gaza and area "A" of the West Bank.

On another day of our sojourn, we drove with the minister of the Scottish church, who was able to travel freely in the West Bank because he had diplomatic plates on his car, to the 99 percent Muslim town of Jayous, where he was presenting the mayor with a donation for a town daycare. My Jewish husband was not the only one nervous about his travelling in the West Bank. The image of the slaughter of two Israeli Jewish soldiers who were captured and taken to the police station in Ramallah and then torn apart, the assailants coming to the window to show off their blood-drenched hands, beggars description.[9] As the principal provocateur of our trip to the West Bank, I felt a terrible responsibility for his safety.

When we got to the town, the mayor showed us around. We adults stood on a cliff overlooking the new "security fence" that was being dug into the West Bank and patrolled by Israeli soldiers in jeeps, cutting the town of Jayous off from important parts of its agricultural lands. My son, for whom I had recently bought in Jerusalem's Arab Market a cheap yo-yo that lit up as it descended and mounted, almost immediately found himself surrounded by a swarm of Palestinian boys who, speaking in excited Arabic, wanted to trade their homemade slingshots with Noah for his yo-yo. Although the negotiations were conducted through no shared language, it was clear what was being offered, yet I could not convince my son of the spectacular deal that he was passing up: to leave the land of David and Goliath with a homemade slingshot.

On the short drive back to Tel Aviv that night, Harry asked me to refrain from telling his relatives that he had been in the West Bank, certain that they would not understand and might even find his curiosity a betrayal – perhaps more so mine, for I was a gentile whom they had warmly welcomed into their family.

In this chilly and distant climate of enforced separation, it is hard to begin to conceive of similarities between the cultural and existential meanderings of Montreal's remaining anglophones and the radically distinct groups and spaces of Israel/Palestine. Yet Meron Benvenisti captures a possible response to the settling reality of this uneasy on-the-ground situation that persists despite endless efforts toward a more intentional negotiated peace. As he notes, "the status quo that has emerged, though it appears chaotic, is in practice quite stable and could be characterized as *de facto* binational"[10] – a marriage despite all protestations to the contrary.

I embarked on the conference that constitutes the central event of this monograph, then, knowing how deeply and understandably fraught the topic of a binational state is for Jews and for Jewish Israelis; aware, too, that it is not the preferred outcome for Palestinians who feel their deepest longings for self-determination compromised by the sharing of a land that they feel unjustly turfed off and squeezed out of. I embarked on it also knowing that the Canadian binational model – and its remarkable success despite the cynics who hold the binational model up to an ideal of perfect harmony that can have no place in a world of complex identities – is in many ways hopelessly ill suited to tensions in the Middle East that amplify my childhood experience of national insecurity a thousandfold. Yet I also embarked on an intellectual exploration of the one-state model knowing that, in the event of the utter failure of the two-state solution (a position that appears to be increasingly inevitable), the Canadian model at least speaks, albeit faintly, to other ways of imagining the real.

Acknowledgments

I owe a debt of gratitude to my publisher and editor. Although the content of this book is controversial, UBC Press did not waver in its support for the book.

Research funding for this book was provided by the Social Sciences and Humanities Research Council. That funding is gratefully acknowledged.

UNTHINKABLE THOUGHTS

Introduction

This book is not about the years of fieldwork that I carried out in Israel/Palestine on mixed legal jurisdictions. Perhaps somewhat strangely, given that a good part of the book is taken up with the theme, this is also not a book about the one-state model for Israel/Palestine. This is a book about academic freedom – a doctrine that is less a fixed rule than a historical concept and therefore a labile one that is often hard to grasp without having it tethered to particular circumstances and historical moments. As Alan Chen notes, "academic freedom represents not a doctrine, but a multitude of analytical approaches that vary widely across the spectrum of academic speech ... It is almost as if the only useful enterprise in examining academic freedom is 'description by infinite itemization' rather than generalization."[1] In detailing what happened to one particular scholarly event – the Mapping Models of Statehood in Israel/Palestine conference held at York University in the summer of 2009[2] – this book presents one more crucible in which the refractories of academic freedom are routinely tested. The fraught field of Israel/Palestine – as a geopolitical space and as a terrain of study – has become a rich and recurrent testing ground for contemporary understandings of academic freedom as the endless political intrigues around the subject generate a multitude of concrete departure points for some of the most enduring intellectual tensions in the contemporary academy between orthodoxy and innovation, between knowledge and politics.

The depth of the controversy stirred by the Mapping Models conference was astonishing – and not only to the conference organizers. By the time that the furor reached the federal government, the treatment that this academic event received took many academic and non-academic members of Canadian society aback. At the height of the frenzy (and less than three weeks before the conference, two years in the planning, was to take place), the federal minister responsible for overseeing one of Canada's leading academic funding agencies threatened to withhold federal budget funding for the agency over its decision to fund the conference.[3]

By the time that the government intervened, the Organizing Committee had already been battered by a year of assaults on our scholarly integrity. The first stirrings were more local, with a colleague at Osgoode Hall Law School (where two of the conference organizers are faculty members) questioning our scholarly credentials to hold an academic conference. As this intervenor put it,

> My colleagues, the organizers of the conference, are sound academics of high reputation in their respective areas. However they have no credentials whatsoever to organize a true academic inter-disciplinary conference on Israel-Palestine. Certainly they are entitled to express their views and invite likeminded people to express their views; certainly professors ought to be encouraged to raise their voice in the public interest. And yet a line is to be drawn between public interest and academic activity. The latter requires specialization that the organizers of the conference lack. Certainly, Middle East Studies are remote to their specialization.
>
> I am told that one of the organizers did a study on mixed marriages in the West Bank. This qualifies her to deal with peace in the Middle East exactly in no superior way than my extensive work on the payment system in Sri Lanka qualifies me to organize a conference on the Sinhalese/Tamil conflict there (regardless of the fact that unfortunately nobody is interested in the subject anymore). I would never claim to have such credentials.[4]

The local interventions were not only horizontal; we were also subjected to vertical pressure from the administration of one of the sponsoring universities: York.[5] At one point, the then dean of Osgoode Hall Law School (vice-president academic and provost of York University from July 1, 2009) intervened with suggestions for the conference program.[6] When we insisted that we alone were in charge of the scholarly content of our event and selected our own keynote speaker rather than one vetted by a shadow advisory committee that, unbeknownst to us, was providing feedback on the program to the dean and one of the university's assistant vice-presidents, the dean sent us the following email:

> What your email now indicates is that you are not in fact going to add another speaker but, instead, have decided to elevate one of your existing speakers to be a keynote. This is not what we agreed in my office. More importantly, from my perspective, by using up the additional keynote slot on an existing speaker, you now have made it virtually impossible to attract any additional major scholars to the conference.
>
> Even more troubling is the fact that you have already gone ahead and invited Lustick as a keynote, without any further consultation or discussion with me. So from my perspective this is presented as *fait accompli.*
>
> I would have thought it appropriate and necessary to at least discuss this revised plan with me before acting on it, particularly since it was inconsistent with what we had agreed. So I have to ask, why would you do that, without consulting or discussing it with me? I have to conclude that you don't see meeting with me or discussing these issues in advance as helping you.
>
> ... I remain open to discussing this further with you, and working with you on improving the conference. But you have to want to work with me. That involves more than just meeting or sending emails. It requires actual cooperation on your part, where you want to work with me in a positive and constructive way, seeing me as a collaborator rather than as a threat. Can I also suggest, gently, that you need some help at this stage – and that you would benefit from my involvement?[7]

The belief that our conference-organizing abilities were questionable was echoed by lobby groups ranging from the Jewish Defence League to B'nai Brith to the Canadian Council for Israel and Jewish Advocacy (CIJA). The latter urged its constituents to "make clear to the administration of York and Osgoode that events like [the Mapping Models conference] should not have the sanction of the university." CIJA believed that work like ours "leads to an increased sense of insecurity for those who should feel free to express their support for Israel."[8]

By the time that the Mapping Models conference eventually opened on June 22, 2009, the conference Organizing Committee had acquired an intimate sense of how exceptional the Middle East was as a topic of intellectual scrutiny. Many of the ordinary conventions surrounding academic life were suspended in our case, particularly those that relate to academic freedom. If we were ultimately resistant to the onslaught of efforts to bring us into line with political visions that were not our own, this was not a straightforward endeavour. As this monograph lays out, the ways in which pressure was brought to bear were subtle as often as they were coercive.

The topic of Israel/Palestine happens to be not only a contemporary but also a challenging topic with which to test whether and/or how academic freedom is resistant to pressure – or not. In the first instance, the conflict in the Middle East is notoriously complex, intractable, and uncontained by the geographic territory of the region. It bleeds into the domestic spaces of many nations around the world and thereby touches many local lives in ways that are potentially incendiary. The roots of the conflict also inflect many of our core understandings of democracy and human rights that derive their contemporary resonance from abysmal histories of anti-Semitism, racism, and Islamophobia – radioactive phenomena that are still present on the current landscape. Our most intimate understandings of oppression, recognition, and security reverberate to the tuning fork of the Middle East. For many of us, Israel/Palestine can cut close to the bone even while it is geographically remote. Furthermore, its contentious history is still being made.

As a result of this proximity to a time and place that spawns ideas in the contemporary moment, it can be hard to see how the treatment of those ideas impinges on cognate values of a democratic society such as academic freedom. It is easy now to see that a fear of communism warped what was thought to be reasonable in the academy, or that religious biases in the early twentieth century inappropriately skewed what was thought to be appropriate scholarly conduct, or that the losing side of the civil rights movement attempted to distort values central to the academic mission. We have enough distance from an itemization of the past's travails that the certitudes about the doctrine of academic freedom that emerged therefrom seem almost like ahistorical truths. On these topics, we are all now indignant. It is much harder to disengage from something as close and vexed and complex as the Middle East as a topic of scholarly scrutiny. The contemporary conundrum – now sophisticated by virtue of prior lapses, commonly accepted as such, in academic freedom – has generated all manner of exceptions to and special pleadings for that common sense.

A clear example, to us on the Organizing Committee, of the exceptional way that scholarship on the Middle East is treated arrived early in our planning for the event. At a meeting to which the dean called the two Osgoode faculty members, he asked us to remove the Palestinian citizen of Israel, a doctoral student at Osgoode, from our conference Organizing Committee. This was one of the more shocking interventions in the organization of the conference. Two years after that event, I was carrying out fact checking for this book and provided Provost Monahan with an opportunity to clarify this intervention. He did not distance himself from the suggestion that we remove Mazen Masri from the Organizing Committee; rather, he provided a defence for it, one generated not in the crucible of spontaneous decision making but in the calm afforded by two years of reflection on the events. He justified the request for removal by remarking that, at the time that he had made the request, he had been "surprised to learn ... that the organizing committee included Mazen Masri, a graduate student who had played a prominent and public role in various organizations that are politically active in relation to the politics of the Middle East." To his mind, it was evident that Masri's "participation would likely lead to criticism of the event on the grounds that it was a political rather than an academic exercise."[9]

The former dean is unabashed in declaring that it was Masri's extramural political involvement that provoked him to propose a curtailment of Masri's scholarly work. This might still strike readers (as it struck the former dean) as a legitimate defence – rather than an embarrassment – and, to the extent that it does, this illustrates precisely how the background thrust of the current political climate goes without saying in providing the status quo with the imprimatur of reality. It is hard to imagine, now, a university administrator suggesting that a student involved in the civil rights movement, or with pacifist leanings, or active in socialist politics, or active on campus in the boycott movement against South African apartheid be removed from an academic event because his or her presence might "jeopardize the willingness of some scholars to participate" in it. Indeed, it is hard to imagine a dean proposing the removal of a Zionist student from some scholarly endeavour on the basis that his or her "participation ... could undermine the goal of creating a robust scholarly dialogue,"[10] and it is certainly hard to imagine that such a request would be met with silent indifference from organized Jewish groups. That it is only certain political positions that are problematic – and, more to the point, that the former dean is not particularly circumspect about stating this – illustrate how difficult it is to rise above our contemporary horizons.

It is tempting to reach for Archimedean points in the face of the hall of mirrors that the present moment presents in order to ascertain that by which academic freedom is constituted in and of itself, tempting also to affirm that academic freedom and the academic mission comprise an abstract concept that always has the same content and configuration that can be understood apart from particular instances in which its parameters come into play. In response to the perception that academic freedom is a perpetually slippery dialectical concept, honed by an ongoing historical dialogue between the academy and its surrounding society, it is tempting to devise ahistorical criteria for the nature of academic discourse. Proper academic endeavour might get characterized, for example, by civility, by respectful exchange, by neutrality and dispassion, and by balance; scholarship might be construed as distinct from politics, based on clear principles of expertise, and disciplined uniquely by the intellectual fields that constitute the academy. Academic freedom, it might appear, protects these eternal hallmarks of the scholarly form of life.

For this understanding of academic freedom, it is not necessary to examine how these characteristics come into play and are used, and thereby given meaning, in particular circumstances. Accordingly, it seems possible to write a book about how academic freedom fared with respect to a particular event – a conference – without referencing the content of that event. Academic freedom looked the same in McCarthy-era America as it does in twenty-first-century Toronto.

This book does not begin from the premise that academic freedom can be understood abstractly. It begins from the assumption that the multifarious interests that interact with, and within, the academy can be wily and cunning and that society intersects with the university in increasingly sophisticated ways, and vice versa. The core doctrine that shores up the practices of the academy – academic freedom – is fragile as a result and kept on its toes by a subtle attunement to contemporary challenges. Among those challenges – as this monograph seeks to lay out – are the very concepts of civility, respectful exchange, balance, apolitical scholarship, discipline, and expertise. It is a further assumption of this work that grasping those challenges is virtually impossible without instantiations of how they come into play.

Part 1 of this book lays out an unintended ethnography that emerges out of the events surrounding the Mapping Models conference. It begins with a chronology as told through the developments that transpired outside academia in relation to the conference (Chapter 1). The sources of pressure external to the university include groups within the organized Jewish community, from the Jewish Defence League to what was then called the

Canadian Council for Israel and Jewish Advocacy.[11] They also include the Government of Canada through a Conservative member of Parliament, Gary Goodyear. And they include the Social Sciences and Humanities Research Council (SSHRC). I begin the book with a narrative that traces the ways in which these external sources interacted with an academic event and institution in order to provide the reader with a historical pivot around which the rest of the work can turn. A good deal of this material is already on the public record because a good deal of it was covered in the media, both in Canada and in Israel. And there have now been two reports that cover these events, the Iacobucci Report, which York University commissioned,[12] and a report for the Canadian Association of University Teachers (CAUT), carried out by Professor Jon Thompson.[13]

In order to make sense of why the Mapping Models conference was so fraught in the view of those outside academia, the second chapter of Part 1 is devoted to laying out the central theme of the Mapping Models conference that apparently made the event so extraordinarily fraught – the one-state model for Israel/Palestine. Although other critiques were levelled against the conference, the fact that it was open to an examination of this charged idea was the original, paramount, and persistent feature that made it so contentious to a faction of Canadian society. Whether or not the idea merits the intrigue generated by being a forbidden one, the one-state model was perceived by many to be an unthinkable thought. Understanding the significance of the idea, then, becomes critical to understanding how seemingly innocuous and abstract concepts such as civility, respectful exchange, balance, apolitical scholarship, discipline, and expertise can become fairly deft political tools in the service of a distinct agenda – and not in the service of scholarly goals. It is hardly possible to understand the ways that academic freedom is provoked without understanding the specifics of difficult ideas. Academic freedom, and its challenges, are best understood when the doctrine is situated. The context external to the university constitutes Part 1 of this unintended ethnography.

Part 2 of the unintended ethnography concentrates on the context closer to the home university that housed the conference – York University. Chapter 3 provides a bridge between the thematic content of the Mapping Models conference (statehood in Israel/Palestine) and the ways that on-the-ground tensions (acute both in Israel and in Canada) associated with the one-state model impinged internally on a foundational doctrine of the university – academic freedom. The chapter lays out the links between a foreign conflict and Canada's foreign policy on that conflict and how domestic foreign policy was marshalled to guide efforts to line up domestic thought, including academic thought. These materials bring the conflict home.

In Chapter 4, I return to the same historical chronology laid out in Chapter 1, the same sequence of beginning, middle, and end. But this time around I cover the events that were happening inside the university as those external pressures were unfolding and intensifying around us. The movement from domestic lobbying within Canada on a foreign conflict to the foreign conflict itself – the trajectories of Chapters 1 and 2 – moves in the opposite direction in the two chapters that constitute Part 2 of the book: from domestic foreign policy associated with paradigmatically public figures (Chapter 3) to the more local public figures associated with university administration and the more personal communications engaged at that level (Chapter 4). External and internal pressures, then, bracket the thematic content of the conference that gave rise to the conflict arising on Canadian academic soil in late June of 2009.

Most of the materials presented in Chapter 4 are somewhat personal; they derive from emails sent and received, not only between university donors and government funding agencies, but also between university administrators and me. Although some of these emails issued directly from my inbox, many more were tracked down through a request under Ontario's Freedom of Information and Protection of Privacy Act, R.S.O. 1990, c. F.31. This piece of legislation enables members of the public to hold university administrators to account by ensuring that their written communications are available for public scrutiny. The documents released pursuant to a request under the law are also drawn upon to corroborate the history laid out in Chapter 1.

Chapter 4 – a more or less chronological narrative composed of the voices of those involved in, or reactive to, the conference – is more strictly ethnographic, as is Chapter 1, which also reverberates with the voices of local actors. Using the intimacy of those voices, both chronicle particular *overlapping* fields. Although they generate some low-to-the-ground analysis (especially conjoined with the historical work and political analysis of Chapters 2 and 3), they more critically provide multitudinous instantiations of the subtle and overt coercions to which research agendas are subjected in twenty-first-century Canada. Chapter 4 constitutes an itemization of the fate of academic freedom in particular contexts and vis-à-vis particular issues without which it is difficult to apprehend what is at stake in its compromise.

These materials present data that have personal valence. This account of what happened to the Mapping Models conference is an insider's account from one of the conference organizers at the centre of a good deal of the data. Although this might be an unusually intimate and perspectival presentation of materials, the events surrounding the Mapping Models conference have generated their own Rashomon of tales. Just as the Iacobucci Report, in coming to its conclusions, digested a slice of the events surrounding the conference (principally those that relate to our responsibilities as academics) and digested an earlier manuscript draft of this account that I submitted to the Iacobucci Review, this book digests the Iacobucci Review and Report and absorbs their meaning and import. It also absorbs the findings of Thompson's *No Debate,* which focused on the responsibilities of university administrators and scholarly funding agencies and in its turn (before my final absorption of all prior consumptions in this book) digested the Iacobucci Report. These reports are folded into the part of the manuscript devoted to making sense of what transpired. And this first level of analysis that absorbs the reports constitutes the initial chapter (5) of the third part of the book, which is dedicated to making sense of the data. This also involves making sense of the nature of this kind of research project that deals with a referential world composed not only of social phenomena but also of individual, identifiable, responsive, and accountable participants.

I have followed the ethnographic work of the first two parts of the book with a set of materials dealing with methodological, epistemological, and ethical concerns that come out of this kind of work. The question about how I came to know what I came to know, and what the nature of that knowledge was, emerged as a theme in the process of fact checking and clarification. The same facts can give rise to different, sometimes contending, interpretations of the significance of events – and even the facts themselves can be contested. The epistemological issues of accounting for the events of the Mapping Models conference find an easy counterpart in the contending histories of and perspectives on the Middle East. It seemed auspicious to focus on what it means to have multiple accounts of an event and what it means to provide an accurate or true account. It is not difficult to see that ascertaining "the truth" in the kind of account constituted by this book is a matter of central importance. And Chapter 5 is preoccupied with how my particular account of local events, as well as accounts of the larger world, reckon convincingly with the referential world.

The troubling of the relationship between narrative truth and historical truth gives rise to the final chapter of this book, Chapter 6, a more sustained dissection of the doctrine of academic freedom. It is here that the question that courses through the work about how to discern the worthiness of ideas is addressed. The concept of expertise – used (and misused) in ascertaining what makes ideas worthy of serious thought – is examined. Here is where questions about what restrains the work of academics are answered, where the very purpose and features of the doctrine of academic freedom are addressed. I also venture a response to the common critique that followed on the heels of the complaint that we were examining the one-state model – namely, that we engaged activists and polemicists rather than scholars to carry out the intellectual work. Chapter 6 examines what it means for academic work to be engaged and the implications of an apparent intermingling of goals – knowledge and political outcomes.

In this unintentional ethnography (for I did not set out to examine the field of academia when I began to organize the Mapping Models conference), important voices are squeezed to the margins because this is a sole-authored work. The conference Organizing Committee was composed of four members whose scholarship, both before and during the conference, left a mark on the event.

I embarked on my intellectual journey that took me to Israel/Palestine in 2000 as I was studying the literature in preparation for a major grant application. With Professor Sharry Aiken, a law professor at Queen's University working on international human rights, I formed a reading group at Osgoode composed of faculty members and graduate students on the topic of Israel/Palestine. Professor Aiken's specific research interests are in refugee law as well as citizenship rights in ethnically divided societies. Part of this research involved a series of ethnographic trips to Israel in which Professor Aiken conducted interviews with a broad cross-section of Israeli intellectuals and activists. A Canadian Jew, she has spent most of her adult life preoccupied with issues relating to minority rights and concepts of security. Despite the above assertion by a colleague that "nobody is interested in the subject [of Sri Lanka] anymore," Professor Aiken has been intensively involved in the Sinhalese/Tamil conflict, both as an activist and as a scholar.[14]

The intellectual community of the first reading group was enhanced the following academic year by a second reading group focused on Islamic and Talmudic law, in particular in the domain of the family. This group drew more widely from the York community of faculty members and young scholars. That year I was also awarded a significant research grant to carry out extensive ethnographic research in the Middle East with a focus on mixed marriages in the mixed legal jurisdiction of Israel/Palestine. In the course of this research, I embarked on seven separate ethnographic expeditions to the region, starting in the extremely tense period of 2001 and ending in 2006 as the Second Lebanon War (known in Lebanon as the July War) exploded around me.

In view of my intellectual formation during Canada's near loss of its own binational heritage, I naturally gravitated to questions relating to similar possibilities and limitations within the context of other mixed jurisdictions such as Israel/Palestine. As it happens, in the past ten years or so, this coincides with a growing intellectual curiosity (one that has been present in some form even before the creation of the state of Israel) among Western, Israeli, and Palestinian scholars about whether a single binational democratic state for all of Israel/Palestine might best embody the human rights ideals and the concepts of citizenship and democracy deeply entrenched in Western self-conceptions of the West's greatest virtues.[15]

In the fall of 2007, I initiated a final reading group on these topics with an Osgoode colleague, Professor Bruce Ryder, together with three graduate students, each with research interests in Israel/Palestine and each completing graduate theses on topics directly related to the question of legitimate statehood. Mazen Masri, a doctoral student at Osgoode, was one of these three students.

Masri, eventually one of the members of the four-party Organizing Committee for the Mapping Models conference, is a Palestinian citizen of Israel who has been extensively involved with political issues in Israel/Palestine. As a Palestinian citizen of Israel, he has been living with the impasse in the Middle East since his birth and has been preoccupied with the political challenges that face his homeland for his entire life.

After graduating from Hebrew University Law School with an LLB and then from the University of Toronto Law School with an LLM, Masri went on to become a legal adviser for the Negotiations Affairs Department of the Palestine Liberation Organization. During his work as a legal adviser, Masri dealt with a wide range of issues pertaining to the peace process. Although he was mainly in charge of doing research on and developing negotiations strategy for the Palestinian refugee problem, he was involved in doing research and developing positions regarding other outstanding permanent status negotiations files such as settlements and the status of Jerusalem. His doctoral research is on human rights and citizenship within Israel. As an Israeli citizen, Masri is fluent in both Arabic and Hebrew.

This latter point about language fluency is worth emphasizing given that one of the conference critics (a colleague from York University's Centre for

Jewish Studies) who challenged our credentials to hold a conference on Israel/Palestine stated in an email sent to the Osgoode listserv that "I think a person who wants to organize a conference about Israel/Palestine, or a person who wants to express a view about whether an Israel/Palestine conference was really academic, should have training in the Middle East and should read Arabic and Hebrew."[16] Most Jewish Israelis, indeed most Jewish Israeli scholars, are in fact not fluent in Arabic. If they speak a second language, it tends to be English or some other European language. Most Palestinian Israelis, on the other hand, because of compulsory Hebrew language education in conjunction with their mother tongues, are completely bilingual. Adding irony to the critique, it was "suggested" by York's administration that we remove the Palestinian Israeli member from our conference Organizing Committee, but doing so would have greatly reduced our ability to access both Hebrew and Arabic literature and scholars.

Professor Ryder, the fourth member of the Organizing Committee, is a constitutional scholar who has extensive expertise in examining issues arising from his studies in civil and political human rights, Aboriginal rights, federalism, and comparative constitutional law. From this comparative constitutional background, it was natural for Professor Ryder to engage with the range of constitutional models that might provide a just and viable solution to the Israeli/Palestinian impasse.

Out of this final reading group, as we explored the emerging academic literature on models of statehood for Israel/Palestine, came the idea of holding an academic conference on a topic that was beginning to attract much greater scholarly attention. Professor Ryder, Mazen Masri, and I asked Professor Aiken to join us in this enterprise, and from this seed grew the conference Israel/Palestine: Mapping Models of Statehood and Paths to Peace, successfully held on June 22-24, 2009.

Each of the other members of the Organizing Committee approached this conference with a unique understanding of the issues and their complexities. That range provided the often provocative and stimulating planning meetings for the June conference over the preceding year and a half and sustained us through the unsettling and distressing intrigues that arose around it. The other members have their own stories to tell of what the conference meant to them, though our long-standing involvement and friendship with each other suggest that these tales might have many overlaps with my own.

However, this particular narrative (in the preface and introduction and throughout the rest of the book), by its nature, is peculiar to my own personal and intellectual proclivities. Like my colleague, who remains convinced that I have "no credentials whatsoever to organize a true academic interdisciplinary conference on Israel-Palestine," this account (like his) is stamped with the limitations (and egresses) of an individual background.

AN UNINTENDED ETHNOGRAPHY

PART 1

1
Outside Academia

Boycott, Divestment, Sanctions

The scholarly backgrounds of the four conference organizers – comparative law, constitutional law, citizenship and immigration law, human rights law – composed a complement of diverse academic backgrounds that facilitated a complex interdisciplinary approach to the conference themes. The personal backgrounds of the organizers – Montreal anglophone, Scottish Canadian, Jewish Canadian, Palestinian citizen of Israel – also provided rich and informed perspectives on the issues to which the conference gave rise. These four streams of intellectual and personal engagement on themes relating to Israel/Palestine manifest a long-standing commitment to intellectual and moral inquiry in this field.

We began conference planning in the fall of 2007. As soon as the Organizing Committee was formed, we set about pulling together an international Advisory Committee. Constituting this committee was the most laborious task of the first nine months of organizing. Because we did not want a conference that had one constituency speaking to a roomful of the converted, the Organizing Committee was committed, from the outset, to ensuring that all of the relevant constituencies were represented on the Advisory Committee. We wanted to stimulate a debate on the topic of models of statehood in Israel/Palestine. To this end, we were determined to secure an international Advisory Committee that would represent different key perspectives on the themes and solicited participation from Israelis and

Palestinians living in the Middle East and from Jews, Israelis, and Palestinians living in the Diaspora.

We had little difficulty getting Israelis and Palestinians from the region to participate. And we had little difficulty getting advisers from the pool of diasporic Jewish and Palestinian scholars on the Middle East who were living outside Canada. What took nine months of diligent pleading and imploring was getting a single Canadian Jewish scholar on Israel/Palestine to agree to sit on an Advisory Committee for a conference that would raise, *inter alia,* the question of the justice and viability of one-state models. We approached a long list of public intellectuals and well-recognized scholars; we arranged many meetings and conference calls in our efforts to get the local Jewish communities involved – particularly those who might be critical of the one-state model or strongly Zionist. We absorbed many recommendations for modifying our vision statement and preliminary program to make the idea of the conference more palatable to this one – seemingly unreachable – constituency. Those who cited reasons for their reluctance noted that raising the idea of a one-state model for Israel/Palestine, even in the context of a discussion of multiple models of statehood, was politically and emotionally fraught, and they could not participate in an event that raised the viability of the binational model as a legitimate topic of scholarly inquiry.

Those nine months of effort were thought by all of us on the Organizing Committee to be indispensable to our aspiration to have plural voices on the conference themes. We were not prepared to proceed until this foundational requirement was met. By early September 2008, with the addition to the Advisory Committee of Ed Morgan, a University of Toronto law professor and the former national president of the Canadian Jewish Congress, we had finally secured a full complement of outstanding and internationally recognized scholars from all of the relevant constituencies.

When joining the Advisory Committee, Professor Morgan was provided with a copy of the conference vision statement and title and with the names of the other members of the committee. The final composition of the committee was posted on the conference website, and shortly thereafter, at the end of September 2008, we issued a call for papers, consistent with the requirements of our main funding source, the Social Sciences and Humanities Research Council (SSHRC).

The Advisory Committee consisted of an impressive group of twelve leading scholars representing diverse personal, geographical, disciplinary, and intellectual positions on the issues. The names and biographies of eleven of them can be found on the conference website.[1] One member of the committee asked us not to make her identity known because she expected that doing so would hinder her ability to travel to Israel, where she was conducting research.

Beyond the September 2008 call for papers, we targeted invitations to leading scholars whom we thought might represent a range of views. The paper proposals that we received were vetted by both committees on the bases of their academic merits and the academic records of the authors. We issued invitations to contribute an abstract to all scholars who were suggested to us by members of our Advisory Committee and by other colleagues. Specific outreach was undertaken with a number of Jewish community organizations to allay possible anxieties about the conference and solicit suggestions for possible speakers.

Throughout, decisions central to the thematic development of the conference were made after receiving feedback from the international Advisory Committee, including decisions related to the conference vision statement, the call for papers, the acceptance or rejection of abstracts, the conference program, and the annotated bibliography.[2]

These elements comprise some of the standard means by which academic conferences ensure integrity: the scholarly backgrounds and interests of the organizers (from tenured faculty members to graduate students), an Advisory Committee of experts in the field (from different disciplines and not only law) vetting all major decisions, and the broad dissemination of an open call for papers soliciting abstracts. These processes and mechanisms are *maximally* designed to ensure that the academic standards expected of scholarly conferences are met. Not all of these elements are necessary to ensure the academic integrity of scholarly events. Many academic conferences are planned without relying on an Advisory Committee; others do not put out general calls for papers but target particular presenters with special expertise.

Although not all academic conferences have in place all of the features that we put in place to ensure the integrity of our process, all do have in common one necessary element: they are designed and organized by scholars at the university.

The September 2008 call for papers generated immediate pressures on the conference. One of my Osgoode colleagues sent an email to the dean of the law school complaining that the law school and university were sponsoring a conference on the one-state model. The call for papers also apparently generated pressures on our Advisory Committee.

In response to the above email (on which Ed Morgan, one of our Advisory Committee members, had been copied), Morgan weighed in on the original title of the conference – One State or Two? – concerning which he had not voiced objections when he had joined the project a month and a half earlier. It now occurred to him that the words *one state* were a code for something almost as vile as the "'Final Solution.'" By his interpretation, "most of the people who deploy it [the phrase] mean the 'Destroy The Jewish State By Another Means Solution.'"[3]

In light of the concerns raised by Professor Morgan about the conference title, we reconsidered whether our original title best reflected what we were trying to accomplish with the conference: a measured analysis of a range of models of statehood. Furthermore, we were starting to receive some outstanding abstracts that reflected the complexity of the topic of statehood in Israel/Palestine, taking us beyond the one-state/two-state binary. Taking into account all of these considerations, we decided to change the title of the conference to Israel/Palestine: Mapping Models of Statehood and Paths to Peace. When we communicated this modification to Professor Morgan, he gave it his imprimatur.

In meeting with my colleague who had made the original complaint, I both explained the scholarly ambitions of the conference and communicated the change in title. This was the last that we heard from him until after the conference. (After the conference, on the faculty listserv, we heard quite a bit.) Following my 2008 meeting with him, he sent us an email (also copied to the administration) expressing his gratitude that we had attended to the sensitive points that he had raised, including the change in title. As he noted,

> I strongly believe that this name change will only enhance the reach of the program in terms of being a forum for constructive views endeavouring to bring an end to the conflict.
>
> ... I recognize that a name change for a conferene is not an easy task, and yet it is only another indication of your good faith and non-partisan attitude. Indeed, the "one-state" term has acquired a secondary meaning that perhaps was not all that pronounced at the time the program title was originally selected. Surely, a recgonition of changing circumstances is only a good sign for any academic endeavour.
>
> As I orally explained to you, I am satifsfied with what you conveyed to me and remain available for feedback as may be needed; the cause of the conference is certainly my cause.[4]

With the complaints from Ed Morgan and the Osgoode colleague, we inaugurated a program of meeting with those who voiced concerns about the conference in an effort to both alleviate and address their concerns and see whether we could accommodate them.

Also coincident with the call for papers, one early source of pressure from a very distinct faction of the Canadian Jewish community emerged. The president of York University received an email complaint from the Jewish Defence League of Canada (JDL) on October 4, 2008, and this email was forwarded to us. In an alternative iteration of the boycott, divestment, sanctions (BDS) campaign led by Palestinian supporters, the JDL proposed its own BDS movement in response to the call for papers – against York University. The email read as follows:

> It has come to my attention that York University will be hosting a conference in June which will focus on Israel. The official website that promotes the conference states the following, "Israel/Palestine: One State or Two? [the original title of the conference] is co-sponsored by Queen's University and York University, and is an official U50 initiative, part of York University's 50th Anniversary celebrations."
>
> I am writing to inform you that I have received many calls from Jewish Students for York U that have received threats and feel very threatened as a result of anti Jewish/Israel activities on campus. Racism should have no place on campus. And this conference will only serve to encourage a negative perception of Jews.
>
> This conference should not be sponsored by York University. I would welcome a meeting with you to discuss this issue further. A university should be a place to learn about ethics, not the promotion of double standards which results in attacks on Jewish students. The Jewish Defence League of Canada is discussing the possility of leading a campaign against York U, calling for boycott, divestment and sanctions. It is my hope that such a campaign will not be required, but we refuse to stand by and allow Jewish students to feel threatened.
>
> ... Meir Weinstein National Director Jewish Defence League of Canada.[5]

According to a backgrounder by the American Anti-Defamation League, the JDL was founded by Meir Kahane under the stated goal of "protect[ing] Jews from anti-Semitism *by whatever means necessary*" (emphasis added).[6]

The JDL is considered by the FBI to be a "violent extremist Jewish organization."[7] It is an open supporter of the Kahane Chai ("Kahane Lives" or Kach) party, banned in Israel. According to the American Anti-Defamation League, "in Rabbi Kahane's gross distortion of the position of Jews in America, American Jews were living in a fiercely hostile society, facing much the same dangers as the Jews in Nazi Germany."[8]

After a long absence, the JDL resumed its activities in Canada in 2006. The Canadian branch of the JDL was originally founded in 1979 by Meir Halevi, who also goes by the name Meir Weinstein (né Marvin).[9] Weinstein became politicized in his early twenties by the writings of Meir Kahane, the original founder of the JDL in the United States and the Kach party in Israel. The Kahanist ideology is far-right wing, promoting the idea that Arabs remaining in the West Bank and Gaza Strip should be expelled and Israel transformed into a religious state.

Weinstein, who told the *Jewish Press* in 2008 that he "will always be a loyal disciple of Rabbi Kahane,"[10] used to be the spokesperson for the Kach movement in Canada before it became a listed entity under the Anti-Terrorism Act in 2005, one year before the rebirth of the JDL.[11] In Israel, the Kach movement was barred from participating in Israeli elections under the Knesset Elections Law, which bans parties that incite racism. It was banned outright in 1994 when Baruch Goldstein, one of Kahane's followers, gunned down twenty-nine Muslims at prayer in a mosque in Hebron. Weinstein's response to the Hebron massacre was that "Our organization [Kach in Canada] does not condemn the attack. It condemns the Israeli government for not providing adequate protection for settlers."[12]

If JDL Canada has a reputation for violence, its leader, Weinstein, has made comments over the decades while he has led Kach and the JDL that tend to confirm that view. As the leader of the JDL in its first iteration, he admitted in a *Globe and Mail* interview that "we have guns ... and we're learning how to use them ... We go to farms outside Toronto ... We practice in fields."[13] The JDL Canada website continues to offer "Elite Security Training" on a weekly basis.[14] And in a 2010 *Fault Lines* interview with Avi Lewis, Weinstein affirmed that the JDL stood for the principle of helping Jews everywhere through "all necessary means: strength, force, and even violence."[15]

From the moment of its first email complaint to the president of York University, the JDL led almost weekly protests against the conference in front of York University; its interventions, to which I will return, escalated as the conference grew closer.

As part of the community outreach that conference organizers conducted in the fall of 2008, both the Council for Israel and Jewish Advocacy (CIJA) and the Canadian Jewish Congress (CJC) were approached to address concerns and seek input into conference planning. This involved Professor Aiken in several detailed meetings and communications. The Organizing Committee had no intention of meeting with the JDL, particularly in light of the extremity of its positions and tactics, which we thought put the JDL beyond the pale of rational discourse and mainstream lobbying. To our surprise, both the CIJA and the CJC urged conference organizers to meet with the JDL to hear its concerns; indeed, they set up a meeting between the organizers, themselves, and the JDL in the offices of the CJC for that purpose. Despite being taken aback by the invitation to meet with the JDL, Professor Aiken attended the meeting to hear what the three organizations wanted to communicate.

Beyond this outreach to members of the organized Jewish community outside York University, we also inaugurated a series of meetings with concerned university colleagues. This included meetings with the chair of the Centre for Jewish Studies at York University, who had also voiced concerns about the conference, and four of her colleagues. As a result of these meetings, and taking into account our own sense of ways in which to incorporate our growing understanding of the complexity of the issues, we modified our vision statement and website welcome page. In fact, we had already issued invitations to virtually all of the people whom they suggested as speakers, and to the remainder we sent further invitations. We also invited the Centre for Jewish Studies faculty, the chair of which we had been told was agitating actively against the conference, to consider nominating a member to our Advisory Committee.

Before any papers were accepted – and without any forewarning to or conversation with the Organizing or Advisory Committee about his disquiet – Professor Morgan published an article in the *Canadian Jewish News*, later reprinted in the *National Post*,[16] outlining his anxieties about the range of papers that might be submitted. In particular, Morgan suggested that the conference could become a platform for "cynical" and polemical "anti-Israel grandstanding." These publications took us aback. His hesitations were aired in the national media without any forewarning to us. We had accommodated his concern about the original title, the only concern that he had voiced to us. Furthermore, before we began working with the Advisory Committee on the conference, we asked that deliberations remain confidential so that ideas might circulate freely. It was troubling to have this request disregarded. A few days later, despite our entreaties, Professor Morgan decided to withdraw from the Advisory Committee.

It became extraordinarily difficult to get other local Jewish scholars to join the Advisory Committee or participate as presenters after Professor Morgan's very public withdrawal. Somewhat ironically, despite the reluctance of members of the Canadian Jewish community to participate, the strong Jewish Israeli contingent on the Advisory Committee did not waver from its commitment to oversee conference planning.

Beyond the flurry of pressure that arose from Ed Morgan's public denunciation of the conference in the fall of 2008, it was not until the spring of 2009 that the conference came under particularly intense political pressure.

Sadly, in the months leading up to the conference, several confirmed speakers called to inform us, with regret, that they were withdrawing their papers. The Jewish community organizations with which they had otherwise been associated had informed them that they were not to associate themselves in any way with the conference. In one case, this applied to a participant who was no longer in the employ of the organization, but it was believed that he had recently enough been associated with it that his participation could be read as an endorsement on behalf of the organization of the conference's legitimacy.

Despite the damage from Professor Morgan's article, we remained unrelenting in our solicitation of local Jewish scholars, in particular strong Zionist supporters of the dominant two-state model. We kept up a vigorous search, following up on leads for suggested speakers, until the last two weeks before the conference. David Dewitt was among the scholars to whom we turned, particularly for assistance in securing a strong advocate of the two-state model. As the associate vice-president of research and innovation at York University, he had awarded us one of the original funds for the conference based on a proposal that focused exclusively on the one-state model under the title Imagining a Bi-National Constitutional Democracy in Israel/Palestine. We stopped seeking his input and involvement on April 15, 2009, when his advice turned to shrinking the prominence of speakers advocating or deliberating on the one-state model and minimizing the conference as a whole – an intervention to which I will return.

As part of our outreach campaign, through the diligent efforts of Professor Aiken, the internationally recognized York scholar on refugees, Howard Adelman, agreed in the fall of 2008 to present a paper on refugee issues as they related to the conference themes. By the end of March 2009, however,

Professor Adelman had decided that he no longer wanted to participate in the conference. Although he later appeared to revise his negative assessment of the conference,[17] at this juncture in March he withdrew his abstract and, much like Professor Morgan, circulated a letter, apparently quite widely, defending his decision.[18]

The strange *volte-face* was puzzling to the organizers. After all, Professor Adelman had many laudatory things to say about the conference. He noted, for example, that "a clear majority of the scholars are reputable and do excellent work and whether I agree or disagree with them, I respect their work ... Based on the abstracts, the organizers should be congratulated for attracting a large number of first rate scholars." Despite these and other favourable comments, Professor Adelman justified his withdrawal on the basis that "it was the inclusion of five papers of unequivocal Israel bashers in the neocolonialist and apartheid language mode that determined that I should definitely not be there ... I did not want to be soiled with approaches that I believe use academic idioms to blacken a state."[19]

Adelman's statement circulated widely enough that it came to the attention of the then chair of York University's Board of Governors. As the latter noted in an April 12, 2009, email to the president of York, "I got cornered on this issue thurs nite at a seder when someone gave me a copy of a memo prepared by [Howard] Adelman explaining why he withdrew from the conference."[20] At this juncture, the chair of the Board of Governors had a measured reaction to the conflict that had literally been thrust into his lap. He noted that, "When I read the memo the next day, it didn't seem to me be much different than the usual academic infighting that goes on all the time at York and at all universities ... [Unidentified] briefly mentioned this conference to me some weeks ago and he seemed to feel it had an Israeli bashing bias, but didn't seem to feel it warranted a dramatic response by the administration."[21]

Adelman's letter also appeared to have triggered a more general campaign of complaints to the university and the law school. In an April 21, 2009, email accessed under the Ontario Freedom of Information and Protection of Privacy Act (FIPPA), a partner at a prominent Bay Street law firm wrote to the dean and indicated that he "simply cannot understand how York and Osgoode can allow this conference to proceed. Its insidious delegitimation of the idea of a Jewish state should be seen for what it is. I ask that you do all in your power to stop this abhorrent conference from taking place." The author of the email justified his proposal in the following manner:

> What troubles me about this conference is its very premise which is essentially to discuss whether Israel should continue to exist as a Jewish State. By implicitly opening to question whether the Jewish nation-state established with UN Recognition 61 years ago should continue to exist as such, this conference reopens the long-settled question of whether the Jewish people has the right of self determination afforded other peoples under the UN charter and international law. Moreover, there appears to be no recognition whatsoever in the loaded language that describes the theme of the conference that if the two-state solution has indeed "failed," it is demonstrably because of its consistent and repeated rejection by Arabs and other Moslems who simply don't want a non-Moslem state in the neighbourhood. (e.g., the 1947 rejection of the UN resolution dividing the remnants of mandatory Palestine (most of it having been already granted to the Palestinian Arabs by the establishment of Transjordan in 1922), the Khartoum Declaration of the Arab States after Israel's victory in the 1967 six-day war, and the unilateral rejection by the Palestinian Authority of the Clinton Camp David and Taba proposals for a two-state solution, etc.)

Despite his request of the dean that the university prevent the conference from taking place, the author noted that he "personally feel[s] very strongly about free speech." Nevertheless, "the consideration of whether the State of Israel should continue to exist as a Jewish State is simply not a legitimate premise for an academic conference given its discriminatory nature. Discrimination against Jews is commonly referred to as anti-Semitism and that is not a tolerable sentiment in our society."[22]

This email was just one of many that began to arrive in the dean of Osgoode's inbox. Another author, whose email was also accessed through a FIPPA request, indicated that he had contributed to Osgoode in teaching, advisory, and financial terms since he had graduated from Osgoode over thirty-five years earlier, and he noted that he was

> very surprised and dismayed that Osgoode would allow its name and reputation to be associated with a conference of this nature which is clearly discriminatory for the reasons [Adelman] has summarized. It is based on a veiled platform of anti-Semitism that should be apparent to any objective person. As someone who knows the high standards and non-discriminatory principles that you ordinarily are aligned with, I cannot understand how this has evolved under your leadership.[23]

Yet another email sent to the dean of Osgoode asked in its subject line, "is it true that one of the topics for this conference is whether the State of Israel should continue to exist?!?" The email continued thus in its body: "Is the question of the continued existence of israel really one of the topics? If it is, then despite my family's history of graduating from Osgoode and my own years of teaching there, I really just can't continue to support Osgoode financially anymore, as I have to the tune of $3000/year these past 3 years."[24]

The question of whether the state of Israel should continue to exist was never one of the topics of the conference, though in the frenzy of rumour and anxiety that was emerging the truth of the matter seemed to be increasingly irrelevant to those who began voicing alarms and protestations.

The dean responded to the deluge of emails coming into his office. In one dated April 11, 2009, to which he offered a personal response, he strongly encouraged his correspondent to wade more thoughtfully through the frenzied rumours buzzing around the conference:

> [I]n my view the email you received is a totally inaccurate and unfair characterization of this conference. It is not calling for anything, and certainly not the end of Israel as a Jewish state. It is, rather, a serious academic conference that will feature over 40 speakers from around the world, including many from Israeli universities. The purpose of the conference, as is explained on the conference website, is to explore whether there are new solutions that might be explored in the middle east in an attempt to find peaceful solutions to the conflict there. This will involve the exploration of controversial ideas, and I know that the conference has been controversial within some elements of the community here in Toronto. But a serious academic institution has to encourage free inquiry ...
>
> Here is a link to the conference website.
> http://www.yorku.ca/ipconf/.
>
> I encourage you to look at the website and see for yourself the range of opinion that is going to be canvassed at the event.
>
> The fact that it received a grant from an independent committee at the SSHRC is evidence of the scholarly character of the conference. That is why it is mentioned on the conference website. In fact the SSHRC committee, which is made up of scholars from other universities, gave the conference the highest possible ranking as a scholarly conference. I do not know why your correspondent would take that as something to criticize.[25]

Beyond Morgan and Adelman, the first organized public assault on both our conference and academic freedom came from a May 12, 2009, statement issued by CIJA.[26] This statement singled out the fact that the conference would explore, among other issues related to models of statehood, the viability of a one-state, binational solution to the conflict between the Israelis and Palestinians. For the drafters of the statement, the only way to read such an intellectual exploration was that its "imposition ... would spell the end of Israel as a Jewish state." Raising the very question of the viability of a one-state model in an academic setting, particularly one that was part of the jubilee celebrations of the university, was a matter of serious concern to CIJA.

The council went on to question the judgment of the university in hosting such a conference and impugned the conference as lacking in academic integrity and good scholarship. CIJA then urged its constituents to write to York's administration with the following complaints:

- Events like this should not have the sanction of the university.
- These events only serve to further the already degenerating situation at York University surrounding the Israel/Palestinian issue.
- These events lead to an increased sense of insecurity for those who should feel free to express their support for Israel.

In keeping with Adelman's critique of the backgrounds of particular presenters, CIJA objected to the inclusion of "a number of speakers who are recognizable for their roles as organizers and outspoken proponents of 'Israel apartheid week' and the Israel boycott movement." Like Adelman, CIJA recognized that we "procured a few balanced speakers of high repute," but this accomplishment was offset by the inclusion of others with whom CIJA, like Adelman, had philosophical and political disagreements.

Almost immediately after release of the May 12, 2009, CIJA statement, York University began to receive complaints. A mere fifty-three minutes after the statement came out, an email was sent to the president's office threatening to withdraw apparently significant donations to the university:

> I have not had the pleasure of meeting you in person but by way of introduction, my husband ... has been proud to be one of York University's major donors. [He] and I have been following with great dismay the situation at York as it pertains to Jewish students. Frankly we are frightened and appalled by what we have heard. I recently had lunch with a professor Jewish

> Studies at York who told me that she considers her top priority as an educator to be: "protecting her students from violence." This is totally unacceptable as I'm sure you would agree. I have now learned that the university is planning yet another Israel-bashing conference in June entitled: Israel/Palestine: Mapping Models of Statehood and Paths to Peace. It seems obvious that such pseudo-academic conferences whose true and sole purpose is to denigrate and demonize the state of Israel will only add to the atmosphere of fear and academic intimidation that has already been established at York. It saddens me that my husband has donated [$X] to an institution which has so boldly positioned itself as an enemy of tolerance and mutual understanding. As recently as last month [$X]. But such donations will now end until we are convinced that we are indeed supporting a liberal and academically free institution where all students, regardless of faith or heritage, may feel free to express themselves intellectually without fear for their physical safety. I urge you to reconsider the sanctioning of anti-semitic conferences on campus.[27]

The donor must have been an important one to the university. The president and CEO of the York University Foundation offered to help the president with this intervenor in any way. The president himself indicated in a follow-up email of May 12, 2009, to the president of the York University Foundation that he would like the latter to arrange a meeting with this donor, which was done.

In a demonstration of principle and courage in the face of this threat to the financial security of the institution that he governed, the president went on after expressing his wish to meet with the donor to note the following: "That said, you know I am sensitive to the donations issue. If I meet them, I will be very firm on the issue of donations. We will do everything possible to fight anti-smitism as a principle not because of donations. Reference to donations makes a just cause cheaper than necesaary."[28]

Shortly after CIJA issued its statement and the university began to receive the complaints that CIJA had urged, York University's president issued a public statement on May 21, 2009, that underlined the paramount place of academic freedom in the university's mission.[29] Presumably, in the face of York University's stand on both academic freedom and its refusal to intervene to penalize it, the campaign moved on to other venues of pressure, notably the government of Canada and the Social Sciences and Humanities Research Council, which had funded the conference.

Warping SSHRC

An acknowledgment from SSHRC that it subjected the Mapping Models conference to extraordinary procedures as a result of the pressure that it was under from the federal government does not appear to be forthcoming. However, among themselves, SSHRC's senior executive officers appeared to be ready to concede (in records accessed under freedom of information acts) that the manner in which they were treating the conference was "outside the norm."[30]

At least two groups within the Canadian Jewish community, the Jewish Defence League and B'nai Brith, lobbied Minister for Science and Technology Gary Goodyear to review the SSHRC conference grant that had been awarded in January 2009. The minister for science and technology, under the umbrella of the minister for industry, is responsible for the oversight of research-funding agencies such as SSHRC.

The original SSHRC application submitted in the fall of 2008 was subjected to a blind peer-review process consistent with the means by which academic excellence is measured in order to maximally eliminate bias. Our peers at SSHRC ascertained that our application was stellar and justified funding to facilitate the creation of a forum for scholarly debate on an important topic. The conference application scored remarkably high. It was ranked 9th out of 120 conference grant applications adjudicated by a SSHRC committee in the latest round, with a score of 86.833/100 (a full 10 points higher than the average of funded conferences in that round). In the normal course of events at SSHRC, there *is* no process for subjecting grants to a second level of peer review once the first stage has been passed. The post-award process requires that grant holders submit a report after the event is finished outlining how the funds have been spent.[31]

This is the normal process in the relationship between research-funding agencies and grant holders who have passed the peer-review process. However, the pressure on the government by organized pro-Israel groups sought to disrupt the critical arm's-length nature of the relationship between the government and research-funding agencies.

The JDL petition, which requested the immediate withdrawal of Canadian government sponsorship from the conference, garnered roughly 600 signatures. B'nai Brith issued a community alert to its listserv JewishCanada urging constituents to "urge the Minister to direct the SSHRC to immediately withdraw its funding from this sham of a conference." The alert levelled grave and unfounded accusations that the conference would be a "blatant exercise in anti-Zionist propaganda. Its entire thrust calls into question the Jewish State's very right to exist, and promises to be a veritable 'who's who' of anti-Israel propagandists."[32]

To our astonishment, the minister responsible for overseeing SSHRC responded to this pressure. While (perversely) recognizing the fundamental principle that governs the relationship between the government and academia, Minister Goodyear issued a statement on June 5, 2009, that began cynically by noting that "Our government is committed to the principle of academic independence and the independent, arms-length, peer review process for assessing applications for research grants." The rest of the statement went on thus:

> It has come to my attention that following a recommendation of a peer review board earlier this year, the Social Sciences and Humanities Research Council provided $19,750 under its Aid to Research Workshops and Conferences Program to a conference at York University entitled "Israel/Palestine: mapping models of statehood and prospects for peace."
>
> Approval of this funding was based on an initial proposal that did not include detailed information on the speakers at the conference. Since funding was provided, the organizers of the conference have added a number of speakers to their agenda.
>
> Several individuals and organizations have expressed their grave concerns that some of the speakers have, in the past, made comments that have been seen to be anti-Israeli and anti-Semitic. Some have also expressed concerns that the event is no longer an academic research-focussed event.
>
> Therefore, I have spoken to the president of the Social Sciences and Humanities Research Council to bring these concerns to his immediate attention and asked that Council give them full consideration. In particular, I asked that the Council, once they have seen this information, to consider conducting a second peer review of the application to determine whether or not the conference still meets SSHRC's criteria for funding of an academic conference.[33]

We discovered this statement on a website by one of the individuals associated with the JDL who had been actively campaigning against the conference for months. The statement had not been issued publicly through a general press release. We called the Canadian Association of University Teachers (CAUT) to see whether it had heard about the statement, and

CAUT confirmed (by calling Goodyear's office) that Goodyear had indeed issued the statement to select audiences. The *Jewish Tribune,* alerted, picked up the story.

It subsequently came out that the minister had not only breached his self-proclaimed obligation to maintain an arm's-length relationship with a granting council but also, at the same time, threatened federal budget funding for SSHRC over the agency's decision to fund our conference. This revelation was contained in an email, marked "Extremely Urgent," sent by SSHRC's communications manager, Trevor Lynn, to SSHRC president Chad Gaffield that described what he had just been told by Goodyear's chief of staff, Phillip Welford: "He [Welford] said that this is a serious issue and is so serious that it will make it hard for the Minister to recommend increased funding for SSHRC in the next budget."[34]

SSHRC responded to the politicization of independent funding decisions. On June 10, 2009, Craig McNaughton, the director of knowledge mobilization and program integration at SSHRC, contacted Professor Bruce Ryder, the member of the Organizing Committee listed as the applicant on the conference grant, to request that he submit a report identifying any changes in the conference since the time of the application submitted for the November 1, 2008, competition. McNaughton referred Professor Ryder to SSHRC's post-award procedures, in particular the guidelines relating to major and minor changes in conference plans since the original grant was issued.

In the Grant Holder's Guide for the Aid to Research Workshops and Conferences program, SSHRC outlines post-award procedures that grant holders need to follow, particularly in cases in which conference plans have changed since the original application. The guidelines are clear that minor changes such as the replacement of a guest speaker or the addition of a new topic do not require prior SSHRC approval provided that the conference plans remain essentially the same. Approval for major changes, such as changes to the theme or focus of the event, must be requested in writing to SSHRC. If the grant holder is uncertain about whether changes are minor or major, he or she is instructed to consult with a SSHRC program officer.[35]

Nothing in the guidelines addresses a situation in which outsiders have questions about whether the conference plans have undergone major or minor changes. The guidelines indicate that the decision to inquire and report rests with the grant holder, whose independent judgment about whether changes are minor or major and whether to contact a program officer will be respected. Despite this, the funding agency requested an interim report from the grant holder identifying "all" changes in the conference since the time of the original application. The basis for such a request is not apparent in the SSHRC guidelines and is, as far as we know, unprecedented. Given that the request came several days after the minister's statement requesting a second peer review of the conference grant, and given that the conference program and list of speakers (available on the conference website) clearly had not changed in any major respect from the original grant application, the conclusion is inescapable that SSHRC's request was a response to political pressure.

Senior officials at SSHRC were aware that what they were asking us to do in submitting an interim report before completion of the funded event was "outside the norm" of regular procedures at SSHRC. In an email from SSHRC's corporate secretary, Christine Trauttmansdorff, to the vice-president, Gisèle Yasmeen, and the executive vice-president, Carmen Charette, there is an acknowledgment that the response of SSHRC to our situation was extraordinary. As she noted, "In the normal course of things, questions or concerns about projects we fund are directed to the grant holder and the institution and that's the end of it. This case is outside the norm."[36]

As noted, SSHRC requested on June 10, 2009, that the grant holder's report be submitted by the following day, which it was. The dean of Osgoode and York's vice-president of research and innovation, in strongly advocating that we comply with the request for the report, stressed that its submission was only a means of allowing SSHRC to save face by ascertaining that changes had only been minor. They further assured us that we could expect an indication from SSHRC that all was in order by June 12. This did not turn out to be the case. Having received the report, SSHRC submitted it to a review, the process of which was never clarified, despite a letter from two members of the Organizing Committee asking for answers to the following questions:

1 What is the process that SSHRC is engaged in to review the report?
2 Where in SSHRC's policies, procedures, and guidelines is such a review authorized?
3 Who is conducting the review? What are their qualifications?
4 Will our report be shared with the Minister of Industry, the Minister of Science and Technology, and/or any of their staff members? During the review process, what will be the nature and extent of communication between the government and SSHRC?

We received no answer from SSHRC regarding the process of review to which it subjected the report.

Along with academics from across the country, the Osgoode Hall Faculty Association seized the opportunity to send an open letter to the president of SSHRC. It was signed by the overwhelming majority of faculty members.

> We are writing as members of the faculty of Osgoode Hall Law School at York University to express our extreme dismay that SSHRC appears to be acceding to political pressure by revisiting its decision to fund the above-noted academic conference ... Your decision as SSHRC president to require a special pre-conference accounting from the conference organizers, outside the normal post-conference reporting procedures for conference grants, raises the much larger question of your agency's integrity as a funder and promoter of independent university-based research in Canada.
>
> As a group we have extensive experience with the organization of academic conferences and with SSHRC granting procedures. We believe there is no basis at all for the suggestion that "major changes" were made to the plan for this conference after the grant application had been peer reviewed and funding granted. Nor do we believe that you could possibly see any basis for this suggestion. Rather, it appears that the special accounting was demanded of our colleagues in direct response to the unprecedented and entirely inappropriate political intervention of Minister Goodyear.
>
> We believe that SSHRC made a serious error in acceding to political interference in this manner ... [B]y intruding into the planning of an academic event after a funding decision has been made, SSHRC's actions are likely to have a most unfortunate chilling effect on academics considering the exploration of controversial or unpopular topics. In addition, by casting doubt on the integrity of its own procedures, SSHRC has empowered those who would devalue academic research and discourse by insisting that academic freedom be reserved only for those who happen to share their point of view.
>
> We hope that SSHRC will very shortly stand up to defend its own granting procedures and the values of academic excellence and autonomy they are designed to protect.

While we waited for a response from SSHRC, B'nai Brith also seized the moment to place a full-page ad on June 13, 2009, in the *National Post* constituted by a "Report Card." It handed out failing grades to York University on "subjects" such as "preventing anti-Israel agitators from spewing hatred," and it claimed that York was "now in danger of becoming infamous for enabling rabid anti-Israel and anti-Jewish sentiment."

Behind the scenes, York's senior administration, led by Dean Monahan, decided that a public response was necessary. He sent the president a letter that said, "Richard [York's chief marketing officer] and I believe a response from the university leadership is required, since this is an unprecedented attack on the entire institution. I have asked Richard to start thinking about the outline of an appropriate response."[37] The discussions that ensued led to the second presidential statement on academic freedom of June 15, jointly signed by the president and the outgoing and incoming board chairs of York University.[38]

SSHRC's occult review completed, the funding agency issued a brief statement on June 15 indicating that it accepted our "assurance that planning for the conference is proceeding in a manner consistent with provisions of the Grant Holder's Guide for the program."[39] Since the information provided in our report was readily available on the conference website, according to the logic of SSHRC's own guidelines, neither a written inquiry from the grant holder seeking clarification of the distinction between major and minor changes nor, *a fortiori,* the extraordinary report itself should have been required.

This did not appear to be SSHRC's preoccupation, however; the funding organization appeared to be worried about how to spin the story. In cooperation with the Conservative government, SSHRC officials worked on crafting a question-and-answer document that the Conservatives could use in the House of Commons during Question Period to respond to any public outcry that might arise over the government's intervention with SSHRC and the latter's intervention with us.

Notwithstanding after-the-fact assertions that SSHRC was always regarded by the government as an arm's-length agency and that there was no ministerial interference by the government in SSHRC, the CAUT report, *No Debate,* concludes that there was government interference through the action and statement by Minister Goodyear. Professor Thompson concludes that "the government's interference was inappropriate and constituted a serious adverse precedent for the independence and integrity of academic research in Canada, with potential adverse implications for all three granting councils and the research communities they support. Among such implications is an atmosphere of uncertainty as to which type of research project might next bring interference."[40]

As for SSHRC itself, *No Debate* concludes that it "acted outside of its own procedures, and that this followed the government's interference. It is to SSHRC's credit that it did not conduct a second peer review, but there also was no basis in its policy for it to have demanded a pre-conference account from the grant-holder. I conclude that this demand by SSHRC to Professor Ryder was inappropriate."[41]

An Increased Sense of Insecurity

Letters of complaint about the conference continued to arrive at York University and Osgoode Hall Law School, some of them manifesting an unbridled disregard for the principle of academic freedom. One email in this period, under the all-caps subject heading "ANOTHER SH-T STORM COMING," asked, "Why in hell do we have to have this stuff on our campus after all our public relations problems this year." The message continued in all caps: "THIS THING WILL NOT END WELL AND SHOULD BE STOPPED." The president personally intervened and noted that "Everyone (on all sides) agree that the organizers had no political objectives or agenda. Their interests are academic." He went on:

> Typical of academic conferences, the organizers issued an open call for papers. It is now obvious that many (but certainly not all) the papers submitted tended to discuss the so called "one-state two-nations" solution. I became aware of it as we started to receive messages from the community who appeared to believe that conference is promoting this particular solution. This is not true. This is an academic conference where participants debate ideas and issues freely and the conference does not issue statements in support of any resolution.

The president went on to lay out clearly that there was more than one dimension to the issue and more than one constituency to which a university has to attend: "We cannot cancel the conference and cannot appear to interfere any further without triggering another serious problem by the academics all over the country regarding academic freedom. I assure you, this is a real threat." Seemingly oblivious of the fact that he was writing to the president of a university and not some organization for which fundamental intellectual principles are irrelevant, the correspondent replied in all caps: "I DON'T CARE A FIG ABOUT ACADEMIC FREEDOM. I DO CARE ABOUT YORK – AND WITH OUR PROBLEMS THIS YEAR THIS IS TROUBLE WITH A CAPITAL T."[42]

Meanwhile, grim as the extraordinary interventions by both the federal government and SSHRC were, the campaigns from organized Canadian Israel advocates did not end with a rebuff by SSHRC. CIJA, the CJC, and the JDL were joined by B'nai Brith in the campaign to shut the conference down in the spring of 2009. On June 12, B'nai Brith issued a community alert to its listserv JewishCanada. The alert accused the conference sponsors and funders of hosting Holocaust deniers. B'nai Brith arrived at this conclusion by attributing the following quotation to one of the presenters, who was also a member of the conference Advisory Committee:

> "Zionist leaders, academics, and propagandists are actually professional, malicious liars as much as they are violent, merciless murderers." From that premise, [name deleted so as not to reinforce the defamation] reasons: "[I]f lying is Israel's best policy ... shouldn't the world ... doubt the Zionists' official stories about ... the holocaust?"

The community alert went on to accuse several other presenters of "advocating for the destruction of the Jewish state," "rejecting compromise," and "justifying terrorism." It arrived at these grave accusations by lifting snippets of quotations out of their original contexts or collating them from different places in the original texts. Not only did this treatment distort what the authors had said, but also the quotations were framed under the above headlines in a manner that levelled serious charges against the presenters. B'nai Brith went on to accuse the sponsors and funders of hosting Holocaust deniers and those who rationalize terrorism: "The veil of academia provided by these sponsors should not fool anyone. No academic body should lend its imprimatur to a conference where several of the speakers are actively engaged in Holocaust denial, rationalize terrorism, and are infamous anti-Israel propagandists."

It took two minutes of electronic research to discover that the attribution of the quotation about Holocaust denial to the conference presenter was false. It was in fact written by someone else in an electronic article and then misattributed to the presenter on a second website. The presenter discovered the misattribution in the fall of 2008 and, with the intervention of a lawyer, demanded that the host of the second website remove the misattribution. Despite his intervention, the very damaging misquotation circulated on the Internet. B'nai Brith exercised no due diligence in reproducing the misattributed quotation.

Within hours of issuing the community alert on June 12, B'nai Brith realized that it had circulated defamatory material and sent a fax to York University and Queen's University noting that the quotation "does appear to be attributed to him erroneously." The extent of its retraction was to note quietly to both university administrations that "We have corrected our records and documents accordingly and ask that you do the same."[43]

The Organizing Committee hired one of the country's best defamation lawyers to deal with the impugning of the presenter charged with Holocaust denial and the other presenters' reputations and the reputations of the conference organizers and sponsors. B'nai Brith's original position in response to our demand for an apology was unacceptably weak. B'nai Brith was prepared to acknowledge the following:

> On June 12, 2009, B'nai Brith Canada issued a community alert through its list serve JewishCanada setting out its concerns about the nature of the above conference.
>
> It has since come to our attention that the quote regarding Holocaust denial attributed to [Mr. X], which our student intern located on current live websites, is attributed to him erroneously. We corrected our records and documents accordingly, and will send this clarification over JewishCanada.
>
> B'nai Brith Canada regrets this error due to incorrect material on the website and any misunderstanding in this matter affecting any party.
>
> Our amended alert can be found at our website www.bnaibrith.ca including the full text of the quotations cited therein.

Given the unacceptability of this non-apology, we persisted in our demand for a meaningful apology. B'nai Brith agreed to modify the apology by adding the following:

> On June 12, 2009, B'nai Brith Canada issued a community alert through its listserv JewishCanada regarding the conference. The alert set out a list of concerns including a claim that the conference would be hosting Holocaust deniers. This particular concern arose from a quote regarding Holocaust denial attributed to [Mr. X], ... one of the presenters and a member of the conference's advisory committee. The quote was found by our student intern on current live Web sites.
>
> It has since come to our attention that this quote was and continues to be erroneously attributed to Mr. [X] by such Web sites. The quote that we

> attributed to Mr. [X] appears in an article written by somebody wholly different than him and in no way associated with him. On learning this, we immediately corrected our records and documents, removed the mistaken information from our Web site and notified the universities involved. This statement is also being sent over JewishCanada.
>
> B'nai Brith Canada regrets this specific error and apologizes to Mr. [X], the conference organizers, York University, Queen's University and the other sponsors and funders for any confusion or distress that this mistaken attribution may have caused.[44]

However, the apology went on to reproduce the extremely damaging claims made about the other conference presenters. We had provided a web page with all of the quotations in their contexts to the organization as a remedy. B'nai Brith refused to use the full quotations without the use of repetition and editorializing.

As noted earlier, since the conference call for papers was issued in the fall of 2008, the Jewish Defence League had made it a priority to demonstrate and agitate against the conference. The JDL went beyond B'nai Brith in the circulation of outlandish and unsubstantiated charges against the conference and its organizers:

> York University will sponsor an International Conference that promotes a "One State Solution." That "solution" supports the goal of Radical Iran – No Jewish State. The roster of speakers will attempt to defame the Torah, the State of Israel and the Jewish People. One of the main advisors for this conference will argue that the Jewish People of today are not authentic Jews and therefore have no real claim to Israel. Other speakers support denial of the Holocaust and compare the IDF to the Nazis and the Arabs of Gaza with the Warsaw Ghetto resistance fighters.

York Security, knowing the self-avowedly violent reputation of the JDL[45] and aware of its concerted efforts to shut the conference down, had to engage the services of the 53rd division of the Toronto Police Services to supplement security efforts in order to keep conference participants safe. In the twenty-four-hour period prior to the opening night, sniffer dogs combed the campus to ensure that there were no bombs on the premises. As part of our planning for this conference, we had to prepare drills for bomb threats. Preparations included securing a safe room equipped with first-aid equipment to which organizers could flee in the case of direct assaults and/or injuries.

With grim irony, in light of CIJA's concern that events such as our conference "lead to an increased sense of insecurity for those who should feel free to express their support for Israel,"[46] by the time that the conference opened on June 22, we felt a deep sense of insecurity, not only with respect to the integrity of scholarly agendas, but also with respect to our physical integrity.

Despite the travails leading up to the conference, the event itself went smoothly – indeed successfully. The sense that the conference was successful was shared by the vast majority of those who attended it. On the last day of the conference, we distributed evaluation sheets, and the vast majority of participants "agreed" or "strongly agreed" that they were pleased to have participated in the conference. One senior scholar from a Canadian university took the time to email us separately about his experience of the event:

> This was an important conference, dealing with a crucial issue. It was about as balanced as a conference in this area could be, given the propensity of participants to self-select around these issues. I emerged with a much better sense of the issues and of the fundamental stumbling blocks to a resolution than I had possessed going in.
>
> I know that there was controversy among some Canadian Jewish organizations with respect to this conference. What became clear, however, is that the Israeli participants, of whom there were many and of varying opinions, defined the permissible scope of discussion much more broadly than the diasporic groups ... Virtually all of the Israeli participants defined themselves as Zionist, in the sense that they believed deeply in a distinctively Jewish state (or at least an identified Jewish political unit of a confederal state) in Palestine. But it is clear that accepting such a definition of the state – essentially embracing a self-consciously Zionist mission in Palestine – is very difficult for many Palestinians. This is true even of those untainted by anti-Semitism (and I saw no evidence of anti-Semitism among the Palestinian participants at this conference). A number would certainly be committed to a state open to all, without a distinct identity attached to a particular people. There even appeared to be potential common ground around some kind of confederal entity (either structured as two states with transnational cooperation or as one decentralized federal state), with the confederal nature designed to accommodate the division between Jewish

> and Arab. But affirming a distinctly Jewish identity of the state was difficult for many Palestinian participants, especially given the presence of other groups. Getting a clear sense of this sticking point, and considering the solutions posed in light of it, was itself an important insight for me.[47]

Despite the broad sense of those in attendance that the conference was a success, one participant, Na'ama Carmi, who teaches law at Haifa University as an adjunct professor, was publicly upset by it.

Carmi had accepted our invitation to present a paper on a panel dedicated to the issue of the right of return. Two weeks before the event, possibly influenced by the boycott campaign that had been launched against the conference in both Canada and Israel, she voiced hesitations about participating and wanted to withdraw because she had begun to believe that the event might turn into an "academic Durban." She was ultimately convinced of the importance of having multiple voices on the panel devoted to this deeply contentious topic.[48]

Over the course of the three-day conference, a handful of audience members shouted out comments in the midst of presentations. Na'ama Carmi was one of the most frequent of these intervenors. She was sufficiently impassioned about what she was hearing from panelists that she felt free to comment loudly.

Carmi subsequently wrote an op-ed about the conference in the *Toronto Star* that spoke to her passionately held beliefs and her anxiety that they were being silenced.[49] Her article has been widely cited by those who did not attend the conference but wished to attach their critiques of it to someone who had been present and could testify against it. Her op-ed made arguments about rude and raucous dissent. She noted that "a hostile atmosphere toward people with different views ... was created. At times, those presenting a different view were subject to abuse and ridicule." Carmi had "never before in [her] whole academic career encountered the rudeness that [she] experienced at this conference."[50]

A handful of participants at the conference thought that some of the ideas floated so deeply offended truths that they held dear that they would be complicit in perpetuating them if they did not object vociferously (and indecorously). Carmi's article spoke to how such conduct might be construed: "If one has good arguments," she noted, "one doesn't need to resort to such tactics. As an Israeli politician once reputedly wrote on the side of his written text: 'Here the argument is weak, raise your voice.'"[51] The Iacobucci

Report refers to Carmi's own conduct at the conference, including the following detail: "Professor Carmi did not follow the normal decorum at academic conferences and at times left the room abruptly, knocking over chairs, or loudly interrupted the presenters whose views she disagreed with."[52]

Leo Panitch, a Canada research chair and professor of political science at York University, attended the conference. He sent a letter to the editor in response to Carmi's op-ed:

> I am puzzled by Na'ama Carmi's claim that the York University conference on Israel/Palestine was characterized by an unacademic atmosphere. I was there for one of the two full days of the conference (the day after Carmi spoke) but what she describes is certainly not what went on the day I was there. I attended two plenary sessions and here panels and all were characterized by a respectful academic atmosphere ... The only two people who showed any slight measure of disrespect the day I was there were Carmi herself and one Palestinian woman academic who were seated not very far from each other (and me as it happened) and who were both muttering under their breath at the opening plenary when things were said they didn't like. I suspected the two of them had set each other off the day before.[53]

History has no doubt generated too many appalling ideas to be complacent about the necessity of deference, decorum, and respect. It is worth leaving latitude in the scope of free speech for boisterous dissent. Sometimes it is the most appropriate response, particularly to ideas that are appalling and come garbed in respectability. The idea that "respectful discourse" characterizes legitimate academic discourse is something to which I will return when I examine the Iacobucci Report.

Outside the conference hall, the anticipated busloads of protesters, on either side of the conflict, did not materialize. As predicted by the conference Organizing Committee in meetings that we had with York Security, there was not a single Palestinian supporter demonstrating outside the event. Indeed, there were rarely more than twelve pro-Israel supporters at any given time. As Jon Thompson observes in *No Debate,* "the only event approximating a protest altercation was between two pro-Israeli groups, as reported in an email exchange between two senior York Media and Communications staff that afternoon. In response to the question, 'any protests today?' the answer was, 'Two sets. Appears that Hasbora was here first noontime but that some squabble transpired that they did not want to stand in arm with JDL.'"[54]

CIJA and the CJC, on the other hand, had earlier invited the JDL to stand side by side with them in the offices of the CJC to voice their collective concerns about the Mapping Models conference. They had, indeed, specifically arranged for us to meet with the JDL. B'nai Brith and the JDL stood arm in arm with each other in a bid to have our SSHRC funding removed. And the Canadian government and our funding agency lined up with these groups, unified in their lobby against an academic event, to demand that we submit to extraordinary measures in the pursuit of our scholarly goals. In attempting to examine a fraught but timely idea, we had run up against a wall. Or, rather, we had run up against one of many concentric walls built up around a subject.

2

The Forbidden Question

"One State or Two?"

Gezerah: A rabbinical enactment issued as a guard or preventive measure; also a prohibition or restriction generally; from the root "gazar" (to cut; to decide). The term is especially applied to a negative ordinance which the Rabbis instituted as a guard or a fence ("geder") to a Biblical precept. [pl: *gzerot*].

– *JEWISH ENCYCLOPEDIA*[1]

Gzerot: Fencing the Unbroachable

As much as I was aware going into the organization of the conference that the topic of binational constitutionalism in Israel/Palestine was fraught, the lengths pursued to ensure that it not be bestowed with the legitimacy conferred by being a subject of academic inquiry were staggering to us. Merely *asking* about the viability of the one-state model for Israel/Palestine – and particularly raising the question in the rigorous and searching forum of academia – apparently legitimated a forbidden intrigue.

The history of academia is cluttered with ideas and questions that have been discarded, if not forbidden, not all of them worthy of thought. Some of these forbidden ideas and questions have gone on to lay down new foundations for the construction of the common knowledge of humanity. I will return to questions about how we distinguish worthy from unworthy ideas, particularly when our contemporary horizons limit our powers of discernment; I will also return to the development of the doctrine of academic freedom that runs like the bed of a river alongside the efforts to stem the flow of ideas. First, however, I want to trouble further the particular idea that generated the external pressures on the conference: namely, the one-state model for Israel/Palestine. The venue of an academic publication offers a more tranquil clearing for the emergence of ideas.

Of this book, this is a forbidden chapter. It canvasses a forbidden idea. The words in its title are forbidden.

That appears to be the central lesson of the field notes from the June 2009 conference on models of statehood for Israel/Palestine. The first and third parts of this monograph deal with the mechanisms engaged to enforce the proscription of the one-state topic; the third part deals with the concept of academic freedom; this part deals with the forbidden history and content of the one-state model.

When the call for papers for our conference went out in the fall of 2008, it was immediately met by one of my colleagues at Osgoode Hall Law School, who noted, in a letter of complaint to the dean, that "politically the 'one-state solution' has become a code word disguising a call for the destruction of Israel."[2] Explaining why he thought that Osgoode should not sponsor a conference that, to his mind, would only bring controversy and dissension, he rhetorically asked the dean these questions:

> Is there any legal issue per se in connection with the establishment of "one state" in Israel and Palestine? Aren't the models simple and obvious? Why hide then behind the number of states to be created? Isn't it that the real issue, other than security, is the repatriation of the 1948 Palestinian refugees to their old homes in Israel? Will this objective not be facilitated by the one-state, certainly much more easily than in the framework of two states? Isn't it self-explanatory?[3]

From this analysis, the *gezerah* around the one-state model protects the more deeply forbidden idea of the Palestinian refugees' right of return to the place that they consider their homeland – a right that, if exercised, would undermine the Jewish majority in the state of Israel and, with presumably inexorable logic and pragmatics if the state of Israel is to remain democratic, the Jewish nature of the state. The impossibility of a Palestinian right of return is thus a fence around the more forbidden idea that the state of Israel might not be Jewish. The verboten one-state model operates as one of the outer rings of prohibition protecting concentrically increasing sacrosanctity.

As we experienced, the fence around the one-state model is itself circumscribed by expanding rings of outer structures that ranged from demands for "balance" in discussions on Israel/Palestine to requisite thresholds of civility and scholarship supposedly attendant upon the topic.

The centrality of how fraught any discussion on the one-state model would be (at least in the Canadian context[4]) recurred as a theme from before that first email complaint until the day of the conference and beyond. As the Organizing Committee sought to gain the participation of local Zionist and two-state proponents on our Advisory Committee – it had been relatively straightforward to secure the participation of Israeli scholars – we were informed by those whom we approached that the topic of the one-state model was too charged for local participation. Immediately after the letter of complaint went out from my Osgoode colleague, one of our Advisory Committee members, who had been copied on the email, raised an issue with us regarding the title of our conference that had not occurred to him before:

> But words exist, as Stanley Fish would say, within an interpretive community. The "One State Solution" has become a euphemism. It's not as vile as the "Final Solution," but it has a similar impact on the reader and listener, and it simply cannot be used without signalling its now commonplace meaning. Most of the people who deploy it mean the "Destroy The Jewish State By Another Means Solution" ... Unfortunately, no amount of bona fide explanation by the conference's organizers can rid the phrase of the use which its most aggressive proponents have made of it.[5]

The title of the conference (One State or Two?) was apparently a code for something far more ominous. It appeared that there could not be a space for discussing alternatives to the more orthodox two-state model without triggering concentric rings of security alarms. As a result, it appeared increasingly as though the only legitimate discussions that could take place about statehood in Israel/Palestine were those that had already been received.

The four members of the Organizing Committee not only had a broad scope of views on models of statehood among them but also shared a fair amount of skepticism and ambivalence about any of the models presented. From the outset, we actively sought the participation of scholars who could represent a range of, if not polar opposition between, conceivable ways out of the Middle East impasse. When the call for papers was answered by a far more complex range of models than suggested by the original title – One State or Two? – we changed the title to reflect the diversity and richness of papers that were beginning to come in.[6] Neither the conference vision statement – explicit in its aspiration to canvass diverse positions – nor the change in title could shake our critics' preoccupation with the one-state model as a scholarly topic of inquiry.

That the one-state model was the central anxiety of the conference's critics was reinforced throughout coverage. The perception that it would be natural for significant swaths of the Canadian Jewish community to react to inquiries into the one-state model was well captured by the media consultant that York University hired to manage the conference Organizing Committee's communications with the media. As the furor was mounting in the weeks before the conference began, Jane Shapiro of Hill and Knowlton – a professional tasked to put her finger on the pulse of the controversy – lamented that "even mainstream Jewish groups can be expected to take issue with the notion of a single state solution, in which the Jewish population would quickly become a permanent minority, and wonder why York is providing a platform for this discussion."[7]

Shapiro's assessment of the conference's core irritant was prescient. The Canadian Council for Israel and Jewish Advocacy (CIJA) issued a statement several weeks before the conference stating that "the conference aims to explore a one-state, bi-national solution to the conflict between Israelis and Palestinians, the imposition of which would spell the end of Israel as a Jewish state," and it called on people to "write to the President of York University making clear that [e]vents like this should not have the sanction of the university."[8] On the first day of the conference, the *National Post* published an article by Stephen Scheinberg and Neil Caplan on what they presumed was the "original political objective of the organizers": namely, promotion of the one-state model:

> We believe that frustration with the lack of progress toward a two-state solution does not provide a sufficient basis for advocating a one-state solution. Current calls for a one-state solution mask a desire for the disappearance of Israel as a Jewish state. They not only reinforce the demands of fundamentalist groups like Hamas, but also cater to demagogic seekers of "justice" and anti-Israel campus groups.[9]

Some time after the conference, in an article in the *Canadian Jewish News* announcing a review of the conference by the president and provost/vice-president academic of York University to the Jewish community, the one-state model in the themes addressed by a roster of speakers and as a topic of scholarly debate remained central to the Jewish community's concerns:

> Another issue that concerned many members of the Jewish community was the York-sponsored conference in June called Israel/Palestine: Mapping Models of Statehood and Paths to Peace. The concern stemmed from the fact that a large majority of the speakers promoted a one-state solution to the Israeli-Palestinian conflict – a solution that would mean the end of a Jewish state.[10]

Although not all of the furor that arose around the conference was focused on the perils of raising the one-state model as a subject of inquiry, the vast bulk of the expressed anxiety was provoked by this stimulus, the associated concerns about activism, advocacy, and imbalance being hinged to this particular conference and its content in ways that they are not for other scholarly events.

The successive proscriptions embedded in the forbidden one-state topic fit well with the Talmudic analogy to *gzerot* established to protect a biblical precept. As with biblical commands within a world of religious pluralism, there is a contingent, contested, and at times radically incommensurable quality to the topics that different communities take – internally – to be indisputable. The contingent nature of *gzerot* – the quality of being deeply and meaningfully proscriptive to insiders while being potentially perplexing, if not arbitrary or even vexatious, to outsiders – is manifest in the history of these devices.

Gzerot – rabbinical, and therefore human, commandments designed to shore up the sacrosanctity of the divine commands given in the Torah – emerged most prolifically after the fall of the second temple in 70 CE when the centre of Jewish lawmaking moved from the land of Israel to the dispersed communities of the Diaspora, and the Torah itself became interpretively surrounded by the *mishnah*[11] and the *mishnah* by the spiralling complexity of the Talmud. When the Jews of Europe were enclosed in ghettos – segregated communities that had earlier been preferred by Jews wishing to settle in new towns but that became imposed during the Renaissance – the authority of rabbinical leaders became entrenched as the ghettos became autonomous and corporate law-making jurisdictions.[12] Rabbinical law flourished commensurately, and the distinctiveness of the Talmudic legal tradition was massaged to respond to a plethora of disputes and conundrums both ponderous and mundane. The structure of rabbinical jurisdiction solidified as the threat of excommunication from a familiar space was given the edge of banishment to a surrounding world of pervasive and persistent anti-Semitism.

When the walls of the ghettos were taken down in the nineteenth century under the ideals of the Enlightenment and the expansion of the French Revolution through Napoleon, Jews dispersed from the corporate and segregated world of ghettos and aspired to equal citizenship in their surrounding societies. As a result of the dispersal and the promise of integration, the jurisdictional scope that the ghettos had afforded the integrity and development of Talmudic law was commensurately diluted. Not only did many Jews assimilate rapidly and sometimes successfully into non-Jewish society, but also Jewish law lost the solidarity and jurisdictional enclosure that enable many legal traditions to flourish. This disruption was significant enough that, as Celia Fassberg notes, commentators have observed that, by the end of the nineteenth century, "the rabbinical establishment had missed the opportunity to develop Jewish law in a number of areas crucial to modern life – contracts, torts, commercial institutions, and the like."[13] The waning robustness of Jewish law is one among several reasons that Jewish law did not play a significant part in the legal system of the new Jewish state.

Not only did integration play a role in retarding the development of Jewish law by dispersing the legal authority from theretofore highly localized communities with steep enforcement mechanisms for non-compliance, but the Jewish Enlightenment (Haskalah) that followed release from the ghettos also fractured the prior cohesion of the Jewish people. Where orthodoxy prevailed by default and by imposed context prior to the Haskalah, the Enlightenment's dispersal of Jewish communities simultaneously fractured the religious community into distinctive clusters that accommodated, to greater and lesser degrees, elements from Europe's emerging and surrounding modernity.

Beyond the religious fracturing that increasingly dwindled Orthodox Judaism's monopoly over observants, the free and critical inquiry at the core of the Enlightenment further dispersed Jews into the secularism that was spreading throughout Europe. Throughout the nineteenth century, the conception of authority that had governed Jews – steeped in revealed truths and rooted in deeply historical sources, many with absolute validity – gave way to a persuasive authority whose sources were far more plural and hybrid and contentious. The paradigm of fences built around absolute truths by authorities whose expertise clustered around a highly distinctive set of sources and methodologies shifted, for Jewish as well as non-Jewish

Europeans. The corporate pluralism of the Middle Ages and Renaissance gave rise to a far more scattered and complex pluralism just as the concept of citizenship held the promise of embracing far more diverse swaths of society.

As Amos Elon has poignantly laid out in *The Pity of It All: A Portrait of the German-Jewish Epoch, 1743-1933,* this promise was devastatingly betrayed for Europe's Jews.[14] The Haskalah transformed the viciously stigmatized and ghettoized Jewish population into a stunningly successful and seemingly fully integrated part of the upper echelons of German society. Having taken seriously the promise of full and equal citizenship in the European community of nations and the prospects of fecundating millennia of Jewish thought with the fruits of the Enlightenment (and vice versa), Jews found themselves transformed in the European imaginary into deadly threats to national integrity. Jews no longer had the security of ghettos to retreat to, and the pervasive and seemingly ineradicable anti-Semitism of European society exploited the vulnerabilities that arose from the openness of integration, assimilation, and hope. The pedagogy of the Holocaust appears logically and overwhelmingly to install a new absolute around which multiple fences are required, emerging as they do out of the seemingly indelible historical truth of deep-seated anti-Semitism: no state but Israel can ultimately protect Jews, and the state must be Jewish to provide that protection. This is the logic of an unspeakable pain and grief that is hard to deny. This is a historical logic that, while contingent, is so virtually unassailable and so immediately evocative, also to outsiders, as to render it a seeming necessity. It is hard to imagine a group whose terror of dependency on the goodwill of others is more justified.

At this post-diluvial point in history, however, the Jews are dispersed and fractured – both geographically and intellectually – and have been as deeply and widely infused with the Enlightenment's core value of critical inquiry as the rest of us. Perhaps the best illustration of this is the high level of contestation and disputation tolerated within Israel proper, for example in its media and universities, a tolerance that is often unparalleled in other Western democracies.[15] Some of the most vocal critics of pronouncements on the unassailable nature of the Israeli state come from Israel itself. When Professor Neve Gordon of Ben-Gurion University called for a boycott of Israel, the group leading the furor to have a tenured professor fired was a Jewish community of Los Angeles.[16] Although the president of Ben-Gurion was highly critical of Gordon's position, she was also clear that, "like it or not, Gordon cannot be readily dismissed. The law in Israel is very clear, and the university is a law-abiding institution."[17]

The recurrent commitment to the Enlightenment values of secularism and critical inquiry is also seen in the enduring tension in Israel itself over the place of secularism in the state. Very few states have this tension as an omnipresent part of national dialogue.[18]

In this much more complex post-Enlightenment/post-Holocaust context, in which Jewish and non-Jewish communities are riddled with contradictions and seemingly irreconcilable tensions over competing core values, we are no longer innocent of the power of persuasive authority over the force of revealed authority. The pluralism of the contemporary world makes it hard to see one people's history as rooted in a bedrock of universal truth while another people's history is rooted in imagination. However much necessity our shared understanding of history generates, it is hard for children of the Enlightenment not to see that it all could have been otherwise – and it all might be otherwise. *Gzerot* are ultimately fragile defences against this need to know.

Post-Haskalah/Post-Holocaust *Gzerot*

This excursus into the nature and history of *gzerot* returns me to the two embedded verboten topics in my Osgoode colleague's email – the Palestinian right of return and the Jewish nature of the state of Israel. These two fences provide classic examples of modern bedrock indubitabilities that, from another perspective, appear to be considerably less grounded in a universal reality. One does not have to adopt a position vis-à-vis either topic to recognize that these are hotly contested ideas that are far from having received judicial notice from either the community of nations or the community of relevant players.

Notoriously, the right of Palestinians to return to what they consider their homeland is one of the – if not *the* – most intractable issues of the Israeli/Palestinian conflict. Although there are at least models for the final status of Jerusalem that appear to have achieved some consensus and recognition in peace negotiations,[19] the right of return appears to generate virtually no common ground between the Israeli government and Palestinian negotiators. In every internationally recognized peace initiative, the right of return has been left off the table for final negotiations in light of the profound irreconcilability of the parties' positions on the matter.[20] The vast majority of Israeli citizens are adamant that a Palestinian right of return cannot, or does not, exist.[21] As Minister of Defence Ehud Barak framed the issue from the Israeli side, "the demand for the right of return, in the deepest sense, is a demographic mechanism to achieve Israel's destruction."[22] More than 73 percent of Palestinians in the occupied Palestinian territories are equally determined that the right of return has never been forfeited and is a basic right guaranteed by international law.[23] Without necessarily agreeing on the practical details of how the refugee question should be dealt with, at a minimum Palestinian leaders insist on the need to recognize the refugees' right of return, "lest the agreement lose all legitimacy with the vast refugee constituency – roughly half the entire Palestinian population."[24] The current official position is that of the Arab Peace Initiative: namely, that "a just solution to the Palestinian refugee problem [is] to be agreed upon in accordance with UN General Assembly Resolution 194."[25] Neither negotiating partner can afford to compromise its position on the issue without courting the massive and debilitating disaffection of the population that it claims to represent.

Not unsurprisingly for such a contentious issue, there is a vast body of scholarly literature on the right of return, much of it sorting out the complex and thorny international law on the topic.[26] Reasonable people might disagree about the existence and scope of the right of return – and world-class scholars who have devoted their intellectual energies to the topic do indeed disagree.[27] However, precluding scholarly debate on the right of return by transforming it into a transgressive topic not only shuts down rich openings for fair resolution of the impasse but also threatens to narrow the range of intellectual perspectives on, and illustrations of, the meta-themes that drive the development of refugee law and international law.

The proscription at the core of both the forbidden one-state model and the right of return is the inviolable conjunction of the state of Israel with its Jewish nature. This conjunction is sufficiently sacrosanct that the Israeli Knesset recently considered legislation that would criminalize opposing Israel's status as a Jewish state.[28] Under the proposed bill, those who do not support Israel's identity as a Jewish, democratic state could be punished by a sentence of up to a year in prison. The Knesset member who initiated the bill, Zevulun Orlev, said by way of justification that "words very quickly lead to actions." This shoring up through the criminal law against threatening ideas found the support of forty-seven MKs, with thirty-four MKs voting against the proposed legislation on its first reading.[29]

Such heavy-handedness with respect to speech clearly underlines how untouchably foundational is the Jewishness of the state of Israel for Jewish

Israeli citizens, if not for the vast majority of Jews in the Diaspora. These concentric stockades around the *Ka'aba* of much of contemporary Jewish life, however, do not transform the core idea into an unshakable bedrock. Here, too, reasonable people can and do disagree. Again, one does not have to agree with proponents or opponents of the Jewishness of the state of Israel to recognize that this is the case. Some of Israel's favourite sons have questioned the link.

Breaking from the dense solidarity surrounding the indissociability of the state of Israel with its Jewishness, one of Israel's most renowned novelists, A.B. Yehoshua, recently published a comment in *Ha'aretz* – "Why Do We Insist on a 'Jewish' State?" – that transgressed this precept of Israel's fundamental nature.[30] The gist of the article turned around MK Ahmed Tibi's ironic remark that "the state of Israel is Jewish for the Arabs and democratic for the Jews." Yehoshua interrogated whether the incessant incantation of the democratic nature of the state is a foil for a much deeper uncertainty about the implications of making it Jewish. As he noted, "no Dane, no Italian, no Irishman, and no one belonging to any other people feel the need to repeat over and over like some kind of oath 'democratic Danish state' or 'democratic Italian state' or 'democratic American state.' The prefix 'democratic' is completely superfluous." A strong intimation of the potentially oxymoronic nature of the combination "Jewish and Democratic" was underscored by the superfluity of the conjunction in other democratic states.

The "hostile and offensive"[31] nature (to the non-Jewish citizens of the state) that Yehoshua deciphered in the phrase "Jewish state" has implications beyond the borders of Israel. The insistence that Israel be recognized as a Jewish state has now spilled over into external relations in light of Israel's recent insistence that Palestinians recognize Israel as a Jewish state as a prelude to peace negotiations and a condition for the creation of a Palestinian state.[32] Ariel Sharon was the first Israeli prime minister to explicitly fix recognition of the Jewishness of the state to peace negotiations when he noted in a 2002 speech that "Israel's desire is to live in security and in true and genuine co-existence, based, first and foremost, on the recognition of our natural and historic right to exist as a Jewish state in the Land of Israel."[33] This position on recognition not just of the state of Israel but also of its Jewishness was taken up by Prime Minister Olmert, who transformed it into a clear precondition. As he is quoted as saying, "Israel is a state of the Jewish people. Whoever does not accept this cannot hold any negotiations with me."[34] This precondition has now surreptitiously entered the lexicon of discussions.

This formula, and its timing, seem poised to poison the prospects of peace negotiations. As Ian Lustick notes about Palestinian resistance to this formulation,

> for Arabs there is ... a crucial difference between acknowledging rights of an existing entity and recognizing that it was right for that entity to come into existence. This distinction is also present in Yasser Arafat's 1993 letter to Prime Minister Yitzhak Rabin, which did not recognize Israel's "right to exist," but rather its "right to live in peace and security" (given that it does exist and no matter whether it originally had a right to exist or not).[35]

Furthermore, though the Palestinians, through the Palestinian National Council, recognized Israel's right to exist in 1996, the new demand that they go further and recognize it as a Jewish state appears to manoeuvre linguistically around one of the thorniest substantive issues of the conflict: namely, the right of return.[36] Prime Minister Netanyahu's seemingly unshakable insistence following his election on the precondition for a Palestinian state[37] has led to speculation that Israel has little intention of undertaking peace negotiations, given how this phrase is artfully linked to the intractable issue of the right of return. Recognition of the Jewishness of the state by Palestinians and other nations would compromise, if not preclude, a right of return to Israel proper, for such an influx would, in one model of the state, demographically undermine its factual Jewishness. This model of statehood – which, as Canada's constitutional structure attests, is far from the only one possible – determines nationality by numerical majority.[38] By the means of Israel's subtle lexical superfluity, fences are linked and secured by further fences as the foundational proscription regarding the Jewishness of the state is linked to the supposedly forbidden right of return.

Echoing Yehoshua's point on the domestic scale, *Ha'aretz* journalist Gideon Levy asks, with respect to this new demand on the international scale, "is it conceivable that France would demand recognition as a French state? Or Italy as an Italian state?"[39] In light of the possibilities of internal Israeli dissent over this charged issue, as evidenced by Yehoshua's own query, it is not surprising that the Palestinian peace negotiators feel the same way when they are called upon to define the internal identity of an independent state. As Palestinian peace negotiator Saeb Erekat noted, "Israel can define itself however it sees fit; and if it wishes to call itself a Jewish state, so be it. But the Palestinians will never acknowledge Israel's Jewish identity."[40] The demand requires not only Jews but also Palestinians, including those living outside the state of Israel, to be avowed Zionists.

The attempt to shore up by fiat what cannot be established by agreement underlines how shakable the foundation really is. The unsettled nature of the Jewish state is uncannily underscored by the insistence that its nature is beyond question. The perturbation caused by the concept is magnified by the fact that it is principally from the Palestinians in the West Bank and Gaza that the demand for recognition is called. As Levy continues, "and from whom are we demanding the recognition? From those who have been groaning under the boots of the occupation for more than 40 years now."[41] Indeed, compelling the Palestinians to recognize Israel as a Jewish state has more painful implications when the full mandate of the Palestine Liberation Organization (PLO) is taken into account, given that it represents Palestinian refugees as well. The requirement would amount to compelling the refugees to acknowledge that their expulsion was justified.

In general, it is fair to assume that, if reasonable people can and do disagree about the importance of the Jewishness of the state of Israel, then a plethora of scholars will have examined the issue from a variety of angles, having taken the intrigue in the disagreement to unfathomed depths. And this is exactly the case. Whether one agrees or disagrees with the positions taken, the question of whether the joint aspirations of a Jewish and a democratic state are irreconcilably at odds with each other has been vetted from within a range of scholarly literatures.[42] Not only does this literature spotlight why so many of the issues in the Middle East are intractable, but it also contributes to the more general literature on issues of citizenship, the nature of democratic states, and the place of nationalism within them.[43]

Just as rendering the Palestinian right of return into an unexaminable topic impoverishes our understanding of the related body of international law, so too placing the Jewishness of the state of Israel beyond the bounds of acceptable discourse impoverishes a much broader intellectual community and set of general inquiries. The logic of excluding scholarly debate on the one-state model by virtue of presumably inexorable trajectories to the anxiety-provoking right of return and even more anxiety-provoking skepticism about the legitimate Jewishness of the state of Israel should be dubious to all but those already convinced of the righteousness of current orthodoxies on one side of a very complex set of issues. Again, one does not need to subscribe to any particular view on either of these proscribed topics to believe that they are worthy of intellectual consideration.

The analogy to *gzerot* works well given how a foundational command (the Jewishness of the state) is fenced in by secular state law's most powerful sanction – criminal punishment – and then, concentrically, by rabbinical-like enactments against intellectually vetting the right of return and the one-state model. It also works (at least for outsiders) to get at the ultimately contingent and arbitrary nature of the proscriptions – things could have been otherwise. For Palestinians and other outsiders, there is no universal logic to these articles of faith, just as for atheists and non-monotheistic religions, and even for followers of the other Abrahamic faiths and indeed for many secular Jews, the 613 *mitzvot* in Leviticus have little grounding in reality if one is not already a member of the community of believers. This is the case even if an equivalent of customary international law has arisen around these issues – that is, an analogy to the "rules of law derived from the consistent conduct of States acting out of the belief that the law required them to act that way."[44] Collective practice can be an extremely powerful foundation for the truths that dwell among us. Indeed, from such a source can arise a number of peremptory norms, fundamental principles of international law that are accepted by the international community of states as norms from which no derogation is ever permitted. However, even this strong level of international certitude still leaves the articles of faith tied to a community of understanding, however broad, and not to a more natural, less human, foundation of indubitability.

Some distance from peremptory norms, the Jewishness of the state of Israel, the status of the Palestinian right of return, and the unassailable wisdom of the two-state model are substantially less settled, despite vigorous efforts to settle them persuasively and forcefully. The fact that these precepts are so persistently and heatedly contested – by outsiders, by those deeply embedded in the community of opponents, and by those who have devoted their diplomatic and intellectual energies to the dispute – underlines how reliant each precept is on one's status as an insider. The fact that repression and asymmetries of force have been resorted to for their persuasive force (the criminalization of ideas and the "say uncle" nature of current peace negotiations) underscores a nervousness about the universality of the goods that they contain.

This is the case even though some of the most reasonable and wise among us believe unshakably that the state of Israel, for sound and compelling reasons, should remain Jewish and be recognized broadly as such, that the Palestinian right of return is not viable because it would undermine that necessity, and that the two-state model is the only realistic way out of the current impasse. They are more likely to be regarded as wise and reasonable – at least more broadly so – when they rely most consistently on persuasive, not brute, force.

Driving the Unthinkable into Thought

Leon Wieselthier has written a bitterly critical response to Tony Judt's 2003 article in the *New York Review of Books* proposing that we take seriously into account the merits of the one-state model.[45] Wieselthier begins his critique with a clever pastiche of the idea that the one-state model is academically and otherwise forbidden.

> "The time has come to think the unthinkable." It is almost an iron law of intellectual life that any idea that is advertised as unthinkable has been thought many times before. The promotion of an idea to unthinkability says nothing about the merit of the idea; many "unthinkable" ideas are not worthy of serious thought. It is not the veracity of the thought that the appeal to unthinkability seeks to establish, it is the courage of the thinker. Only truly free minds think the unthinkable. The rest are shackled by dogmas and sentiments and clichés and interests. The thinker of the unthinkable may even envy the others their intellectual tranquility, but now "the time has come," he has no choice any longer but to wound the others with the truth, to utter something bold and new, to "speak out" or "tell truth to power" or otherwise indicate that the unpopularity of his opinion is evidence for its correctness. Is it dissent? Then it must be right.[46]

Wieselthier is of course correct to deflate any frisson of intrigue associated with the unconventionality of an idea. However, the intensity of the opposition that our conference generated to a full airing of the alternatives in the infamously boxed-in context of the Middle East appears to suggest that it was not that unthinkable ideas were unworthy of serious thought but that their serious consideration was precluded from the outset. The following sections of this chapter provide an overview of the concepts at stake in discussing one state versus two for Israel/Palestine, alongside a range of other models.

One of the most compelling reasons for scholars and others to open up to the possibilities of a model with less currency than the middle ground's current orthodoxy (the two-state model) is that, if the former is unrealistic and utopian, the latter appears to be increasingly so in the contemporary context. Despite fatigued and cloying photo ops at the United Nations of Netanyahu shaking hands with Abbas in front of Obama,[47] all of the signs point to the conventional routes of the peace process, built around the two-state model, having ground to an immovable halt.[48] What is increasingly taking its place on the ground, while the empty sham of negotiations is cynically paraded in a parody of movement, is so starkly anti-democratic that a gulf is spreading between Western understandings of democracy and Israel's claim to share those understandings. As a result of this flourishing on-the-ground reality, a more realistic baseline around which to congregate thinking about the future is the prospect that the status quo will prevail for the foreseeable future – or worse, by analogy to acceleration rather than velocity, an intensification of the injustices inherent in the status quo. This increasingly abysmal status quo might well be the real comparator for assessing the merits of the one-state model – an important consideration for all of those with prior intellectual commitments to Enlightenment and democratic ideals.

Without belabouring the exhaustingly familiar arguments about who is missing an opportunity and who is responsible for past failures, it is not hard to see that the parties' existentially foundational worldviews are radically incommensurable. The staggering improbability of success for the current peace process, premised on the two-state model, should be evident from the irreconcilable opening positions on each side. Following his 2009 election, Netanyahu insisted that Palestinian negotiators not only recognize Israel's right to exist (which they have already done)[49] but also recognize that Israel is a Jewish state: that is, that the Palestinian right of return (which, according to the Oslo Accords, is considered a final status issue)[50] should be compromised as a precondition of Palestinian statehood. This is the same position that he arrived at after the 2010 direct peace talks were squandered by the lifting of a brief moratorium on settlements in the West Bank and East Jerusalem: namely, that he would renew the moratorium if the Palestinians forfeited the right of return prior to negotiations.[51] When Palestinian negotiators responded by swearing that "the Palestinians will never acknowledge Israel's Jewish identity,"[52] the prospect of reconciling these conflicting opening positions seemed to be extremely remote.

Just as troubling, if not more so, is the seemingly radical incommensurability of each group's foundational national narrative and how that incommensurability is becoming officialized. As noted above, the unspeakable horror of the Holocaust and the ineradicable pedagogy of distrust that flows with seeming necessity from that cataclysm lead almost inexorably to the conclusion that there is no state in the world but a Jewish state that can protect Jews from the persistence of anti-Semitism. Holocaust denial is both an extremely disturbing provocation to this existential truth and an anguishing reminder of the axiom regarding the necessity of a Jewish state.

It can hardly be other than profoundly troubling, then, for Israeli Jews to hear that, among the Palestinians who have been living with them as co-citizens within the state of Israel, more than 40 percent of them claim that the Holocaust never happened, a drastic increase from the 28 percent who denied the Holocaust a mere three years earlier in 2006.[53] If Palestinian citizens of Israel are increasingly denying the paramount existential raison d'être of the state, then how can one hope that Palestinians who want to form a state next to Israel – let alone have the right to flood back into the state in accordance with a Palestinian right of return – would begin to accept this foundational narrative?[54]

The author of the survey, Professor Sammy Smooha, interprets this increasing rate of Holocaust denial among Palestinian Israelis as a protest more than an actual disbelief in the Holocaust. The constant refrain of anti-Semitism and the experience of the Holocaust that discussion of Israel evokes are, to Palestinians and Arabs in general, unrelated to what Zionism and Israel have meant in the Palestinian experience. Although the historical link between anti-Semitism and Israel is part of the history of Zionism – a critical link that became the driving force behind modern Jewish nationalism – the Palestinian aspect of Zionist experience (its most recent) cannot be understood solely in terms of what happened in Europe. Rather than a consistent trend of radicalization over the past thirty years, Smooha perceives a long-term adaptation of Israeli Arabs to Israel's existence. The sharp increase in Holocaust denial, by his interpretation, reflects the fact that, "to the Arabs, the Holocaust is a legitimization of Israel's right to exist as a Jewish state. If you say there was no Holocaust, you're protesting this [Israel's existence]. This is a way of saying that the Jews use the Holocaust to portray themselves as the victims, when in truth, we [the Arabs] are the victims."[55]

Smooha might be correct in his interpretation. But it is not hard to imagine the anguish and unsettling impact of these statistics on Israeli Jews (and on Jews in the Diaspora) who have gone through the Holocaust – or, more pertinent to this historical moment, for their children and grandchildren. They convey a terrible harbinger of the prospect of peace, or indeed cohabitation, under the auspices of such a profoundly attenuated common ground – and an ominous augury of the place of Jews in the world more broadly.

The devastation of the Holocaust, however, is not the only constitutional narrative threatened by a radical undermining by the other side. Nakba denial – the denial of the foundational narrative of the Palestinian people – has now been elevated to the level of a possible state position in Israel.

Since the Israeli archives were opened fifty years after the founding of the state of Israel, a school of Israeli historians has revisited the official history of the founding of the state on the basis of this newly available documentation.[56] The orthodox history of Israel is founded on the story that the Palestinians fled the territory voluntarily during the War of 1948 – the war in which Israel's status as a state was consolidated – principally under the sway of Arab leaders who convinced them that they could return victorious after the hostilities ceased.[57] Based on the newly released Israeli military and governmental documents from the period, the New Historians make a compelling case that concerted political and military efforts to evacuate the land of Palestinians by the terrorization of indigenous civilians in order to ensure a demographic majority for Jews in the newly formed state of Israel might have had as much as or more to do than any other factor with the flight of 700,000 Palestinians from their homeland.[58]

This disaster, the Nakba, sundered the Palestinian population in two – those remaining within the state of Israel who constitute 18-20 percent of the Israeli population[59] and those (less than a third in refugee camps) scattered throughout the West Bank, Gaza, and the Middle East and the larger Palestinian Diaspora.[60] This catastrophic evacuation of Palestinians from their historic homeland is a defining tragedy of the Palestinian narrative felt acutely by those Palestinians left behind – those who lost their families and co-patriots to the dispersal and who often feel like second-class citizens in their homeland.[61] It is an anguish felt daily by those refugees who, more than sixty years later, are still living tenuously in refugee camps, often in intense squalor, poverty, and hopelessness, yearning to return to their lost Jerusalems.[62]

These Palestinians did not need the New Historians to inform them of the accuracy of the history that they had lived through. The New Historians, however, facilitated a broader recognition of Palestinian foundational truths among those who had erased them, with seeming intentionality, from the shared narratives of humanity.

This long history of denial that Israel's War of Independence was also a violent catastrophe of ethnic cleansing recently found a counterpart to the 40 percent of Israeli Palestinians who deny that the Holocaust occurred. The Israeli minister of education, Likud's Gideon Saar, recently decided to remove references to the phrase "Nakba" (or "catastrophe") from textbooks for Arab schoolchildren. "No other country in the world, in its official curriculum," he stated, "would treat the fact of its founding as a catastrophe."[63] Prime Minister Netanyahu went so far as to claim that "the word 'nakba' in Israeli Arab schools was tantamount to spreading propaganda against Israel."[64] That the pedagogy of official history would preclude the experience and perspective of close to a quarter of the population cannot but make the latter feel that the country being taught about in their own schools is not their own.

This move to deny the Nakba in the educational system was one item of a raft of proposed bills recently placed before the Knesset led by the Likud coalition in its first months of business.[65] One of the more poignant of these bills proposed that Palestinians be forbidden from commemorating the Nakba, on pain of a jail term of up to three years for violators.[66]

This effort to outlaw collective memory and the foundational narrative of a people – a narrative that is inconvenient for many aspects of Israel's founding narrative – has all of the anti-democratic taint of the proposed bill criminally outlawing critical thought and speech related to the Jewishness of the state of Israel. Far more ominously, however, it is also darkened by the growing shadow of the threat of a population transfer of Palestinian Israelis, construed as a fifth column within the Jewish state since the original flight and transfer of more than half of their population from the land in 1948. The raft of Likud bills cited above was led by coalition member Avigdor Lieberman, important enough in Israel's government not only to sit in the cabinet but also to have been designated under Netanyahu as the Israeli foreign minister.[67] Under the previous government, Lieberman's Yisrael Beiteinu ("Israel Is Our Home") party proposed a plan to strip citizenship from Israelis based on race, transferring through a redrawing of Israel's borders with the West Bank the dense concentration of Palestinians living in a cluster of Israeli Arab towns and villages adjacent to the green line.[68] The endorsement that Lieberman's party received in the most recent Israeli elections emboldened both Lieberman and the Likud coalition, in which he played a kingmaker role, to operationalize the platform of Israel being exclusively one people's home.

The transfer platform – in conjunction with a bill aimed provocatively at Palestinian Israelis that proposed hinging citizenship on an oath of loyalty (anomalously, for democratic states, hinging civil rights on the performance of duties)[69] and in conjunction with the host of bills policing ideas, collective memories, and pedagogy – underscores an extremely troubling and distasteful anti-democratic trend in Israel proper. This trend not only portends but also illustrates in real time Israel's exponentially increasing alienation from predominant understandings of democracy and citizenship prevalent in the Western world.

Although the Knesset's Ministerial Committee on Legislation approved the draft law outlawing the commemoration of the Nakba by majority vote, the legislation did not pass and was met by a vocal protest among both Jewish and Palestinian Israelis.[70] However, whether these disturbing laws passed or not, their purpose seemed to be exquisitely designed to undermine the Palestinian reality in the region as well as to threaten any Palestinian sense of being at home, as equal citizens, in Israel.

The conjunction of logically impossible peace negotiations in light of (apparently intentionally) irreconcilable opening positions and the entrenchment of incommensurable narratives of the past appears to leave the two-state model drifting further toward utopia while increasingly losing touch with realities on the ground. The illusion of the pursuit of an increasingly elusive two-state solution, while the accelerating anti-democratic thrust of Israel's governance proceeds in the practical world, is jarring for those whose democratic and humane sensibilities incline them naturally and sympathetically to the hope for a state founded on a profound awareness of the Holocaust's complete annihilation of those ideals.

The bedrock of Never Again – not for Jews or any other people – created a broad new community of concern, vigilance, and commitment. This community, which operates on both international and domestic levels and has some internationally pedigreed spokespeople, has accumulated an array of instruments and institutions to shore up the lessons of the Holocaust and other humanitarian disasters and wars. It has thrown up new *gzerot* and entrenched others around that terrible pedagogy. These *gzerot* include proscriptions around the violation of fundamental human and civil rights – and they are designed with acute circumspection about the applicability of preference for some peoples and not others.

If the direction of the status quo in the Middle East appears to be veering troublingly toward a democratic deficit and depletion of the equal distribution of civil rights for all citizens in Israel proper, on the international scale it is increasingly hard to square the proscriptions around human rights abuses and the laws of war with the nihilistic practices of both sides. In light of these practices, both sides should expect a drastic loss of support from the larger communities that were and are at least ideologically instrumental in maintaining international law's fences around inhumanity – including the United Nations, the United States, and, as this story unfolds here, Canada.

Because Israel has been almost unwaveringly supported by the United States since 1967[71] – and has asymmetrically enjoyed Canadian support since the Conservative government came to power in 2006[72] – it seems to be the least prepared for international indignation and condemnation when it breaks basic humanitarian and human rights laws. As with Israel's slate of anti-democratic bills, recent history need only be courted to demonstrate this troubling direction – both the violations and the responses to outside criticism.

One of the world's revered archetypes of respect for the rule of international law is Richard Goldstone, a former South African Constitutional Court judge. As the chair of the Goldstone Commission, which inquired into public violence and intimidation in the waning years of South Africa's apartheid regime, Goldstone played a critical role in bringing home to "white" South Africans the extensive violence being done in their name.[73] He is also intimately familiar with the legal and factual thresholds relevant to the determination of war crimes and other violations of international law, having served as the chief prosecutor of the International Criminal Tribunal for the former Yugoslavia and Rwanda.[74]

Goldstone was appointed by the United Nations in April 2009 to head an independent UN fact-finding mission "to investigate all violations of international human rights law and international humanitarian law that might have been committed at any time in the context of the military operations that were conducted in Gaza during the period from 27 December 2008 and 18 January 2009, whether before, during or after."[75] This was a conflict in which between 1,387 and 1,417 Palestinians were killed and in which there were fourteen Israeli fatalities, of whom four were civilians and ten were soldiers, four of whom died as a result of friendly fire.[76] The conflict happened just months before the Mapping Models conference and added to a general sense of despair and urgency regarding the impasse in the Middle East.

Goldstone fits classically the paradigm of one schooled extensively in the pedagogy of the Holocaust, including its universal lesson of Never Again. As a Zionist who loves Israel, he was shocked as a Jew to be appointed to head the mission.[77] However, as he was quoted as saying in explaining the emotional and juristic resources from which he drew to assess the Gaza conflict,

> he viewed the Holocaust as a unique occurrence because of how it affected judicial protocol on war, as well as international and humanitarian judicial approaches. The laws that had been in place before the Holocaust were not equipped to deal with crimes of the Holocaust's scale and therefore sought to define a new crime, which they labeled a crime against humanity. These crimes were so great, he explained, they went beyond their direct victims or the countries in which they were perpetrated, to harm humanity as a whole.[78]

The characterization of Goldstone by Richard Falk, a professor of international law at Princeton University, seems apt: "He has deep emotional and intellectual links to Israel but he also has a professional attachment to the rule of law."[79]

The Goldstone Report makes it clear that both sides violated international law during the conflict. The report begins its consideration of the Palestinian side of infractions by noting the continuing violation of the Third Geneva Convention on the Laws of War in the ongoing detention of Israeli soldier Gilad Shalit, captured in 2006 by an armed Palestinian group. As a prisoner of war, Shalit should have been protected, treated humanely, and allowed external communication as appropriate according to that convention. Furthermore, the International Committee of the Red Cross (ICRC) should have been allowed to visit him without delay.[80] The report also references intra-Palestinian actions during the war that violated basic human rights such as the targeting of Fatah affiliates by security services under the control of the Gaza authorities.[81]

The principal complaint against Palestinian armed groups whose forces were directed against Israel and Israeli soldiers was the launching of 8,000 rockets into southern Israel since 2001. Between June 18, 2008, and January 18, 2009, three civilians were killed inside Israel. Over 1,000 civilians inside Israel were physically injured as a result of rocket and mortar attacks, 918 of those during Israel's military operations in Gaza.[82] Given that the mortars fired were incapable of being directed at specific military targets and were launched into civilian areas, the Goldstone Report is clear that they were indiscriminate attacks on the civilian population of Israel and as such constituted war crimes and could amount to crimes against humanity.[83] A primary purpose of the attacks was to spread terror among the civilian population, a violation of international law. The express intention to target civilians as a form of reprisal for Gaza's civilian fatalities was also found to be contrary to international humanitarian law.[84]

Although the report describes violations of international law on both sides, it focuses on the larger violations of international law committed by Israeli forces – paralleling the massively disproportionate losses between Israelis and Gazan Palestinians.[85] This component of the report begins by describing the economic and political isolation imposed by Israel on the Gaza Strip since the electoral victory of Hamas in February 2006. Pursued as an ongoing policy for three years before the conflict, the blockade included restricting the importation of goods into Gaza; the closure of border crossings for people, goods, and services; cuts in the provision of fuel and electricity; and a reduction of the Palestinian fishing zone and a buffer zone around the strip that reduced agriculture and industrial capacity.[86] As the report notes, "the military operations of 28 December to 19 January 2009 and their impact cannot be fully evaluated without taking account of the context and the prevailing living conditions at the time they began. In material respects, the military hostilities were a culmination of the long process of economic and political isolation imposed on the Gaza Strip by Israel."[87] Problematic in its own right as a collective punishment of the entire population of Gaza – and a violation of the Fourth Geneva Convention – the long-standing blockade, the report notes, weakened the capacities of the population and of the health, water, and other public sectors to respond to the emergency created by the military operations. The report urged Israel to cease this violation of the Fourth Geneva Convention to ensure the supply of food, medical and hospital items, and other goods to meet the humanitarian needs of the population of the Gaza Strip.[88]

The Goldstone Report is very telling in its delivery of a broader context for the Gaza War. The concluding section of the report provides an even broader context than Gaza alone and makes it clear that the war was not an isolated event in which the only considerations were the Qassam rockets from Gaza and the Israeli military response to them. Goldstone indicates that the Gaza War was part of a "continuum" linked to the occupation of Palestinian territories for more than forty years. As the report notes, "Israel's military operation in Gaza between 27 December 2008 and 18 January 2009 and its impact cannot be understood or assessed in isolation from developments prior and subsequent to it. The operation fits into a continuum of policies aimed at pursuing Israel's political objectives with regard to Gaza and the Occupied Palestinian Territory as a whole."[89]

The continuum to which Goldstone refers is evident in the Israeli blockade of Gaza preceding the military operations that was imposed in order to isolate and weaken Hamas after its electoral victory in 2006. As Goldstone notes, prior to the Gaza War, "men, women and children were psychologically suffering from long-standing poverty, insecurity and violence, and enforced confinement in a heavily overcrowded territory. The dignity of the people of Gaza had been severely eroded."[90]

The Goldstone Report, however, goes much deeper than an examination of the blockade of Gaza[91] and insists that the continuum that constituted the more pressing context of the 2008-9 operations connected to other pre-existing Israeli policies with respect to the occupied Palestinian territories, including the West Bank and East Jerusalem. The report lays out an array of these policies that makes it difficult for Israel to isolate Gaza and the Qassams and claim (as it did as part of its enduring resistance to the Goldstone Report)[92] that it was legitimately defending itself, or in the words of Tzipi Livni, the minister of foreign affairs during the war, a country under attack "must respond in a way that returns the intimidation."[93] The report anticipates Israel's justification of self-defence by noting that

> several measures adopted by Israel in the West Bank during and following the military operations in Gaza also further deepen Israel's control over the West Bank, including East Jerusalem, and point to a convergence of objectives with the Gaza military operations. Such measures include increased land expropriation, house demolitions, demolition orders and permits to build homes in settlements, greater and more formalized access and movement restrictions on Palestinians, new and stricter procedures for residents of the Gaza Strip to change their residency to the West Bank. Systematic efforts to hinder and control Palestinian self-determined democratic processes, not least through the detention of elected political representatives and members of Government and the punishment of the Gaza population for its perceived support for Hamas culminated in the attacks on government buildings during the Gaza offensive, most prominently the Palestinian Legislative Council.[94]

The Goldstone Report lays out the longer continuum between Israel's military operation in Gaza and the antecedent forty-one years of occupation, stressing that the former cannot be understood without assessing it as part of this larger oppressive context.

Beyond this contextualization of the military operations, the report itemizes grave violations by Israel of international war. They included attacks by Israeli forces on government buildings and persons of the Gaza authority, including police,[95] and attacks on the foundations of civilian life in Gaza, such as the destruction of industrial infrastructure, food production, water installations, sewage treatment plants, and housing.[96] Also cited are the inadequate precautions taken to protect the civilian population and civil infrastructure in Gaza, including the instruction to the populace to move to city centres for safety when the centres themselves had been subjected to intense attacks during the air phase of the military operations.[97] As reported to the mission, there was a pervasive sense in Gaza that there was "nowhere to go." "The nature of the attacks in the first week had caused deep shock. The widespread attacks created a dilemma not only about where to go but about whether it was safe to leave at all."[98]

The report also complains about indiscriminate attacks by Israeli forces resulting in loss of life and injury to civilians. And, most troubling, it details multiple incidents in which Israeli armed forces launched direct attacks against civilians with lethal outcomes and no justifiable military rationale. These attacks included the shelling of a house in which Palestinian civilians had been forced to assemble by Israeli armed forces and the shooting of civilians while they were trying to leave their homes to walk to a safer place, waving white flags and, in some cases, following an injunction from Israeli forces to do so. These actions were aggravated by the subsequent refusal of Israeli soldiers to allow the evacuation of the wounded or to permit access to ambulances. In another incident, a mosque was targeted with a missile during early evening prayers, resulting in the deaths of fifteen people, and an attack with flechette munitions on a crowd of family members and neighbours at a condolence tent killed five.[99] These actions "constitute[d] grave breaches of the Fourth Geneva Convention in respect of willful killings and willfully causing great suffering to protected persons and, as such, give rise to individual criminal responsibility. It also finds that the direct targeting and arbitrary killing of Palestinian civilians is a violation of the right to life."[100]

The Goldstone Report was released in September 2009. It provided a very painful account of violations of international law and war crimes on both sides of the conflict. Ultimately, it recommended that each side be given until the end of 2009 to conduct fully independent internal investigations into its violations of international law, failing which Goldstone recommended that the report be referred to the UN Security Council for prosecution at the International Criminal Court.[101]

Given the disproportionate number of citations and indictments against Israel, their gravity, and the overwhelming asymmetry of force between the two sides, the Goldstone Report was poised to offer a piercing analysis of any pretension that Israel was the most vulnerable party, morally justified, and somehow rational in its deployment of force. No doubt foreseeably, the report was greeted in Israel and in much of the Jewish community in the Diaspora with fury and charges of anti-Israel bias.[102]

The immediate response of the Israeli government was to attempt to marshal international opinion against the report. Prime Minister Netanyahu asked world leaders to "come out now, condemn this report and act to quash its consequences now." He further called on the world to oppose the conclusion that formal charges could be brought against Israeli soldiers, officers, and leaders at the International Criminal Court. Although various prominent Israelis urged the government to set up the commission of inquiry recommended in the Goldstone Report in order to preclude a referral to the UN Security Council, Netanyahu opted to put his energies into convincing the international community that a referral to the International Criminal Court would sound the death knell of the peace process.[103]

There are certainly voices within Israel and the Jewish Diaspora[104] who condemn the strenuous efforts to place Israel outside the pale of the community of nations and the collective legal norms and resources that emerged before and, more concertedly, after the Holocaust to govern nations. Journalist Gideon Levy writes in *Ha'aretz* that,

> for almost a year, Israel has been trying to argue that the blood spilled in Gaza was merely water. One report followed the other, with horrifyingly identical results: siege, white phosphorous, harm of innocent civilians, infrastructure destroyed – war crimes in each and every report. Now, after the publication of the most important and damning report of all, compiled by the commission led by Judge Richard Goldstone, Israel's attempts to discredit them look ludicrous, and the empty bluster of its spokespersons sound pathetic.[105]

The defensiveness of the official Israeli reaction, however, is indicative of a growing insularity that speaks to a turning away from a beholdenness to any other but internal norms, to a defiance toward the *gzerot* of the larger collective, which are prerequisite in many ways to advancing the two-state model given how such a model is dependent on both the recognition of collective international norms for its moral weight and the recognition of the basic reality of the other.

This sense of insularity has been well captured by Ian Lustick in a seminal article entitled "Abandoning the Iron Wall: Israel and the 'Middle Eastern Muck.'"[106] Lustick compares the positions of earlier Israeli governments with those of recent years. The paper was written before the election of the current Likud coalition and before the Gaza War. Events such as the coalition's raft of anti-democratic bills and reaction to the Goldstone Report consolidate the article's underlying concern for the increasingly solipsistic direction in which Israel is headed.

Some early Zionist leaders recognized that they had no reason to expect Palestinians and others in the Middle East to greet the building of a new Jewish national home with anything but intransigence and violent opposition.[107] The solution (Jabotinskian in origin) was to erect an iron wall. This, as Lustick notes, was "the systematic but calibrated use of force to teach Arabs that Israel, the Jewish 'state-on-the-way,' was ineradicable, regardless of whether it was perceived by them to be just."[108] Force was the necessary prelude to negotiations based on acceptance of realities rather than rights. As he remarks, this strategy served Israel well until the end of the twentieth century. He indicates that Israel is abandoning that strategy and that, rather than asserting itself forcefully as an inextricable part of the Middle East, its leaders and much of the population as a whole are fundamentally withdrawing "from the realities of the Middle East and from a commitment to engage and change those realities, whether through force or diplomacy."[109] This position derives from an expansion of distrust, despite the victories of force, fed by an unanswerable suspicion that even moderate Palestinian positions camouflage a desire to regain the territory in stages. The ineradicable distrust drives an expansion of demands by the consistently victorious side, particularly because the use of force drastically – and equally ineradicably – increases the sense of injustice on the other side.

The position of escape also derives from a flaw in Jabotinsky's reasoning about the pedagogy of force – not with regard to the defeated but with regard to the victorious. As Lustick notes,

> [Jabotinsky] did not realize that while a normal nation does produce moderates willing to compromise when it is regularly and painfully defeated for

> trying to achieve what it feels is just, a normal nation (such as the Jews) that experiences victory after victory over an apparently impotent foe will tend to eliminate moderates within itself, empower maximalists, and search for reasons to avoid negotiations and compromise in the expectation that fulfilling all its dreams simply required the dogged and ruthless exercise of power.[110]

The increasing scope for maximalism in the face of the massive asymmetry of force between Israelis and Palestinians has encouraged an increasing insularity and enforced separation between the two groups.

The increasing insularity and maximalism to which Lustick alludes can be seen in the new demand for Palestinian recognition of the Jewishness of the state of Israel; in the imagery of the Arab other as irrational, brutal, violent, and intractably anti-Semitic and deceptive; in a deep pessimism about the prospects for a two-state solution conjoined with fantasies about Greater Israel or paying Palestinians to leave Israel and the occupied territories or enlisting Jordan and Egypt to absorb both the refugees and eventually the residual Palestinian fifth column of a Jewish state; and in the escape from the Middle East by Israelis leaving the country or the border zones of contact with the Arab world by an influx into Tel Aviv.[111]

Although Lustick was writing before the 2009 Gaza conflict, he speaks to a further departure from the idea of compelling the surrounding (and embedded) Arab world to accept the reality of the Jewish state in its midst whether or not it is just. The Gaza conflict – and the official reaction to reports of abuses in its conduct – consolidate Lustick's assessment that the non-rational use of violence by Israel, beginning with the invasion of Lebanon in 1982, portends its departure from an aspiration to create a Jewish state that could conceivably exist within the context of the Middle East.

As Lustick notes, "Zionism's use of violence against Arabs was traditionally conceived as a pedagogical device to convince Arabs of the Jewish National Home's indestructibility, and then to persuade some among them to negotiate mutually acceptable deals based on the alternative of suffering painful defeats."[112] The transformation from the rational use of violence (marshalled to this end of forcing a recognition of realities over rights) arises with the deep pessimism of the past twenty years about whether, despite the consistent deployment of force, Arabs and Muslims can come to accept a Jewish state in their midst. As a result of this shift, the rationale for violence also changes:

> Instead of being conceived as a persuasive instrument in service of political or diplomatic aims, force against Arabs and Muslims is increasingly treated as a kind of *rattonade*. This was the term used to characterize the French practice in Algeria of entering casbahs and other Muslim quarters, killing inhabitants, and then quickly returning to European areas or bases. Its literal meaning is "rat hunt." More generally, it refers to a violent strike against the enemy "on the other side of the wall" for purposes of punishment, destruction and psychological release.[113]

The lack of rational military or political objectives was evident in the Second Lebanon War. This much was underlined by Israel's official and internal investigation of that war, the Winograd Commission.[114] Such military action can be emotionally gratifying – as evidenced by the Israelis who "stood with their children on the hills around Gaza and cheered on the carnage-causing bombs" in the Gaza War.[115] However, as Lustick notes, "specific evaluation of these measures based on their political rationality – i.e., the likelihood that they might enhance or undermine chances for progress toward a peace settlement – is almost entirely absent."[116] The fact that Netanyahu asked world leaders to condition their support for peace negotiations on the burial of Goldstone's findings of injustice – in the form of war crimes and crimes against humanity – speaks to an abandonment of Zionism's earlier commitment to a pedagogy of coercion. The earlier wager that a Palestinian (and consequently Arab and Muslim) recognition of a Jewish reality in the Middle East could be tied to both the forceful reality of the Jewish nation and sufficient political, economic, and legal Palestinian satisfaction has given way to the singular predominance of the former. The only reality to be reconciled to is the endless, arbitrary, and punitive use of force – a pedagogy that international law not only will not learn from but is also committed to confront.

Lustick relates the demise of this wager to one last element that seemed (even writing before the 2009 Israeli elections) to foretell the death knell of the two-state model. As he notes, "it is the centrality of this wager [the provision of sufficient political, economic, and legal satisfaction conjoined with the iron wall reality of Israel's existence] to the integrity of the Zionist project that has made the question of *de facto* annexation, and whether Israeli settlements have obliterated chances for a real Palestinian state solution, so crucial and so painful within Israel."[117] Because Lustick was writing before the initially bold, but now failed, efforts of the first Obama administration to bring a halt to Israeli settlement activity in the occupied territories in order to reinvigorate the peace process and before the triumphalist and successful refusal of Netanyahu's government to do so, his pessimistic speculation that a two-state solution has been rendered impossible has only become more grim. The stark choice that he laid out in 2008 between engagement with the real Middle East and the demands that it makes on Israel for justice, democracy, and territory – or escape from it – seems already to have been clearly cast.

This grim prognosis for the two-state model was echoed by a recent op-ed in the *Washington Post* by another archetype of the international post-Holocaust community, former American president Jimmy Carter.[118] His 2007 book *Palestine Peace Not Apartheid* was received with the same suspicion and defensiveness that the Goldstone Report met.[119] Yet, since the Camp David Accords of 1978, Carter has been working assiduously on first a proto-two-state model based on the recognition of both peoples' rights to security and self-determination and later the now orthodox two-state solution.

Controversially (beyond the charged use of the word *apartheid* in the book's title), Carter lays a great deal of the blame for the impasse on Israel. As he notes, "peace will come to Israel and the Middle East only when the Israeli government is willing to comply with international law, with the Roadmap for Peace, with official American policy, with the wishes of a majority of its own citizens – and honor its own previous commitments – by accepting its legal borders."[120] One central issue that Carter returns to throughout his argument – one implicit in this citation – is Israel's long-standing refusal to honour UN Security Council Resolution 242 of November 22, 1967.[121] It is the ongoing breach of this resolution over the past forty-five years that Lustick, above, laments might have rendered the two-state model impossible. And it is the current Israeli government's defiant disregard for it that appears to have contributed to Carter's pessimistic movement between the 2007 publication of his book and his September 2009 *Washington Post* op-ed (to which I will return).

UN Resolution 242 was approved unanimously at the Security Council, is still applicable, and serves as the foundation of peace negotiations and treaties from the Camp David Accords onward. It was approved immediately after the 1967 War in which Israel occupied the West Bank and Gaza as well as the Golan Heights and the Sinai Peninsula. The resolution stipulates that every state has the right to live in peace with secure and recognized boundaries free from threats or acts of violence.[122] It calls for a just settlement of the refugee problem.[123] And, most critically, through a linking of Article 2 of the Charter of the United Nations to the resolution, it is premised on the foundation that Israel's acquisition through force is illegal in international law[124] and that Israel must withdraw from the occupied territories.[125] Not only is UN Resolution 242 the most referenced resolution to end the conflict, but this cornerstone of the international diplomatic community has also been the foundation of American policy on peace negotiations from the Camp David Accords to the Road Map for Peace – a relevant fact due to the almost exclusively pivotal role that the United States has played in the Middle East for the past forty-five years.

The settlement of Israelis within the occupied territories exacerbates the violation of UN Resolution 242 (which calls for the withdrawal of Israeli forces from the occupied territories) and the antecedent international law upon which the resolution is based.[126] An abundance of international legal scholars,[127] UN resolutions,[128] and diplomatic interventions[129] has affirmed that the ongoing settlement of the territories, including the settlement of East Jerusalem, violates Article 49 of the Fourth Geneva Convention, which states that "the Occupying Power shall not deport or transfer parts of its own civilian population into the territory it occupies."[130] The fundamental illegality of settling Israeli citizens in the occupied territories (including East Jerusalem) was also clearly decided in 2004 by the International Court of Justice.[131] The court held that, despite Israeli arguments to the contrary, Article 49 of the Fourth Geneva Convention applies to the occupied territories[132] and that "the Israeli settlements in the Occupied Palestinian territories (including East Jerusalem) have been established in breach of international law."[133]

In light of the broad international consensus on the illegality of the Israeli settlements, the relentless and escalating relocation of Israeli citizens by the Israeli government in the occupied territories (and East Jerusalem) inflames Palestinian feelings of insecurity, injustice, and hopelessness. This campaign is also catastrophic for the prospect of the two-state model, predicated as it is on the coexistence of two viable states living alongside each other, with state capitals in West and East Jerusalem respectively. Carter lays out just how bleakly the settlement policy (and the physical and military infrastructure that has been installed to shore it up) has undermined the prospects for a viable Palestinian state:

> There is a zone with a radius of about four hundred meters around each settlement within which Palestinians cannot enter. In addition, there are

> other large areas that would have been taken or earmarked to be used exclusively by Israel, roadways that connect the settlements to one another and to Jerusalem, and "life arteries" that provide the settlers with water, sewage, electricity, and communications. These range in width from five hundred to four thousand meters, and Palestinians cannot use or cross many of these connecting links. This honeycomb of settlements and their interconnecting conduits effectively divide the West Bank into at least two non-contiguous areas and multiple fragments, often uninhabitable or even unreachable, and control of the Jordan River valley denies Palestinians any direct access eastward into Jordan. About one hundred military checkpoints completely surround Palestine and block routes going into or between Palestinian communities, combined with an uncountable number of other roads that are permanently closed with large concrete cubes or mounds of earth and rock.[134]

In this passage, Carter writes about the period following the failed 2000 Camp David Summit. The settlement project has proceeded unabated since that time, compounding the sense of hopelessness, generated by the ongoing settlements, about the prospects for the two-state model.

The 2009 election of Netanyahu multiplied the grimness. He ran for election on the platform of scuttling the two-state model of the Road Map for Peace, endorsed by the quartet of the United Nations, the United States, the European Union, and Russia.[135] He has also, contrary to the broad consensus in international law, declared that Jerusalem is the indivisible capital of Israel[136] – nullifying the viability of East Jerusalem as the capital of the sovereign state of the Palestinians. And, despite a seemingly courageous and strong American affirmation of its long-standing policy with respect to UN Resolution 242 and the settlement by Israelis of the occupied territories, Netanyahu defiantly refused to recognize President Obama's call for a complete cessation of settlement activity.[137] With the swift demise of the peace negotiations initiated by Obama in the late summer of 2010, a ten-month lull in permits for new settlement homes in the West Bank came to an end on September 27, 2010, with 238 permits expeditiously issued for East Jerusalem alone.[138] The situation in the Middle East has continued on the same inauspicious trajectory since that time.

The PLO insisted that it cannot negotiate while the settlement project continues, and the Israeli prime minister refused to renew the freeze unless the PLO recognized Israel as a Jewish state, but, for the reasons outlined above, that was clearly a non-starter.

The PLO, observing the effectively complete demise (yet again) of the peace process and the implications for the PLO of the dispute being "managed" into the foreseeable future along the lines of a grossly unfavourable status quo, decided to seek membership in the United Nations directly and not by way of negotiations.[139] September 2011 was chosen as the deadline for this project in light of the statement by President Obama in the UN General Assembly that he wanted to see a Palestinian state at the United Nations by 2011. The Arabic name for the campaign at the United Nations is "September's obligation," implying that this is a commitment owed to the Palestinian people by the American government and the world community. However, both Israel and the United States opposed the UN bid.

In the fall of 2011, after weeks of discussions at the UN Security Council, the United States seemed to manage to avoid invoking an embarrassing Security Council veto of the Palestinian bid by strong-arming Bosnia and Colombia into sinking the resolution. Although the resolution continues to be debated, that appears to be the likely outcome for the bid.[140]

In the meantime, Palestine was admitted to the UNESCO. This development was followed by an announcement by the United States that it would therefore cut its annual contribution of roughly $60 million. And, as a result of the UN bid, Congress debated cutting aid to the Palestinian Authority (PA), with the Israeli prime minister intervening, ironically, to oppose the motion because most of the aid goes to the PA security forces that meet Israel's security interests in the West Bank.[141]

The Arab Spring, roiling the entire region in which Israel/Palestine is embedded, has done little other than generate the occasion for a greater entrenchment of power. In a speech delivered by Prime Minister Benjamin Netanyahu on November 23, 2011, he referenced the rising tide of historical demands in the Arab world for fundamental freedoms and human rights and concluded that

> the earth is shaking. We do not know who will take over any land that we give up, not tomorrow, not this very afternoon. We see this reality everywhere. Whoever does not see it is burying their head in the sand. But that did not stand in the way of people suggesting that I give in. I said that we want to reach an agreement with the Palestinians because we do not want a bi-national state, but we must insist on having stable and secure foundations, we have always wanted that, but now we need it more than ever.
>
> I will not ignore reality, I will not ignore the dangers, I will not ignore history, I will not ignore the present or give up on any of our security

> requirements that have increased because of the recent crises and not diminished. This is not the time to yield them, it is not the time to rush into things, it is the time to be cautious in our connections with the Palestinians.[142]

Israel appears to be very remote from the desire to cohabit with others in the region that Israelis call home. The entire situation speaks to a poverty of hope for the two-state model.

Although Carter has long been a strong advocate for the two-state model, he is clear in *Palestine Peace Not Apartheid* that there are other models, some of which are unacceptable in international law and to the minds of many supporters worldwide of the fundamental tenets of democracy. Netanyahu's Likud coalition appears to be taking Israeli society toward the most egregious of these options: a Greater Israel that annexes the occupied territories onto Israel.

Of the three logical leading alternatives for the future of the Middle East, the first that Carter addresses is the forcible annexation of the West Bank and Gaza Strip and their legal absorption into Israel. Although this alternative might coincide with Israeli visions on the far right of a Greater Israel, without the transfer of a large swath of the Palestinian population from this larger territory it is just as, if not more than, foreseeably linked to a one-state model in which non-Jewish citizens acquire the right to vote and live as equals under the law.[143] This vision of Israel as a single state of all of its citizens is, as pointed out by the critics of our conference, a totally unacceptable direction for the future for most Israeli and diasporic Jews. However, the alternative subset of this future – the transfer of Palestinians from this vision of Greater Israel or the incorporation of them as second-class citizens into a single Jewish state – is wholly unacceptable to both international law and the international community.[144]

The second future, as Carter notes, is "a system of apartheid, with two peoples occupying the same land but completely separated from each other, with Israel totally dominant and suppressing violence by depriving Palestinians of their basic human rights."[145] Carter courted a furious backlash from diasporic Jewish communities and Israeli Jews[146] for going on to remark that "this [apartheid] is the policy now being followed, although many citizens of Israel deride the racist connotation of prescribing permanent second-class status for the Palestinians."[147]

The third and, to Carter's mind, most attractive option, "and the only one that can ultimately be acceptable as a basis for peace,"[148] is the two-state model, which Carter has been promoting since he managed to convince both Egyptian and Israeli counterparts to the Camp David Accord of 1978 that the Palestinian people should be recognized therein as a separate political entity with the right to determine their own future.[149] This was a major step toward a Palestinian state, and hence the two-state model, which thereafter became the increasingly accepted model for peace in the Middle East from the Oslo Accords through the Arab Peace Initiative of 2002, the Geneva Initiative of 2003, the Road Map for Peace first outlined by US president George W. Bush in 2002, and the current attempt by the Obama administration to marshal Israeli and Palestinian parties into negotiations.

These were the foreseeable options that Carter outlined in 2007. Following a visit to the Middle East in the late summer of 2009, Carter, while still endorsing the two-state model, appeared to be far bleaker about its prospects in light of many of the issues outlined above. In his op-ed piece, he echoes Goldstone's deep concerns about Israel's violations of the Geneva Convention through the blockade on Gaza. He calls Gaza a "walled-in ghetto" and notes that "Israel prevents any cement, lumber, seeds, fertilizer and hundreds of other needed materials from entering through Gaza's gates. Some additional goods from Egypt reach Gaza through underground tunnels. Gazans cannot produce their own food nor repair schools, hospitals, business establishments or the 50,000 homes that were destroyed or heavily damaged by Israel's assault last January."[150] He notes with despair that (consistent with Netanyahu's settlement policy and the policy of successive Israeli governments from 1967 on)[151] "settlement expansion is continuing apace, rapidly encroaching into Palestinian villages, hilltops, grazing lands, farming areas and olive groves." He notes the "even more disturbing expansion"[152] taking place in Palestinian East Jerusalem, a development catastrophically linked to the demise of the two-state model.

While Carter was both laying out the alternatives in 2007 and strongly endorsing the only one that he found acceptable as a basis for peace (the two-state model), in 2009, still a strong advocate for that model, he had a different prognosis for the resolution of the impasse, one that, echoing Lustick, is deeply pessimistic about whether the conditions for a two-state model any longer exist:

> A more likely alternative to the present debacle is one state, which is obviously the goal of Israeli leaders who insist on colonizing the West Bank and East Jerusalem. A majority of the Palestinian leaders with whom we met are seriously considering acceptance of one state, between the Jordan

> River and the Mediterranean Sea. By renouncing the dream of an independent Palestine, they would become fellow citizens with their Jewish neighbors and then demand equal rights within a democracy. In this nonviolent civil rights struggle, their examples would be Mahatma Gandhi, Martin Luther King Jr. and Nelson Mandela.[153]

Scheinberg and Caplan, cited earlier in this chapter, believe that "frustration with the lack of progress toward a two-state solution does not provide a sufficient basis for advocating a one-state solution."[154] However, in the grim context of decades of frustrated peace negotiations framed by the two-state model, and in the context of a status quo with an accelerating asymmetry of force, the basis seems to be increasingly compelling to those who draw from the foundational moral and legal resources of the post-Holocaust world, a foundation based on Never Again – not for Jews *and not for any people.* It is hard (though by no means impossible)[155] to characterize Carter as one who "cater[s] to demagogic seekers of 'justice,'" to use Scheinberg and Caplan's phrasing.[156] As Carter intimates with his connection of the one-state model to other civil rights struggles around the world, the structure of the current impasse might indeed make it harder to continue putting quotation marks around "justice" (as Scheinberg and Caplan do) – at least without making impassioned appeals to the prejudices and emotions of the populace.

Postscript on Richard Goldstone

Richard Goldstone published a brief comment in the *Washington Post* on April 1, 2011, in which he laments the failure of Hamas in Gaza to investigate the allegations of its war crimes and possible crimes against humanity but in which he also partially distances himself from his earlier findings, indicating that, "had [I] known then what I know now," the Goldstone Report would have been a different document.[157] Although sufficiently brief to be somewhat cryptic, he claims that investigations published by the Israeli military and recognized by a follow-up UN committee report chaired by Judge Mary McGowan Davis "indicate that civilians were not intentionally targeted as a matter of policy." What makes the claim oddly incomplete is that the McGowan Davis Report in fact questions the Israeli investigations and finds them to be lacking in impartiality, promptness, and transparency.[158] As John Dugard, a South African professor of international law and former UN special rapporteur to the UN Human Rights Council on the situation of human rights in the occupied Palestinian territories writes, the McGowan Davis Report "paints a very different picture of Israel's investigations of 400 incidents" than is warranted by Goldstone's confidence in those investigations. As Dugard observes, the investigations of those 400 incidents of possible human rights abuses "have resulted in two convictions, one for theft of a credit card, resulting in a sentence of seven months' imprisonment, and another for using a Palestinian child as a human shield, which resulted in a suspended sentence of three months." Dugard concludes that "there are no facts that exonerate Israel and that could possibly have led Goldstone to change his mind."[159] His post hoc reopening of his report was baffling to many observers, and, given that he has not elaborated it, it remains a strange and troubling insertion into the public record.

In the conclusion of this book, I bring up some other troubling developments, with painful personal implications for Goldstone, that also followed the publication of his report.

Troubling a Forbidden Idea

Jimmy Carter's association of the binational state model and historical civil rights struggles was not a new concept in the mainstream. *New York Times* columnist Thomas Friedman made exactly this point in 2003, though his emphasis was on the dissonance and discomfort that the connection was likely to arouse:

> Rather than create the outlines of a two-state solution, this wall [encircling the city of Qalquilya] will kill that idea for Palestinians, and drive them, over time, to demand instead a one-state solution – where they and the Jews would have equal rights ... This transformation of the Palestinian cause will be very problematic for Israel. If American Jews think it's hard to defend Israel today on college campuses, imagine what it will be like when their kids have to argue against the principle of one man, one vote.[160]

Both Carter and Friedman were pointing to three emerging ways in which the one-state model is being increasingly addressed. The first relates to the moral poverty of the status quo; the second to the practical poverty of the two-state model in the context of a status quo moving along an impossible trajectory; and the third to the greater resonance of the one-state model with ideals broadly shared in the Western world of democracy, civil liberties, and human rights. All of these themes are intertwined. This more recent incarnation of debates on the one-state model also speaks to a movement away from nationalist discourses of self-determination and sovereignty that characterize the two-state solution.

The moral foundations of the one-state model were most commonly voiced by Jews prior to the foundation of the state of Israel, the majority of Palestinians perceiving neither reason nor need for them to share their homeland or their worldview with incoming Zionists and Jews. This perception of the reasonableness of the Palestinian position was shared by the early Jewish binationalists, who sought to reconcile Zionism with Palestinian nationalism. Arthur Ruppin, the founder of Brit Shalom (the small Jewish-Palestinian Peace Alliance founded in 1925), a group dedicated to the early binational movement, noted that "one need not be a maximalist, i.e., demand mass immigration and a state, to be a faithful Zionist ... What was vital was a recognition that both nations were in Palestine as of right."[161]

This sense that a failure to recognize the at least equal rights of the Palestinians to the land would lead to severe friction and eventually war was shared by a small minority of prominent figures in the prestate political and academic establishments. These figures included philosopher and Jewish theologian Martin Buber and a key founder and the president of Hebrew University, Judah Magnes. To these early binationalists, the idea of creating a Jewish majority in the land, later fortified by Jewish political domination through the creation of a Jewish state, was tantamount to the promotion of a racist agenda in which a Palestinian commonwealth would be an outpost of European civilization in which the native population was to be civilized.[162] Both Buber and Magnes argued that, since both Jews and Arabs had national claims to Palestine, it could be neither an Arab nor a Jewish state but should be a binational one in which each group shared power.[163]

I have already alluded to the awareness of early Zionists of the naturalness of the Palestinian sense of injustice to the establishment of a new Jewish national home in Palestine. Jabotinsky's iron wall policy, whereby "the systematic but calibrated use of force would teach Arabs that Israel was ineradicable, regardless of whether it was perceived by them to be just,"[164] was predicated on recognition of the naturalness and legitimacy of Palestinian intransigence and violent opposition. However, the sense of the early binationalists that this Israeli use of force could not be justified and was potentially disastrous for the Zionists was shared by the early founders of Israel, who, whether out of conviction or for tactical reasons, supported the binational program.[165] Israel's first prime minister, David Ben-Gurion, declared in 1927 that "we have no right to discriminate against a single Arab child, even if thereby we attain everything we desire. Our work cannot be based on depriving anyone of his rights."[166] Four years later Israel's first president, Chaim Weizman, claimed that he had "no sympathy or understanding for the demand of a Jewish majority ... The world will construe this demand in only one sense, that we want to acquire a majority in order to drive out the Arabs."[167] The foreboding of the early binationalists that the paramountcy of force over justice would corner Zionism in intractable hostilities is echoed in the contemporary situation; more to the point, the sense that the binational model represents a just outcome that accounts for the prestate realities of the land had currency, even among leading Zionists, and speaks to what is now more evidently a perennial thread of legitimacy for the idea. In light of how Middle Eastern history has played out over the past sixty years, it is abundantly clear that Palestinians can never hope to win on the field of arms against Israel. However, the field of morals and rights, to use Helena Cobban's phrasing, appears to be ever nascent.[168]

The more recent justifications of the one-state model build on the simpler idea that it represents a just (though perhaps unrealistic) outcome; proponents characterize the current stalemate as leading to the conclusion that the one-state model is indeed a response, however reluctant, to reality. The "walled-in ghetto" of Gaza and the seemingly unretrenchable "honeycomb of settlements" with its "interconnecting conduits" that divide the West Bank into "non-contiguous areas and multiple fragments"[169] represent facts on the ground that are just as realpolitik as the counter-realpolitik opposed to the one-state model.

This latter discourse on the diversion of the one-state model took on greater weight even before the state of Israel was founded in 1948, which alone appeared to doom the binational model to political oblivion. As Tamar Hermann notes, "the wave of violent Arab riots against the Jews in 1929, known as the 'disturbances,' were a severe blow to the binationalists."[170] However, the idea, originally promoted more strongly by Jews than by Palestinians, became seemingly irrelevant after both the formation of the Jewish state and the ensuing bloody war. Thereafter, the fact of Israeli sovereignty based on a Jewish state, recognized by the community of nations, became a fixed response to the binational option.

The weight of this reality is reiterated as one of the leading objections to attempts to refloat the binational option. The movement away from national rights of self-determination, embodied in state sovereignty, and toward some kind of constitutional federalism cannot proceed without taking power away from those who have already embodied their quest for self-determination in a sovereign state.[171] The current framework of international law, rooted in deep respect for the sovereignty of states, is radically opposed to the idea that the sovereignty of a state can be compromised without its consent. As George Bisharat notes, "there is no legal means by which a one-state solution could be directly imposed on the parties to the dispute without violating the respective rights of each group ... As a matter of law, a one-state solution could only come about through the agreement of Palestinians and Israelis and as an exercise of their respective rights to self-determination."[172] The hard reality facing the binational option is that the will of Israelis to participate in this exercise is virtually non-existent, a point made forcefully by Uri Avnery and Ilan Pappé: "Anybody who is rooted in the Israeli-Jewish public knows that this public's deepest aspiration – and here it is permissible to make a generalization – ... is to maintain a state with a Jewish majority, a state in which Jews will be masters of their fate. This takes precedence over any other wish and aspiration."[173]

The realities of both international law and the will of Israelis are compounded by the same deep pessimism voiced by Carter brought about by more than sixty years of conflict and forty years of occupation. As Yossi Klein-Halevi noted in 2003, "the notion that Palestinians and Jews, who can't even negotiate a two-state solution, could coexist in one happy state is so ludicrous that only the naïve or the malicious would fall for it."[174] The intractability of the violence and the seemingly complete irreconcilability of positions lead proponents of a two-state model, based on maximal separation of violently opposed peoples, to conclude that it is the only model that has a remote chance of success.

But it is precisely the aspersions about naïveté and utopianism (and maliciousness) that are regularly reversed in the emerging discourse on the one-state model. Although the moral arguments for the one-state model find proponents who are both Zionist and non-Zionist (if not anti-Zionist), the practical arguments for the one-state model are beginning to find support among those who, like Carter, would prefer a different scenario but have come to conclude that existing geopolitical and demographic realities dictate a binational solution. In this latter camp are two Israeli Zionists interviewed in the aftermath of the failed Oslo peace process, Meron Benvenisti and Haim Hanegbi, the former a past deputy mayor of Jerusalem with roots in the old Zionist establishment[175] and the latter a well-known public figure and journalist of the political left. Both gave scandal-stirring interviews to *Ha'aretz* in June 2003 in which they revealed that they had come to the conclusion that the one-state model is both a moral outcome of the Israeli/Palestinian impasse and a practical inevitability. Both had placed their faith in the two-state model that was the predicate of the Oslo peace process set in motion in the early 1990s but had become demoralized by the ways in which force – and the clear on-the-ground move toward a Greater Israel that would annex the West Bank and Gaza without granting Palestinians citizenship rights – had eviscerated the viability of the two-state model. Hanegbi realized that the settlements had doubled themselves; "I also realized that Israel had missed its one hour of grace, had rejected the rare opportunity it was given. Then I understood that Israel could not free itself of its expansionist pattern. It is bound hand and foot to its constituent ideology and to its constituent act, which was an act of dispossession."[176]

Hanegbi perceived the irreconcilable aspirations of the two-state model with the practical facts on the ground that Israel had structured. "In order," he observed, "for Jewish sovereignty to be maintained there needs to be a uninational framework that will surround itself with a wall and retain its isolation, but such a construct is contradictory to the spirit of our time. Israel as a Jewish state can no longer exist here."[177]

Benvenisti was similarly bleak about what the program of settlement in the West Bank had done to the two-state model as a practical possibility. "At the beginning of the 1980s," he said,

> I already maintained that partition was no longer a viable option, that the establishment of the settlements and the takeover of land had created an irreversible situation here. And at that time there were only 20,000 settlers. Today there are 230,000. So it's clear that the critical mass I was afraid of, which would not permit a change in the status quo, existed even then. Neither Oslo nor the separation fence nor talk about a Palestinian state can change the status quo.[178]

Given that Benvenisti had long been concerned about the settlement project, the change in his thinking revealed in the 2003 interview stemmed from what he called his realization that the Israeli/Palestinian struggle was not a national one but one between natives and settlers/colonizers. This new understanding drove him to the certainty that separation was no longer an option and that the entire land of Israel should be regarded as a single geopolitical entity. Benvenisti was clear, however, that he had not come to this understanding happily. He pessimistically recognized the reality on the ground that no longer lends itself to separationist models.

This pragmatic pessimism has increasingly begun to dominate agitation for the one-state model. In a seminal and highly controversial article in the *New York Review of Books,* Tony Judt came to very similar conclusions about the growing utopianism of the two-state model. As he noted about the conventional consensus that Israel should dismantle the settlements and return to the 1967 borders in exchange for real Arab recognition of those frontiers,

> I suspect that we are already too late for that. There are too many settlements, too many Jewish settlers, and too many Palestinians, and they all live together, albeit separated by barbed wire and pass laws. Whatever the "road map" says, the real map is the one on the ground, and that, as Israelis say, reflects facts. It may be that over a quarter of a million heavily armed and subsidized Jewish settlers would leave Arab Palestine voluntarily; but no one I know believes it will happen. Many of those settlers will die – and kill – rather than move.[179]

There is an emerging sense that what was once a just and possible solution that could gather a conventional consensus – a moral consensus with international backing – has been squandered.

The idea that there is something nefarious about continuing to propagate a utopian two-state solution is also being increasingly added to moral and practical objections. Azmi Bishara, an Arab Christian and former member of the Israeli Knesset, voices Klein-Halevi's sentiment that there might be something malicious in propagating particular models of statehood for Israel/Palestine but from the opposite perspective.[180] As Bishara notes, prior to the first intifada, there were two clear de facto policies that Israel pursued in the occupied territories: there would be no withdrawal, and there would be no annexation. The intifada added another "no" to the realities on the ground: there would be no status quo ante. The Oslo process, with the two-state model at its core, managed these three irreconcilable policies by providing the illusion of progress toward a Palestinian state but within the framework of no withdrawal and no annexation. It proposed a model of "autonomy" for the Palestinians in which Israeli control over the occupied territories would persist but Palestinians would define and police themselves as non-citizens. Bishara, speaking in 1995, identified this as the Gaza model – a bantustanization of whatever residual territory the Palestinians would be allowed to live on:

> Gaza is the model for the West Bank. Look at what Israel is doing on the ground. It is investing millions of dollars for an infrastructure of roads that will link up most of the Jewish settlements and fragment the Palestinian "areas" into so many townships. At the end of the day, we can call these townships a state if we wish. We can call Arafat "emperor" if we wish. But the reality is bantustanisation.[181]

The sense that the peace process itself, under current conditions, amounts to a cruel boondoggle of Palestinian interests finds confirmation not only in the years of absence from negotiations of the American administration under President George W. Bush but also in the surprisingly candid stated ends of this nonchalance by the chief of Ariel Sharon's Prime Minister's Bureau, Dov Weisglass, who negotiated the deal with the United States over the removal of the Gaza settlements in 2005.

> What I effectively agreed to with the Americans was that part of the settlements [i.e., the major settlement blocs in the West Bank] would not be dealt with at all, and the rest will not be dealt with until the Palestinians turn into Finns ... The significance [of the agreement with the United States] is the freezing of the political process. And when you freeze that process you prevent the establishment of a Palestinian state and you prevent a discussion about the refugees, the borders and Jerusalem. Effectively, this whole package that is called the Palestinian state, with all that it entails, has been removed from our agenda indefinitely. And all this with [President Bush's] authority and permission ... and the ratification of both houses of Congress.[182]

An endless peace *process* for the foreseeable future that allows for this reality of separation without withdrawal on the ground makes the two-state model seem like a massive illusion that perpetuates an abiding injustice – a boondoggle that can hardly seem to be less than malicious to those who are its victims.

The emerging view from critics of the direction in which Israel has been headed is that time is running out for the two-state model, both for moral and for practical reasons.[183] This perspective, however, is far from universal. Most explicit in the rejection of the idea that the two-state model has an urgent deadline is Efraim Inbar of Bar-Ilan University. He casually remarks that "time is on Israel's side." Echoing the Jabotinskian struggle to overcome the enemy, he notes that "Israel has become stronger, while its enemies ... have become weaker." To support this argument, he cites Israel's vibrant economy and the fact that most of its social rifts have been bridged (noticeably glossing over the growing religious/secular divide and its relationship to visions of Greater Israel).[184] In the international arena, Inbar remarks on positive developments in the Arab League peace initiative of 2002 and improving diplomatic relations between Israel and a multiplicity of important countries. As he notes, "the ups and mostly downs in Israeli-Palestinian relations have hardly had an impact on how states conduct their bilateral relations with Israel." Inbar comments on the US victories in the Cold War and the 1991 Gulf War, both of which, for him, bode well for Israel, a valued American ally. Finally, he notes, "the Zeitgeist of this epoch that stresses democracy and free market values favors Israel over its Muslim opponents, who continue to grapple with the challenge of modernity."[185]

This view that the future, on its current trajectory, is bright for Israel might be sustaining to some; however, it is not a widespread view and is not even shared by all Israeli leaders. There are indications that the latter are aware of the growing alternative one-state model in the shadows and are spooked by it. Former prime minister Ehud Olmert is among them. Rather than being complacent about time being on Israel's side, Olmert sounded a note of urgency about the perils of the maximalist vision in several interviews that he gave to *Ha'aretz*.[186] As he noted in 2008, "forty years after the Six-Day War, the international community's willingness to accept Israel as a binational state is growing ... Time is not on Israel's side.[187] Beyond this, Olmert is clear that a Zeitgeist stressing democracy will in no way dependably favour Israel over its "Muslim opponents":

> More and more Palestinians are uninterested in a negotiated, two-state solution, because they want to change the essence of the conflict from an Algerian paradigm to a South African one. From a struggle against "occupation," in their parlance, to a struggle for one-man-one-vote. That is, of course, a much cleaner struggle, a much more popular struggle – and ultimately a much more powerful one. For us, it would mean the end of the Jewish state.[188]

This "much more popular struggle," of course, is the same one alluded to by both Carter and Friedman – a move away from national independence and toward constitutional democracy and equal citizenship.

This shift is indeed the focus of a seminal article in the *Boston Review* by diasporic Palestinian scholar Lama Abu-Odeh.[189] Writing in 2002, she noted that for many Palestinians the two-state solution had already lost a great deal of its historical appeal. She cited "the 'unrepresentativeness' of the Palestinian Authority, the lack of meaningful territorial gains, and the lack of progress on the crucial question of the return of refugees" as stimulants of the deep disappointment with the Oslo process.[190] The period since Oslo revealed for many Palestinians the lack of any serious intention by Israel to concede any set of powers or adequate contiguous territory that would allow a nationalist project to succeed. Even the success of the two-state model would provide for an extremely limited payoff for Palestinians. Abu-Odeh advocated a reconsideration of the binational model for Israel/Palestine but from the vantage of a turn away from the model of a progressive liberation of Palestinians from Israeli colonial control (with appeals based on international law) and toward a model of constitutional liberalism with its conception of individuals as equal rights-bearing members of a single political society.[191]

Abu-Odeh called this move a "re-consideration" because the secular, or non-sectarian, democratic state for all of Israel/Palestine was the model originally promoted by Yasser Arafat's PLO, principally from the early 1970s, until a definitive turn to the two-state model in 1988 as a prelude to the Oslo peace process. The promotion of a non-sectarian democratic state became the official stance of the PLO in 1971, having replaced earlier formulations that were more clearly rooted in a nationalist, postcolonial stance geared to reversing Israel's military victories and achieving the total liberation of Palestine through "armed struggle" and destruction of "the Zionist and imperialist presence."[192] Jewish claims to peoplehood – and to a sovereign state that, in that historical period, was the paramount expression of self-determination for a people – were denied. What was sought in the PLO's early aspirations for a one-state model was a Palestinian state in which, following its inauguration, all Jews not resident in the country before the 1917 Balfour Declaration would depart (or presumably, in the face of a Palestinian victory, be expelled or transferred).[193] Following the 1971 meeting of the Palestinian National Council, the idea of a single democratic state became the official position of the PLO "in the framework of the Arab nation's aspiration to national liberation and total unity."[194]

Given the increasing superiority of Israel's military capability, the prospect of an overall victory in a nationalist armed struggle became commensurately remote. The 1970s saw a gradual movement away from this nationalist version of the one-state model and toward an acceptance of partition. This movement toward a two-state model, however, remained linked to a platform of "phased" Palestinian nationalism, to grow from an "independent and fighting authority" in any part of the country "liberated from Israel."[195] This position of constructive ambiguity had both an element of political realism (with respect to the futility of armed struggle) and long-term nationalist aspirations.

The ambiguity of a point somewhere between a one-state solution and a two-state solution gave way in 1988 to the PLO's adoption of the Algiers Declaration, at the height of the first intifada. The impetus for the declaration was a growing desire for a Palestinian state to be created in any "liberated" territory and, after the 1988 declaration, was promoted in terms of a peaceful two-state solution. This position made possible the emergence of the Oslo peace process of the 1990s, with two states grounded along the green line of the 1967 borders. The nationalist and anti-colonialist animus behind the PLO's position gave way in the Palestinian recognition of Israel's right to exist in the Oslo Peace Accord and subsequently the late 1990s with the removal from the Palestine National Covenant and Charter of the provisions calling for Israel's destruction.

Abu-Odeh's proposition reconsiders a return to the one-state model promoted by the PLO from the 1960s to the late 1980s; however, it emerges from a very different historical point and with a substantially different aim. As Abu-Odeh noted, while it would undoubtedly be a substantial achievement for Palestinians to have a state with the trappings of national independence over a formally delineated territory with East Jerusalem as their capital, "the national solution now seems to have reached a dead end ... Even if the two-state strategy succeeded, its payoff would be limited."[196] Although the PLO position from the early 1970s to Oslo might have been characterized by constructive ambiguity, her position is deeply imbued with (reluctant) pessimism about the prospects for the nationalist agenda. The diffuse constitutional liberalism that she proposed would favour the rule of law governing a citizenship of equals over the lack of constraint on a governing model based on the rules of war. The superior military power of the Israelis dooms the Palestinians to accept concessions that the international community finds acceptable between two states at war. Abu-Odeh (echoing Olmert, Carter, and Friedman) noted that, as a strategy to advance the interests of Palestinians, "the mobilizing agenda for political activism would appeal to 'civil rights' rather than the current 'anti-colonial struggle to achieve national independence'" – the former being a struggle that has far greater resonance in the United States, where "most Americans don't quite grasp the racialized and dehumanizing bond between colonizer and colonized ... but do understand well the idea of a civil rights struggle."[197]

In 2001 at the beginning of the second intifada, Abu-Odeh's proposal was inchoate, more the expression of a desired moral outcome than a practical plan for how such a one-state model, based on ideals of democracy, equal citizenship, and constitutionalism, would look. As noted by one of the leading Palestinian critics of the one-state model, Salim Tamari, the binational state model as formulated by Abu-Odeh has several significant defects.[198] Proponents have not yet engaged, as an aspiration, in detailed discussions on the repercussions of creating a single juridical, social, and political regime from the current stalemate of two antagonistic national groups. Furthermore, writing in 2001, Tamari noted that the binational model has no real constituency on either side. Moreover, proponents of the binational model fail to address the problem of overcoming institutionalized Zionism and the cultural resistance of Palestinian nationalism to being incorporated into a Europeanized and industrially superior state. Most pressingly for Tamari, the binational model would entail Palestinians giving up their struggle for independence, for the further evacuation of Israeli military rule, and for the dismantling of colonial settlements – in return for a constitutional arrangement that is bound to be met with hostility by their Israeli neighbours.

A number of Tamari's critiques have been echoed, of course, by Israeli and Jewish critics of the one-state model, including the lack of a constituency (particularly on the Israeli side), the massive hurdles of bridging a divide within one regime of two radically antagonistic national groups, and the aspirational, if not utopian, nature of the model. However, post-Oslo despair, still somewhat nascent at the beginning of the twenty-first century, that launched the quest for alternatives to a failed and increasingly utopian two-state model has (in answer to Tamari's point about serious and detailed discussions canvassing all of the repercussions) spawned more concerted efforts to construct more detailed models of single statehood in the region.[199] These range from the model for a secular democratic state based on constitutional liberalism with a unitary, centralized state, in which the rights of individuals prevail over ethnic-collective rights; to federal and binational models in which both Jews and Palestinians have recognized group rights in addition to equal individual rights of citizenship (akin to the modern federation familiar to Canadians); to models of consociationalism in which elements of shared governance exist alongside strong and permanent commitments to the maintenance of primordial divisions through constituent states (represented by Switzerland's cantonal territorial divisions). Not all of these models have equivalent resonances for the rights of either individuals or ethnic-religious groups.

The complexity of possibilities that began to emerge in the sense of futility about the two-state model responded in many ways – inadequately or not – to the opposing interests on both sides. The early ways in which the single-state model was conceived in the post-Oslo period did not reflect the diversity and nuances that exist among single-state models. In light of the "phased" single-state model promoted by Arafat's "secular democratic state," which aimed first at Palestinian statehood on all liberated occupied territories and ultimately at a single Palestinian state with a Palestinian majority and a greatly reduced or non-existent Jewish polity, the one-state model is freighted with ominous associations for Jews and Jewish Israelis, whether or not this constitutional liberal democratic model is otherwise regarded as one of the world's laudatory state models.

This is the model that drives the Jewish fear behind the demand for equal voting rights for everyone – one person, one vote – that would bring an end to the Jewish state because of the loss of a Jewish demographic majority. This classical liberal regime of individual rights – the regime that replaced the apartheid government in South Africa – might indeed be the one-state model identified with binationalism in which there is no regard for ethnic-collective rights. As Benvenisti notes, "if the Palestinians do indeed force the Israelis to impose such a model, as the blacks did in South Africa, it would indeed spell the end of the Jewish state in the sense of its ethnic dominance and other national privileges."[200] In light of demographic realities in the region of Israel/Palestine, this model would indeed seem to confirm Olmert's (and many of the conference critics') expressed anxieties that the demise of Palestinian nationalism and its replacement with a struggle for one state would mean the end of the Jewish state.

Benvenisti's phrasing indicates that the classic liberal model would not necessarily be a bad thing, but the gist of his 2003 *Ha'aretz* article – "Which Kind of Binational State?" – suggests that other models might be more auspicious for answering the question that, in his view, is "no longer whether it will be binational, but which model to choose."[201]

This sense that the range of options for the one-state model is more diverse and complex than immediately conceived was reflected by respondents to Abu-Odeh's 2001 article in the *Boston Review.*[202] As Lustick noted in his response, the terms "binational" and "secular" are often used interchangeably though erroneously. Adding clarification to the beginning of the discussion on the one-state model, Lustick noted that

> "binational" refers to a country in which two and only two national cultures are afforded pride of place, with juridically entrenched rights of control of shares of the state's resources, positions of authority, symbols, etc. In an Arab-Jewish binational state, Jewish law might apply to matters of marriage, divorce, burial, etc. among Jews, while Christian and Muslim law and practice would apply for Arabs. In such a state Arabic and Hebrew would both be national languages, two national anthems would be sung (or none at all), stamps would honour equally both national cultures, land and other important resources would be allocated according to an agreed formula, and so on. Such a state could go far toward satisfying the specific national, cultural, religious, and symbolic requirements of the two rival peoples.[203]

A secular state, on the other hand, would have to muster a single common identity for the country, something that is much harder to conceive of, particularly in the current context.

However, as the Canadian and Swiss experiences show (and despite the considerable voiced pessimism about the absence in contemporary times of a single successful binational state),[204] federal binationalism and consociationalism would not in principle entail the demise of either a Jewish or a Palestinian state. And both models are consistent with an emerging scholarly literature (not a small part of which is Canadian) that questions the linkage of the international law concept of self-determination for a people with the right to a sovereign state over a defined territory for that people.[205] In the context of the mosaic of peoples in the Middle East, this growing recognition of the difficult and fraught division of territories into ethnoreligiously homogeneous nation-states anticipated by European models of statehood might be particularly apt.

These considerations point to a plethora of legal, political, and moral issues that remain to be canvassed for the one-state model. As noted by Daniel Elazar of the Jerusalem Center for Public Affairs in a 1998 consideration of federal and confederal solutions to the Israeli/Palestinian conflict,

> there are over 100 diverse models of interjurisdictional arrangements: mixed governments, power-sharing and the like presently in operation around the world ... Of the 160-plus sovereign states in the world in the 1980s, only 10 or 11 were ethnically homogeneous. The other 150 ethnically heterogeneous states must reach some kind of intergroup accommodation. The choices range from extermination of ethnic minorities, to forcible assimilation into the majority culture, to serious and innovative efforts to foster and encourage the formation of multi-ethnic societies.[206]

There is a wealth of comparative material to draw on to gauge whether, and which, one-state models have any prospects for responding to the general despair and legitimate anxiety that surround the current impasse in the Middle East. If the one-state model has any prospect for viability in the Israeli/Palestinian context, this broad and deep experience needs to be drawn on and applied with the peculiarities and perils of that setting in mind. The result of all of these puzzles, deliberations, and facts on the ground is that, beyond the writings of journalists and former presidents of the United States, the idea of a single binational state in all of the territory of Israel/Palestine has been gathering what Benvenisti, by 2009, was calling a "sea change among academics and organizations engaged in progressive thinking."[207] And it was an examination of this sea change that the Mapping Models conference contemplated.

Given the emerging complexity of scholarly discussions on the one-state model over the past eight years, the Mapping Models conference aspired to bring together academics and experts to present the developing range of models of statehood alongside the pitfalls and extensive problematics potentially generated by each – a scholarly enterprise that we not only recognized had inherent intellectual merit but also assumed would be permitted to flourish on a Canadian university campus.

Given the fraught content of the conference themes – and the perennially fraught context of the Middle East – we anticipated that the conference would give rise to difficult and challenging ideas. We did not anticipate the intensity of opposition to the airing of those ideas in a Canadian university setting or the individuals, groups, and institutions that would line up to police what was for them – and to their minds should have been for us – a forbidden idea.

The conference website has posted video and audio recordings of virtually all of the presenters at the conference.[208] Given the seemingly intractable conflict in the Middle East (and the current trajectory of the Netanyahu government), it is a fair bet that the scholarly and journalistic literature on the binational option will continue to mushroom.

However, the rest of this book is not devoted to a continued exploration of the one-state model, which will continue to gather momentum – or not. Rather, the remaining chapters move on to a detailed case study of the fragility of academic freedom – an examination of how fences were erected around supposedly forbidden ideas in a liberal democracy such as Canada.

PART 2

AN UNINTENDED ETHNOGRAPHY

3

Mixing Jurisdictions

Academic Foreign Policy

This book covers two separate fields: the conflict in the Middle East and the interested communities that group around it, and the university with its attendant communities of interest. Both fields of practice have principles and ideas that animate the activities of those whose everyday lives circulate within them, and some of these principles are more core than others, more demanding of a kind of shoring up and protection that minimize risk that the core might be compromised. The core of each community is what is perceived to constitute the bonds of that community, such that a failure to recognize a violation of those bonds could constitute a failure of the community itself.[1] Fences are built around each so as to minimize the risk of such a failure.

Because this is a book about academic freedom, I am characterizing the former field – the Middle East and its diverse and far-flung communities of interest – as "outside" the walls of the latter – the academy. The first part of this unintended ethnography covered some of the animating ideas of the outside field and the activities that go into bracing the bonds within that community (diverse as it is, so diverse also in its agonistics). The intrigue coursing through the selected data out of which the accounts of the previous two chapters were composed was set on its course by the more central intrigue of this book: academic freedom. Hence, the welter of data out of which chronologies were pursued was drawn on in order to illuminate and set up how the "outside" impinged upon the "inside" – the latter being the setting in which academic freedom constitutes a vital bond of the community, unrecognized violations of which forebode its failure.

The imagery of an outside and an inside is somewhat contrived – and I will return in the analytical materials of Part 3 of this book, "Making Sense," to what it might mean to encroach on the central practices of the academy and therefore compromise its collective integrity. This part of the unintended ethnography, which continues to set the stage for that analytical turn, moves increasingly inward, from foreign conflicts to domestic policies and eventually, in Chapter 4, to local Canadian politics and the forms of mundane communication that compose a community. Part 2 of this unintended ethnography, then, picks up a thread that ties the Middle East to the university, then pursues it through the interface of the foreign and the domestic (in the national sense). It then retraces the chronology of Chapter 1 but from inside the university that housed the Mapping Models conference.

Governmental Foreign Policy

On York University's website, former president Lorna Marsden issued a statement on the autonomy of universities in which she underlines the importance of the independence of the institution from government.[2] The idea

> that universities are or should be an arm of their national government is a direct threat to academic freedom and should be opposed on principle ... The idea that individual universities should operate some kind of academic foreign policy is anathema to everything that, as academics, we stand for. Universities are not governments operating global policies but academic communities of scholars free to communicate with other academics across the globe in the pursuit of their academic goals.

President Marsden issued this statement in response to the campaign to boycott Israeli universities. "At York," she affirmed, "we stand firm for the autonomy of universities from government and the freedom of our scholars, scientists and artists to pursue their own academic goals unfettered by the dogmatism of others."

When Gary Goodyear, Conservative MP in the federal government, intervened with SSHRC to have the funding for our conference re-reviewed and/or suspended, he was oblivious of the principle that "universities are not governments operating global policies but academic communities of scholars." Because SSHRC and York University capitulated to the pressure to insert "the dogmatism of others" into an academic event, it is important to understand the content of that dogmatism. The following materials provide background on foreign policy positions taken not only by the Conservative government of Canada but also by members of the official opposition.

John Mearsheimer and Stephen Walt, in their book *The Israel Lobby and US Foreign Policy,* provide a brief discussion on why and how they chose the words *Israel lobby* to describe the phenomenon of domestic pressure on American foreign policy to pursue a particular approach to the Israeli/ Palestinian conflict. They are clear that, despite the use of the article *the,* the phenomenon is not monolithic. It is not a single unified movement with a central leadership and a defined membership. And the groups and individuals who make up the broad coalition that supports the approach have disagreements over particular policy issues. They are equally clear that what they describe is not a cabal or conspiracy. It is a collection of groups and individuals that operates in the open and in the same way that other interest groups do.[3] If there is something remarkably different about this lobby, it is its extraordinary effectiveness.

Meirsheimer and Walt's assessment that the existence of a lobby to promote Israel's interests is perfectly legitimate does not necessarily eliminate anxieties among those for whom use of the term has unsavoury connotations. Despite the name of the organization, the Canadian Council for Israel and Jewish *Advocacy* – renamed the Centre for Israel and Jewish Affairs under the same CIJA acronym in 2011 – objected to use of the phrase "Israel lobby" by Jon Thompson in his report on the conference on the grounds that "it's a slur that is designed to promote the myth that anyone who supports Israel controls the actions of government and other institutions. It's a deplorable term, and we object strongly to its usage and all that it implies."[4] Thompson responded to this critique by noting that "members of the so-called lobby 'denounce critics of their activities for saying that there is an Israel lobby, but at the same time, boast on their website that they are very effective in influencing government policy.'"[5] This is well illustrated by B'nai Brith's involvement in the conference and its pride in getting the federal government to intervene with the conference funding source. The organization did not hesitate to take credit for its success "subsequent to our appeal to the Government on this matter" and asked readers of the community alert trumpeting this success to write to the minister to convey their thanks and appreciation for his action as well as to "urge the Minister to direct SSHRC to immediately withdraw its funding from this sham of a conference that seeks to delegitimize the Jewish State and its supporters here at home."[6]

It would be incorrect to say that groups such as CIJA and B'nai Brith "control" government, but that they seek to "influence" government appears to be a core aspiration of organizations engaged in Israel advocacy.

Although groups such as CIJA aspire to represent "the Jewish community," Meirsheimer and Walt are also clear that "the" community is considerably more diverse and fractured than those aspirations can reconcile. They point out that the general policy thrust of the lobby does not capture the sentiments of all Jewish Americans or even those with favourable attitudes toward Israel. As they note, "the authors of this book are 'pro-Israel,' in the sense that we support its right to exist, admire its many achievements, want its citizens to enjoy secure and prosperous lives, and believe that the United States should come to Israel's aid if its survival is in danger. But we are obviously not part of the Israel lobby."[7] For Mearsheimer and Walt,

> to be part of the lobby, in other words, one has to actively work to move American foreign policy in a pro-Israel direction. For an organization, this pursuit must be an important part of its missions and consume a substantial percentage of its resources and agenda. For an individual, this means devoting some portion of one's professional or personal life (or in some cases, substantial amounts of money) to influencing US Middle East policy.[8]

They group within the lobby powerful hard-line organizations such as the American Israel Public Affairs Committee, the Zionist Organization of America, the Conference of Presidents, and the American Jewish Committee.

In their elaboration on the definition of the "Israel lobby," they make clear that it is a movement with fuzzy boundaries. However, their comments about being pro-Israel make clear how delicate this exercise in describing the ideological thrust of the lobby can be. That the lobby works to move American foreign policy in a "pro-Israel" direction begs the question of what it is to be a friend of Israel. If former American president Jimmy Carter is correct that time is running out *fast* for the two-state solution and that the folly of Greater Israel will lead inexorably to Israel's international status as a pariah state, then the discomfort aroused by his association of the current trajectory with an apartheid state might be the kindest intervention in the current impasse. The Goldstone Report, which refuses to allow Israel to see individual incidents of the conflict in isolation from the continuum of oppression constituted by over forty years of occupation, might be a leading Zionist intervention for the twenty-first century – particularly coming, as it does, from one with deep emotional and intellectual ties to Israel and with a professional attachment to the rule of law schooled in the pedagogy of the Holocaust. Indeed, in the moral bleakness of the current impasse, those who wade into the "sea change among academics and organizations engaged in progressive thinking"[9] to contemplate rigorously a single binational state for Israel/Palestine might be the ultimate guardians of a place for Jews, the Jewish nation, and the Jewish state in the Middle East. Mearsheimer and Walt, who advocate for the two-state solution, believe that the direction that the Israel lobby has successfully urged on the United States over the past several years has been not only harmful to American interests but also damaging and counterproductive to Israel.[10]

Canada has been influenced by the American Israel lobby, and a shift in Canadian foreign policy toward an "Israel, right or wrong," approach has been discernible since the beginning of the twenty-first century. According to Paul Heinbecker, a former UN ambassador and foreign policy adviser to both Liberal and Conservative governments, successive Canadian governments have long pursued a "fair minded and principled" policy on Israel/ Palestine, "calling the issues as they saw them."[11] This approach earned Canada a reputation for bringing a constructive attitude to international problem solving reflecting the domestic absence of colonial and racist baggage and a unique history on the world stage of successfully recognizing and integrating minorities. Heinbecker also notes that Canada's international reputation for putting domestic politics ahead of diasporic politics and not favouring the cause of one group over another has facilitated domestic harmony.

The stance that Canada began to take under the Conservative government in 2006 aroused a very public critique of a felt shift in Canadian Middle East policy: namely, that Canada was losing its reputation as an honest broker in the Middle East,[12] particularly after the stance became more strident when Prime Minister Harper stated in the context of the Second Lebanon War that "it's not unfair to liken Hezbollah to the Nazis because both stand for the destruction of the 'Jewish nation.'"[13]

Liberal MP Irwin Cotler, who lined himself up squarely with the Conservative position on that war, might well be correct that Canada has never taken a position of "neutrality" in the Middle East (or elsewhere in the world for that matter) and that foreign policy principles, "as affirmed by successive governments, require us to 'take sides,' to eschew even-handedness and to raise our voice as a moral interlocutor in a principled way."[14] Cotler's analysis comports with Heinbecker's view that Canada's position has always been fair-minded and principled. What differs between Heinbecker and

Cotler is the substance of their assessments of what constitutes a fair-minded approach. In Heinbecker's analysis, in lining up, as the Harper government did, with the uncritical post-9/11 approach to Israel of the George Bush administration's War on Terror, Canada sacrificed its ability to render judgment on Israel's domestic and foreign policies (and actions in the occupied territories) and to assess aspects of Israel's nefarious role in contributing to conflicts in the region. This shift did not start, however, with the Conservative government.

The fair-minded policy that used not to hold Muslims, Arabs, and Palestinians primarily if not uniquely responsible for both the conflict and Israel's actions began to shift under Paul Martin's Liberal government in 2004 when Canada changed its voting pattern at the United Nations and began to tilt toward Israel. Previously, in UN votes requiring Israel to comply with its obligations under international law and withdraw from the territories that it occupied in 1967, Canada had abstained. However, under Allan Rock, the Canadian ambassador to the United Nations, Canada began to vote alongside the United States, Israel, Palau, Micronesia, and the Marshall Islands and apart from the majority of other democracies in the United Nations. This progressive alignment of Canadian foreign policy with that of the Bush administration coincided with both domestic American dissatisfaction with American foreign policy and growing international animosity toward the United States. In light of Canada's antecedent reputation for principled fair-mindedness, and the impact of a tilt toward Israel both domestically and internationally, Heinbecker is clear that the "Israel, right or wrong," position that has influenced the American approach is "not a policy worth emulating."[15]

The minority Conservative government that brought down the Liberals in 2006, led by Stephen Harper, not only leaned into the tilt pursued by the Martin Liberals but also sought to distinguish themselves by shifting the spectrum even further to the right. Two days after Harper became prime minister, Hamas won elections in the West Bank and Gaza. The latter elections were both Canadian monitored and regarded globally as having been fair.[16] Canada distinguished itself as the first country to cut off assistance to the Palestinian Authority.[17] In doing so, Canada aligned itself with the policy of Israeli adviser to Ehud Olmert, Dov Weisglass, who said that "the idea is to put the Palestinians on a diet, but not to make them die of hunger."[18] The hunger pangs were intended to force Palestinians to pressure Hamas into recognizing the state of Israel and renounce violence and/or to force Hamas from power.

The policy, which punishes Palestinians for having voted the "wrong way" in a democratic election, has had devastating effects, particularly in Gaza. Gaza has been described for decades as an open-air prison. However, the cessation of funds flowing into the aid-dependent Palestinian Authority produced a paralysis of Gaza's commerce and severe shortages of basic foods as Gaza's economic lifeline, the Karni crossing into Israel, supposed to handle 1,300 containers of merchandise and food per day in order to sustain 1.5 million people, was effectively shut down save a small and intermittent trickle. The severe food shortage was compounded for Palestinians in Gaza when the aid-dependent Palestinian Authority was unable to pay its staff's wages as a result of the suspension.[19] This dire predicament forced on the citizens of Gaza forms part of the continuum of policies aimed at pursuing Israel's political objectives with regard to Gaza and the occupied Palestinian territories as a whole, to which the Goldstone Report refers.[20]

The Second Lebanese War erupted just months after Harper took power in 2006 and provided a second opportunity for the Conservative government to distinguish its policy on the Middle East. The bombing of Lebanon by Israel severely damaged Lebanese infrastructure and killed about 1,000 people, with close to 1 million civilians caught in the war zone. While the United Nations called for an immediate ceasefire, Harper made clear his strong support for Israel by refusing to back the plan and commenting controversially that the bombardment of Lebanon was a "measured" response.[21]

Shortly after these two interventions, the Harper government established an Israel Allies Caucus to mobilize support for the state of Israel along the lines of its American counterpart, the Congressional Israel Allies Caucus.[22] The latter, along with the Knesset's Christian Allies Caucus, formed with the expressed purpose of strengthening ties between the state of Israel and Christian Zionists to mobilize Christian support for Israel. The caucus is constituted by members of the Canadian Parliament under the auspices of a mobilization of support for Israel and the promotion of Judeo-Christian values. Headed by Conservative MP James Lunney[23] (also the chair of the Canada-Israel Interparliamentary Group [C-IIG]),[24] the caucus was officially announced in Ottawa in the presence of Prime Minister Harper and Canadian and Israeli parliamentarians.[25]

The Declaration of Purpose of the International Israel Allies Caucus (IIAC), of which the Canadian parliamentary caucus is a member, is deeply rooted in Jewish and Christian theology, founded on the declaration that "the Ten Commandments and the Hebrew Bible, or Torah, have served for three thousand years as a cornerstone of Western civilization and serve today as the moral foundation for societies around the world."[26] The policies adopted by the IIAC not only are right wing but also run counter to the peace process pursued by the international quartet of Russia, the European Union, the United Nations, and the United States. For example, the caucus maintains that "Jerusalem is, and should be, the undivided capital of Israel and the Jewish People, and in recognition of this all of the nations of the world should locate their embassies in Jerusalem."[27] The IIAC also states that, "while we all yearn for peace, we recognize that pressure on Israel from the international community to negotiate and make concessions with those sworn to its destruction has not led to peace; we regard such attempts as futile."[28] A leading policy that the IIAC pursues is the resettlement of Palestinian refugees in Arab countries, and to that end it urges the cessation of funding from member countries such as Canada to the United Nations Relief Works Agency (UNRWA), which deals with Palestinian refugees and is the main agency in Gaza that supplies food and other emergency services to aid-dependent Palestinians.[29]

Mearsheimer and Walt elaborate on the linkages between Christian Zionists and other Christian Evangelical organizations with the Israel lobby in the United States and with the US Congress.[30] The Canadian Israel Allies Caucus, with a Conservative MP as chair, suggests that these linkages exist within Canada as well under the Conservative government.

The shift in foreign policy toward an uncritical pro-Israel stance can also be seen in the response of the Conservatives to the Gaza War of 2008-9. The Canadian government put the blame for the conflict squarely on Hamas's continuing assault on Israel. Echoing the enduring Israeli position on the military operation – that Israel's actions can be isolated from the continuum of events preceding it and that it was a measured reaction of self-defence – Minister of Foreign Affairs Lawrence Cannon issued a statement at the height of the conflict that called for a halt to "all rocket attacks on Israel" and said that "Canada maintains that the rocket attacks are the cause of this crisis."[31]

This pre-emptive laying of blame squarely on Hamas was echoed by Conservative MP Peter Kent, minister of state for foreign affairs of the Americas, who stated that "the position of the government of Canada is that Hamas bears the burden of responsibility for the deepening humanitarian tragedy."[32] He is also quoted as saying (again at the height of the conflict and without evidence) that "it is the Hamas practice to use civilian infrastructure and civilian population as shields for their terrorist activity and they certainly bear the burden of responsibility for behaving that way again here."[33] This is a claim for which Goldstone did not find any corroborating evidence:

> The Mission's attention has been drawn to a well-known incident in which women and children followed calls to gather on the roof of the house of a Palestinian man who had been informed by the Israeli authorities that his house would be targeted. This incident has been documented in video footage in the public domain and is referred to in submissions received by the Mission as evidence of the use of human shields. The Mission notes, however, that the incident occurred in 2007. No such incidents are alleged by the Israeli Government with regard to the military operations that began on 27 December 2008. The Mission received no reports of such incidents from other sources. On the contrary, in one case investigated by the Mission, a Hamas official received a phone call from the Israeli armed forces to the effect that his house would soon be targeted. He evacuated the house with his family and alerted the neighbours to the imminent threat so that they, too, were able to leave their homes before the missile did indeed strike.[34]

The factual content of the Goldstone Report leaves the strong impression that rumours circulating about Hamas's purported use of human shields were not only unsympathetic to the natural and terrible fear faced by Gazans as the homes in which they were sheltered with their families were being bombed from the air but also racist for their dehumanization of the civilian victims.

In fact, Goldstone reported that the mission investigated four incidents in which

> the Israeli armed forces coerced Palestinian civilian men at gunpoint to take part in house searches during the military operations. The men were blindfolded and handcuffed as they were forced to enter houses ahead of the Israeli soldiers. In one of the incidents, Israeli soldiers repeatedly forced a man to enter a house in which Palestinian combatants were hiding. Published testimonies of Israeli soldiers who took part in the military operations confirm the continuation of this practice, despite clear orders from Israel's High Court to the armed forces to put an end to it and repeated public assurances from the armed forces that the practice had been discontinued.[35]

The Goldstone Report ends up condemning *Israel's* use of human shields, prohibited under international humanitarian law and a war crime.

Although the Conservatives have adopted an "Israel, right or wrong," foreign policy, this position was echoed by Liberal leader Michael Ignatieff (whose adviser as special counsel on human rights and international justice was MP Irwin Cotler),[36] both during the Second Lebanon War and during the Gaza War. When asked whether he was concerned about the loss of civilian life in the former conflict, Ignatieff stated that he was not "losing any sleep" over it, a statement that he later acknowledged was a mistake.[37] During the Gaza War, again at the height of the conflict and with no evidence of the Palestinian use of human shields, Ignatieff echoed the Conservative opinion on the conflict and stated that "Hamas is to blame for organizing and instigating these rocket attacks and then for sheltering among civilian populations."[38] The Liberal tilt initiated by Martin and amplified by the Conservatives is evident in a general thrust among Canadian parliamentarians.[39]

The work of the Conservatives to promote the Israel lobby in Canada has not gone unnoticed by Canadian Jewish organizations. In May 2009, the Canadian Jewish Congress awarded Prime Minister Harper the Saul Hayes Human Rights Award, the first time that it was given to a sitting prime minister.[40] In June 2008, B'nai Brith awarded Harper the organization's International Presidential Gold Medallion for Humanitarianism Award, the first Canadian recipient of the award. In accepting it, Harper used words resonant with the Declaration of Purpose of the International Israel Allies Caucus. Although the Canadian Charter of Rights and Freedoms has been used and cited innumerable times by lawyers and others, it is rare that the preamble to the Constitution Act, 1982 (which has no legal force) gets cited. When it does, scholars tend to be critical of the ethnoreligious bias that it manifests, which goes against the grain of Canadian multiculturalism and secularism and is offensive to Aboriginal Canadians.[41] Harper, however, noted in his acceptance speech that "the preamble of the Canadian Charter of Rights and Freedoms [states] that 'Canada is founded upon the principles that recognize the supremacy of God and the Rule of Law,'" and he went on to postulate that this roots the Canadian Constitution in Judeo-Christian values and that the preamble "is rooted in our common theistic tradition and the covenant at Sinai."[42]

All of the recent foreign policy interventions by the Liberals and Conservatives amount to a tilt in a five-year period away from Canada's longstanding reputation as a fair-minded and principled (and therefore honest) broker in the Middle East. Richard Falk, Princeton University professor emeritus of international law and UN special rapporteur for human rights in the occupied Palestinian territories, echoes the sentiments of former Canadian ambassador to the United Nations, Paul Heinbecker, to the effect that Canada has damaged its moral reputation in this regard, both domestically and internationally. In words similar to Heinbecker's, Falk says,

> I think Canada has a great potential role as one of the most respected countries, with strong internationalist credentials. But on these issues, the present [Conservative] government has not pursued a helpful policy, in my view ... It has damaged Canada's moral reputation most dramatically by coming out in full support of Israel's unlawful attack on Gaza last winter, where the whole international community viewed this attack as a moral and legal outrage. Only the United States and Canada, as far as I know, were unconditionally supportive[,] so that if Canada is to play a constructive role, it has to re-establish its credentials as a fair and balanced interpreter of the developments that affect both sides.[43]

Not only is the shift to an uncritically pro-Israel stance evident in recent Canadian foreign policy, but it also explains an important part of the context for understanding what happened with the Mapping Models conference after the organizers had consolidated their intellectual goals and aspirations and began to execute them in the form of an academic event.

Prior to the conference, it might have seemed inconceivable that an academic conference might run afoul of the political policies of government. This opening contextual material about federal domestic and foreign policy would have seemed tangential and irrelevant to the independent research activities of scholars, except to the extent that their research focused on such policies, which our conference did not. However, this political background came to play an ominous role in the ways in which academic freedom is situated in Canada in the early twenty-first century. This is the inward aspect of Falk's point about Canada's international reputation that Heinbecker stresses when he notes that "our international reputation is part and parcel of our domestic harmony. One reason we have been able to enjoy our peace, order and good, albeit not always good enough, government has been that we have put Canadian interests above Diaspora politics. The more we appear to favour the cause of one group over another, the more we put that peace at risk."[44]

The Treatment

Mearsheimer and Walt are clear that the organized efforts to marshal the government (be it of Canada or the United States) in the direction of uncritical support for Israel are wholly legitimate.[45] This is what lobbyists, with special interests, do. Although the government of Canada, for example, registers and regulates the activities of lobbies, these activities fall completely under the realm of the legal. There is nothing nefarious (or, worse, conspiratorial) about the Israel lobby in and of itself.

Mearsheimer and Walt are equally clear that the lobby engages in objectionable tactics[46] and clear that governments, which must represent the greater interests of the state as a whole (including in their foreign policy), need to resist the urge to capitulate in an unprincipled way to this extraordinarily powerful lobby. These objectionable tactics – relevant to this monograph – include heavy-handed attempts to change substantively the discourse on university campuses and the abuse of the charge of anti-Semitism (and, as we will see, grotesque misuse of the charge of Holocaust denial).

As Mearsheimer and Walt point out, the Israel lobby provides the link between governments and university campuses. Campus activity, as a result, appears to be wired directly into national politics, and this was apparently the case with the Mapping Models conference. Yet the wiring is not direct. In Canada as well, the circuit is heavily charged by Jewish organizations that represent the values of a particular faction of the more diverse Canadian Jewish community. And this organized Canadian Israel lobby operates, as it did in our case, directly in campus affairs.

While Mearsheimer and Walt lay out the objectionable influence of the Israel lobby on American campuses, a recent article by *Tikkun* provides a more resonant overview of the ways in which the lobby has attempted to pressure academic discourse.[47] In the article, "The Trial of Israel's Campus Critics," David Theo Goldberg and Saree Makdisi talk about "strident, even furious, attempts to silence or stifle criticism of Israeli policy on American college campuses."[48] The article could have been written about the Mapping Models conference and the fury that built around it.

The campaign to promote uncritical support for Israel on university campuses is organized, in the United States, under the umbrella of the Israel on Campus Coalition (ICC). This coalition shelters thirty-three distinct organizations under its wings, including the American Israel Public Affairs Committee, the Zionist Organization of America, the Anti-Defamation League, and the American Jewish Congress. The mission of the ICC is not merely to monitor campus activity as it relates to Israel; it is, rather, to generate "a pro-active, pro-Israel agenda on campus."[49]

In the wake of this agenda, Goldberg and Makdisi remark that "insinuation, accusation, and defamation have become the weapons of first resort to respond to argument and criticism directed at Israeli policies. As far as these outside pressure groups (and their campus representatives) are concerned, the intellectual and academic price that the scholarly community pays as a result of this kind of intervention amounts to little more than collateral damage." They observe that one of the means of undermining academic critiques of Israeli and domestic foreign policy has been cavalierly and maliciously to misrepresent those scholars, "mostly through *ad hominem* attacks on their characters, reputations, and careers." These attacks have the effect, if not the intent, of making others think twice before speaking out. In the case of the Mapping Models conference, the assaults included insinuation and accusation, but they also bordered on defamation.

Ad hominem attacks are but one of an array of tactics used by the ICC that makes up what Goldberg and Makdisi call "the treatment."[50] Beyond character assassination, other aspects of "the treatment" include selective misquotation, the wilful distortion of the record, the fabrication of falsehoods, and an utter disregard for the truth. Most, if not all, of these tactics were used against the organizers of and participants in the Mapping Models conference, as Chapter 1 documented.

When attempts at shaming are not immediately fruitful, or simply employed as a simultaneous means of "shap[ing] memory, disposition, and arguably – in the long run at any rate – the policy process itself," outside pressure is brought to bear on university administrations to intervene in the research activities of independent scholars. "Some of [these administrations]," Goldberg and Makdisi note, "seem to have yielded to coercion, while trying to 'balance' calls for responsibility with commitments to academic freedom. Some senior university administrators seem willing to take for granted the misrepresentations and fabrications by boisterous supporters of Israel, and have done so merely on the strident assertion of those making these claims."[51] The Mapping Models conference was no stranger to these stresses.

An aspect of this pressure brought to bear on university administrations operates at a more subtle level and involves a co-optation of the language of both responsibility and civil discourse – respectfulness – each of these lofty words being marshalled to publicly shape "acceptable" and "inappropriate" discourse. For example, the ICC put out a discussion paper in 2007 under the innocuous-sounding title "Academic Rights, Academic Responsibilities: A New Approach."[52] The report starts out with an anodyne discussion of the ICC agenda – "how to create a campus climate that enables the open, civil and objective study and discussion of complex and charged topics."[53] The report is predicated on the notion that academic freedom – a central tenet of the university community – by itself is not sufficient to protect a thriving academic environment; the teleology of the university should be seen through a new prism: a responsibilities-based approach. It goes on to propose the imposition of a set of responsibilities on academics that would bind the academy to external political influences from both governments and lobby groups. As the report notes,

> outside parties want a voice in this discussion [about what constitutes suitable academic content]: Off-campus constituencies are becoming increasingly determined to take part in discussions about the campus environment. Campus stakeholders traditionally have opposed such forays, but, due to a number of trends, the time has come to consider the best ways to include outside voices in discussions about campus life. As a part of the broader community, a university cannot insulate itself altogether from the priorities and concerns of members of that broader community, especially those who have ties to the university.[54]

The report is clear that universities should accept public oversight of the activities of scholars to ensure that they "maintain certain standards of inquiry and discourse."[55] Given the ICC's mandate to generate "a pro-active, pro-Israel agenda on campus," it is not difficult to decipher which types of discourse public overseers should be directed to discourage.

In a passage ominously reminiscent of what happened with the Mapping Models conference, the report alludes to the "review of funding allocations by a government body that would determine whether the goals of funding are being met. While many campus stakeholders decry any efforts to attach strings to federal funding, ultimately each school has the option of declining the grants and the conditions that accompany them." The thrust of the report indicates that a "responsibilities-based" approach would leave both universities and individual academics accountable to the most powerful political forces of the day.

This language of responsibility and respect has resurfaced as a component of "the treatment" to which critics of Israeli and foreign policy are now subject. Just as ad hominem attacks and pressure on the university administration became staples of "the treatment" to which the Mapping Models conference was subjected, so too this language of responsibility to outside voices and of "civil discourse" became part of the tactics brought to bear to fence in a forbidden topic.

The result of all of these interventions is that, in the words of the *Tikkun* article, "what is taking place in the academy today is an extension of what takes place on Capitol Hill and in the corridors of (real) power."[56] However, the influence of the Israel lobby on both institutions – Capitol Hill and the academy – suggests that activity in both locales is an extension of an outside agenda brought to bear, very successfully, on both. In the case of the Mapping Models conference, the loop got closed as the government intervened, on behalf of groups such as B'nai Brith, the Jewish Defence League (JDL), and other Canadian groups agitating for a particular vision of Israel.

Goldberg and Makdisi approach their material from a strictly American point of view, referencing events taking place at American institutions of higher learning and addressing the types of pressures on academia specific to the United States over the past ten years. The sources of pressure are not, however, unique to the United States, nor are the tactics used, and nor are the responses of both government and university. Given the legality and legitimacy of special interest lobbying in Canada as well as the United States, the need for universities and governments to respond in forceful and principled manners to these pressures is just as pressing.

There is little written scholarly material about Canada's equivalent to what Mearsheimer and Walt call the Israel lobby. This might be due in part to the relatively recent emergence of a reorganized central pro-Israel lobby in the country and the very recent formation of a Canadian organization kindred to the American Israel Public Affairs Committee (AIPAC). Both of these organizations, the Canadian Council for Israel and Jewish Advocacy (CIJA) and the Canadian Jewish Political Affairs Committee (CJPAC), emerged just prior to, and in tandem with, the shift in Canadian foreign policy toward Israel.

A June 2005 article in *Toronto Life* magazine chronicles the emergence of CIJA and lays out the connections between the lobby and the Liberal government when the Martin Liberals shifted Canadian foreign policy toward Israel.[57] On the eve of Paul Martin's election as prime minister, two of the key creators and funders of CIJA, Heather Reisman and Gerald Schwartz, threw what constitutes the largest single political fundraiser in Canadian history, an event at which they flaunted the history of their friendship with Martin and talked "about sitting around the kitchen table with [him]."[58] CIJA was the response of Reisman and Schwartz to events that had taken place two years earlier at another Canadian campus, Concordia University in Montreal, in which a speech by then former prime minister of Israel Benjamin Netanyahu was cancelled due to protests. They marshalled Hershel Ezrin, the CEO of CIJA at the time of the conference (who later issued the public statement against our conference cited in the introduction), to conduct a poll that confirmed that Israel was losing ground in the war for public opinion. These results in hand, Reisman and Schwartz set up the new lobby with Ezrin as CEO to make the case for Israel with more conviction and financial muscle, a move that has been described as "essentially a takeover of the country's Jewish institutions."[59]

Although there were certainly organized Jewish groups operating prior to the creation of these two umbrella organizations (principally the Canadian Jewish Congress and the Canada-Israel Committee), the 2002 formation of CIJA and the 2005 formation of CJPAC consolidated and focused efforts to clarify a Canadian Israel policy and injected a considerable amount of new funding into that project. As Brent Belzberg, co-chair of CIJA, noted in a 2004 *Canadian Jewish News* article, "before CIJA's creation, including the Congress, the CIC and national campus organizations subsisted on a combined allocation of $5.3 million. Since then, the agencies' combined budget has grown to $10.4 million, while the dollar amount spent on administration has not grown."[60] CJPAC (which grew out of its antecedent, CIJA-PAC) is not only well funded but also structured as a lobby group along the lines of its American counterpart, AIPAC. Both participate directly in the political process by working with all elected officials, regardless of political affiliation, to advance a particular version of pro-Israel advocacy. The policy thrust of each lines up with a right-wing politic (in Israeli political parlance). In the case of CIJA and CJPAC, as is evident from the tilt in Canadian foreign policy beginning in 2004, and no doubt in large measure as a result of how well endowed each organization is, they have "the ear of those who make decisions," in the words of CIJA co-chair Belzberg.[61] As the *Toronto Life* article noted in 2005, "CIJA can already claim political dividends. Last fall, Martin's government switched Ottawa's votes on two United Nations resolutions that had long been a thorn in Israel's side ... In foreign policy circles, the turnabout qualified as a diplomatic bombshell."[62] As John Ibbitson observed in the *Globe and Mail,* "in case you missed it, our Mideast policy has shifted."[63]

Although the links between the American Israel lobby and the Canadian Israel lobby are not difficult to trace,[64] the patterns in how each government has responded and, more to the point, the ways in which the lobby has had an impact (or at least has tried to have an impact) on university discourse on the topic of Israel/Palestine are strikingly similar.

In the case of the Mapping Models conference, one does not have to believe that there is an overlap between CIJA-PAC (or CJPAC) and AIPAC, the latter shaping and instructing the policies of the former, to see the direct overlaps in tactics between the Canadian and American organizations. The ways in which the Mapping Models conference was received and treated by CIJA and other Jewish organizations such as B'nai Brith and the JDL make clear that they are all on the same side of this issue.

In the material that follows, it is hard to avoid the irony of the insistence on responsibility and civil discourse – and the critique of boycotts – by those agitating, in the words of the Israel Campus Coalition, for "a pro-active, pro-Israel agenda on campus" when juxtaposed against the tactics invoked.[65] The irony compounds, and renders more complex, what it means to agitate for responsibility in academic freedom. It throws into relief a passage from the statement by the president of York University published in response to groups such as the American ICC. In that passage, President Shoukri notes that "with academic freedom come certain obligations. Scholars' academic activities must be based on evidence, rigorous thought and extensive research."[66] The proposition that questions the presence of evidence, rigorous thought, and extensive research should be subjected to review for things such as funding and a place within the university by "outside voices" and "off-campus constituencies"[67] is left open by this passage. What follows examines, in narrative form, what those off-campus constituencies were prepared to do to promote their agendas and should give pause to where academia properly turns to make those determinations.

The Mapping Models conference appears to have received a Canadian version of the *full* treatment. The pressures brought to bear to sanction the conference or to bring about its cancellation altogether appear to have fallen on fertile soil with this particular government. The Social Sciences and Humanities Research Council (SSHRC) seemed to be similarly compromised. And, despite former York University president Marsden's emphatic remark (in the context of boycott campaigns against Israel) that the "idea that individual universities should operate some kind of academic foreign policy is anathema to everything that, as academics, we stand for,"[68] York

University president Shoukri's administration appeared to be amenable to tilting toward an academic foreign policy for the Mapping Models conference and setting aside what was otherwise anathema to everything that universities stand for.

4

Inside Academia

Chapter 1 of this book laid out the history of the external pressures brought to bear on the Mapping Models conference. It covered the efforts to align an academic query with foreign policy. Wrong-headed, unprincipled, or outrageous, the voices raised were external to the immediate community that housed the conference, the university itself. This chapter takes much the same historical frame laid out in Chapter 1 and chronicles the events happening coevally inside a community subjected to pressures to align thought with politics, a community for which such an alignment is problematic.

What would it look like, in its minutiae, for foreign policy to operate on academia (to borrow former president Marsden's phrase from the last chapter)? What tone in communications, what precise phrasing of words, what behind-the-scenes manoeuvres, what marshalling of collective intellectual resources, what play on officialdom, what internal justifications, what subtle distortions of authoritative voice would be consistent with efforts to make universities an arm of national (and foreign) governments? What would a university do right in fending off such manoeuvres? What public face would it present? What affirmations would it offer internally? What lines would it refuse to cross? The following material presents a case study of exactly those quandaries. It reviews the external and internal pressures to which the Mapping Models conference was subjected and the responses of the relevant academic players to those pressures.

Although off-campus constituencies were extraordinarily vocal in their opposition to the conference, and although the Canadian government itself became involved in our academic activities, the administration of York University appeared to be resolute in its commitment to academic freedom. In many respects, the president of York University could not have made a clearer and more eloquent defence of academic freedom than was contained in his May and June 2009 statements on academic freedom.[1] The statements encapsulate many of the principles of academic freedom enunciated by associations of university professors.[2]

The Organizing Committee had one meeting with the president, on May 13, 2009, in which he veered not an inch from the position articulated in his statements on academic freedom. The meeting was barely a month before the start date of the conference and roughly a week before his first statement appeared on the York University website. At that meeting, the president assured us that the university took clear lines on academic freedom and that he had no intention of crossing them. He expressed regret that we might at any time have been left with any other impression.

However, by that time, we had been given a fair amount of indication that those lines were not as clearly demarcated as we might have wished. The following materials track developments of the university administration's interventions in the Mapping Models conference in (more or less) chronological sequence.

Academic Anathema

Spring 2008

The first nine months of organizing were principally dedicated to the composition of an international body of experts qualified to serve as our Advisory Committee.[3] Another aspect of the early planning exercise involved securing funds to enable us to launch conference planning in earnest. To that end, in the spring of 2008, Professor Sharry Aiken sought funds from her home faculty (Law) and institution (Queen's University). Professor Bruce Ryder and I requested start-up funds from a range of administrative bodies at York University.

For fundraising purposes, and to provide prospective members of the Advisory Committee with some background, the Organizing Committee gave the conference a title and drafted an early vision statement for the conference as well as a preliminary draft conference program. Emails circulated as part of our fundraising efforts made it clear that we were in the early stages of planning a conference for the following year. We noted that the conference program that we attached to the email was "a tentative draft" and noted on the draft conference outline that the titles of the conference panels were suggestive.

The actual title, structure, and vision statement of the original conference proposal that we circulated in our early fundraising efforts bear emphasis (for the original conference proposal, see Appendix 16). The proposed conference, Imagining a Bi-National Constitutional Democracy in Israel/Palestine, was originally focused almost exclusively on the one-state model. The purpose of the conference was clear in the circulated vision statement: "to explore the possibility that a single binational constitutional democracy in Israel/Palestine is the most promising path to future peace and security in the region." There was no impulse in the original formulation to ensure that discussion of this model be "balanced" against arguments in favour of the two-state model. Indeed, the original vision statement noted that "a growing number of scholars are reaching the conclusion that the chances of reaching a just two-state solution are increasingly remote."

The vision statement made passing reference to a phenomenon that indeed became the preoccupation of the conference: "The existing one state scholarship is devoted primarily to convincing those with an aversion to even considering the idea." Although we were aware at the outset that this "aversion" distracted attention from many of the other complex issues related to this model of statehood, we had not fully anticipated the ferocity with which it could consume efforts to thoughtfully address our original intrigues, such as "specific issues of constitutional design" and an exploration of "the possibility that a state shaped by federalism, equal citizenship and respect for linguistic, cultural and religious rights could provide greater protection than the current situation to the long-term security and right to self-determination of both Israelis and Palestinians in the Middle East."

The draft conference agenda itself also appeared to be almost completely unconcerned about a full vetting of the viability of the two-state model. Both we and those who approved early conference funding were apparently nonchalant about any putative obligation to affirm its importance or to dignify it with solemn headings. The only panel in a two-and-a-half-day conference that would canvass the outlines of the two-state model was formed under the title Is One State in Israel/Palestine Inevitable? This panel proposed canvassing the two-state model only to the extent that, in considering the one-state model as a viable alternative for the region, it "canvasses its history, and assesses its prospects against the background of the current poverty of hope in the two-state solution." Against this background and a stated perception that "the prospects of a lasting peace under the two-state model appear increasingly remote, if not impossible," the first panel was the only one that proposed a detailed examination of the "current prospects of the two-state model." But the suggestive four subheadings of that particular panel, for which we were hoping to find speakers, were the following: Trials and Tribulations of the One State Proposal, Divorced Till Death Do Us Part, The Dusk of the Two State Solution, and Finding the Pulse of the Two State Solution. In 2008, it seemed to be permissible not only to be concerted about examining binationalism in Israel/Palestine but also to be frank ("poverty of hope") and flip (Finding the Pulse).

Beyond this residual consideration of the "impossible prospects" of the two-state model, the rest of the panels were devoted to in-depth explorations of binationalism. I have laid out the entire conference program, under its original title, as an appendix that I invite the reader to consult.[4] The original vision demonstrates what relatively unbridled scholarly imagination might conjure up. It also lays out exactly what early funders thought was a reasonable and worthy endeavour, indeed an "interesting," "provocative," "challenging," and "ambitious" one – including those who apparently drastically re-evaluated their judgments over the twelve months that followed.

The other addition made to this draft proposal was the suggestion of Desmond Tutu as a keynote speaker; we were, in fact, attempting to secure him as the sole keynote for the conference. Ultimately, he was unable to arrange his schedule to accommodate the conference. The prospect of engaging this particular keynote speaker did not raise any concern among our early funders. However, one of our Advisory Committee members, an Israeli scholar, ultimately expressed relief that the invitation had been declined in that Tutu's name on the program would have greatly diminished the number of Israeli scholars who would have felt comfortable attending the conference in light of his public description of Israel as an apartheid state and his early affiliation with the boycott, divestment, sanctions (BDS) campaign in support of the Palestinian cause.[5] His possible affiliation with this group and his public description of Israel as an apartheid state were not among our motives in considering Tutu as a prominent speaker. Rather, his involvement in a peaceful transition to binationalism (or multinationalism) in South Africa constituted his central appeal for us. However, we never contemplated that his involvement in the BDS movement – which, after all, is a prototypically non-violent form of resistance – might somehow disqualify him.

These titles and the accompanying blurbs on the thrust of each proposed panel conveyed the scope of what we wanted to examine in the process of our appeals for funding. Given that we were applying for a SSHRC grant (which obliges researchers to issue a call for papers and draw up a conference program on the basis of the response to that call), we did not expect the final program to correspond to this structure. However, the document gives a clear sense of what we wanted to examine, what we thought were legitimate topics for examination, and, perhaps just as important, what those who originally agreed to fund the conference thought we were designing as an academic event.

In response to a request to fund this proposed conference, Queen's University was immediately and generously forthcoming, as were several sources at York University, including the office of the associate vice-president of research and innovation (AVP). The AVP, David Dewitt, affirmed at that point that the conference seemed to be "an interesting, challenging and provocative" event.[6] Having vetted the vision statement and proposal, he voiced no hesitation (quite the contrary) regarding the proposed keynote speaker.

On March 3, 2008, we sent Dean Patrick Monahan an email asking for a meeting in order to ascertain whether Osgoode Hall Law School could provide us with financial assistance. As per our protocol, we provided the dean with the preliminary draft of the conference program. We flagged for him that we had already secured funds and sponsorship from Queen's University's Faculty of Law. The dean responded to our email by indicating that he looked forward to meeting with us "to discuss this interesting and ambitious proposal."[7] The meeting was called for March 26.

At that meeting, Dean Monahan noted that it was salutary, in light of tensions at York University, that a scholarly event (specifically of the nature of the above proposal and with its proposed keynote speaker) would be held on Israel/Palestine and might model how these issues could be aired as part of an academic exercise.[8]

There was no discussion at this juncture on "genuine forums" for scholarly dialogue or any stress on or requirement that the conference have "internationally recognized scholars or public figures" – claims that the dean made retrospectively in his July 13, 2009, "Preliminary Review" of an earlier draft of this unintended ethnography.[9] There was no discussion on the conference representing a "balanced range of opinions on the issues to be discussed." Far from it. If by balance what is meant is some proportionate representation of one-state and two-state models, or even an extensive negative critique of the one-state model to offset arguments that would advance it, the original model was almost single-mindedly focused on the binational one and an exploration of its prospects and possibilities. And the leading internationally recognized public figure on the proposal was a strong advocate of, indeed activist in, the boycott, divestment, sanctions campaign. He was not an academic, and indeed, apart from his pastoral work, Tutu might be considered a consummate advocate and activist. The first time that the dean raised these types of concerns regarding balance was in his meetings with us in April and May 2009, after he began receiving intense pressure from a faction of the Jewish community both at York University and externally.

The principal funding source to which the dean directed us was the U50 Campus Committee established to approve academic events officially to become part of the fiftieth anniversary celebrations at York University. This group was tasked to conduct peer reviews of all U50 applications and composed in the majority by our academic peers at the university. The above draft materials prompted the dean to suggest that our project was a model event for York's fiftieth anniversary celebrations.

We thought that our chances of securing U50 funds were close to nonexistent given the potentially controversial nature of the conference's themes. Nevertheless, we submitted our U50 application on April 11, 2008, accompanied by the above unmodified vision statement and draft conference proposal. The dean signed off on this application without speaking further with us.

We found out in the spring of 2009 that we had been approved for U50 funding. We were cheered that the U50 Campus Committee, along with the university itself, had not been deterred by the potentially controversial nature of the conference's themes. This gave us faith in the academic integrity of York University.

Despite our pessimism about being placed on the funded roster of 50th anniversary celebration events, given the standard protocols for university funding of academic events it would have been surprising, if not alarming, to learn that sponsorship came with stipulations for administrative involvement in the content of such an academic activity.

The dean later confirmed that he shared our understanding that sponsorship meant nothing more than the provision of funding. In an April 24, 2009, email to an external party who had complained about Osgoode's and York's co-sponsorship of the event, Dean Monahan responded,

> As for the issue that it is "sponsored" by Osgoode, the organizers applied to a York committee to be designated as a York 50th event, which meant that they got some money from a fund created to celebrate the 50th anniversary of York. I supported their application, based on the vision statement. And really I had no other realistic choice but to support them. I supported every application that was put forward by my faculty members ... So that is what the "sponsorship" consists of.[10]

From the moment that we secured U50 funding and the approval of our application by Dean Monahan, we shared his view that he had supported our application in a perfunctory way and without constraint on our academic freedom. However, in justifying his subsequent interventions in the conference, he drew considerably on what he construed as an "agreement" between himself and the Organizing Committee that supposedly gave justification for interventions aimed at promoting balance in the program. These justifications can be found in the several submissions that he returned to me in my request for feedback on my assessment of events as well as in the feedback that he provided to the CAUT Inquiry.

In his July 2011 response to my request for feedback, Provost Monahan noted that,

> because this particular conference was approved and sponsored by the University as one of the select number of York 50th events, the University had an interest in its conduct and success ... At all times the organizers and I were aware that issues relating to statehood in the Middle East are extraordinarily complex and arouse strong emotion from those involved. I believe we all understood that any effort to promote genuine academic debate and dialogue needed to be sensitive to the range of competing academic perspectives on these matters. This need for "balance," in the sense of ensuring a wide range of scholarly perspectives on the issues, was a shared goal of the conference organizers and the University from the very beginning of my discussions with the conference organizers in spring 2008.

Provost Monahan noted several times in his feedback that there was an "agreement" between the organizers and his office or that there was "a commonly accepted basis upon which [he] had agreed to sponsor the conference from the beginning" and that this "agreement" secured the justification for his subsequent involvement to ensure that the two-state model had a more prominent place in the program and that advocates of the one-state model be offset by advocates of the two-state model – that is, balance in the sense that Provost Monahan began to use the phrase once the conference came under intense political pressure.

Professor Jon Thompson in *No Debate* rejected Provost Monahan's characterization of the arrangement between the conference Organizing Committee and York University (by way of the dean) as a quasi-contractual one.[11] Thompson found no persuasive evidence for the assertion of a quasi-contract stemming from our agreement that "the University had an interest in [the conference's] conduct and success." As Thompson confirmed, our U50 application nowhere spoke of balance as a driving aspiration for discussion of one-state and two-state solutions. Furthermore, the draft program, proposed conference title, and vision statement seen by the dean in March 2008 and signed off by him in our U50 application were clearly focused on the one-state, binational model for Israel/Palestine. The two-state model was considered only by way of recognizing its historical demise.

The application further evinced no reluctance to showcase non-academic "activists" especially when the original keynote speaker was someone who, whatever other stellar qualities might underscore his appeal, was known for drawing connections between Israel and the apartheid regime of South Africa and who was affiliated with (if not one of the early leaders of) the boycott, divestment, sanctions movement in support of the Palestinian cause. The pages of the original draft conference proposal provided the parameters for what would constitute a diversity of perspectives on the topic of Israel/Palestine.

In his July 2011 feedback, the dean also found a quasi-contractual obligation of the Organizing Committee in the Memorandum of Understanding (MoU) to the U50 grant signed by the dean and Professor Ryder. He noted that,

> because this particular conference was approved and sponsored by the University as one of the select number of York 50th events, the University had an interest in its conduct and success. It was for this reason that all York 50th events had to be approved by the Dean of the relevant faculty, and that all event organizers were to report regularly to their Dean on their plans and progress. These commitments were understood and accepted, as set out in a July 18, 2009 Memorandum of Understanding signed by Bruce and me, setting out administrative arrangements, planning time-lines and reporting expectations.

The Organizing Committee did not recall there being any obligation on us set by the MoU to allow administrative oversight of the content of our conference or, indeed, any reliance on it drawn by Dean Monahan in his communications with us about the conference. Professor Thompson reviewed the MoU, and his findings conformed to the place that the MoU had in our work on the conference. As he noted, "from a review of the MoU, it was a generic document for U50 events, concerned with administrative matters to help ensure the timely and successful mounting of each event. It was not concerned with the academic standards or program content of the particular event." Professor Thompson concluded that the MoU provided no effective support for Dean Monahan's position that his interventions to ensure balance in the conference program derived from any quasi-contractual undertaking on our part to ensure balance in our work.[12]

From these considerations, it seems reasonable to conclude that Dean Monahan did not secure any greater interest or right of intervention in the Mapping Models conference than is normally allowed university administrators by virtue of his approval and sponsorship of the U50 event. It remained fully up to the Organizing Committee and the Advisory Committee to determine what we meant by "principled conversations" or by "a wide range of scholarly perspectives on the issues," free of administrative interference or oversight.

Fall 2008

The first interaction with Osgoode's dean that was troubling to us arose around the confluence of events in the fall of 2008 that included the call for papers, our colleague's email to the dean complaining about the conference,[13] and the article that Ed Morgan published in the *National Post*. At the same time as the call for papers went out, an international speaker series at Osgoode – Putting Theory to Practice – was set to host a seminar on a Canadian case relating to a violation of the Fourth Geneva Convention. The case arose from the construction of residential buildings by a Canadian company in the occupied Palestinian territories. Bil'in, a village in the West Bank, was seeking damages and an injunction ordering the company to stop its allegedly illegal activities. Two speakers were to address the issues in that case. The doctoral student on our conference Organizing Committee, Mazen Masri, had organized the Bil'in seminar with the cooperation of a faculty member at Osgoode, the associate dean of graduate studies (ADRGS), under whose auspices the speaker series was organized.

Our colleague, who complained about the sponsorship of our conference, wrote a second email to Osgoode's dean to complain about this seminar.[14] Concerned about such events poisoning the institutional atmosphere by discussing sensitive political issues, our colleague asked whether, for the sake of balance, the law school would "also be arranging for a seminar on illegal funding and active support for terrorist organizations; illegal terror organizations, supported by UN members, which occupy territory, conduct terror attack from it, incite for mass-murder (if not genocide), are committed to the destruction of a neighbouring state, and even do not claim to be bound by international law." As conference organizers, we were copied on this email, and allusion was made to political issues being aired (in both the conference and the seminar series) with a supposedly very thin and illusory disguise of scholarship. Our colleague finished by noting that, if the faculty seminar convener and we decided to discuss the Israeli/Palestinian conflict, "is it too much to expect it [the discussion] to be balanced and comprehensive?"

The third event that occurred at the same time as the call for papers and the Bil'in seminar was an article on York University featured in *Toronto Life* magazine. Under the title "York's Middle East War," the article focused on other tensions on campus relating to the politics of Israel/Palestine. As the article announced, "the Israel-Palestine conflict is poisoning York University with violent demonstrations, riot cops on campus, lawsuits, even a Human Rights Commission inquiry. The school's new president – the first Muslim head of a Canadian university – wants to make peace. Does he stand a chance?"[15]

Dean Monahan responded to the confluence of our colleague's emails about our conference and the Bil'in seminar with the imminent publication of the *Toronto Life* article by calling to his office the two Osgoode professors on the Organizing Committee to discuss the various brewing controversies, particularly as they related to our conference. He indicated that he "would appreciate a chance to speak about these concerns."[16]

It was not the Organizing Committee that asked for this meeting (the first of many) to address his concerns. Structurally, as faculty members, we were being called into the dean's office not as colleagues or personal acquaintances; we were formally being called, under administrative auspices, to address institutional concerns.

Dean Monahan sent us a follow-up email forwarding a copy of the article in *Toronto Life* magazine, very damning to the university, about the politics relating to Israel/Palestine on the York campus. He labelled this preparatory email "Background for our discussion on conference."[17] He saw our conference as linked to other events on campus.

At that October 9, 2008, meeting, the dean sought further information on the conference. He had read and approved of the title and vision statement when he signed our application for funding to the York fiftieth anniversary celebration events – as he did when he signed off on our SSHRC application. Now he wanted to know more about the Organizing Committee.

We told him about Professor Aiken from Queen's, a Jewish scholar whose doctoral work included a comparative study of human rights and citizenship in Israel. We told him that Mazen Masri was the fourth committee member, a doctoral student whose research centred on human rights in Israel. We indicated that Masri was a Palestinian citizen of Israel with an LLB from Hebrew University and an LLM from the University of Toronto. He had also been a legal consultant to the PLO and hence was well versed in the legal issues relating to the conference themes.

At this point, the dean requested that we remove Masri from the Organizing Committee. The composition of such a committee frequently changes, he argued. Masri was only a doctoral student. His ejection from the committee would improve the optics of the conference.

Since we balked at the suggestion, the dean said that, if we found ourselves unprepared to remove Masri, we should put someone else on our committee to balance his presence. He proposed that Professor Ed Morgan, or someone like him, should join the Organizing Committee.

Dean Monahan subsequently confirmed our fears that he was serious by emailing us that he was intending to raise the question of us rearranging our Organizing Committee with the president in a meeting between the two of them the following week. As he noted, "When I meet with the President and the VPA I will be indicating that I have requested an adjustment in the membership of the organizing committee. Plse let me know what you decide to do in that regard."[18]

As noted in the introduction to this book, Dean Monahan affirmed that he requested us to remove Masri from the Organizing Committee and justified this intervention by remarking that, at the time of his request, he was "surprised to learn ... that the organizing committee included Mazen Masri, a graduate student who had played a prominent and public role in various organizations that are politically active in relation to the politics of the Middle East." To his mind, it was evident that Masri's "participation would likely lead to criticism of the event on the grounds that it was a political rather than an academic exercise."[19]

After the October 2008 meeting, the Organizing Committee regrouped and assessed which accommodations we could make without violating the academic integrity of the project. We were distressed enough after that meeting that we had discussions on how to make accommodations that were insignificant to our work but would appease the dean's desire to restructure our committee. We proposed a community liaison officer for the Organizing Committee, a thankless position that we had little chance of filling but would allow us to present an accommodating gesture to the dean.

In an October 10th memo to the dean, we presented arguments about why it was wrong-headed to add another member to the Organizing Committee to meet his political concerns:

> The organizing committee meetings at this point are very pragmatic events. At our weekly two hour meetings there is little if any heated discussion. In fact we are far more focused on arranging the multifarious details than having political discussions. We are concerned that adding another member whose function is to provide "balance" will inject a political tone which has the potential to not only derail the planning, but also has the potential to become disruptive. If this committee (which we believe has much less prominence than the advisory committee) becomes politically derailed and polarized, the political fall out from that could be far more pernicious than the status quo, particularly if those difficulties become public.

In our memo to the dean, we also noted a change to the title of the conference and flagged the series of meetings with concerned university colleagues that we had undertaken.

As noted above, between the complaint from our colleague and the first iteration of the conference title in the spring of 2008 (Imagining a Bi-National Constitutional Democracy in Israel/Palestine, with a program focused almost exclusively on the one-state model), we had already changed the title of the conference to Israel/Palestine: One State or Two? on the advice of one of the Israeli members of our Advisory Committee, who had suggested that we might get a broader range of scholars attending if we broadened the title and range of focus for the program. This title change had been approved by all of the Advisory Committee members. Our colleague was now complaining about the presence of the one-state model in our conference program at all. In his mind, there was not "any legal issue per se in connection with the establishment of one state in Israel and Palestine."[20] As discussed above, Advisory Committee member Professor Ed Morgan also weighed in (shortly before leaving the committee) to note that the very words *one state* in the context of Israel/Palestine were a code for something almost as "vile" as the "Final Solution."[21]

Since the title seemed to be the most superficial aspect of the conference program and easy enough to compromise when weighed against the dean's request for "an adjustment in the membership of the organizing committee," and since we were in fact receiving responses to our calls for papers that spoke to a broader range of models than conceived of even in the second iteration of the conference plan, we changed the title a second time to its final one: Israel/Palestine: Mapping Models of Statehood and Paths to Peace.

The dean responded favourably to these accommodations and expressed gratitude for our willingness to compromise. He shared this memo with the president. The position of community liaison officer, not surprisingly, never came to fruition. For the time being, the conference was again on a stable footing with the institution.

If we had concerns about our dependence on the dean's goodwill for the conference, they were played out with respect to the Bil'in seminar that Mazen Masri helped to organize. In response to our colleague's October 5th email to the dean, which strongly criticized the law school over the seminar, Dean Monahan contacted the then associate dean of graduate studies and research (ADRGS), who had organized the event.

On October 6th, Masri was sent an email by the research coordinator in the associate dean's office that asked for background on the presenters, and then a follow-up email from the associate dean arrived:

> It may be that we, due to the politically heated nature of the topic, have to complement the two litigators with an adequate representative of a differing view. This would likely create a more mini-symposium like event, but we think this might be a more fruitful context for a talk in this area. The central concern here is that we should be hesitant to provide a scholarly platform for a non-scholarly presentation of an on-going litigation without providing for a balanced context.[22]

On October 6th, another colleague intervened to propose that he would moderate the seminar and that Ed Morgan be added to the seminar since he was representing the plaintiff in the *Lebanese Canadian Bank* case, also out of Quebec, in which the bank was being sued for its facilitation of Hezbollah.

On October 14th, when it appeared that Morgan would not be available on the originally planned seminar date of October 30th, the associate dean wrote to Masri: "After deliberations at the Law School, we want to postpone the pttp talk from 30 October to the Winter term. We believe it will be a much more worthwhile event if prepared with more lead time. Ed Morgan expressed his enthusiasm for the event, but is unable to make it on that date."[23]

Masri, understanding the "postponement" to be a de facto cancellation, responded to Osgoode's administrative intervention by pointing out that,

> Given that this event is taking place at other universities (University of Ottawa, University of Toronto and Harvard), and given that organizers there are under the same political pressures that we are facing here, if Osgoode cancels, it will be clear that this is the result of pressure that Osgoode could not withstand in a principled manner. This may not reflect well and may paint Osgoode in a negative light, a thing that we all, as members of the Osgoode community, should do our best to avoid.[24]

Masri further indicated that he would have a student organization host the event given that the presenters were available only on the preplanned date.

At this point, I also intervened and went to the associate dean to express my serious concerns about how the seminar was being handled by the law school. In my recollection of the conversation, he explained to me that the rationale for the administrative concern arose from a policy that the law school did not invite discussion of ongoing litigation.

In response to these events, and in conjunction with Masri, I marshalled another senior colleague to convince the associate dean to resist the dean's intervention in the seminar. With Masri's agreement, we suggested that this senior colleague offer to moderate the seminar at the scheduled time. This alternative was accepted, and the seminar went off without a hitch.

As part of the fact-checking process integral to the creation of this book, in March 2011 I sent a letter to the current dean of Osgoode, Lorne Sossin, to inquire whether or not Osgoode indeed has a policy about inviting discussion of ongoing litigation. Provost Monahan, apprised of my inquiry, responded by stating that

> [The associate dean] and I discussed the fact that a lawyer representing a client in litigation has a duty to his/her client which limits the extent to which the lawyer can express independent views on the matters that are before a court or tribunal; thus if, as in the case of this seminar, a lawyer

> is invited to present a seminar on a matter that is before the courts (and in which the lawyer is acting), it is desirable to ensure that there is an independent, academic perspective presented on the matter, along with the views of the lawyer.

He also noted that he "did not suggest to [the associate dean] that the law school has a policy of not holding seminars on matters that are the subject of on-going litigation."

I found this response of Provost Monahan puzzling because it did not correspond with the regular pedagogical and scholarly practices that I had observed at the law school. In a cursory manner, I canvassed eight of my colleagues and discovered that the majority of them (six) invite lawyers to present on ongoing litigation or on cases in which they have been involved without feeling any need to invite the "other side." Some of these colleagues talk in class about cases in which they are actively involved. Many of our adjunct professors talk about cases in which they are or have been actively involved. The "desirability" of providing the "other side" with an opportunity to respond and/or ensuring that there is an "independent, academic perspective presented on the matter" is, presumably, more acute in the case of the classroom, where there is a captive audience. The majority of the colleagues whom I canvassed also cited instances in which they asked lawyers to present at conferences/seminars on cases in which they were or had been actively involved without feeling the need to bring in the "other side" – indeed, some thought that doing so would be positively undesirable.

In the correspondence between Provost Monahan and me about whether or not he had said that the law school had a policy about the use of lawyers in legal pedagogy at Osgoode, I twice asked him to cite examples of other cases during his tenure in which lawyers were presenting and he intervened to ensure balance and an academic perspective. In the first email, sent March 23, 2011, I asked,

> Of all of the seminars (and classes) that take place at Osgoode, can you think of other instances in your tenure, Patrick, in which on-going litigation is being discussed in which you intervened as dean to the conference convener (or instructor/professor) to insure that there be an independent "academic" perspective? Could you provide me with specific examples? Or other examples of seminars being held at Osgoode over the course of your tenure where the issue of "balance" and "academic perspective" came up and over which you intervened?

In my second query, sent March 24, 2011, I asked,

> In light of how often law profs [have lawyers present on cases they are or have been actively involved in] and how often this happens at the law school in conferences and seminars, can you tell me of another circumstance in which you intervened the way that you did with the Bil'in seminar? Why did you get involved in the Bil'in seminar when it appears there is a healthy amount of practice (in the possibly more worrisome context of the classroom) where you refrained from doing so?

I got no response to these queries at that time.

In following up on these queries in his July 2011 feedback, Monahan indicated that he "did not see the relevance of this line of questioning." He also noted that he himself engaged in the practice of inviting lawyers involved in litigation to present at academic events and regarded this as valuable "provided that it was presented in an academic context."

I also asked three times whether the only prompt for the dean's intervention in the Bil'in seminar had come from our colleague's email. I got no response to these queries, though in his July 2011 feedback Monahan noted that he had intervened "in response to concerns raised by certain colleagues" (a response that was ambiguous in its suggestion of a plurality). Apart from our colleague on the record, the identity of any other colleague who might have lodged a complaint about the Bil'in seminar remains a mystery. He or she appears nowhere in the records.

Provost Monahan also acknowledged in his July 2011 response that he "may have made reference to the political sensitivities surrounding discussion of Middle East issues on campus" when he first contacted the associate dean about the Bil'in seminar the day after our colleague sent the dean's office an email complaining that it would poison the atmosphere at Osgoode by bringing in sensitive political issues.

It does appear that there is no policy at Osgoode that controls the use of lawyers in the law school or in academic events that take place at the law school. The university setting itself provides the academic context.

April 2009

We received over 120 submissions to our call for papers. Over the next several months, the Organizing and Advisory Committees vetted the abstracts and biographies and, through a process of agreement (and disagreement), winnowed the list of confirmed speakers down to roughly fifty. The central criteria invoked to sift accepted from rejected abstracts were the scholarly merit of the proposed papers and the relation of the abstracts to the conference themes, also taking into account the scholarly background of the speaker. At the end of November, we began to post confirmed speakers to the conference website as they became available.

Pressures on Jewish participants at the conference began to escalate in the spring of 2009. As noted above, we were aware of at least two cases in which confirmed speakers who were also members of Jewish community organizations were told by these institutions that they had to withdraw from the conference, which, with regret, they did.

As also noted above, at the end of March 2009, Professor Howard Adelman's circulating memo found its way to the chair of York's Board of Governors,[25] the president, and the dean. At the beginning of April, the dean again contacted us and told us that it would be helpful for him to understand how the conference planning had evolved in order to respond to such concerns in an informed manner. We drafted a memo that provided an update on the work that we had been doing to ensure that the conference would be a success. We noted our regret that Professor Adelman felt that he could no longer participate in the conference, particularly since his participation would have enhanced the multiplicity of voices for which we had been striving from the outset. The dean, grateful for the update, shared the memo with the president. He also sent an email to the president indicating that he did not think that the university administration should initiate any discussion with the "broader community" at that point.[26] This despite the recommendation of the chair of York's Board of Governors that the university take a proactive approach and meet with (Jewish) community leaders to indicate that university administrators had thought about the situation even if their conclusion regarding the conference was not what the community wanted to hear.

Within days, the landscape changed yet again. We received a second email from the dean stating that he had begun to receive communications from both inside and outside the university expressing concerns over a lack of balance among the speakers and presenters.[27] In response to these communications, he had reviewed the list of abstracts and decided that there were serious concerns over the content and overall direction that the contributors appeared to take on the issues. He asked to meet with us to discuss his newfound concerns. As he indicated, the conference was provoking a major reaction "in the community." He wanted to impress upon us the seriousness of the situation that we (the organizers and the university) were facing. He saw the conference as shaping up to be an event that could spin very badly out of control.

As also flagged above, we received an email from AVP David Dewitt on April 15th (from his administrative email account) that changed our willingness to solicit his feedback on the conference.[28] Although he had originally supported with funding from his office the conference in its original conception as an almost exclusive investigation of the one-state model under the title Imagining a Bi-National Constitutional Democracy for Israel/Palestine, a year later he concluded that he could no longer participate in it because of the presence on the program of individuals "who by their past actions have been tarnished by ideology and polemic." He was now concerned that a baseline of acceptable questions for the event had been crossed.

More troubling to us was that the AVP also provided advice on how we should manage the conference thenceforward, and his proposal struck us as contrary to the requirements of the SSHRC grant that we had already received. Our grant was predicated on the event being a conference and stipulated that, while keynote speakers could be invited, all others were to be culled from a call for papers. This requirement explains why the conference changed in focus from an examination of the one-state model to a more multipolar look at models (in the plural) of statehood. The title more or less changed to keep pace with these developments, hinged to SSHRC funding. Despite our funding requirements, AVP Dewitt asked us to modify our project significantly. He proposed the following:

> S[i]nce your SSHRC grant is insufficient to cover the expenses of the conference but its rules require this to be "public" (ie., not restricted to "by invitation only"), and since you already seem pretty confident that you have about a dozen or so strong contributions by recognized and worthy individuals, why not notify all that due to financial constraints (and everyone now knows about those!) the program has had to be reduced to a shorter time (one day perhaps or day plus a morning) for the presentation of those 12 or so papers, and only those individuals will receive financial support and be on the program. Others are certainly invited to attend in the audience and to participate from that vantage point, but not to present.
>
> You do that and even though you (and York and Osgoode) may still face some "community" difficulties, you will have diverted the situation to one of managing some unhappiness while being able to move forward with your project, including the book. You also will be able to do another revision to

> the website which would allow you to clarify as you deem appropriate both the core of the undertaking while confirming some fundamentals which could allay those who wish to think badly of what you are trying to do. You will never be able to satisfy those whose minds are fully made up, but you should be able to fulfil your academic responsibilities to SSHRC, accomplish much of what you are hoping for in terms of serious engagement, and come out with a respectable book.

This proposed modification to our event (just months before it was to be held) would have had serious implications for SSHRC, the major funding source for the conference.

Professor Thompson, in *No Debate,* affirms our sense at the time that AVP Dewitt's proposal would have been seriously ill advised. It would have constituted a "major" change to our program and could have placed the grant, or at least the amount of it, in jeopardy, despite his advice that we "should be able to fulfil [our] academic responsibilites to SSHRC." Adding to the concern over the sustainability of the proposal was the suggestion that we attribute the modification to a fanciful rationale: namely, that financial constraints provoked a reworking of the conference program (and vision statement). Given that AVP Dewitt was interacting with us as an administrator, Professor Thompson finds his intervention with the Organizing Committee to be inappropriate.[29]

Just as decisive for us in our decision to cease conferring with AVP Dewitt after April 15, 2009, was the ideological commitment that he expressed and that prompted him to propose a lineup of "worthy" presenters that coincided with this commitment. As he laid out the terrain in his April 15th email,[30]

> In the socio-political context in which Middle East affairs is now presented, and given the legacy of nationalism and state building not to speak of imperialism and colonialism in the region, posing the theme as has been done for this conference and giving space – both intellectual and physical/material – to individuals, some with serious academic credentials, others who by their past actions have been tarnished by ideology and polemic, your well-meaning effort to unpack the challenges facing both Israelis and Palestinians is being hijacked.

The presentation of his commitments as neutral in phrases such as "serious academic credentials" and his judgments captured by phrases such as "tarnished by ideology" rendered AVP Dewitt sufficiently overcommitted to be of little further serious assistance. He had now embraced a distinct political vision for the conference that was inappropriate to our scholarly goals. He further noted in his email that "I personally see nothing wrong with asking some very tough and fundamental questions about 'models of statehood or of national aspirations' so long as it is very clear that we are not entertaining the elimination of the Jewish national homeland or questioning the legitimacy of the State of Israel or its right to live within secure and recognized boundaries." In this passage, he was essentially providing us with the contours of what is allowed academically and what is not. He was providing us with a range not only of "reasonable presenters" but also of "reasonable questions."

No Debate captures well our fatigue with the posturing that we had been encountering from all corners to the effect that those with whom one disagrees are "activists," "ideologues," or "polemicists" and those with whom one agrees are "serious scholars" or "experts." Professor Thompson points out that

> ideologies are common in scholarship and, far from necessarily tarnishing it, an ideological perspective can be fundamental to progress in a field (although it can lead in some cases to tendentious, even spurious, work). Simply to label a scholar's approach to her or his work as ideological (or even to establish that it is ideological) does not by itself establish anything about its quality. A similar comment applies to claims that a scholar's work is polemical.
>
> However, in some instances, scholars who espouse competing ideologies or disciplinary perspectives have been known to discount the quality of substance of work by those seen to hold opposing views. Gabriel Piterberg made an observation that is ironical, illuminating, and relevant: "It is well known, of course, that critical works about Zionism or Israel are 'polemical' (or worse), whereas favourable ones are scholarly."[31]

AVP Dewitt's proposal reflected a commitment with respect to content – one that verged itself on polemical – suggesting that Dewitt would be useless in future deliberations. Moreover, we viewed his assessments as insulting to presenters whose abstracts had been vetted by us and our international Advisory Committee. If we had known that the president had asked Dean Monahan to work with Professor Dewitt in addressing issues regarding the conference – which the dean acknowledged in his July 2011 feedback and which had not been made known to us until the FIPPA request revealed it – we would have indicated at that time that Dewitt was not an appropriate consultant and in fact had shown signs of being perilous to the exercise.

April 15, 2009, appears to have been an important turning point in the administration's response to our conference for a number of reasons. Before that date, the dean, other administrative staff, and the Board of Governors of the university were receiving a swelling tide of complaints about the conference. However, the approach adopted appeared to defend our right to hold the conference. The chair of the board, Marshall Cohen, seemed to be calm and matter of fact in his response to events. Dean Monahan provided context and presented the difficulties with how complainers were framing things.[32]

On April 15th, this resolution in the face of pressure appeared to fold. Marshall Cohen sent out an email to the president and dean in which he flagged a wish to remove our conference from campus, to modify our program, and to "populate the audience with observers &/or participants to ensure a balanced dialogue."[33] This email was sent in anticipation of a meeting that day with the president and dean. After that meeting, Dean Monahan sent out an email to university history professor Irving Abella under the subject heading "Speak more about conference" and wrote, "Irv I have looked at the website in more detail and understand better the concerns. I want to get involved now in a more direct way and would like to speak with you, this evening if possible. Where can I reach you?"[34] Dean Monahan copied the Honourable Madame Justice Rosalie Abella on his April 15th email to Professor Irving Abella at her email account at the Supreme Court of Canada. Later that night, Dean Monahan updated President Shoukri and Marshall Cohen on his conversation with Abella.[35]

At the same time that we received the dean's concerned note, we received notice from the fiftieth anniversary celebrations committee that we might not have access to the venue that we had booked for the conference. Although we had reserved Glendon Campus in July 2008, and had been assured at the time that no other activities had been planned for the site, we were now informed that Glendon's convocation conflicted with our conference. As Professor Ryder recounted to the CAUT Inquiry, he was "stunned" – as were we all on the committee – to find that the venue for the conference was now being moved.[36]

We investigated and discovered that Glendon's convocation was in fact scheduled a week *after* our conference. In response to this point, we were told that it was convocation *setup* that would displace us, and the Board of Governors had decided that they wanted to have their year-end board meeting and "Hail and Farewell" dinner in one of the buildings on Glendon Campus on the second night of our conference.[37] We pointed out that the conference had no planned activities that night. We also pointed out that, if the non-overlapping events could not be accommodated, the board often met at a downtown location or at the other York campus throughout the year and that surely it would be less disruptive to move a dozen or so board members, who had no particular expectation where any given meeting might take place, than to displace a conference of 200 participants from a venue that had been booked the previous summer.

When we met with the dean on April 17th, the proposed shift in venue two months before the conference had still not been settled. At that time, he stated that the Board of Governors wanted us off *all* York University campuses. (Dean Monahan's perception of the board's wishes appears to have been well founded. Marshall Cohen, chair of the board, sent him an email to that effect on April 15th before a meeting with Dean Monahan and President Shoukri later that day.[38]) Two days later, on April 17th, Cohen sent a second email to Monahan in which he noted his surprise that we were willing to accommodate the request to move off campus: "I can only assume that you put the fear of all 3 gods involved here into them! Good work." It was in this email that Cohen revealed that removing us from campus was "Plan B." "Plan A" was for Dean Monahan to continue pressuring us until Cohen and the senior administration were "comfortable" that the conference would be "balanced" and that "people" would perceive it to be so.[39]

Although the conference was fast approaching and we were thus alarmed by this news, we indicated a willingness to move off campus but also a lack of funds to do so. Money was no object, the dean told us. If we could book an alternative venue off campus, the university would pay for it. The dean followed up our meeting by writing an email to the chair of the Board of Governors confirming that the latter had proposed that our conference be moved off campus:

> I met with the organizers ... today to impress upon them the seriousness of the situation and ... had a productive discussion ...
>
> [T]hey are open to moving the conference off-site to a hotel, subject to cost. I am having someone investigate the availability of a modestly price[d] hotel option ... [Y]ou [chair of the Board of Governors] raised this idea – do you think it worth it to invest the additional money needed to move it off-campus?[40]

The dean also expressed his grave concern over how the conference was shaping up in terms of confirmed speakers. He was convinced that we needed to secure more speakers, in particular strong advocates of the two-state model.[41] We explained how diligently we had been courting two-state advocates, and he offered to meet with two senior Jewish administrators at York (Stan Shapson, the vice-president of research and innovation [VPRI], and David Dewitt, the associate vice-president [AVP]) in order to "strong-arm" them into rallying more participation in the conference from the Jewish community.

The president also later came up with this idea, apparently independently, of strong-arming the AVP into participating in the conference. He sent a May 9th email to the dean asking, "What do [you] think of the idea that I personally put intense pressure on [the AVP] to present a paper. He has to decide if he is a member of the team or not (I am not going to put it in this language)."[42]

By this time, the dean had apparently encountered some resistance from us about his plans for our conference. He began his response to the president by noting that AVP Dewitt was not an expert in the areas covered by the conference: "I'm not sure this would be fair to [the AVP] since the topic of the conference is not really in his area." He went on to note that "in any event the organizers have not been demonstrating the required flexibility. I am still going to try to work with the organizers and see if we can make any progress."[43] In his observation about our lack of "required flexibility," he manifested awareness that we were not always receptive to his interventions. Something seemed to be required of us that the dean felt comfortable demanding. This contrasted with his later claims (in his July 2011 feedback to me) that our discussions with him had always been collegial and suggested that it would have been reasonable for him to anticipate an eventual critique rather than being "stunned" to learn that his interventions were not always appreciated (as he states in his feedback to *No Debate*).[44]

Although the offer to "strong-arm" members of the Jewish community constituted an unsavoury form of pressure (presuming that Jewish administrators have an obligation to draw on their connections to their own community and that they can be "strong-armed" into using them), we were already aware from our own initiatives that it was naive to presume that any reluctance to participate came from a lack of effort.

We had been meeting and communicating regularly with one of these administrators, AVP Dewitt, urging him to participate. At our most recent meeting, hearing his concerns about how the conference had been framed and his resulting reluctance to participate in it, we invited him to form a panel of critics from the concerned Jewish academic community at York University and in Toronto, the theme of which would be a scholarly critique of the framing of the issues, both in the conference and in the larger debates on models of statehood. This invitation was not taken up.

As noted above, on April 15, 2009, we received an email, from the AVP, stating that he would not participate in the conference and suggesting instead that we condense the event from 2.5 to 1.5 days, highlighting the scholars whom he approved of and backgrounding the others.[45]

Coming out of the April 17th meeting, the only authorization that the dean had to approach the VPRI and AVP on our behalf was to see whether the latter might make an effort to secure more scholars for the conference. The dean's mandate from us did not extend to seeking ongoing (or indeed any) advice for us from the VPRI and AVP. In fact, if we had been apprised of a further role for AVP Dewitt in our conference preparations, we would have emphatically opposed it given the turn that he had taken to strong ideological and polemical opposition to the conference and its participants.

The dean walked away from that meeting with a different understanding of his mandate from us to involve the AVP and VPRI in deliberations about the conference. In an April 21st email labelled "Re: Durban 11" sent by the dean to both the president and the chair of the Board of Governors, the dean wrote that he met with the VPRI and AVP, "and we are working on a plan to try to rework the agenda and mitigate the damage. [The AVP] and I are meeting with the organizers on Thursday morning to explore the possibilities and try to find a path forward."[46]

When the dean informed us shortly thereafter that he had, unsolicited, set up a meeting between us and the AVP, we became concerned, particularly in light of recent revelations from the AVP about his ideological commitments. We actively resisted this imposition when the dean kept insisting on the AVP's involvement.

As noted above, anxious that this meeting had the aura of a mediation in which the dean would ask us to entertain the idea of shrinking the conference as a compromise, we asked to meet first with the dean independently to flag our reluctance to go along with this plan and to include the AVP in conference deliberations. We also knew that we had an Advisory Committee to help us determine the scholarly content of the conference and that to subject *content* to the arbitrary review of someone who was resolutely critical, while being just as resolute about not participating, was baffling. It was also in the backs of our minds that David Dewitt was married to Susan Davis, the executive vice-president of CIJA, an organization that was becoming increasingly hostile to the aims of the conference and that would shortly release a statement asking its constituency to sanction the university for hosting the event.

Resistant to our request *not* to meet with the AVP in the dean's office, the dean responded that the conference was no longer an Osgoode issue – it was now a university issue. Our request for a meeting with the dean alone, without the AVP, was disturbing to him because it appeared to reflect a lack of understanding of the nature of the challenge that "we" faced. As he noted, he had tried to "be supportive and to work with you, but you have to work with me and try to search for solutions" to the things that he regarded as problems.[47]

It took multiple emails from me before the dean relented on his insistence that the addition of the AVP was an appropriate intervention in conference planning.[48] When I told him that we wanted to set up an independent meeting with him and noted that "We are growing increasingly troubled by some of the developments around this conference," the dean responded by noting that the "underlying tone" of my message gave him concern. He went on to say,

> so please forgive me if I emphasize again how challenging this event is becoming in its current form. I do believe that it is essential that you be open to exploring ways to structure the event so as to mitigate some of the concerns that have arisen and continue to emerge. I want to help in finding a creative solution. I understood you to be open to changes when we met and, on that basis, met with [the VPRI] and [the AVP] on Monday. But, with respect, if the purpose of our first meeting is to explain why the concerns are wrong, or why you should not consider changes in your plans, I fear that our meeting is not going to be productive or help us to get to a place that is workable. I am assuming that you are willing to think about changes, as we discussed at our meeting on Friday.

I responded by insisting that we thought it more appropriate to postpone the meeting with the AVP in favour of a meeting of Osgoode colleagues alone.

The dean responded with an insistence on the importance of greater administrative oversight. I had to insist a third time that we strongly believed that it would be in the best interests of both Osgoode and York if the meeting with the AVP were delayed in favour of a meeting with the three Osgoode faculty members, himself included. After this vigorous insistence, we prevailed, and the AVP was not present at the meeting.

I sent three separate emails to the dean in response to the meeting that he had called for us with AVP Dewitt indicating that I was troubled by recent developments – in particular the scheduling of a meeting with the AVP without our knowledge or input. Alert to the way in which Osgoode's and York's reputations might be at stake should the AVP's inappropriate administrative conduct, and now clear ideological commitments, come to light and Osgoode be too closely affiliated with the AVP, I noted that "We are very much of the opinion that it would be in the best interests of both Osgoode *and* York University if the meeting with the VPRI were delayed in favour of a meeting with the three of us (you, Bruce, and me)."[49] In his July 2011 response to my fact checking, the dean clearly grasped that I had not been pleased with his impromptu invitation of the AVP to further discussions about our conference. He indicated in his feedback that he "was concerned by the threatening tone of this email."[50] Notice to the dean was accumulating that we did not always welcome his interventions, and he himself indicated that he began to feel threatened by our responses to them.

Patrick Monahan's July 13, 2009, preliminary review of the first iteration of this book states that he "worked openly and transparently with the organizers at all times."[51] If there was uncertainty about whether or not we wanted the AVP involved in our conference-organizing plans before this repeated expression of reluctance, any communication between the dean and the AVP about our conference beyond this point clearly occurred behind closed doors and with neither our knowledge nor our consent.

At this point, the issue of the conference venue remained unresolved. Many off-campus alternatives were unfeasible due to either lack of availability or cost.

At the April 23, 2009, meeting that the dean had set up – and from which the AVP was excluded – the dean made several suggestions for how the conference could be improved, in his opinion, including by emphasizing leading scholars in plenary sessions and side-lining controversial ones in concurrent sessions – a proposal that was suggestive of the advice of the AVP. Although he stressed that it would be our choice which scholars we wanted to highlight in plenaries, when I asked him how he felt about us emphasizing the scholars whom conference critics found objectionable, for example Jeff

Halper and Ali Abunimah, he noted that I was not "working with" him and needed to do so. He also stressed that he thought we needed him.

The dean also suggested that we swiftly court a handful of strong Zionist two-state supporters to whom we could offer keynote speaker positions, funding for which could be provided by the university. He suggested the name of a scholar whom we had not contemplated, Professor Michael Bell, indicating that he would support our invitation if we were agreeable. We indicated that we were prepared to accept any suggestions from the dean that were consistent with what we understood to be the academic integrity of the event. The invitation of Professor Bell struck us as well advised.

The dean indicated, as he later confirmed, that he would also be willing to intervene to secure Glendon Campus for us if we agreed to add keynote speakers whom he regarded as suitable. He also briefly floated the AVP's suggestion that we shrink the conference to a day and a half but relented on this issue when we resisted.

At the end of this meeting, I expressed my concerns to the dean about the implications of this course of conduct on academic freedom. I made it clear that, though I would take his suggestions into consideration, I was also prepared to speak to CAUT, the Osgoode Hall Faculty Association (OHFA), and York University's Faculty Association (YUFA) about my concerns. The dean noted in a subsequent meeting with us on May 12, 2009, that he was sensitive to the prospect of me bringing a complaint against him to CAUT. And, indeed, in an email sent by the dean to the president and chair of the Board of Governors updating them on our April 23rd meeting, he stated that

> The bottom line is that we have made some progress, although perhaps not as much as I would have liked ...
>
> I have to say that I pushed them very hard, even to the point where Drummond on Thursday said that I was pressuring them inappropriately and infringing their academic freedom. She suggested they may have to raise the matter with CAUT and with the Faculty Association. I don't think that will happen, but I just wanted to indicate that I have to be very cautious now in making suggestions, as opposed to demands.[52]

In light of my clear statement that I was prepared to involve the relevant faculty associations to restrain the dean from further interference in our academic event, it seems reasonable to doubt that the dean was consistently under the impression that we were all working "collegially" and in a "constructive fashion" (in the terms of his July 2011 feedback on this book). The dean himself recognizes that he "pushed [us] very hard" and that his previous interventions were "demands" rather than "suggestions," which he thought more auspicious an approach against the spectre of a complaint to CAUT. The dean's remark in July 2011 that "the organizers were free at all times to accept or reject any of the suggestions that were made" should be read in light of these exchanges.

As the dean also avers in his July 2011 feedback on expressions of "gratitude" from the Organizing Committee members for his efforts on a variety of occasions, he intervened several times in the conference in ways that indeed warranted our sincere gratitude. For example, he secured funding for the event at the early planning stages and supported our application to the U50 funds, he assisted in the drafting of two public statements by York University when the support of our institution was critical, and he delivered a compelling opening speech at the conference that underlined the importance of academic freedom. Our gratitude was unqualified for this assistance. However, it would be a stretch to interpret as complicity other communications of ours that prefaced resistance with expressions of gratitude. These forms of intervention are more credibly interpreted as politesse and deference to the office.

Dean Monahan also apprised the president and chairman of the Board of Governors in that April 25, 2009, email that we had "gotten [our] backs up on the idea of moving off campus ... Ryder," he went on to observe, "(who is the more reasonable of the two) was particularly exercised on this point."[53]

The chair of York's Board of Governors responded to Dean Monahan's update on his pressures on us by saying,

> that's good progress but we're not home safe and sound yet. My thought for the moment wld be to wait and see whether they can get enough new speakers to ensure a balanced program. If they can't, then you will have to turn your mind to a Plan "B."
>
> This issue may come up at the Board mtg to-morrow. Or you may wish to use the occassion to initiate some comments and thereby send a "public" message. Either way, you shld be prepared and give some careful thought to what you say at this juncture, especially since we don't yet know whether we will end up with Plan A or Plan B.[54]

Plan A was to coerce us into changing the program for our conference. Plan B was to keep us off all of York's campuses.

After the April 23rd meeting, the dean started to repeatedly contact Professor Ryder by cell phone, apparently avoiding the more "unreasonable" opponent of his interventions.

In the above email to the president and chair of the Board of Governors, the dean also confirmed that, despite our resistance to the involvement of the AVP, he continued to pressure us to adopt the latter's vision for how our conference should be structured:

> They also don't want to shorten down the conference. This was a suggestion from David Dewitt (with whom they ultimately refused to meet., but that is another long story that I can share if you want), but I don't think it makes a lot of difference whether it is 1.5 days or 2.5 days. The key is to get this kind of rebalancing that will ensure that the conference is a legitimate academic conference.

The AVP's suggestion was the one that the dean had floated by us on April 15th, one that we had rejected.[55]

Several hours after this meeting with the dean, he secured the apparently unavailable Glendon Campus for us. He awaited word on what we would do to secure two strong Zionist keynote speakers for the restructured program that he was proposing. The dean later confirmed by email the connection in his mind between securing Glendon Campus and our compliance with his suggestions for keynote speakers:

> When we met in my office a couple of weeks ago I thought we had agreed that it was important to add another significant speaker to the program as a keynote speaker. The reason is that, given the current lineup of speakers, there is a perceived lack of balance in the approaches being taken ...
>
> As you know, offering someone a keynote slot is an important way to attract senior scholars. For a number of reasons I think it unlikely, although not impossible, that you will be able to attract significant scholars to participate in this conference at this stage. So adding a new speaker as a keynote was a very important and constructive decision on your part. I was encouraged by your agreement with this and, *based on that, (as well as on the idea of plenary sessions to highlight the strongest scholars), I facilitated the securing of the space in Glendon for the conference.*[56]

In fact, Glendon Campus did not require securing on April 23rd or thereafter. The president of the university, on April 20th, had his senior executive officer send university counsel an email in which she stated that

> The President has asked that I touch base with you about having the Board of Governor's meeting (and by extension H and F) moved from Glendon College to either Keele or Downtown. He would like to make sure that the Osgoode Conference stays at Glendon and that the Board meeting is not held in the same location as the conference. Would you please let me know where the meeting will be moved to?

At one point, in the week of May 4, 2009, the dean called Professor Ryder at night by cell phone and told us that he had heard rumours that busloads of Palestinian protesters were going to arrive at the gates of Glendon Campus for the conference. He wanted our response to this rumour. Apparently, he had come across this "information" on the Jewish Defence League's website.

Within several days of the April 23rd meeting, Professor Ryder and I met with York University historian Irving Abella as the culmination of our continuing efforts to understand, respond to, and solicit assistance from those who had concerns about the conference. We had been told for months that Professor Abella was upset about the conference from the moment that the call for papers had been issued and that he was in fact centrally active in the campaign against it in the Jewish community both in Canada and abroad. *No Debate* references an email that I sent to Dean Monahan on April 15th in which I noted that Professor Ryder and I had "met with David Dewitt a couple of weeks ago. He suggested that we meet with Irving Abella who, David indicated, was leading the campaign against the conference."[57]

In the middle of our meeting with Professor Abella, he told us that he had heard we were trying to get Michael Bell to participate as a keynote speaker. It had not been our intention to mention this to Abella because we were well aware that invitees were vulnerable to pressures from certain sections of the Jewish community not to participate. We had in mind the growing number of Jewish participants in the conference who had felt forced to withdraw as a result of these pressures and wanted to avoid the invitation to Bell being pre-empted in this way.

The dean had not, at this point, brought his communications on the conference with the AVP to a close; indeed, he appears to have intensified them after this point. After our meeting with the dean, he copied David Dewitt on the invitation letter that went out to Michael Bell. Dewitt sent the dean an email on April 27th in which he thanked him for being kept in the loop and continued with a lengthy missive about how to continue managing our conference. He offered the following observations to the dean:

> I very much like that the letter specifically encourages [Bell] to offer a "principled address of the two state solution" which, in one variant or another, is the status quo with adjustments made through negotiations. You may have been following some of the debates which have been occurring within Israel as well as between Israel and the US, among others, in addition to the more common positions expressed by others in the Middle East and the Muslim countries, about this. Most recently in today's Ha'aretz (the most "progressive" of the Israeli newspapers) there was an effort to lay out the profound constraints about moving forward on peace based even on a two-state solution, with the alternatives non-starters. The position of that author was that while ultimately it must end up being a two-state solution, at the moment the Palestinians simply are unable and their supporters unwilling to deliver on that, while Israelis under even a right wing government have moved in that direction, only to be rebuffed or worse. For that author, an end-state that is not a two-state is simply not possible if Israel is to survive, and the intent to eradicate Israel is the strategy of both moderate and more extreme Arab leaders. Michael Bell is, in my view, very well placed to unpack such arguments, examine alternatives, and I would guess whether for principles or for pragmatic politics, argue why a two-state solution is the only possible path should peace and security be the shared goal.[58]

The dean responded to this email by noting that he himself was not an academic specialist in the Middle East: "This is not my area and I need some guidance as to whom we should be seeking to include in (and, conversely, to exclude from) the plenaries. I'm hoping you can help me with that."[59]

Professor Ryder and I had clearly indicated at the April 23rd meeting with the dean that we were not prepared to entertain the AVP's suggestion that we shrink the conference down and exclude presenters. As the dean noted in his April 25th email to the president and chair of the Board of Governors, we were not inclined to work with AVP Dewitt, particularly in light of the proposal that we exclude some presenters.[60] Our reluctance to plan the conference with the AVP was not shared by the dean. In an email that he sent to Dewitt on May 2nd, he forwarded a letter that we had sent to the dean, asking him to keep it strictly confidential. In forwarding this email to the AVP and underlining its "strictly confidential" nature, he noted that

> It is therefore absolutely essential that if you share this information (and not [the] actual email) with anyone you must have 100% guarantees from them of confidentiality. Don't let me down on this. We have a chance to shape this in the right direction, but just one chance.[61]

May 2009

Shortly after the April 23rd meeting with the dean, we heard from him that Professor Bell possibly had a scheduling conflict. The dean sent us a letter informing us of this and suggested that we immediately try to solicit federal politician Bob Rae to be another keynote speaker, a prospect that we had considered. From the outset, we had viewed it as a poor idea to have sitting politicians present papers: we were concerned that they would be constrained by party discipline and the need to appeal to their constituencies. Furthermore, *here* balance would be appropriate. If we asked a Liberal, then we would need to ask at least a member each of the Conservative Party, the New Democratic Party, and the Green Party. And we had already informed the dean in a memo of April 3rd that we had decided not to invite politicians to speak at the conference.[62]

We had conferred as a committee and agreed on Bell, and we asked the dean to give us a chance to decide as a committee whom we wanted as a keynote speaker. Three times the dean implored us to act immediately to secure Rae. Why didn't we want Rae *regardless* of whether Bell accepted? the dean asked. "He would add a huge amount of credibility. With or without Michael you should be wanting him."[63] Three times we insisted that we be able to make the decision about keynote speakers as a committee of the whole. In the end, despite our objections, the dean unilaterally went ahead and did his own recognizance on whether Bob Rae and Irwin Cotler could attend the conference (Cotler being another sitting politician whose name had been floated and eventually, for the same reason, dismissed by us).

By the time we did meet as a committee, three days later, Bell had indicated his lack of availability. We reconfirmed our view that we did not want sitting politicians presenting papers at a scholarly event. Given the extraordinary efforts that we had put into trying to get local (York University and Canadian) strong Zionist two-state proponents to participate, and given that the conference was now six weeks away, we selected from among our list of confirmed speakers a senior scholar of Israel with impeccable scholarly credentials, Professor Ian Lustick – a member of our Advisory Committee whom we were independently pleased to showcase. We selected a second keynote speaker from our confirmed list of scholars for the second spot who was an eminent Palestinian critic of Israeli policies, Professor George Bisharat.

Having made these decisions, we communicated them to the dean.[64] In that communication, we also flagged that we were concerned that Professor Abella, whom we knew to be utterly hostile to the conference project, appeared to be privy to deliberations between us and the dean on the format of the conference. We asked for assurance that discussions with the dean on the program and speakers be kept confidential. We did not get a response to this request for confidentiality.

We had a lengthy discussion at our May 8, 2009, Organizing Committee meeting on how troubling we found the dean's involvement in the conference. We decided to meet with the president of York University to discuss our concerns about the way that the conference was being handled by York's senior administrators. Right after the meeting, I sent the president an email, copied to the dean, on behalf of the Organizing Committee requesting a meeting.

Our email to the president, the first move that we made to go over the dean's head, prompted a May 9th email from the dean to the president in which he laid out his reasons for why the president should not meet with us:

> [S]et out below is an email that was sent to you last night by the organizers of the June conference. They are asking to meet with you to discuss the "progress" they are making. I think you should not meet with them at this stage for a couple of reasons.
>
> First, when I met with them a couple of weeks ago they agreed to add a prominent keynote speaker who would defend a 2-state solution in the Middle East. They proceeded to invite Michael Bell. Unfortunately Bell has said he can't do it. Without further consultation or discussion with me, the organizers decided that they are not going to add any speakers to the conference program, contrary to what they had agreed with me last week. Instead they are going to have one of their existing speakers, (Ian Lustick), serve as a keynote. They proceeded to invite Lustick and presented that to me last night as a fait accompli.

> Second, they have emailed you seeking a meeting with you to discuss the conference, also without discussing this with me. This I interpret as an attempt to do an end-run around me and perhaps to complain to you about me.[65]

If this email to the president indicated that the dean had strong feelings about us deciding unilaterally to meet with the president, his email to *us* gave us considerable concern.

The dean's response to our May 8th email, which came on May 10th, offered no assurance that the dean was not, nor would be, sharing deliberations with members and leaders of the Jewish community who were adamantly opposed to the conference; however, he did express strong disapproval of the committee having decided on our keynote speakers without first consulting him.[66]

The dean reiterated what he took to be an agreement with him on our part to add a keynote speaker to remedy "a perceived lack of balance in the approaches being taken." He was bothered that we had decided to elevate one of our existing speakers – which was not "what we agreed in my office." By using up the additional keynote space on an existing speaker, he remarked, we had now made it virtually impossible to attract any additional major scholars to the conference. Even more troubling to him was the fact that we had offered a keynote speaker position without any further consultation or discussion with him: "So from my perspective this is presented as *fait accompli.* I would have thought it appropriate and necessary to at least discuss this revised plan with me before acting on it, particularly since it was inconsistent with what we had agreed." Returning to a theme that had been raised in the fall of 2008, the dean again suggested that we "seek some other form of outside participation on your committee, someone who could bring a fresh perspective to your work and help you get to where I think you need to be."

The idea that the dean had an "agreement" with us to add keynote speakers whom he sanctioned (and apparently whom AVP Dewitt sanctioned and perhaps a professor from an Israeli university who was also the head of the right-wing NGO Monitor sanctioned) requires some examination. As has already been laid out, and confirmed in *No Debate,* there was no agreement that the dean had a right to intervene in the content of our scholarly work that derived from our original application to the U50 grant or from the Memorandum of Understanding that accompanied it. The CAUT Inquiry reviewed six separate submissions from the dean in response to requests for clarification about his role and actions. These six submissions included the former dean's responses to my own requests for clarification in the production of this book, which the former dean returned to me and copied to the CAUT Inquiry. Professor Thompson comes to the following conclusion regarding the supposed "agreement" to which the dean referred:

> On April 17 [2009], [the dean] gave [the Organizing Committee] to understand that it was the wish of the board of governors that the conference not be held on university premises ... When [Ryder, Drummond, and Monahan] met on April 23, Ryder and Drummond both expressed opposition to moving off campus. Monahan made more specific suggestions about program changes than he had made on April 17, and the organizers agreed to discuss them with their fellow committee members.[67]

That we were stunned by the possibility that the event could be removed from campus is captured by Professor Ryder: "This was April 17th; the conference was June 22nd. So we were extraordinarily upset, distraught about this ... The getting booted off campus, so to speak, the threat of getting booted off campus is, I'm not sure where it came from ... I don't think he [the dean] was the [original] source of the pressure."[68]

Professor Thompson goes on in *No Debate* to argue that, with respect to any supposed "agreement" between the Organizing Committee and the dean about the ultimate shape of our program,

> regardless of what his intentions may have been, or the particular words used to characterize his involvement, Dean Monahan conducted through the senior administrative office he held a process wherein two professors in his faculty were given to understand that the prospect of the university's withholding a campus venue – a prospect he communicated to them in meetings – could be avoided through his intercession, subject to their acceptance of program changes he proposed. He himself termed the outcome of this process an "agreement." I ... conclude that his action in this matter was inappropriate.[69]

In his email, the dean seemed to have some awareness that we (or at least I given that his May 10, 2009, email was addressed to me) thought his interventions were heavy-handed. As he noted, "Whether intentional or not, the underlying message that I take from both of your emails is that, for some reason, you do not seem to appreciate that I have been attempting to assist you in your efforts to improve the conference. On the contrary, you seem to regard me as somehow threatening or undermining your efforts."[70] Indeed, I did find his interventions to be both threatening and undermining.

Any suggestion that the dean's interventions had a threatening tone might be read in light of the CAUT finding that withholding the campus venue could be avoided through his intervention, and the following passages in the May 10th email might be read in that light:

> I would have thought it appropriate and necessary to at least discuss this revised plan with me before acting on it, particularly since it was inconsistent with what we had agreed ...
>
> I have said throughout that I want to be able to continue to support you in this endeavour, both within the university and publicly. But this is premised on my being comfortable that the necessary balance had been achieved. I have to tell you that at this point I very much doubt that I will be able to personally support the conference ...
>
> I remain open to discussing this further with you, and working with you on improving the conference. But you have to want to work [with] me. That involves more than just meeting or sending emails. It requires actual cooperation on your part, where you want to work with me in a positive and constructive way, seeing me as a collaborator rather than as a threat.[71]

I found this email to be highly threatening even while garbed in the language of collegiality, support, and cooperation.

The FIPPA request revealed that, before the May 10th letter was sent to me, my colleague Professor Ryder vetted it for Dean Monahan on May 9th. The rest of us on the Organizing Committee became aware of this vetting only through the FIPPA release in the fall of 2009. Dean Monahan had contacted Professor Ryder the night before (May 8, 2009) by phone. Professor Ryder followed up on this call with a lengthy email to the dean, which was not released on the FIPPA request (and which therefore did not come to the attention of the Organizing Committee until I asked my colleague for feedback in December 2011).

My request for feedback from Professor Ryder was stimulated in part by Provost Monahan's July 2011 feedback, which noted that, "Since there is evidently a significant difference of opinion between Susan and my views on these particular matters, I believe it appropriate and necessary to consult with Bruce to confirm the accuracy of Susan's accounts of these conversations."[72] As a result, some of the following revelations date to December 2011.

The May 8, 2009, phone call was one of several made to Professor Ryder in this period that he said "left me deeply distressed." He "felt strongly that some of what Patrick said to me the night before [May 8th] showed a lack of understanding of, or a lack of respect for, our scholarly objectives and efforts."[73]

Professor Ryder's May 9th email to the dean[74] noted that "I haven't spoken to anyone about the content of our conversation last night ... and don't intend to. Confidentiality about that conversation, and this email exchange, strikes me as essential to keeping us on a constructive path." I have asked Professor Ryder to tell me about the content of that conversation that the rest of us were not aware had transpired until my December 2011 request for feedback prompted him to send the email to me. He is not prepared to disclose to me what transpired.

Professor Ryder's May 9th email was lengthy. In light of the fact that, on May 8th, the Organizing Committee had sent an email to the president asking for a meeting (copied to the dean), Ryder offered the dean some advice on how that meeting could unfold. He also reiterated the Organizing Committee's commitment to securing more strong two-state supporters on the conference program and noted our openness to receiving suggestions from the dean but underlined that "The organizing committee needs to make decisions based on academic criteria and in light of the academic goals of the conference, in consultation with the advisory committee when appropriate, taking seriously any suggestions we receive from you and others. Any hint that we are being dictated to, as opposed to being given suggestions to consider in our collective deliberations, will erupt."

Dean Monahan appears to have raised, in the May 8th phone call to Professor Ryder, the prospect that Osgoode and the U50 committee could withdraw sponsorship because Ryder observed (next to an underlined subheading "Withdrawal of Osgoode and U50 Official Sponsorship") that "I think this would be a complete disaster for the university. I'd prefer to talk about it further on the phone. I'm really upset about it even being contemplated at this late stage, a month before the conference."

I asked Provost Monahan to respond to the mention of removal of university and law school sponsorship of the conference when I found out about this intervention in December 2011. And I wrote that

> Bruce also notes, at the top of his May 9, 2009 email "I haven't spoken to anyone about the content of our conversation last night ... and don't intend to. Confidentiality about that conversation, and this email exchange, strikes me as essential to keeping us on a constructive path." Would you like to comment on that May 8, 2009 phone call that you had with Bruce?

Provost Monahan's response to this inquiry was first of all to declare that,

> with respect to your December 22 email, the paragraph you propose to insert in your manuscript [i.e., the above paragraph starting with "Dean Monahan appears to have raised"] is incorrect and misleading. The University was not proposing to withdraw sponsorship of the conference in May 2009, or at any other time, and your description of my discussion with Bruce is inaccurate.[75]

The provost provided no further details to facilitate making sense of the lengthy May 9, 2009, email that he received from Professor Ryder. The conversation of the night before that Ryder alluded to – the one that struck him as requiring confidentiality between the two of them thereafter – remains occult.

Whoever raised the issue, it is hard to decipher any possible basis for the spectre that Osgoode and the U50 committee could withdraw sponsorship of the conference. York's own inquiry – the Iacobucci Review – makes it clear that the Organizing Committee participated fully in the U50 oversight process and in other meetings organized by the U50 office.[76] Dean Monahan affirmed to SSHRC in June 2009 that there had been no major changes to our program since our funding award had been granted. We had done not a thing to put us in bad academic standing at Osgoode Hall Law School. Withdrawal of sponsorship – which in the case of the U50 grant would appear to involve the withdrawal of funding as well – might well have constituted a breach of contract by York University. That Professor Ryder so strenuously resisted this proposition (unbeknownst to the rest of us on the Organizing Committee – who were also unaware until December 2011 that the spectre had even been raised) might well have saved the university a good deal of grief.

Professor Ryder's email response to the May 8, 2009, phone call from Dean Monahan went on to address an argument – and a criterion for academic events – over which the Organizing Committee and the dean were at odds in this period:

> The Balance Concern: The argument that the conference lacks academic integrity because it lacks balance rankles. We did not hoodwink our academic sponsors – SSHRC, the Nathanson Centre, various York offices, Osgoode, U50, Queen's, Queen's Law. We were forthright about our goals with everybody from the outset, and have worked incredibly hard to achieve them. Many have congratulated us on what we've been able to achieve on such an incredibly difficult topic.
>
> Our goal from the outset has been to promote a scholarly debate between two-state proponents and one-state proponents, and supporters of models between and beyond. It is not about "destroying Israel," in the not-so-thoughtful formulation used by critics of the conference. It is about transforming a de facto binational reality, one that a large and growing number of scholars acknowledge is not sustainable over the long term, into a more secure future for Israelis and Palestinians alike. With the rise of religious fundamentalism and racist discourses in both Israeli and Palestinian political circles, the conditions are not propitious, to put it mildly, for a settlement of the conflict based on either a two-state or a single binational state model. Authors like Benny Morris, with whom I agree on this, acknowledge as much, and are interested in reviving discussion of the possibilities raised by the promotion of federal or confederal institutions in the region. In the face of the huge obstacles to one state or two state models achieving support on both sides of the divide in the near future, it makes sense for supporters of both to be challenged at a conference like ours, and for proponents of in-between approaches (for example, step-by-step incremental development of federal institutions to address various urgent governance issues, like water) to be given a forum in which to develop their ideas.[77]

Professor Ryder's response reflected the overall response of the Organizing Committee: the argument about balance rankled us, whether it came from the dean or from other directions – but perhaps most acutely when it came from the dean. We were actively courting a fruitful diversity of views among the conference panelists, views sufficiently different from one another to ferment an academic dialogue. Our criteria for diversity were framed in terms of what would stimulate this dialogue. In pursuit of this end, we sought a range of perspectives on theoretical, methodological, and substantive orientations, not political positions per se. The dean was viewing the issue of balance in political terms and, in particular, in terms of how the program would look to interested outsiders – outsiders of a particular kind, given that nobody was voicing concerns over what Palestinians might think of the conference program. This latter understanding of diversity (or balance) ran counter to what we were trying to accomplish as academics.

The dean's preoccupation with balance in our program was also addressed in *No Debate.* Professor Thompson made it clear that "there is no general requirement in Canadian universities that the membership of a research team be balanced or that a research project be balanced in a political or ideological sense, nor is there any such requirement in SSHRC regulations." One of the emails from SSHRC accessed through the FIPPA search confirmed that this was indeed the view of the funding council. In one of the email threads from June 2009, Vice-President Yasmeen asked, "do we oblige our conf applicants to have an event with balanced views ie folks both for and against stuff or does this come up in the review or do we just not have a policy on that?" To this query, Director Craig McNaughton replied, "no Policy – I would say a question like that is one for peers to decide as a function of their assessment of the scholarly quality – eg in relation to the criterion on 'appropriateness and quality of the conference's scope and program in relation to its theme or themes.'"[78] This reference to "peer review" is the standard means by which academic events are assessed.

Professor Thompson was clear in his findings that the pressures from York's administration with respect to balance were "inappropriate" and that "the criticisms had no significant academic or administrative basis." Where we referred to balance in any of our own communications, our understanding was that it was reflected in the composition of our Advisory Committee, which would be assisting us in determining appropriate balance, not York's administration. Thompson ultimately found that

> deans may appropriately raise questions with researchers or research teams in response to concerns brought to their attention. However, academic content decisions regarding a research project are properly those of the researchers, not an administrator.
>
> An exception would be a case in which the researcher(s) had voluntarily undertaken to accept academic assessment of the project and academic involvement in it by an administrator. In the case of the York/Queen's conference, there was no such undertaking. Yet Monahan made academic assessments regarding "balance" for both the research team (in October 2008) and the program of speakers (in April and May 2009). Moreover, he involved himself academically on the basis of this assessment.

> I conclude that Dean Monahan did not respect the principle of administrative neutrality in [this] specific instance.
>
> I note that the dean acknowledged ... that he lacked expertise in the specific topics of the conference. Thus he had no direct academic basis on which to come to his conclusions as to need for balance in either the committee or the conference program. Even if he had such expertise, he was not a member of the specific research team, and so his comments about the academic content of the project would still be contrary to the principle of administrative neutrality.[79]

The May 9, 2009, email of 3:37 from Professor Ryder in which he eloquently defended the conference against the spurious criterion of balance for evaluating academic events was issued around the same time as an email from Dean Monahan to Professor Ryder on May 9th, sent at 2:11 p.m. The first time that members of the Organizing Committee saw this email (and the one that Professor Ryder sent in response) was when they were released on the FIPPA search. This one was under the subject heading "Confidential draft email to you and Susan." The dean, referring to my email to the president asking for a meeting with him, said, "Bruce I have reflected further on our discussion and set out below a draft of an email to you and Susan in response to hers of last night (which I assume you have already seen.) I would appreciate your input and advice before I send this." (The final letter was sent on May 10th and is in Appendix 32.) Below this message, Dean Monahan inserted an earlier draft of the above May 10th email that I found highly threatening. Professor Ryder responded to this draft at 4:04 by remarking to the dean, "I think it is clear and constructive – the only thing I would add is that we continue to seek out strong two-staters, who are under-represented in the list of confirmed speakers as a whole, to participate in all aspects of the program (ie, in addition to a keynote)."

When I discovered this exchange on the FIPPA release in the fall of 2009, I found Professor Ryder's response to the draft of the dean's May 10th email (and, indeed, the fact that it had been vetted in this manner) baffling and troubling. And Ryder, in a December 2011 communication, came to the same conclusion. He found his assessment puzzling "as I don't find the tone and content of Patrick's draft message constructive as I reread it now."

> Patrick sent his email with the draft to me at 2:11 pm. I sent him a long email at 3:37 pm explaining the current state of conference planning in detail and

> reflecting on a troubling conversation he and I had had on the evening of May 8 ... [It does not] appear to me that I gave his 2:11 pm email a careful enough read before I responded at 4:04 pm. It looks to me like I responded hastily having already shared my views at length on the state of conference planning the day before and then again at 3:37 pm earlier that afternoon.
>
> The only thing I can imagine that I found "constructive" about Patrick's draft, as I put in my May 9 4:04 pm message, was its focus on the importance of our shared continuing efforts to find prominent scholars who are supporters of the two-state peace process (like Michael Bell) to add to the program. Hence my comment in that email that we continue to seek out strong two-staters to participate in all aspects of the program.
>
> Still, there is so much more I should have repeated from my earlier emails, and perhaps did later by phone. I should have pointed out, as I had in emails to Patrick on May 8 and a half hour earlier on May 9 (3:37 pm), that you and I had never agreed to anything other than to take any suggestions made to us back to the OC as a whole for our collective consideration. Also, I should have reiterated what I had said in my email on May 8, that our decision to elevate Ian Lustick to a keynote made eminent sense given his stature, his insights into the issues, and his support of a two-state resolution, and that his elevation was a decision all members of the OC fully supported.

The dean's sense of where he thought we needed to be – as evidenced in his May 10th email to me – did not derive from his own judgment – or at least not uniquely. Throughout this period, Dean Monahan and AVP Dewitt had extensive conversations about a range of issues relating to our conference. With neither our knowledge nor our consent, in fact over our opposition, Monahan and Dewitt conferred on May 9th over the feedback that they had sought about our conference program from a shadow advisory committee that they had set up.[80] The AVP presented "the list of possible plenary speakers" to this group of anonymous advisers. Hours after the dean sent us his May 10th email, Dewitt sent Monahan an email under the subject heading "PRIVATE & CONFIDENTIAL."[81] While we on the Organizing Committee were structuring our own program independently (and, of course, properly), Associate Vice-President Dewitt was consulting with unnamed external academics on "who might make up the so-called 'plenary day.'" "I'm still waiting to hear from two more senior academics I've contacted regarding their assessment of the conference lineup," the AVP noted.

> To date, the two have had mixed comments: one is fundamentally critical, and while recognizing that there are "a few" credible scholars, even they are well known – including or especially the Israelis – as being extreme critics, and among their colleagues often are seen this way as a means of reputation building and desiring notariety. The other colleague was somewhat more positive; about half of the plenary candidates he would join on the podium even though he likely would not agree with their views; a quarter he would not be seen with; and the remainder he doesn't really know either them or their work sufficiently well to comment one way or the other.

To this email, the AVP attached a draft op-ed written by Gerald Steinberg, a right-wing chair of political science at Bar Ilan University in Israel,[82] a university that has a reputation for being right wing itself. Steinberg monitors NGOs such as Human Rights Watch and lobbies to get them defunded. He is also associated with the Jerusalem Center for Public Affairs, an extreme right-wing think tank. His reputation was well known to us and presumably to most other people who had any experience with the political conflict in Israel/Palestine. Professor Thompson in *No Debate* described his reputation in the following manner:

> Steinberg is well known as the founder and president of NGO Monitor (www.ngo-monitor.org). It is apparent from articles by Steinberg or NGO Monitor, posted on their websites or published elsewhere, that they have taken on a function somewhat analogous to that of Daniel Pipes and his Campus Watch organization in the United States: namely, denouncing persons or organizations they regard as critical of Israel or its policies, and conducting campaigns against events or organizations they regard as not in Israel's interests. Israeli political commentator and former Mossad agent Yossi Alpher, writing in the *Forward,* in late 2009, made the following observations:
>
> NGO Monitor ... is not sticking to its Web site's slogan of "promoting critical debate and accountability of human rights NGOs in the Arab Israeli conflict." Rather, it seems dead set on eliminating human rights monitoring of Israel entirely and smearing anyone who supports this vital activity. In so doing, NGO Monitor is running roughshod over some important organizations that are working to maintain Israel's integrity in the context of its ongoing occupation of the West Bank.

In the body of his email, AVP Dewitt brought the draft op-ed to the dean's attention: "[Steinberg], a very well known senior Israeli academic who often writes in various Canadian and US newspapers, plans on submitting, probably to one of G[lobe]&M[ail], [Toronto] Star, [Ottawa] Citizen, or [National] Post."[83] As Thompson noted in *No Debate,* the AVP did not alert the dean that Steinberg was "also well known as the president of NGO Monitor."[84] Dewitt's unqualified recommendation of Steinberg as "a very well known senior Israeli academic" confirmed the concerns that had arisen for us since his April 15, 2009, email about the AVP's judgment and ideological motivation. Although, according to the dean's July 2011 feedback, the president had appointed Dewitt as his point man on the conference, we would have explicitly raised the perils of seeking further input from him had we been apprised of that ongoing involvement.

Dewitt went on in his email to which the Steinberg op-ed was attached to indicate that "He has sent it to me out of 'courtesy,' I presume, indicating that under separate cover he also will be sending it to Jason Kenney and Irwin Cotler in the context of SSHRC funding issues."[85] The dean responded by saying, "I'm meeting tomorrow morning with Susan and Bruce. Can I show them this piece, without indicating how it came to me?"[86]Dewitt responded by writing in all caps, "PLEASE DO NOT SHARE THIS." He went on to say,

> I think not. Even without telling them from whom it came, they will suppose it is either from me or from someone else with whom you are connected within a group of individuals interested in undermining them. Let them see it in the newspapers if/when it appears. I also think that given what I understand to be their views and how they have not kept one or more aspects of the agreement you thought you had with them, it puts you in an unfavourable position.
>
> I don't think that they should need to see this op ed piece in draft form to understand the issues, including what they may well put you, Osgoode and YorkU through. The issue is not the topic but the quality of the invited and paid for speakers.
>
> If the op ed piece comes out, there will be lots of time for all of us to have to respond, should that be necessary.[87]

As a result of this request from AVP Dewitt that the dean not share with us Steinberg's plan for a more prominent assault on the conference, or share an alert that Steinberg was about to contact members of the federal government about the conference in the context of our SSHRC funding, we were left in the dark about these upcoming threats. We only became aware of Steinberg's op-ed on May 19th, when one of the members of our Advisory Committee brought it to our attention after Steinberg emailed it to him. Steinberg wanted to confirm that our Advisory Committee member was actually participating. He put the article on his website on May 22nd, the first time that we were able to read it, and the article was finally published (with an additional blistering attack on York University and the stand that President Shoukri and the Board of Governors were taking on academic freedom – see below). It was a senior administrator at York University (the email was sent from David Dewitt's administrative address) who was keeping us unaware of significant upcoming challenges.

That AVP Dewitt did not share this information with us (and constrained the dean from doing so) is discussed in the findings of *No Debate*. The report flags the position that these two senior administrators left us in: namely, "not only would the conference likely be criticized in a newspaper op-ed, but also in a communication to a federal minister and another influential MP known to be strongly supportive of the State of Israel. Yet the AVPR and the dean agreed not to disclose this information to the organizers." Thompson also noted that Dewitt made a submission to the CAUT Inquiry in defence of his conduct:

> I passed on his draft op-ed to Patrick because as the Dean of the sponsoring faculty of a U50 event, he was the key central administration person in this matter. He deserved to be kept informed on matters that could involve his Faculty and the University ... I did what was necessary and appropriate to ensure that my colleagues in the senior administration and their colleagues as the conference planners were aware of the fact that there may be an adverse op-ed piece published, thereby allowing them to be in a position to prevent unfair criticism of their work.[88]

This is similar to the response to my own request for feedback that I received from David Dewitt in December 2011:

> With respect to the Steinberg op-ed, my role as AVP Research was to inform the then Dean, Patrick Monahan, and Stan Shapson, then VPRI, of information relevant to the conference and issues of concern that had emerged. I did so. I also met with the President. I was aware that Dean

> Monahan and the President's office were working towards issuing a statement concerning academic freedom. What Steinberg sent me was a draft opinion piece that he intended to submit to a Canadian outlet. I passed the draft on to Dean Monahan for his consideration. There was no need to do more, nor any obligation.
>
> Had I shared a copy of the unsolicited draft op ed with you and Bruce Ryder, I was concerned that you would have interpreted this as an indication that we in the administration were somehow collaborating with the critics of the conference.[89]

Thompson arrived at a different interpretation of Dewitt's conduct: "Instead of ensuring that 'the conference planners were aware of the fact that there may be an adverse op-ed piece published, thereby allowing them to be in a position to prevent unfair criticism of their work," Dewitt requested of Monahan: 'PLEASE DO NOT SHARE THIS,' and the dean agreed. Thus ... Dewitt did not do what he himself asserted in February 2011 'was necessary and appropriate.'"[90]

Where Dewitt went on in his submission to the CAUT Inquiry to state that it would not have assisted us to know the identity of Steinberg as the author of the op-ed, in light of the dean's subsequent use of Steinberg's piece in his deliberations with us, Thompson went on to note that "knowing that the author was Steinberg could have been of assistance to Drummond and Ryder in their May 12 meeting with Monahan because Steinberg was not only 'an academic colleague' of Dewitt, he also was president of NGO Monitor."[91]

Professor Thompson concluded that the AVP, as an administrator, had a responsibility to ensure that we were aware of the prospect of the adverse op-ed being published so that we could be in a position to prevent unfair criticism of our work. He also should have ensured that, at a minimum, we were informed that Steinberg might be sending his op-ed to Kenney and Cotler in the context of our SSHRC funding. In Thompson's words, "AVPR Dewitt failed to live up to a responsibility of his office and, therefore, he ... acted inappropriately."[92]

In the May 11, 2009, correspondence between the dean and the AVP, the latter went on to attach, for the dean's information and in confidence, a number of comments from "senior academics" from whom he had solicited assessments of the conference participants. He had done this work on behalf of the dean, noting that the information was "about the names you were interested in."[93]

In a later email from Dewitt to Monahan, the AVP offered verbatim commentary from one of the secret "advisers" to our conference: "The organizers are motivated by their own war against Israel and that is what this is really about. All the rest is camouflage. This in essence is not a scholarly exercise but political advocacy under the guise of scholarship – the high jacking of academe to promote the undoing of Israel." This critic could not have known what motivated us, particularly given the complex range of positions and hesitations on the conference themes that each member brought to the Organizing Committee. The writer added a comment on our presenters: "For what qualifies as scholarship these days one could hardly fault any one of them for not being a real scholar."[94] Given the anonymity of the scholar's comments, we have no way of assessing whether his or her own body of work would qualify as "real" scholarship, whatever that means, or whether anybody should credit these opinions as worthwhile.

No Debate raises questions about the dean absorbing without question the assessments of the conference critics provided to him by Professor Dewitt and Professor Abella – both known critics of the conference – in light of his avowed lack of expertise in the subject area of the conference. Professor Thompson noted that it was open to the dean to consult with one or more members of our international Advisory Committee about the speakers whom we had selected. "Its members," the report notes, "had been asked to serve because, to a greater or lesser extent, the conference topic *was* in their area of expertise." The dean had been apprised of the existence of the Advisory Committee when he had signed off on our original U50 application in the spring of 2008, and we had drawn his attention to its existence on other occasions. Thompson went on to find that

> the approach Monahan adopted to solve the perceived problem or, in his words, to "mitigate the damage," included trying to add additional academic speakers to the program who would be strong supporters of the two-state model, or strong supporters of Israel in order to provide "balance" he considered was needed. He asked Abella, and later also Dewitt, to provide him with advice on the conference program. Of these two professors, he wrote in emails to Shoukri: "This [conference] topic is not an area of [Abella's] expertise," and "The topic of the conference is not really in [Dewitt's] area."

> Between April 15 and May 12, 2009, Dean Monahan should have made an effort to consult with at least one expert involved in the development of the [conference] program, or with an independent expert. This would have been important because he himself was not an expert, he doubted the judgment of Professors Ryder and Drummond, and Professors Abella and Dewitt were strong critics of the program.[95]

In response to the strong email of May 10, 2009, from the dean, we asked for a meeting with him ASAP. This meeting was set up for May 12th – the meeting that immediately preceded the one with the president in which he regretted that we had ever held any other impression than that the university was deeply committed to academic freedom. Dean Monahan sent the associate vice-president a note referring to this request for a meeting: "They may be feeling the pressure. I sent them a strong email over the weekend and Susan's email reply to me was a bit cryptic. But the armour may be cracking. On the other hand that may be wishful thinking and they may be coming to lodge a complaint."[96] Again, the perception that we had "armour" that needed "cracking" suggests that the dean was aware that our conversations were neither unreservedly collegial nor mutual and aware that we were resisting his overtures. The atmosphere around such phraseology suggests that some circumspection is warranted when the dean noted, in his July 2011 submission, that "it was at all times up to the organizers, and not the administration, to determine the program and the focus of the conference. This was always clearly understood by everyone involved." It seems just as reasonable to infer that it was "clearly understood by everyone involved" that the administration believed that some armour needed cracking and conducted itself accordingly.

Unbeknowst to us, Dean Monahan was guided in his conversation with us at the May 12, 2009, meeting by Gerald Steinberg's op-ed, which he had in hand as a result of AVP Dewitt's connection. As he noted in his correspondence with the AVP just prior to his meeting with us, he intended to "use the substantive points [in the Steinberg article] as the basis of my discussion."[97] The notoriously right-wing views of this Israeli professor were setting the intellectual tone for discussions on whether there were problems with a scholarly event taking place on a Canadian university campus.

At that May 12th meeting in the dean's office between Professor Ryder, me, and the dean, Monahan reiterated the positions that he had been taking with us with increasing force since the middle of April.[98] He predicted that the president would have to make a statement on the conference and said that this statement would be based on the academic merits of the conference. The dean made it clear that his own central concern over the conference was its academic quality. In his estimation, some of our speakers were very strong, but many of the remainder were "polemicists" and "activists," not academics, or they were graduate students.

In response to his preoccupation with the university's reputation vis-à-vis the Mapping Models conference and his determination to assess its academic qualities and merits and to possibly have the president similarly weigh in with a substantive statement, I pointed out that, because the university's reputation hinged on academic integrity, I thought that it would be ill advised for the university itself to assess the academic merits of the conference. In the dean's view, the university's academic integrity did not mean endorsing the substance of the event, with which I readily agreed, but he went on to claim that the university *had* in fact endorsed it because the conference was part of the fiftieth anniversary celebrations.[99]

Another of the dean's concerns was that posting of the conference program was delayed and that we did not have a draft of the program or agenda ready for review two months prior to the event. (For review by whom was not made clear to us.)

The dean also wanted to stress that the Organizing Committee did not have the academic credentials to be involved (single-handedly) in bringing about a conference of this nature. When he opined that neither I nor Professor Ryder is a scholar on the Middle East and that this was not an area in which we had been working, I pointed out that I had previously won a significant, peer-reviewed research grant to examine mixed marriages in Israel/Palestine in the context of mixed legal jurisdictions. I had been publishing the results of that work. Shifting ground, he then responded that my work had not been focused on the *political* conflict in the Middle East, an assessment of the nature of politics that is at best dubious.

When I pointed out that Professor Aiken's doctoral work was a comparative study of citizenship in Israel and Canada and that Aiken had been the Rabin Scholar at Hebrew University, the dean said that he did not think her work was on the *politics* of the Middle East.

In response to the fact that Mazen Masri, the doctoral student on the Organizing Committee, was doing his research on human rights and citizenships in Israel/Palestine, the dean noted that Masri was only a doctoral student.

The recurrent theme of the meeting stalled on the dean's assessment of the conference's scholarly merits despite his avowed lack of expertise.

Monahan repeated that he had heard concerns from "serious, respected scholars of the Middle East" who thought that the quality and nature of the confirmed speakers were inadequate. On their authority, he had come to the same opinion himself. And, as provost-designate of the university, he planned to share his opinion with the president to assist him in formulating a public statement on the conference. He noted that, given his judgment as provost-designate of what we had accomplished, we probably would not be terribly happy with the president's eventual statement.

Apart from the "polemical" thrust of the speakers, the dean considered that there would be very few people at the conference who would be seen as *strong* defenders of Israel. Furthermore, he noted, many of the speakers coming from Israel itself tended to be from one side of the political spectrum (the political left – understood in Israeli terms as a litmus test of where one stands on the Israeli/Palestinian impasse), and as a result we did not have the full range of speakers from Israel. At no point did the dean suggest that having "the full range" of speakers from Israel/Palestine entailed the inclusion of the voice of a representative of Hamas, the democratically elected representatives of the West Bank and Gaza since 2006.

Having thus framed his own judgment, the dean proposed that we "postpone" the conference. In the interim, we were to meet with the AVP and Professor Adelman. The dean acknowledged that they would ask us to do certain things that we might not want to do. They might tell us to remove certain speakers from the conference program. The dean could see the president telling us to go into a room, sit down, and try to work out a compromise. Surely, he noted, a compromise could be reached on how a conference should be run. If we were amenable to this proposal, the dean would be happy to try to facilitate the meeting, to ask what is fair and reasonable, and to flag that it is fair to ask this but not that. By this process, the dean wanted to see if we could broker a deal to bring Adelman and the AVP back on board. However, he was clear that doing so we would have to make compromises.

We made it clear that what the dean was proposing was unrealistic and reiterated how we had spent the past ten months urging Professor Adelman and AVP Dewitt first to participate and then not to abandon the project. The dean then moved on to the suggestion that he had made in the fall: namely, that we needed to involve another member on our Organizing Committee. He reiterated his opinion that we were a small group, none of whom he considered a scholar on the Middle East. He suggested that we needed some fresh perspective on the committee because we were too close to the issues.

When we pointed out that a new committee member would not be capable of adding significant changes to a planning process that had been unfolding for sixteen months, and that likely a new member would not want to be publicly associated with a conference that he or she had not had a hand in shaping, he suggested that what we needed was a confidential "special adviser" who would vet our program and provide us with feedback. The dean himself would be eager to speak independently to this adviser after we selected him or her. We were not averse to this suggestion, provided that the adviser was someone whom we would have picked ourselves to provide advice. We agreed to seek out such an officer. In the end, foreseeably, the adviser never materialized since the person whose counsel we were prepared to seek was not available.

Immediately after our May 12, 2009, meeting with the dean, he rushed over to meet the president, who had, earlier that day, cancelled a trip to New York. Two hours after our meeting with the dean ended, CIJA posted its statement against the conference, attacking the academic integrity of the institution and claiming that it did not qualify academically as a first-class institution. Hershel Ezrin went on to recommend that CIJA's constituency write to York's president and dean to make it clear that events such as our conference should not have the sanction of the university, that such events "only serve[d] to further the already degenerating situation at York University surrounding the Israel/Palestine issue," and that events such as our conference "lead to an increased sense of insecurity for those who should feel free to express their support for Israel."[100] The statement directed readers to CIJA's executive vice-president, Susan Davis, if they had any questions.

Later that evening Professor Ryder received a phone call from the dean stating that the president might ask us at our meeting the next day to "postpone" the conference in order to avoid a "disaster," and he communicated that he was proposing the name of a facilitator/mediator to work with us, Adelman, and Dewitt. In his submission to the CAUT Inquiry, Professor Ryder characterized the phone call by noting that "the proposal [of earlier that day to postpone the conference] was in effect escalated into what appeared to be a demand ... on the basis of the tone and content of the dean's remarks."[101]

The phone call from the dean left us with profound uncertainty about where things stood. We were uncertain whether sponsorship by the law school, the university, and the fiftieth anniversary celebration committee would all be pulled if we did not agree to a postponement. We were unsure whether funding that had already been committed by these groups would also be withdrawn, leaving us with participants' already booked airfares and hotel accommodations to pay. Given that the university had already come close to rescinding our use of the campus venue, which we had booked the previous summer, we were deeply anxious whether we could continue to hold the conference at all in these circumstances.

We posted the program to the Internet the next day, wanting to make it clear that our conference program was not subject to mediation by some external party – as per the remark by the dean that he would propose to the president a mediation between us and Professors Dewitt and Adelman. We had been peer reviewed, we had an Organizing Committee, and we had an Advisory Committee whose task it was to vet our program.

Unbeknownst to us, the dean sent an email to the president after the phone call in which he urged us to postpone the event.[102] As he noted, "I think the organizers are not going to agree to postpone the conference. I spoke with one of them this evening and he was very hostile to the notion. I don't think it will fly with them. And we can't force them to delay it. That will only hurt us." Running up against our intransigence appears to have finally led the dean to the position on academic freedom that we had been repeatedly urging on him: namely, that the university's integrity hinged on its stance on academic freedom and that the university should neither endorse nor critique the academic merits of scholarly events. In his communication to the president, the dean noted that he had been "trying to think of a way to finesse this." He had arrived at the following approach to academic freedom and the conference:

> The source of the problem, really, is that the conference has been designated as an official York 50th event. This is being interpreted as the university somehow endorsing the views expressed at the event. But this is not the case. The views expressed at the conference will reflect a range of opinion, and the university does not necessarily endorse the views of any of the participants.
>
> I am wondering whether we couldn't issue a disclaimer of some kind, clarifying this point. In effect we would say that this is an independently organized academic event; that the views expressed at the conference are those of the participants and will reflect a range of opinion; and that these views do not necessarily ref[l]ect those of the university.
>
> This is a standard disclaimer that is not exceptional since the university does not generally endorse the particular opinions of faculty members. This reality seems to have been lost in the current context.

> This does not suggest that we are withdrawing our sponsorship of the event as a York 50th event, just that we are clarifying that this financial support does not imply support of the substantive views and opinions expressed at the event.
>
> If we put out such a statement, then we would just let them proceed with their event as they wish, without attempting to make any further changes.
>
> I think we can defend this position academically from criticism from both sides.

This email appears to have led to the brief and reassuring meeting with the president that we had the next day, mentioned earlier, in which he commented that the university was not in the business of counting heads at a scholarly event and that there were clear lines that the university took on academic freedom that he had no intention of crossing.

From the known record, there was at least one more juncture at which Israeli activist Gerald Steinberg played a role in the Mapping Models conference. President Shoukri posted a very eloquent and strong message in support of academic freedom on the York University website on May 21, 2009. The FIPPA record, and his own July 2011 feedback, reveal that Dean Monahan was instrumental in crafting this statement, for which the Organizing Committee was very grateful. It provided public and much-needed support for our academic endeavour, and, in light of the intense pressure that the university and law school had come under, it is hard to construe the position taken by the president (and the dean) as anything other than courageous.

On May 21st, President Shoukri circulated the first draft (ready for release) of his statement on academic freedom. It appears that it was posted but not made fully public (i.e., it was not released on *Yfile*, the electronic university newsletter) until May 22nd.

Just minutes after the dean got notice on May 21st that the statement was published in the media archive and on the president's web page, he sent AVP Dewitt an email under the subject heading "President's message on academic freedom posted," flagging for Dewitt that the statement, which he attached, was posted and would go fully public the next day. He wrote to the AVP, "David as per our discussion can you follow [up] with GS? Thanks." It becomes evident in the next chain of emails that GS was Gerald Steinberg, by this time a known adversary of the conference.[103]

Later the same day (Israel time) Steinberg sent Dewitt a revised version of the draft op-ed that Dewitt had brought to the dean's attention on May 11th. The subject heading of this email was "2ND ARTICLE: YORK UNIVERSITY VS. ISRAEL: ACADEMIC FREEDOM OR ACADEMIC FARCE?" Steinberg prefaced his revised blog with "Draft for comment before blog posting: 22 May 2009." Dewitt immediately forwarded Steinberg's request for comments on his blog to the dean and VPRI Stan Shapson.[104]

Steinberg's draft op-ed (eventually published in the *National Post* on June 9th) now contained a scathing critique of President Shoukri's statement on academic freedom, which, on the dean's behalf, AVP Dewitt had just forwarded to Steinberg. Steinberg wrote,

> The President of York University in Toronto has issued a statement attempting to defend his university's sponsorship of an event headlined "Israel/Palestine: Mapping Models of Statehood and Paths to Peace," scheduled for June 22 to 24. This response to intense criticism of the program attempts to portray serious criticism as an attack on academic freedom. However, in examining the details and the debate over this event, and in the context of vulgar anti-Israel activities and physical intimidation of Jewish students at York, these bland words are a diversion – a straw man aimed at deflecting criticism, and blocking the important public debate over the role of university campuses as battlefields in the Arab-Israeli narrative wars that perpetuate the violent conflict.[105]

Steinberg's op-ed/blog ends by calling York University an accomplice in a crime: "the vicious warfare and mass terror which has taken the lives of tens of thousands of Israelis, Palestinians, and others, and is escalating into nuclear confrontation."[106] This draft blog that Steinberg sent to Dewitt for feedback the morning of May 22nd was posted later that day on his blog. Where York University had not been the focal point of assault by Steinberg in his pre-May 22nd op-ed, it now came under direct critique – focused on the presidential statement – in his May 22nd redrafting. This occurred on the very day that the presidential statement on academic freedom was issued publicly on *Yfile*.

I was troubled to learn of these developments when this batch of FIPPA documents was released. I sent an email to both Provost Monahan and AVP Dewitt on April 18, 2010, underlining that I was finalizing a manuscript that placed on me "an extra obligation – to the story and to you as well – to get the account right." I did not hear back from either of them regarding my questions about what was happening in this sequence of events. I found it baffling that these two senior York administrators would forward the president's statement on academic freedom to a known adversary – one who immediately turned around and launched a blistering attack on both York University and the president's statement. I wanted to know why the dean had asked the AVP to forward the president's statement to Steinberg. I wanted to know about the "discussion" between the dean and AVP alluded to in the May 21st email. I wanted to know whether either party had provided feedback, oral or written, on Steinberg's draft blog. I asked for documentation of these possible exchanges given that there was nothing in the FIPPA record.

When I did not get a response to my questions from AVP Dewitt and Provost Monahan in April 2010, I followed up with an email to the president of York University. I asked for an explanation of why Steinberg, Dean Monahan, and AVP Dewitt appeared to have been involved in a consultation at that juncture. President Shoukri responded on April 20th:

> I was made aware of the draft of the Steinberg op-ed by the Provost last May. In discussion with the Provost, I authorized the sharing of my statement with Professor Steinberg who I believed might share some of the values of academic freedom which I had expressed. I hoped Steinberg might consider modifying his proposed article; specifically, that he might soften his attack on the university's decision to support the conference. Of course that is not what he chose to do. I hope this helps clarify that issue.[107]

No Debate notes that Dewitt responded to the CAUT Inquiry's query about his involvement in the article's production, and Dewitt stated that he had not provided comments to Steinberg on the draft. Dewitt also responded to a follow-up query of mine on these matters in December 2011, noting that "I neither saw it before it was published nor knew where or when or if it would be published until it was brought to my attention. No one in the Office of the VPRI or in Dean Monahan's office, as far as I know, ever provided any commentary to Steinberg; nor did I."[108] The CAUT Report accepts Dewitt's statement regarding "advice to Steinberg."[109] I see no reason to quibble with this finding. Professor Thompson goes on to remark that "the basis for Shoukri's hope that there was a non-negligible prospect that Steinberg might consider softening his characterizations of the conference is unclear."[110]

As part of my final revisions to this book in December 2011, I sent an email to both Provost Monahan and David Dewitt and asked them to respond to my original questions of April 18, 2009. Both responded by saying that the president's April 20th email was an answer to all of my queries. So I followed up with a further set of questions to each. To Provost Monahan, I asked again about the nature of the "discussion" that he had had with AVP Dewitt on May 21st. And I asked how he had come to the conclusion that Gerald Steinberg was someone whose opinion on these matters was important and could be changed. Specifically, I asked,

> Did you just let David Dewitt convince you, without further rationale, that Gerald Steinberg was somehow relevant to the conference or to York University? If David provided more of a rationale than what is in the FIPPA'd records (just a "say so" – May 10, 2009, Dewitt describes Steinberg to you as "a very well known senior Israeli academic"), what was it that he said that convinced you of Steinberg's relevance? Or did you come to an independent assessment for your judgment? And if the latter, on what basis did you arrive at this assessment?

Provost Monahan answered none of these questions but remarked in response to them that,

> Despite your apparent recognition that you have "an extra obligation – to the story and to you as well – to get the account right," I regret to say that you appear to me not to be approaching this matter in a fair minded way. You make conclusions which are shown to be wrong, which then lead you to make other conclusions of a similar nature which are equally lacking in foundation.

Since I received no other materials from Provost Monahan with which to create a foundation for understanding the strange set of communications that York's administration had with Professor Steinberg, and accepting, as I do, that Dean Monahan was not attempting to undermine the president's statement on academic freedom (which he himself had been extensively involved in drafting), my understanding at this juncture is that he exercised a very different judgment on the matter than the conference Organizing or Advisory Committee would have.

To David Dewitt, I sent the following request for feedback on December 21, 2011:

Patrick presented me, in July of this summer past, with a lengthy document in response to my request for feedback on my manuscript. In that document, he notes, under a subject heading "Events in April 2009," that

> President Shoukri asked me to meet with the conference organizers to see whether these concerns could be addressed in some way, while at the same time supporting the organizers in achieving their goals, and to keep him informed of developments. President Shoukri also asked me to work with Professor David Dewitt, the senior academic within the Office of the Vice President Research and Innovation responsible for matters involving the Social Sciences and Humanities Research Council of Canada (SSHRC), which had provided a grant to support the conference.

It is evident that the President delegated administrative responsibility for staying on top of the Mapping Models conference to Patrick and to you ...

As per the delegation that Patrick mentions in his July 2011 feedback, President Shoukri clearly relied upon Patrick to provide him with wise council relating to the conference. But there is no evidence at all that Patrick exercised independent judgment about Gerald Steinberg. All of the evidence points to Patrick relying wholly upon your judgment in this regard. The evidence also indicates that you thought highly of Gerald Steinberg. In an email that you sent Patrick on May 10, 2009, you describe Steinberg as "a very well known senior Israeli academic." This is, of course, the email in which you forward an earlier draft of Steinberg's op ed to Patrick on the basis of its relevance to thinking about the Mapping Models conference. I don't see any evidence of a critical evaluation from you of Steinberg's views in that May 10, 2009 email to Patrick.

I can tell you for a certainty that, had we been asked, the Organizing Committee would not have come to the conclusion that Steinberg shared "some of the values of academic freedom" articulated in the May 22, 2009 Presidential Statement. And the evidence is there that our judgment would have been impeccable on this question – to wit the actual use to which Steinberg put the Presidential statement that he had a head's up on from you, via Patrick's reliance on your council.

Now that we know without doubt that Gerald Steinberg was not a friend of either York University, or your colleagues Bruce and me, or academic freedom, and now that we also know (I believe fairly conclusively) that you were the administrative delegate who thought he might be, I wonder if you could

> please comment on the judgment you exercised with respect to Gerald Steinberg, most particularly in your advice to the President to forward York University's statement to him. Do you now see it to have been ill-advised? Do you stand by it? If so, how, and why?
>
> What are your thoughts on Steinberg's op ed, now that we are over two and a half years away from its publication, and from the Mapping Models conference itself?
>
> I would greatly appreciate any thoughtfulness you can add to my accounting of events.

I did get a partial answer from Dewitt in December 2011 about how he had arrived at the judgment that Steinberg was someone whose views were worthy of regard:

> I knew Steinberg from his research and publications on arms control, disarmament, and Middle East regional security. The late Prof R B Byers had invited him to speak at York shortly after my arrival, and after that I saw Steinberg a number of times in professional meetings. He knew me from my work on international and regional security related both to the Middle East and to East Asia. He was especially interested in my work on arms control and proliferation issues in Northeast Asia, and approaches to managing the difficult situation concerning North Korea. But that was back in the early through mid 1990s; not since.
>
> During that part of my 1993-94 sabbatical when I was a visiting scholar at Tel-Aviv University, I recall meeting Steinberg once in his capacity as Chair of the Department of Political Science, Bar Ilan University, when I was invited to present at a seminar.
>
> I became aware of his parallel activities involving evidence-based responses to those who he and his colleagues view as inappropriately attacking Israel and/or Jewish academics through a former doctoral student of his who was a visiting post-doctoral researcher at York University as of 2006.
>
> Steinberg's professional credentials – full professor, widely published, department chair, advisor to government and the UN on arms control – attest to his academic standing and it was only in that capacity that I knew him until I was informed of his involvement in NGO Monitor and later his concerns about your conference. While I need not agree with his opinions

> whether professional or personal, academic freedom includes the right for colleagues within the academy to critique as they wish so long as they marshall evidence and argument that can be challenged, is undertaken openly, and does not call for violence.
>
> My point to my senior colleagues at York was that Steinberg was a credible and known senior academic; that remains.

Dewitt chose not to share his reflections on Steinberg's op-ed from the perspective offered by time.

When Dewitt noted that "academic freedom includes the right for colleagues within the academy to critique as they wish," it is not absolutely clear whether he was referring to Steinberg's right or his own, particularly given that Steinberg was never part of our academy. Furthermore, though I do not doubt Steinberg's right to rail against an academic event, circulating through occult administrative channels a draft op-ed for comment on the Mapping Models conference is hard to characterize as "undertaken openly."

Nevertheless, Dewitt was right to suggest that the criteria that he cited – full professor, widely published, department chair, adviser to government and the United Nations – are the hallmarks that academics rely on to facilitate judgment about the worthiness of ideas. A scholar's resumé is also his or her calling card for entry into debate. Because academia tends to demand high levels of specialization and rarified expertise, recognized authority can sometimes be the bedrock of ultimate judgment. But these are also the very indicia that can cocoon ideas from a more reasoned assessment of their worth, which is one of the reasons that peer review is often double blind, with neither the reviewer's nor the author's identity disclosed. Judgments made by reason of authority rather than by authority of reason can lean on sham legitimacy.

Academic credentials also generate the propensity to inoculate the judgment of academics from the scrutiny and skepticism of those who lack the resources by which to assess it on their own. The gulf in judgment exercised by Dean Monahan between graduate student Mazen Masri and full professor Gerald Steinberg is illustrative of this point. For the former, an exceptional candidate for a role on the Organizing Committee of the Mapping Models conference, playing "a prominent and public role in various organizations that are politically active in relation to the politics of the Middle East" (in the words of Provost Monahan's July 2011 feedback) comprised the ground for removal from a properly constituted Organizing Committee; for the latter, unscrutinized credentials eclipsed the administration's view of the clear trajectory of a notorious activist in the politics of the Middle East. Full professors, armed with the hallmarks of the guild, are granted an exceptional authority to confound political and academic work.

As noted above, David Dewitt's claim in his December 24, 2011, email that "academic freedom includes the right for colleagues within the academy to critique as they wish" might just as plausibly be interpreted to be one that he was making in his own defence. I do not otherwise quibble with the view that Gerald Steinberg had the right to critique the conference as he wished; Dewitt, however, was not simply a "colleague," and his own "right to critique as he wished" (if that is what is meant by his ambiguous phrase) was curtailed to the extent that he was not.

First, the AVP had a privileged position from which to marshal strong opinion against the event in that he had been delegated by the president to assist the dean in grappling with concerns. It would be an abuse of the prestige and authority of that position to launch critiques that, from an unprivileged colleague, would be less potent and perfectly appropriate.

Second, the ambiguous phrasing in Dewitt's email echoes a passage written by renowned former president of York University and former dean of Osgoode Hall Law School, Harry Arthurs: "If academic freedom implies the right of professors to make controversial statements, it also implies the right of other members of the community – including the president – to disagree, to condemn and or [to] repudiate those statements."[111] Dewitt, if he was claiming for himself the right to critique as he wished – albeit through an opaque process of marshalling authority, unexaminable by us except through a FIPPA request, rather than reason – appeared to be appropriating through delegation a supposed right of the administration to disagree with, condemn, and/or repudiate the controversial views of fellow colleagues. As we will see in Chapter 5, that passage from Arthurs, if taken out of context, can be badly manipulated – an abbreviation that another of my former Osgoode colleagues, Professor Les Green, called "distressing" when the manipulation was deployed in another context.[112]

Third, and related, a key means of shoring up academic freedom is to draw administrators from the ranks of the professoriate. By that means, external influence over the day-to-day work of scholars is minimized, for the governance structure of the institution remains autonomous in being thus buoyed by the culture – a culture that prizes knowledge over almost all other values. Once culled, however, and when they are thereafter acting in their administrative capacity (even while their collegial involvement might continue in parallel), administrators move out of the horizontal position of collegiality and into the hierarchical one of administration. As I discuss below, the view within Canadian academia is that administrators must observe a principle of neutrality in their dealings with the academic activities of independent scholars. As we will see in Chapter 5, this is the thrust of Arthurs's unexpurgated message. There is some ambiguity built into the dual roles played by university administrators (who, after all, remain part of the collegium); however, ambivalence on that score opens up the sluices to non-academic critique (flow as it might from someone who otherwise has scholarly credibility) – and, as I argue below, the demands of academic freedom are unambiguous at that point: university administrators have an obligation of neutrality where their colleagues do not.

Managing the Message

The May 13, 2009, meeting with the president and dean was not the end of our interactions with York's administration. The university also provided media services to the conference. We also had an exchange with the dean and vice-president of research and innovation, Stan Shapson, regarding SSHRC's extraordinary intervention in our grant application. The following material covers York's intervention in the conference's media policy followed by the manner in which the administration of York University handled the pressure on us from SSHRC.

In May 2009, someone in York's administration decided, without consulting us, that the conference organizers should work closely with not only York Media but also an outside media consultant who specialized in crisis media management. We were called to a meeting on May 13th by York's director of media relations and its chief marketing and communications officer. We went to this meeting immediately after our meeting with the president. York had hired Jane Shapiro of Hill and Knowlton, a strategic communications consultancy "with a successful track record of providing high value public relations and public affairs support to companies, agencies, government ministries and organizations."[113]

For the meeting, Hill and Knowlton and York's director of media relations had prepared a memo for York's chief marketing and communications officer on the subject of the conference. It constituted a "Communications Context and Strategy."[114] It was distributed to us when we arrived.

The context drawn up by the Hill and Knowlton consultant clearly reflected a discomfort with the very idea of the conference, compounded, in her view, by its inclusion in the fiftieth anniversary celebrations. Shapiro cited two passages from the conference vision statement, the first one noting that the purpose of the conference was "to explore which state model would be the best to resolve the Israeli-Palestinian conflict, respecting the rights to self-determination of both Israelis/Jews and Palestinians." She also found problematic a second statement in the vision statement: "The time is right to revisit the one state vs. two state debate in an academic context ... At the same time it will provide an opportunity to question whether a one state option could ever achieve sufficient political support or adequately protect the rights and security of both national communities."

However anyone else might have read these passages, they were clearly troubling to the media consultant that York University had hired for itself and ostensibly us. As Shapiro noted,

> These were highly charged terms of reference so that it was inevitable that the conference, like the topic, would become political and controversial ... Even mainstream Jewish groups can be expected to take issue with the notion of a single state solution, in which the Jewish population would quickly become a permanent minority, and wonder why York is providing a platform for this discussion.

Before preparing her remarks about the strategy that she thought we and York Media should pursue to manage media interaction with the conference, Shapiro noted that, "In retrospect, inclusion of the conference in the 50th Anniversary events was perhaps naïve and, in light of Middle East related tensions on campus, not a good choice. Managing the event will require careful planning and preparation."

The rest of the meeting was taken up with instructing us on the media strategy that we should pursue. The key message of this strategy from the chief marketing and communications officer, the director of media relations, and Hill and Knowlton was that the media should be excluded from the event, a proposal that, as we indicated at the meeting, the Organizing Committee could not agree to given that one of our members was not present.

There was one agreement that came out of that May 13, 2009, meeting with York University's media department. We all agreed that the Organizing Committee would handle all media queries that related to the conference and that York would handle media inquiries about its sponsorship and hosting of the event. Beyond this clear division of roles that limited the involvement of York's media department, Hill and Knowlton stressed to us all the importance of having a spokesperson who would be the *single* point of contact for the media and the community; we agreed that, apart from the circumscribed role for York Media to address sponsorship and hosting, the conference spokesperson would be selected from among the four Organizing Committee members. We designated Professor Aiken as that spokesperson.

After a series of Organizing Committee meetings in which we discussed the approach that we wanted to take with the media, we ultimately decided that we were not in agreement with excluding the media from the conference. We believed that York University's interests and ours with respect to the media did not necessarily coincide. While, as academics, we were in the business of disseminating ideas, York's paramount concern appeared to be to minimize any bad press for the university regarding the event. We sent an email to York Media in which we noted that we had talked over our media strategy and had decided that we wanted to open the event to print media. We indicated that we were in the process of designing a protocol around this decision and would let York Media know when it was in place.

Our efforts to define our own media policy for our own conference were met with fierce resistance by Hill and Knowlton, by York Media, and ultimately by the dean of Osgoode. Hill and Knowlton intervened first and advanced several arguments about why our media approach would be disastrous. The consultant was convinced that we would be turning our conference into an uncontrolled political event, and she recommended that we stick to the original decision (which York and the consultant had made and then urged on us) not to invite the media.

We responded politely but firmly to this growing difference between us and the university and its consultant regarding the place of the media in academic events. Among the members of the Organizing Committee, we had a good deal of experience dealing with the media, particularly regarding controversial events and topics. We laid out our protocol in some detail and our reasoning behind not excluding the media from the event.

We received two more emails on our media policy from the York administration. The chief marketing officer sent us an email under a subject heading in all caps that read "PLEASE RECONSIDER." He reiterated Hill and Knowlton's arguments and said, "I understand your impulses on this but you may well be providing fodder for months and years to come particularly on the internet which, as we know, never forgets."

And, finally, the dean of Osgoode weighed in by telling us that he was "surprised and concerned" and thought that he should at least make us aware of his concern. He urged us to reconsider our decision, which he did not believe was in the interests of the kind of genuine academic inquiry that we proposed to convene. He hoped that we would reconsider and "not go down this road, which will lead you in directions that will undermine what you are trying to do."

We responded to the dean by clarifying that, whatever York University's position on the media might be, we were ultimately responsible for the media policy relating to our conference: "What we would like to do is consider the matter of our media policy/strategy over the next two weeks as events unfold. We will certainly let you know where we end up on this matter and will continue to communicate with York Media on what we consider to be the most appropriate media response."

After all of our efforts to clarify our assiduously arrived at position of institutional independence on matters relating to media coverage of the conference, York University dispatched the director of media relations to attend the conference hours prior to its opening on June 22, 2009. The director appeared early the first day and began to object strongly to the only present faculty member on the Organizing Committee about the fact that we had invited a journalist to the event. This had been loosely organized months earlier before York Media had become involved in the conference.

When all four organizers were present at the conference venue, we had a meeting among ourselves in which we decided that, despite the forceful objections of the director of media relations, we still wanted the journalist to be present. Ultimately, the journalist did not attend because (as he recounted to us) a second journalist from the *Jewish Tribune,* who had seen his nametag on the conference registration table, called him and threatened to write about his presence at the conference.

In the end, the "no media" policy advocated by York University's Departments of Media and Marketing and Communications became a focal point of media coverage of the conference. By June 24th, someone had sent an email to the president asking why

> the media or any reporters were prohibited from sitting in and observing the conference. This in itself scares me the most. If York University really believed that this conference was a good outlet to debate issues of public concern, obviously the media would have been allowed in. I would really like to know the answer to this question.

The president's office forwarded this email to someone with the request "Could you please reply to this email on behalf of the President?" We do not know who was tasked to answer this question; it was not us. The Organizing Committee was in favour of a media presence.

The *Jewish Tribune* ended up doing a front-page story under the title "Is Media Barred from Anti-Israel Conference at York University? B'nai Brith Canada Asks for an Explanation." The director of media relations ended up answering the *Tribune*'s questions about why the media were barred. He did not mention that there was a disjuncture between York's media policy and the Organizing Committee's media policy: "It's a common practice for academic conferences of this nature – in order to provide speakers and audience members with an environment conducive to candid dialogue and debate."[115]

In another response to a request from the *National Post* regarding York's policy and whose decision it was to close the conference to media, the director of media relations again explained the policy. Although it was York's policy and not the Organizing Committee's, he noted that "the Conference Organizing Committee sets the policies for their conferences."

Facilitating Pressure

As noted in Chapter 1, on June 5, 2009, just under three weeks before the conference, the minister of science and technology intervened in the granting council that had assisted in funding our conference. The granting council responded to this political pressure by asking us to submit an extraordinary report on our activities – a report that did not follow the normal procedures for conference grants, which expect reporting only after the event is completed or if the principal investigator determines that there has been a major change in the theme or focus of the event. As noted above, the senior executives of SSHRC conceded (between themselves) that what they subjected us to fell outside the normal procedures. What follows is how the senior administration of York University thought the situation should be handled.

Although deeply troubled by the political interference in our conference funding, we decided to comply with SSHRC's request to report on whether there were major or minor changes to the conference program since our original application. Before we submitted the report, however, we contacted VPRI Shapson – the administrative member tasked to deal with granting councils – and set up a conference call. At his request, the dean joined him and Professor Aiken and me in a June 11th conference call. We initiated the call to ask the university to provide us with institutional support in declaring to SSHRC that our conference was completely in order and that the request for an extraordinary report was unwarranted.

From the outset, Professor Aiken articulated both our commitment to complete the report and our concerns over the precedent set by SSHRC's request to the dean and VPRI. She made it clear that we would respond to SSHRC's request. We remained concerned, however, that complying with the extraordinary demand set a dangerous precedent. She noted that we had in mind the thousands of other university researchers across the country concerned with the degree of government intervention in an academic event. We did not want to be complicit in a process that was dangerous for the future of independent research.

Professor Aiken went on to note that we were, in fact, genuinely concerned that the report might not be the end of the matter. Although we were confident that there had been no major change to the event, given the extraordinary escalation we were worried that the pressure would be unrelenting on both the minister and the granting council. She underlined that we felt extremely vulnerable, particularly since the conference was less than two weeks away. Furthermore, on our word that we would cover the costs, participants had already booked plane tickets and reserved hotel rooms. We worried about our personal liability for these costs. In light of these concerns, we asked for York's support in a more formal way. We made it clear that we were very worried.

The response of the VPRI and the dean throughout the phone conversation was that we should simply comply with SSHRC's request and that, while there were larger issues relating to the implications of a government asking a granting council to intervene in an independent research event, they could be dealt with later. To their minds, there was nothing extraordinary about the SSHRC request.[116] They believed that the council was requesting something of us that fell completely within its normal procedures. The VPRI urged us simply to respond and noted that doing anything else would just raise the temperature. Any residual political issues regarding what SSHRC was doing should be raised at another time, once SSHRC funding was secured and the conference was completed.

Indeed, the VPRI and dean were not only convinced that SSHRC's request was normal but also impressed with how SSRHC was handling the matter. The VPRI noted that SSHRC had not buckled. He thought that it had strategically withstood political pressure. We noted our view that this was not, indeed, normal procedure and asked whether the VPRI had ever seen a case in which a grant was being reviewed as a result of political pressure. He could not recall an instance of this ever happening.

As much as the dean and VPRI urged us simply to comply with the request, they were also emphatic that there had been no major change to our conference according to SSHRC's criteria distinguishing major from minor changes. The dean was explicit about his assessment as he urged us to file the report. He referenced the York U50 application that he had signed off on in the spring of 2008 and declared that the program in it was substantially the same as the program posted on the conference website. If anything, he noted, we had made changes that responded to concerns raised by our critics. He was emphatic that there had not been any material change to the program. He further recognized that, as is typically the case with conferences, the list of speakers had to be adapted as some speakers withdrew and others were added to ensure that gaps were filled. He remarked that in this case, from the point of view of both SSRHC and the university, the former was providing a way for the issue to be dealt with in a discreet way.

Given the strong statements of both the dean and the VPRI that there had been no major change to the conference since our original application and that merely stating so would make the matter "go away," we asked them if they would put their assessment in writing. We made it clear how vulnerable we were feeling and that we both needed and wanted institutional support as an intermediary stage before we submitted the report.

They refused this request for support. As far as they were concerned, we, as individual faculty members, had been asked to submit the report to SSHRC. The university would not normally be involved in reporting to SSHRC. They were confident that their intervention would not, in any event, be of assistance to us. When I responded that I thought it would assist us because it would provide us with the assurance that the university was behind us, particularly given how vulnerable we were at that moment, the dean objected to my doubt that the university was prepared to support us. He stressed that the administration had been trying to work with us from the beginning and had engaged the services of many people at the university to this end.

The VPRI went on to note that nobody was going to abandon faculty researchers or leave them vulnerable. The university, he insisted, protects all faculty members from any case of vulnerability.

Disappointed as we were with the phone meeting, that day we drew up the report as a committee. After the phone call, we sent the dean and VPRI an email summarizing the conversation in which we wrote down their strong orally conveyed view that there had been nothing but minor changes to our SSHRC project since we had submitted our application. We thought that it would be difficult for them to respond in writing that they disavowed the support that we ascribed to them. They did not respond to this email. Before we submitted the report to them for vetting later that day, having contrived to secure their written support, we wrote in it that they were in agreement that nothing but minor changes had taken place (hence the redundancy of the report and, implicitly, the inappropriateness of its request).

The June 15, 2009, statement issued by SSHRC president Chad Gaffield made explicit reference to the assessments of Osgoode's dean and York's VPRI that nothing but minor changes had occurred:

> The grant holder has informed SSHRC that the changes in conference programming since November 2008 are minor and that the aims of the event remain unchanged in their essence. The dean of Osgoode Hall Law School, and the vice-president research and innovation at York University agree with him. SSHRC has accepted their assurance that planning for the conference is proceeding in a manner consistent with provisions of the Grant Holder's Guide for the program.[117]

The inclusion of that line in our report appears to have been instrumental in alleviating the pressure on SSHRC (perhaps also on the government) – and ultimately on us.

The pressure applied by the government to SSHRC, and then by domino effect to York University and us, was not "our" difficulty. SSHRC was in far greater jeopardy of compromising its independence had the issue not been resolved in the way that it was; indeed, its reputation arguably has been damaged by the way that it *did* intervene. In fact, the Canadian Association of University Teachers had assured us that, if SSHRC pulled our funding, CAUT would make up the deficit and our conference would not be held hostage to deeply inappropriate machinations between the government and SSHRC. Just as the university was in jeopardy if it forced us off campus (though York seemed to be oblivious of the damage to its reputation that it was courting), so too SSHRC's reputation of having an arm's-length relationship with the government was in considerable jeopardy.

The dean and VPRI were impressed by the way that SSHRC handled the debacle with us. They thought that SSHRC was not weakening the case of independent research by submitting us to an extraordinary procedure (which they both thought was regular). They thought that SSHRC strategically withstood political pressure and had not just thrown the political problem onto the university's lap. In our view, what the university, SSHRC, and the government had done was throw their political problem onto *our* laps. When we asked for institutional support from York, the administration declined by telling us that we were making things way too complicated and putting way too much tension into the scenario. In fact, the tension on us as individual faculty members was excruciating, and the administration was asking us to continue absorbing it all on our own and desist from asking the university to absorb any of it. Despite protestations that York would not leave any of its faculty members vulnerable and that nobody would abandon faculty researchers, it appeared that that was, in fact, what the university did.

A Successful Academic Event

In large measure due to the intervention of the president of York University following the May 13, 2009, meeting with the Organizing Committee, the conference proceeded as scheduled with the program that the conference organizers and their Advisory Committee had been working on all along. The principal interventions of the president were his two public statements on academic freedom as it related to the conference. The conference was further supported by the Board of Governors and by the 2009 outgoing and incoming chairs, Marshall Cohen and Paul Cantor, both of whom attached their names and the prestige of their office to the statements. And if the large measure of support for the conference came officially from the president's office, all of the FIPPA material as well as repeated statements by the president himself made it clear that Dean Monahan was central to the drafting of those statements and key to the confident and appropriate approach to the conference that the university followed from May 13, 2009, on.

As noted, the CIJA statement against the conference came out on May 12th. In it, the CEO of CIJA asked people to write to the president of York and the dean of Osgoode to voice their opposition to the event. Apart from the comments appended directly to the statement on the CIJA website (removed from underneath the online statement in the late fall of 2011), many people opposed to CIJA's strategy wrote to York in support of the conference and academic freedom. One such writer was Ian Lustick. On May 13th, he sent the following letter, which he copied to Susan Davis, CIJA's contact person for the statement:

> The CIJA statement on the upcoming conference ... is a part of a pattern of misguided, so-called "pro-Israel" attempts throughout North America to suppress debate, run away from challenges, and ignore serious questions confronting Jews and Palestinians in the Middle East. In this particular case ... the statement is formulated in an unusually egregious way that directly and unashamedly defies the principles of freedom of speech and of unfettered intellectual disputation ... The implication here [in the CIJA claim that we had "procured a few balanced speakers of high repute, but (that) this is certainly not enough to characterize the conference as one of high academic integrity or good scholarship"] goes far beyond the (illegitimate) demand that an event at a university be cancelled because the demander does not agree with something that will be said; to a demand that all events should be cancelled except for those featuring an unspecified percentage, perhaps a majority, of speakers that the demander actively approves of as "balanced." There is one and only one criterion that any self-respecting college or university can use when judging whether to host an event or speaker. That criterion cannot have anything to do with the substance of what will be argued, but only whether what will be said or done will contribute to the ability of members of the community to improve their arguments and their analysis. Any other criterion places power in the hands of particular groups with particular opinions and agendas to decide what is right, what is worth considering as possibly right, and what is illegitimate to even question.[118]

The email was also addressed to Dean Monahan. And he clearly read it and took it in. As he noted in an email sent to AVP Dewitt just forty minutes after receiving it, "see below from Ian Lustick. This confirms the wisdom of the approach we are going to take on this."[119] It seems evident from this that the dean had already committed himself to the approach to the conference, and to academic freedom, manifest in the two statements that he drafted and in the moving and supportive welcoming remarks that he gave on the opening day of the conference. It was also manifest in the strong defence of academic freedom that he advocated in response to an email stating that the university should not sanction the conference and claiming that we were proponents of "Israel apartheid week" and the Israel boycott movement. Dean Monahan responded on May 27, 2009:

> In fact, the freedom of individual, independent academics to organize academic events such as conferences on subjects of their choosing – within

> certain limitations – goes to the very heart of academic freedom. It would be inappropriate for the university administration to intervene in or to take responsibility for the academic content of such events ... There are almost 100 events and initiatives that make up the [York] 50th anniversary calendar, and the university has no stake in the academic content of any of them. At the same time, it would be unthinkable to exclude a conference *because* of its subject matter.[120]

It is hard to imagine a more supportive statement – or supportive conduct – on either academic freedom or the right of conference organizers to control their own research and dissemination.

By early June, with the conference around the corner, AVP Dewitt and Howard Adelman also appeared to have modified their assessment of our endeavours, without any changes in what we were doing. We had rejected AVP Dewitt's proposal to shrink our conference down to the presenters whom he thought were "worthy." We had advanced our own keynote speakers for the event. We had continued our original process of determining for ourselves which abstracts were worthy of consideration and continued to grant spaces for participation driven by our own criteria of worthiness. We had not removed a single presenter from earlier postings of the program on the website and never considered using criteria of whether or not they were "activists" or "polemicists" or "non-scholars" to downplay their roles in the conference. All fifteen of the presenters who had been denounced by Gerald Steinberg were still on the program. All seven of the presenters whom B'nai Brith objected to were on the program. The six members of our Advisory Committee whom the JDL denounced in its complaint to the government remained in place, and four of them presented papers. Despite the constant and consistent position of the conference organizers, on June 8th AVP Dewitt wrote to Dean Monahan with the following assessments:

> Last week I went over the conference website and abstracts carefully and concluded that the organizers have improved what was there. While I personally still have some reservations, had what is now been presented six months ago and had they been a bit more careful in how they selected their speakers, I think much of the problems we've encountered either would not have happened or could have been managed ...
>
> I was pleased to note that entirely separately, in speaking with Howard Adelman over the weekend, he had gone through a similar exercise and

> came to much the same conclusion: what is there now is significantly better than before. Still problematic in some ways, but not to the extent previously and certainly within the bounds for what might now be a managed engagement of strongly differing ideas ... It is still not in my mind a high level/quality conference even with some very good scholars present; too uneven and still with some rather dubious individuals. Hence, Gerald Steinberg will still write what he writes, as noted in my previous email to you.[121]

The thematic topic of the conference also appeared to have lost some of its hard edges. On June 5th, Patrick Martin of the *Globe and Mail* published an article under the title "Has the Two-State Ship Sailed?"[122] It covered the various models of statehood for Israel/Palestine in much the same way that our conference was about to do. Echoing our original vision statement, which queried whether the two-state model even had a pulse left, Martin's article covered the stance of the prime minister of Israel, Benjamin Netanyahu, regarding the two-state model. Although international leaders were firmly behind the two-state model,

> Israel's Prime Minister, Benjamin Netanyahu, still doesn't agree, and an impressive gathering of right-wing politicians met in Jerusalem recently to back him up, outlining several reasons why the two-state solution is a failed option, no matter what Barack Obama says, and proposing several alternatives. Ironically, these Israelis have only expressed what many Palestinian thinkers have been arguing for some time: the two-state ship has sailed and it's not coming back ... Are there alternatives to a two-state solution? Sure there are. But a lot of people aren't going to like what they are.

The article devoted considerable space to the one-state model and less space to a less auspicious confederation linking Jordan to the West Bank and Gaza to Egypt. And it concluded by referring to the alternative of the status quo prevailing into the foreseeable future. Martin finished the article by noting that, if neither the two-state model nor the one-state model is capable of working and Netanyahu decides not to adhere to insistence from the White House on the former and Israel carries on with this approach of "managing the conflict,"

> then we can expect to see the further growth of Israeli settlements in the West Bank, probably accompanied by improvements in Palestinians' daily lives – exactly the formula the Netanyahu government has proposed. In

> that event, Israel and the semi-occupied Palestinian territories will begin to look like a single state even if it wasn't intended. It's just that it will be one state for two peoples, but with two different classes of rights.

Here Martin alluded to a future the parameters of which speak to an extraordinarily fraught dispute, one that is becoming more of a debate (i.e., more reasoned and less polemical) the farther down the road Israel moves to the last model that Martin covered. The dispute/debate arises over whether (and at what point) it becomes appropriate to describe Israel/Palestine as an apartheid state. If the characterization is accurate, then the international community could reasonably be called on to boycott it, divest from it, and/or otherwise sanction it in the same manner that South Africa was subjected to that treatment until it abandoned apartheid.[123]

The article by Martin was well received by Dean Monahan and AVP Dewitt. Monahan sent a note about it to Dewitt: "I thought that the piece was very well balanced and suggested that, at the very least, the notion of two states versus one state is a topic for some debate. What was interesting was the fact (according to Martin) that even some of the Israeli right seem to be entertaining a discussion of a one-state solution." Dewitt responded to Monahan's appraisal by noting, "yes, the Martin article was good, and had the initial conference website presented something similar and then managed – by invitation – the speakers, we'd likely not be facing the current situation."[124]

We on the Organizing Committee had also read Martin's piece. Because I had dealt with Martin several times when he was editor of the *Globe and Mail*'s op-ed section, before he departed to his post as its Middle East bureau chief, and since the Organizing Committee had decided to pursue our own media policy rather than the one (of media exclusion) advocated for us by York Media, we decided that I should contact Martin and see whether he could recommend someone at the *Globe and Mail* to cover the conference. I sent him an email in which I provided a link to the conference website and detailed some of the silencing reactions that we had received. Martin responded by noting, "your conference sounds terrific." He recommended someone whom I could follow up with, but that contact did not pan out.

Two weeks later the conference proceeded as and where planned. The dean opened the conference with very moving words of encouragement and recognized "that this conference has attracted considerable controversy in recent weeks." He went on to note that, "as York President Mamdouh Shoukri has so clearly articulated in his recent public statements on this subject, universities exist to provide forums for consideration of the widest range of political issues and debates, no matter how sensitive or controversial the subject matter." Dean Monahan found it opportune at that point to "return to first principles and recall the reasons why open inquiry and debate are so fundamental to a free society." In making this return, he cited John Stuart Mill's 1865 essay *On Liberty:*

> Mill explained that when an opinion is silenced, the injury is not merely a private one, visited upon the individual whose opinion has been suppressed. Rather, Mill argues,
>
> the peculiar evil of silencing the expression of an opinion is that it is robbing the human race, posterity as well as the present generation – those who dissent from the opinion, still more than those who hold it. If the opinion is right, they are deprived of the opportunity of exchanging error for truth; if wrong, they lose, what is almost as great a benefit, the clearer perception and livelier impression of truth colliding with error.
>
> Thus, Mill concludes, all silencing of opinion is an assumption of infallibility. There is the greatest difference, Mill explains, between presuming an opinion to be true because, "with every opportunity for contesting it, it has not been refuted, and assuming its truth for the purpose of not permitting its refutation." It is only the "complete liberty of contradicting and disproving our opinion that provides the condition which justifies us in assuming its truth for the purposes of action."

The dean concluded by stating that he knew "that my colleagues Susan Drummond and Bruce Ryder, along with the other members of the organizing committee, have worked to create an academic forum that will promote genuine dialogue on these challenging issues."

It appears that the dean was ultimately satisfied with the conference. Professor Thompson drew on the former dean's submissions to the CAUT Inquiry to emphasize its affirmation that "there was no appropriate academic or administrative basis for ... involvements by the dean":

- On June 11, 2009, Monahan (along with Shapson) supported Ryder's report to SSHRC that there had been no major changes to the conference program subsequent to the application to SSHRC in autumn 2009
- The list of speakers for the actual conference program of June 22-24, 2009 had only minor changes from the list in mid-April, 2009 when the

dean had concluded the program lacked balance and there was damage to be mitigated

- In his February 2011 submission, Monahan wrote that "the conference proceeded in the manner determined by the organizers" notwithstanding his adverse academic assessments in mid-April 2009 and his subsequent proposals regarding the academic content of the program
- In his February 2011 submission, he stated that "this conference was a success," and that it was "a successful academic event"
- In his July 5 submission, he again stated that the conference was "a success."

Professor Thompson concluded by observing that "Monahan appeared to acknowledge in February and July 2011 that his assessment in April 2009 that the conference was not a 'legitimate' academic event was not well founded academically."[125]

AN UNINTENDED ETHNOGRAPHY

PART 3
Making Sense

5

Accountability and Validity

The tangle of tales coming out of the Middle East – and the results on communities far and wide of submitting to the compulsion of those tales – already provides ample opportunities to scrutinize what might be meant by a "true" account of events and history. Similarly, ethnography, as a discipline, has been preoccupied with what it is to give a "true" account of a field when the account is often constituted from a multiplicity of voices and views, including those of the ethnographer. Questions about how much prior commitment and position inflect understanding and output are legitimately raised in the Middle East and in ethnographic work. And, as was seen in the events surrounding the Mapping Models conference, it can sometimes matter terribly that a tale has truth to it or not.

In the last chapter of this book, I will return to how this epistemological question – what does it mean to give a true account? – relates to academic freedom. In particular, I will examine some contemporary theoretical preoccupations with the doctrine and justification that it finds in the claim that it maximizes opportunities for the advancement of knowledge. In this chapter, I want to address what might be called the story of the story. The materials that follow provide a history of earlier efforts to generate *an account* of what happened – that is, of my early efforts to hold people to account and the account making of Frank Iacobucci for York University and Professor Jon Thompson for CAUT. Each effort was built on the struggle to understand what academic freedom comports and account for how the doctrine related to the events surrounding the Mapping Models conference.

That my efforts to hold parties to account were wound together with my efforts to tell the story – that is, to generate a credible and compelling piece of academic writing – does not undermine the accounting sought. Indeed, when my efforts to secure accountability repeatedly failed at York University, the ability of the published work to fulfill that purpose became all the more critical. The text's vocation as an account does not preclude the text from also being ethnographic – from being a piece of research carried out on (and in) a field of day-to-day life. Rather, it lends ethnographic and academic research a dual role. The text is both a tale from the field and an account of it – and, to the extent that individuals are identifiable, therefore an account of the conduct of those within it. And this has implications for the ethics of generating accounts, an issue to which I will return at the end of the chapter.

The Story of the Account

While we were going through the events surrounding the Mapping Models conference, we were aware that a good deal of what we were being subjected to was unacceptable and an affront to some of the basic institutions and principles of the community of which we counted ourselves members. We were aware that the events gave rise to both a "story" and an "account." The *story* had a compulsion of its own in the narrative threads that we could begin to discern in the events as we were going through them. The events were pregnant with an intrigue. But the *account* held the compulsion of history. The story, in other words, amounted to a cautionary tale – an illustration, once the threads were pulled together, of what ought *not* to happen. In addition to any narrative allure, the story, though capable of standing on its own, could also facilitate a holding to account. As it is reconstructed here, the story is designed, in other words, to generate a pragmatic as well as a discursive result.

Oddly, attempts to tell the story and render the account acquired a history of their own after the June 2009 conference. In the interest of getting the record straight, the production of the manuscript included a fairly extensive process of fact checking and clarification with participants in the story. This formal process began in the summer of 2011 with the distribution of a factual summary of relevant parts of this book to the provost of York University. The former associate vice-president of research, David Dewitt, was approached in December 2011 and responded to my solicitation of feedback and clarification.

My factual summary to the provost prompted his July 2011 release of a thirty-four-page document that provided detailed commentary on each point that I had raised. This document had appended to it a large volume of communications that supported the story laid out in the thirty-four pages. The formal process ended with a series of emails that I sent in December 2011 asking for clarification of a few straggling details. I received responses to several of these emails, leaving some unanswered, but effectively exhausting the back and forth of the process.

The process of soliciting feedback and clarification is not the same as the process that ethnographers engage in when they seek respondent validation of their analysis of the field. Some ethnographers feel compelled to test their accounts against whether the actors whose beliefs and behaviours have been described recognize the validity of the account. The aim of such an exercise is to generate an endorsement of the ethnographer's judgment or to enable the ethnographer to correct the analysis so that assent is no longer withheld. This is a form of triangulation (a concept to which I will return) in which an ethnographer checks inferences drawn from one set of data sources by collecting data from others – in the case of respondent validation, data generated by feedback from the subjects of the account.

Respondent validation is not quite the same as the feedback process that I engaged because ethnographers generally submit for respondent review their assessment of the member's social world rather than a summary of the conduct and statements that will constitute an account. The ethnographic focus on a social world tends to diminish the importance of individual actors and facilitates the anonymization of data. An account that aspires to render individuals responsible for their conduct – as my efforts have been primarily geared to doing – would hardly be possible with anonymization.

Respondent validation and the solicitation of feedback on a proposed account also share similarities. Both ethnographic writing and writing that holds individuals accountable for their actions place emphasis on the *validity* of the accounts. That an ethnography is made up or that an account has been falsified would render the first shoddy and disreputable and the second potentially actionable. This emphasis on validity does not preoccupy other forms of narrative rendering, such as fiction, that rely more for their compulsion on aesthetic finality.

There are also overlaps in that accounts about the actions of identifiable players can reveal the kind of social world that ethnographers seek to uncover. An autobiography or a report on a social event by a participant, if rich enough in detail and if hinged on the interpretation of the meaning, function, and consequences of human actions and institutional practices, can constitute an unintended ethnography, often conveying more about a particular area of social life than the output of a dedicated ethnographic project in the same field.

There are also overlaps between feedback solicitation and respondent validation that derive from the caution with which ethnographers deploy the technique. They recognize that participants in events are not necessarily privileged commentators on their own actions. The meanings of our actions might not be readily apprehended without the benefit of time and might be further occluded by the tendency of social phenomena to "go without saying" – just as they come without saying. Respondents might never have conscious access to all of the elements that prompt and govern conduct in a particular context, not even their own conduct. As Martyn Hammersley and Paul Atkinson note in their book on ethnomethodology, "while people are well-placed informants on their own actions, they are no more than that; and their accounts must be analyzed in the same way as any other data, with close consideration being given to possible threats to validity."[1] Even with the benefit of time, the multiple competing interests that drive an actor can undermine the veracity of the "ultimate insider" account, the latter being an informant commenting on the meaning of his or her own conduct.

As can be imagined, respondent validation as a method of analyzing data can be problematic. As noted by Hammersley and Atkinson, "it may be in a person's interest to misinterpret or misdescribe his or her own actions, or to counter the interpretations of the ethnographer."[2] That is not to say that it is logically or practically impossible for insiders to provide plausible and robust accounts of the fields in which they are immersed. In fact, ethnographers often rely on such insider information and perspectives to build their accounts. However, respondent validation and the responses to a request for feedback to a proposed account constitute only under reservation a compelling sounding board for validity. Respondents are usually heavily invested in the final output in ways that can occlude the struggle for validity.

Both Patrick Monahan and David Dewitt provided responses to my requests for feedback that demanded of me a considerable effort to reconcile my accounts with theirs, a synthesis evident in the final product. Even the conclusions that Monahan and Dewitt generated, which often went against the grain of my own account, needed to be further reconciled with the other things that were known. Thus, the final remarks of the provost in his July 2011 feedback did not carry the truth along with them just by virtue of the assertion that they did so. He concluded his feedback by stating that, "as the above review demonstrates, the contemporaneous written record of events, read fairly, taken as a whole and understood in its proper context, supports only one conclusion":[3] that is, his narrative of his actions is the favourable one. The bare assertion that the data support one conclusion is insufficient, particularly when there are doubts surrounding it. As with all singular pieces of data, reliance on it alone increases the danger of undetected errors in the inferences drawn.

The simple provision of a response rarely on its own constitutes a certification of validity, particularly when accounts contradict other known phenomena from the field. Contending accounts do not mean simply that there are competing versions of reality, neither of which has a greater claim on the truth. Parties to a feedback process can misinterpret or misdescribe their actions as much as interested participants in any social world, and they are endowed with the same proclivity to misapprehend phenomena that both come and go without saying. This book, then, does not simply reproduce the undigested accounts gathered through the feedback process. As with respondent validation, the accounts that came back had to be "analyzed in the same way as any other data, with close consideration being given to possible threats to validity."[4] It is not, then, a test of my account that those described within it recognize (or do not) the validity of that account.

This experience of carefully sifting through feedback responses corresponds to the experience of those who rely on respondent validation in ethnographic analysis: namely, "whether respondents are enthusiastic, indifferent, or hostile, their reactions cannot be taken as direct validation or refutation of the observer's inferences."[5] The feedback process, however, provides an extra validity check. To the extent that respondent validation is not a technique systematically pursued by ethnographers, the feedback process engaged for this account generated an opportunity for more rigorous cross-checking than would be the case for ordinary ethnographic writing. As such, the feedback process formed one point of what sociological and anthropological researchers refer to as "triangulation," and there were many such points of reference for the construction of this account.

Reasonable hesitations about the validity of an account can be analogized to the means by which surveyors and navigators situate their real-world locations against the abstraction of a map – triangulation:

> For someone wanting to locate their position on a map, a single landmark can only provide the information that they are situated somewhere along a line in a particular direction from that landmark. With two landmarks,

> however, exact position can be pinpointed by taking bearings on both; one's position is at the point on the map where the two lines cross. In social research, if we rely on a single piece of data there is the danger that undetected error in our inferences may render our analysis incorrect. If, on the other hand, diverse kinds of data lead to the same conclusion, we can be a little more confident in that conclusion.[6]

The formal feedback process was just one means by which my account cross-checked references from one set of data sources by collecting data from others.

Although the back and forth of the feedback process was foreseeable for an account about identifiable individuals in real events, some of the efforts to still the story and stifle the account were unforeseen. Less formal than this feedback exercise were earlier, and significantly more detailed, efforts on my part to run my account up against the possibilities for correction – both of my account and of the conduct of some of the players in it.

My first "informal" – that is, unguided by legal counsel in the shadow of concerns about defamation – effort to hold the administration of York University to account arose less than two weeks after the conference was over. I swiftly drafted a preliminary version of the materials presented in Chapter 4 as a document that I entitled "Fieldnotes on a Conference." This document, too, was a solicitation of feedback. However, it was not a factual summary but a robust sixty-page paper.

On July 3, 2009, I presented this paper to the former dean of Osgoode (who had become academic vice-president and provost two days earlier) and the president of York University. I had written the document because I was troubled by the interventions of York's administration in the conference and believed that it was important to compose a *post facto* account of what had transpired, especially since I believed strongly that the principle of academic freedom had been seriously at risk.

Because the Organizing Committee had not publicly disclosed any of their experiences with the administrations of their universities, there was virtually no public awareness of how these administrations had conducted themselves. In this vacuum, my document concentrated exclusively on the conduct of York University's administration, particularly on the conduct of the dean of Osgoode, Patrick Monahan. Because two of us on the Organizing Committee teach at Osgoode Hall Law School, the dean seemed to become the conduit for the exertion of pressures (off-campus, administrative, and board-generated pressures) to shape the conference in a manner that coincided with alternative political visions of the conference's subject matter. I presented the president and provost with my document to provide them with an opportunity to respond and allow me to correct any inaccuracies in my record. This document was drawn from my personal experiences of the events and from the emails that had circulated between the administration and my Osgoode email account.

"Fieldnotes" is an apt description of this early intervention. Although I made a stab at that juncture at analyzing my experiences in light of some of the literature on academic freedom, the source of the data on which I built my analysis was primary and derived equally from participant observations and written communications. My immersion in the field about which I am writing brings this book closer to the ethnographic genre. While ethnographies often draw on a wide range of data and sources for their conclusions, the immersion of a researcher in the field of study as a key source of knowledge is usually the *sine qua non* of ethnographic accounts.

As noted above, legitimate questions can arise from this latter component of my research in light of how proximity to the events can warp objectivity in the same way that it does for respondents and informants. Just as respondents can misdescribe or misinterpret their own conduct and experience, so too can an ethnographer, who in principle is no more of a privileged commentator on his or her experiences, only one who is perhaps more predisposed to pay attention to what goes without saying. That an account is first hand does not necessarily discount it, but again reliance on a single source of data increases the risk of undetected errors in any inferences drawn from it.

Getting the story right was the beginning of the process of holding to account. My overture to the president and provost at that time was both candid and private – even though I flagged that I had eventual publication in mind. At that point, the paper had a highly circumspect circulation among my colleagues on the Organizing Committee and these senior administrators. In inviting the administration to participate in the process, I was attempting to minimize embarrassment by providing them with early notice of the issues and giving them an opportunity to consider the most appropriate response without the pressure of scandal. The response itself, in the end, became data for the story of the story since it brought no finality to the intrigue but carried it forward into a different phase of the fieldwork.[7]

In response to the "Fieldnotes" document, the president and provost called me into the president's office on July 13, 2009. The president thanked me for my candour and indicated that he took very seriously concerns raised about academic freedom since he took academic freedom itself very seriously. In the meeting, the issue of my "objectivity" was raised directly. Provost Monahan noted that he himself would not feel competent to write reflectively on events in which he had been a participant, at least not for three years.

Although I was clear that I had eventual publication in mind, I was not then set on the format – and indeed indicated to the president and provost that, particularly in light of the claims about my lack of objectivity, I was willing to work with the provost on a joint account of what had happened, a dialogue that could be seeded by my initial document. This was an idea that the president found congenial but from which the provost shrank.

The president followed up by asking me not to do anything with the paper until he and the provost could conduct a thorough review of events surrounding the conference so that lessons could be learned. I was led to believe that, flowing from my concerns, a review would examine the judgment that the York administration had exercised with respect to the conference, particularly when viewed in light of the critical principle of academic freedom. They told me that they were trying to engage a third party to carry out this review and stressed that the objectivity of my account of things was contaminated because I had been too close to the events. The president followed up in an email on his opinion that I had been too close to events to fully grasp them. He suggested that I might need more time to reflect on my experiences and that it would be beneficial to gain additional distance from the events.[8]

If time alone can bring human beings closer to realities embedded in the past, then ironically this book has been produced after a lapse of over three years from the events surrounding the Mapping Models conference. However, the generation of understanding tends to be more complex than the bare passage of time. And many of the events that followed this meeting generated opportunities to check my original data in my "Fieldnotes" document against other sources of information. The first cross-check was delivered to me at the end of the July 13, 2009, meeting.

Provost Monahan passed me a six-page document that was a response to my "Fieldnotes" document: "Preliminary Review of 'Fieldnotes on a Conference.'" The text adopted the literary device of the third-person omniscient perspective: for example, not "I said," "I thought that," "I decided to," but "the Dean said," "the Dean thought," "the Dean decided," aiming for a point of abstraction beyond the real-world location in which we were also both situated: that is, two human beings who occupied the navigational positions of professor and dean/provost. Since the provost had in hand my first account and passed it back to me with a detailed account of his own, from the outset it can be said, ethnographically, that I engaged in respondent validation. This exchange was the first effort at triangulation – at securing a valid account against both real-world and abstracted referents. Once in hand, I folded the six-page "Preliminary Review" into my next iteration of the account.

While I awaited news of the president's review, another member of the Organizing Committee tried to secure publicly available documents on the story that each of us had lived through. My "Fieldnotes" (of first-hand experiences and communications that I had sent and received) contribute to the account in this book, but ultimately they constitute a small part of the data from which the story unfolds. A more copious source of data was found in documents that were publicly accessible but required a request for their release. The materials in Chapters 1 and 4 document for the most part a story through email communications, accessed through the Ontario Freedom of Information and Protection of Privacy Act (FIPPA). As soon as the conference was finished, Mazen Masri submitted a request to the Information and Privacy Office at York University for those emails and documents drafted and received by the senior administrators of the university that related to the conference. In particular, he sought emails to and from the dean of Osgoode Hall Law School that dealt with the conference up until the end of the latter's term at the end of June 2009.

Beginning in June 2006, in light of the fact that universities are publicly funded institutions, Ontario universities were covered by provincial Freedom of Information legislation with the purpose of increasing transparency and accountability. Communications by those who administer universities fall within the public domain, and parties both internal and external to the institution have a right to survey the documentary workings of that administration.

In a number of decisions, the Ontario information and privacy commissioner has ruled that the identity of an individual who applies for access to information under FIPPA is "personal information" that should not be disclosed by an institution except as permitted by section 42 of that statute. FIPPA section 42(1)(d) permits disclosure of personal information to an officer, employee, consultant, or agent of the institution that needs the record in the performance of its duties and where disclosure is necessary and proper in the discharge of the institution's functions. The commissioner has also stated in a "practice" notice on her website that "employees of an institution responding to requests – generally the Freedom of Information and Privacy Co-ordinator and assisting staff – should not identify any requester when processing requests for general records" and that "there is no reason to identify an individual requesting general records to employees outside the Co-ordinator's Office." The commissioner explains that everyone is "entitled to exercise his or her right to access information ... without being unnecessarily identified and without fear of negative repercussions."[9]

When York's Information and Privacy Office sent an interim acknowledgment to Masri, the letter repeated the names of those from whom he was seeking documentation, including those of the dean of Osgoode for the relevant period (Dean Monahan). On the acknowledgment letter, *Provost* Monahan was copied as the presidential delegate to review the request; however, this entailed that he become aware that his emails for the relevant period of his deanship were being sought along with the identity of the requester, Masri. This was an error by York's Information and Privacy Office and has been acknowledged as such by that office to me in person. Masri sent his request under the tenure of the provost who preceded Monahan, and the acknowledgment letter was sent back to him under the fresh tenure of Provost Monahan, and the information officer failed to notice the fact that, by copying the new provost, she would be alerting him to the identity of the requester.

In response to a request for clarification from Provost Monahan about his involvement in Masri's information request, Monahan confirmed in July 2011 that he had received a copy of the letter in which his own emails were requested. He explained that "[information] requests involving academic matters are normally sent to the Provost for review."[10] That is, the provost is normally an "employee who process[es] requests and privacy complaints," in the language of the privacy commissioner's practice directive.[11] He noted that he had recused himself further from the formal access to information process. However, it is clear that he had absorbed that his own emails were being requested – and by whom.

Upon reviewing the details of the information request, Provost Monahan communicated to Masri's doctoral supervisor at Osgoode, Professor Bruce Ryder, that the request had been made. As Ryder noted to me in personal communications in December 2011, Provost Monahan had expressed his view to him on a number of occasions right after the conference that it would be better if we could put the conference behind us.

Subsequent to Provost Monahan mentioning to Professor Ryder that Masri had made an information request on the former dean's emails, Ryder expressed concern to Masri, as his doctoral supervisor looking out for his best interests, about the FIPPA request. Ryder had been unaware that the FIPPA request had been made and did not approve of this pursuit of information. Masri felt compelled to drop the FIPPA request in these circumstances, and, as a result, both Masri and I subsequently turned to the Canadian Association of University Teachers (CAUT), which embarked on a review of the events surrounding the Mapping Models conference, and urged the association to seek out the same documentation. Given that we made the request through CAUT, we were given access to the same body of documents released to the Thompson Review.

The large body of documents released from SSHRC, the Canadian government, and the senior administration and Board of Governors at York University generated a further source of triangulation, beyond the feedback/respondent validation process engaged in one on one with the provost and former AVPRI. To the two sources of data that went into my preliminary inferences about my experiences – the "Fieldnotes" document and its sources and the provost's "Preliminary Review" – were now added a series of communications to which I had not been privy when I wrote my "Fieldnotes." These emails, to the extent that the request was fulfilled, generally elude the temptations of selective memory and misdescription. What a party actually wrote at an actual time and place is released as part of the public record. Even the provost's "Preliminary Review" would need to be reread and corroborated in light of them.

Many of the documents released were surprising to those of us on the Organizing Committee who read them. They were not surprising with respect to the story that we had lived, which had unfolded in their shadow. They explained and confirmed a good deal of what we had gone through and provided further evidence that our interpretations from the field were correct. They were surprising in how much and in what detail they fleshed out the context surrounding our experience of the events. Using them as landmarks, we were eventually able to pinpoint the positions (also in the ideological sense) of the players with considerable exactitude.

The next I heard of President Shoukri's review and its terms of reference after our July 13, 2009, meeting was on the eve of its announcement on July 30th. Despite the review having been prompted by concerns that I had raised with the president and provost earlier in the month, neither my input nor that of the other members of the Organizing Committee had been sought on how the university could learn lessons from what had transpired. And, though the review had been prompted by concerns over the conduct of the administration, the focus of the "lessons learned" was not on that body.

The third party whom the president and provost had hired for the job was former Supreme Court judge Frank Iacobucci. Dean Monahan and President Shoukri had thought that I – one of the conference organizers – had been too close to the events to speak with any objectivity about how the administration had intervened in the conference. The administration, however, had "engag[ed] an external person with the highest level of credibility to help us in evaluating the lessons learned during these events."

The records accessed through York's Information and Privacy Office indicate that Iacobucci did not come up with the terms of reference for his review on his own; nor did the president of the university. Monahan, in the provost's office since July 1st, assisted in drafting the terms of reference for a review that, in its originating impulse, was supposed to include a dispassionate review of his conduct.[12] These terms of reference excluded scrutiny of the administration's – and therefore Patrick Monahan's – conduct.

The provost also marshalled the material that would constitute that review. One of the defences of the university's conduct presented in Provost Monahan's "Preliminary Review" was that York University had provided a considerable amount of support, both moral and pecuniary, for the conference. Now in the office of the provost of York University, Monahan sent out a memo instructing anyone who had had anything to do with the conference to make a submission or communication for Iacobucci that outlined exactly the support that he or she had provided.[13]

The terms of reference themselves (see below) were problematic, both to the conference organizers and, shortly after their issuance, to the Canadian Association of University Teachers. The Osgoode Hall Faculty Association also took issue with them. After a cursory reference to the obligations of universities, the preamble to the terms of reference states that universities are "obliged to ensure the respectful exchange of ideas based on research."[14]

Respect, as a criterion for determining the parameters of academic excellence, is an often cited and misplaced one in the annals of academic freedom. Many ideas are not worthy of respect. To provide one example from an era from which we are sufficiently distanced that the flimsiness of the idea is illuminated, Robert Post and Matthew Finkin, two leading American scholars on academic freedom, provide a highly salient example of the misplaced emphasis on respect and responsibility that compellingly makes the case for the inappropriateness of hinging academic content to the whims of powerful forces outside the academy. The Alabama Polytechnic Institute in 1958 refused to reappoint an assistant professor of economics because he had published a letter in the college newspaper criticizing its opposition to integration. In dismissing the professor, the institute concluded that he had failed to exercise "appropriate restraint" and to "show respect for the opinion of others" and that he had thus been "irresponsible" and "flouted the 'known opinion of the administration.'"[15]

Canada has its own history of hideous ideas associated with the upper echelons of respectable power that should have been met with resounding and disruptive objection, unconcerned about causing offence. For example, in their book *None Is Too Many,* Irving Abella and Harold Tooper point out that the Canadian government did less than the governments of other Western countries to help Jewish refugees between 1933 and 1948.[16] Only 5,000 Jewish refugees entered Canada during this period, the lowest record of any Western country. The head of immigration in Prime Minister Mackenzie King's administration, with King's full support, actively limited Jewish immigration. Both anglophone and francophone elites in general supported the policy of exclusion. As Abella and Tooper recount, in early 1945, reflecting the prevailing anti-Semitic Zeitgeist of the era, an unidentified immigration agent was asked how many Jews would be allowed in Canada after the war. "None is too many," he replied. It can be profoundly difficult for the disenfranchised to have their just cause heard in "respectable" company. Particularly when conjoined with power, some of the most appalling ideas in history have had an unacceptable amount of respect. Rude and raucous dissent can be the most appropriate response to undeserved demands for politesse associated with them.

The terms of reference went on from the framing device of "respectful discourse" to limit the review almost exclusively to the actions of the conference Organizing Committee. Iacobucci was instructed to

- review the experience with the planning, organizing and delivery of the "Mapping" conference;
- advise on the responsibilities of faculty members and University administrators in relation to conferences of this type, particularly conferences sponsored by the University;
- and to provide advice on best practices for the successful planning and execution of such events in light of York University policies and procedures pertaining to academic conferences.[17]

The entire review exercise framed a discussion of academic freedom around the supposed responsibilities of academics, not the responsibilities of academic institutions.

It was the terms of reference for the Iacobucci Review and their failure to scrutinize the conduct of the administration with respect to the Mapping Models conference that prompted CAUT to conduct its own review, initiated in September 2009, just over a month after the Iacobucci Review was announced.

Beyond the controversial terms of reference for the Iacobucci Review, also objectionable was the fact that the invitation for submissions went beyond those who had actually attended the conference and might have some first-hand knowledge of the event; it even went beyond the York community and invited anyone, anywhere, who had an opinion about the conference to submit it. The Organizing Committee was alarmed by this renewal of attention – at the university's prompting – to the research activities of independent scholars. We were deeply troubled that this structure would subject us to yet another round of inquisitorial scrutiny of our decision to hold an academic conference on a topic of intellectual merit to us but objectionable to others as a legitimate subject of inquiry. We were bruised and exhausted by the unbridled imputations that circulated claiming that we were Israel-bashers, anti-Semites, Holocaust deniers, or self-hating Jews; that we were uncredentialled to hold a conference on the Middle East; that our conference participants were insufficiently scholarly or too activist; or that our topic of inquiry was out of bounds in polite society. The structure of the Iacobucci Review invited our critics to assail us all over again. The invitation to renew the assault was compounded by interviews given by President Shoukri and Provost Monahan in the *Canadian Jewish News* in which they actively solicited submissions on the conference.

We immediately wrote to the president voicing our grave concerns that the conference and its organizers had become the focus of the inquiry's scrutiny, objecting to the implication that our work did not promote "a respectful exchange of ideas based on research." Given the terms of reference, respectful exchange appeared to be the axis around which community groups would intervene. The bulleted items, in particular the second two, reproduced all of the problems to which academic freedom at York University had been exposed throughout the conference and its planning, a conference that had been singled out for extraordinary attention and intervention (including by York's administration) because it bothered a particular constituency.

The reference to "conferences of this type" was troubling, for it suggested that there are particular topics (e.g., Israel/Palestine) that should be treated differently from others. It suggested that there are particular responsibilities of faculty members and university administrators in relation to this topic. What else was this conference's "type"? The reference to "such events" in the third term of reference was similarly troubling. Apart from the conference being an event on the topic of Israel/Palestine, it was hard for us to see what else was being contemplated by this phrase. If the university was considering a review of best practices for academic conferences, then why would a conference on Israel/Palestine be singled out for launching the exercise? Through the terms of reference of the Iacobucci Review, it appeared again that the university was capitulating to the idea that it is legitimate for administrations not only to attend to external critics but also to weigh in positively, and further facilitate a general weighing in, on the substance of an academic event.

After receiving our letters of complaint, President Shoukri agreed to meet with members of the Organizing Committee to hear their concerns. He suggested that we speak with Frank Iacobucci on a "preliminary" basis in order to raise our objections about the terms of reference. Only Professor Ryder took President Shoukri up on this suggestion. Despite Ryder's efforts, no change was made to the endeavour on which the university had embarked. We remained sufficiently troubled by the review that York University had set up that our original position was that none of us would participate in it. As the Iacobucci Review unfolded, and given that its terms of reference were structured to preclude an accounting of what York's administration had done, I sought other venues within York that might conduct the work of accountability.

Beyond the formal feedback process and the informal one that began with my July 3, 2009, submission of my "Fieldnotes" document, I provided the provost with an account with the same basic story line in January 2010. I did this in the window after the creation of the Iacobucci and CAUT reviews (July 31 and September 3, 2009, respectively) and before either report was published (March 2010 and October 2011 respectively). And I did so because the Iacobucci Review seemed to be inadequate to the purpose – accountability – for which I had brought my fieldnotes to the attention of the provost and president. Dismayed that they had taken the opportunity to account for administrative conduct and transformed it into the contentious Iacobucci Review, to which none of the conference organizers was prepared to make a submission, I was also concerned that York University was capitulating its internal possibilities for review to an external party (who is not a member of the collegium) and to the external review that CAUT commissioned in September 2009. I believed that York University had the jurisdiction and resources to carry out an internal review, even without the cooperation of the senior administration.

York, like most universities in Canada, is a bicameral institution, bifurcated between two governing bodies: an administration and a Senate. The latter body, having jurisdiction over academic policy, in my view had the jurisdiction to review independently and dispassionately the conduct of the administration throughout the events surrounding the Mapping Models conference. This could have been a review conducted by academics, moreover York University academics, given that the Senate is composed of faculty members from the institution. Such a review could have been carried out through the creation of an ad hoc Senate committee or the activities of an already existent Senate subcommittee. The Academic Policy, Planning, and Research Committee (APPRC) seemed to be the most auspicious such committee.

To bring the attention of the APPRC to the concerns raised in my "Fieldnotes" document, I created a limited-access website on which I posted the same basic account as contained in this manuscript supported by electronic links to the FIPPA emails that had come into my possession by this point. I submitted the link to this website in January 2010 to the committee as a whole and requested that a review internal to York University be set up under its auspices. Since the provost is an ex officio member of the APPRC, he therefore received the link to the website when I sent it out to the committee listserv.

Because I happened also to be a member of the Senate committee, I had every intention of being at the January 14, 2010, meeting that discussed how the university ought to respond to the account, though I was fully prepared to recuse myself if the other members of the committee who had played a role in the conference did so (e.g., Provost Monahan and AVP Dewitt, who were also members of the APPRC Senate committee). However, I gave birth to my son Jacob on January 13th and could not attend the meeting, recused, as it were, by circumstance. Since the meeting was held in camera, I have no idea what transpired except to say that a decision was reached to defer a response from the APPRC until the release of the Iacobucci and CAUT Reports – a response that to date has not been forthcoming. The provost did not recuse himself from the in-camera meeting. The website came to greater prominence as part of the process of cross-checking data upon the release of the Iacobucci Report in March 2010.

When the copious documentation that issued from the Access to Information request that made up a good part of the ethnographic material became available, I sent Iacobucci an email in which I asked whether he had received the bundle of records that had been released to CAUT.[18] I summarized some of the more disquieting revelations from that bundle. I offered to make the entire database available to him, particularly since it seemed to me to be of paramount relevance to an inquiry into academic freedom.

In response to my offer, Iacobucci said that he had been unaware of these emails. But he went on to say that,

> Although I was given and reviewed a large volume of documentary material and written submissions (in addition to conducting interviews with many individuals), I did not ask to see and generally did not review e-mails. President Shoukri directed all administrative units and invited all members of the community to communicate suggestions and recommendations to me and I received many communications. As we have discussed before, the purpose of my review was not to arrive at findings of fact in respect of or against anyone or any group and, accordingly, my mandate did not require me to obtain or examine all relevant documents.[19]

He had no interest in either those cited emails or other records left by the administration with respect to its interventions in an academic event.

When all of my secondary efforts to have the behaviour of the administration scrutinized failed – including the decision of the APPRC not to conduct a review of the administration's conduct – I felt compelled to make a submission to the Iacobucci Review that the university had initiated. Iacobucci, then, received an earlier draft of this book as my submission to his review. My submission included extensive reference, as it does now, to the FIPPA record.

Even with my monograph in hand, Iacobucci assiduously maintained that he was not mandated "to arrive at findings of fact in respect of or against anyone or any group and, accordingly, ... did not require me to obtain or examine all relevant documents," and hence the data remained silent for the university's reviewer.

One further method by which the data of my fieldnotes were triangulated arose from my submission of the same materials to the Thompson Review.

By the time that I made my submission to each review, not only had I incorporated the first "respondent validation" from the provost (his "Preliminary Review" of my "Fieldnotes" document), but I had also gathered a substantial amount of documentation released on the FIPPA request. Professor Thompson combed through my submission and how it interacted with the FIPPA material from my vantage point in the field. He had access to the same considerable body of documentation from that request, and he thus vetted the selective pickings through the considerable field of communications that I chose to highlight. Effectively, with the latter exercise, and given that I now have the benefit of *No Debate* for my own account, I had my account reviewed by a sophisticated third party who facilitated the revision of my understanding of events. Although I welcomed the same scrutiny from Iacobucci, he refused to modify his frame of reference to include and make sense of highly significant data from the field – the FIPPA material.

Given that Iacobucci's review would not include the FIPPA record, and given that neither the APPRC nor the administration was prepared to reckon with what had happened during the Mapping Models conference, and given that *No Debate* was nowhere on the horizon yet, I decided when I learned in April 2010 of the imminent release of the Iacobucci Report that I would make public the website housing an earlier version of this account, including the FIPPA material, so that the record therein could be held up against the Iacobucci Report and it assessed against that more ample background. I sent a link to the website to the faculty listserv, on which the provost remains a member. The Iacobucci Report was not, as a result, released into a void. The public release of the website generated yet another opportunity for respondent validation since it was now "out there" and amenable to, if not positively inviting of, critique. The respondent feedback (and partial accounting) eventually arrived, albeit several months later and through a circuitous route.

With the existence of two reviews, both of which had access to the same data from the field (though one reviewer refused to examine that data), the possibility arose for more than just cross-checking with respondents, cross-checking between researchers (if I can call Iacobucci and Thompson researchers in this exercise), and cross-checking with data sources (my "Fieldnotes" text with the FIPPA material). Because both reviewers were also operating under particular theories of academic freedom, the opportunity arose to check theoretical approaches against each other. This theoretical interplay arose from the approach to academic freedom advanced by Iacobucci in contrast to the responses of other members of the Organizing

Committee, the Osgoode Hall Faculty Association, and *No Debate*. In a sense, the president and provost's response to my "Fieldnotes" paper of creating the Iacobucci Review, which in turn provoked the creation of the CAUT Review, generated an experiment in which the data relating to the Mapping Models conference would be approached via multiple perspectives and hypotheses. In the language of ethnographic research, the thinking about academic freedom that the president and provost proposed as appropriate to the events could be theoretically triangulated – by reference to other theoretical takes on the subject vis-à-vis the conference – on a map of ideas and pinned down.

The Iacobucci Report, issued in March 2010, confirmed the grave concerns of the Organizing Committee over its structure, purpose, and effect. As much as Iacobucci claimed that his review was only forward looking and not intended to single out "anyone or any group," the entire first half was conspicuous in its detailed and backward-looking examination of the conference organizers and their event. He was not interested in the administration's involvement in the conference and preferred to focus extensively on "perceptions" of the event, particularly those devoted to the conference organizers. The report as a whole serves as a vehicle for assessing the credentials, planning, and execution of the conference Organizing Committee. Although Iacobucci acknowledged from the outset that the primary holders of academic freedom are faculty members and students, the driving thrust of the report focuses not on the freedom but on the responsibilities of academics.

The oddness of Iacobucci's position with respect to the existing record, as well as the damaging and skewed slant of the final report, were taken up by Professor Ryder in recent and earlier critiques of the Iacobucci Report. The report quotes Ryder as saying that he "recognized that the conference presented a number of difficult challenges for the administration, almost from its inception." Iacobucci claimed that Ryder "expressed the view [for the record] that, in the end, the administration had taken all the right steps including the upholding of academic freedom."

I sent an email to Professor Ryder in December 2011 and asked, in light of the recent release of *No Debate*, whether he wanted to provide a final comment on both reports, Iacobucci's and Thompson's. In response to my request for feedback, he wrote,

> I was really pleased with [the Thompson Report]. I thought he did a careful, balanced job throughout and reached measured, thoughtful conclusions.

> I experienced some of Patrick's and David's interventions as disrespectful of our efforts and scholarly objectives and the challenges we had grappled with throughout the planning process. I didn't experience their interventions as inappropriate pressure, because I felt the organizing committee was strong and always in charge. The organizing committee was free to disregard the suggestions Patrick or David or anyone else asked us to consider if we didn't decide to pursue them after deliberating among ourselves and getting advice from advisory committee members and others.
>
> The email trail provides disturbing evidence of a lack of respect for our efforts and scholarly objectives. I haven't changed my mind about the Iacobucci Report since we prepared our collective letter to him about the draft report back in April 2010. I was shocked and appalled when the Iacobucci Report was released without incorporating our comments on the draft in any meaningful way. By repeating ill-informed negative assessments of the conference, many of them demonstrably false, and by ignoring the many scholarly best practices we had followed in conference planning, the Iacobucci Report tread very close to defamation, in my view, and at the very least was deeply disrespectful of our efforts. It was also outrageous that Iacobucci studiously ignored the inappropriate communications by members of the York administration that had come to light. Jon did us all a great service – as I expect your book will too – by dissecting the administration's actions and communications so carefully. I agree with all of Jon's conclusions, including the conclusions he reached about inappropriate behaviour on the part of David and Patrick. Despite the disturbing and disrespectful communications that have come to light, in the end, the conference took place at the time, place and manner we had planned. The university secured the space and supported the conference in many ways, including issuing the statements on academic freedom and paying for the security costs. In the end, despite the inappropriate behaviour along the way that you and Jon have documented, the university did take all of the right steps. The conference was therefore a triumph of academic freedom, as Jon noted and as I said to Frank.[20]

Ryder clearly thought that Iacobucci had not diligently cross-checked his data and analysis against other points of reference and data from the field – the feedback that the Organizing Committee had provided to the first draft of his report. His assessment of both reports and his affirmation of the documentation generated by my website (which, beyond the original

"Fieldnotes" document, is all that he had access to at that point) and *No Debate* provide a form of theoretical triangulation that generates an account from another participant differentially located in the setting. *No Debate* itself takes up the submission that Ryder formally made to the CAUT Review, and, to the extent that this book relies on *No Debate* as a source of data, this adds to the diverse data lending detail and density to the map of events.

The Osgoode Hall Faculty Association (OHFA) echoed the concerns of the Organizing Committee about the Iacobucci Report and sent a strong and clear message to the York Senate voicing their objections on April 26, 2010.[21] By that time, my website, with its cornucopia of FIPPA documents, was publicly available. In light of the collective understanding of the implicit and explicit norms of the institution represented by the OHFA, the critique generated by the association provides a source of common-sense expectations regarding academic freedom, common to the Faculty of Law, which housed three of the players associated with the conference: two professors and a former dean. The views of the OHFA, interpretive in nature, allow for the multiplication of perspectives and hypotheses with which data can be analyzed, generating yet another means to cross-check data.

Where Iacobucci remained unmoved by the documentation released under the Access to Information request, the OHFA was "surprised and dismayed by the role played by several members of the University's senior administration in relation to the Mapping Models conference." On the basis of this documentation, they concluded that "senior administrators were inappropriately pressuring conference organizers to make significant changes to the conference programme and speakers, to submit to internal oversight and review, or to make other modifications of the event or its planning." The released emails "reveal a troubling history of inappropriate interference." Clarifying that the OHFA did "not believe a complete record of the role played by York University officials has yet emerged," their assessment based on the available record revealed activity that went "well beyond the acceptable boundaries of administrative involvement in a scholarly event."

The OHFA had signalled to Iacobucci, when the terms of reference for his review were announced, that, congruent with the concerns of the Organizing Committee, "The Association considered the University's decision to conduct an external review to be a potential threat to academic freedom, not an affirmation of it." On that basis, much like the original impulse of the Organizing Committee, the association had refused to participate in it. In response to the Iacobucci Report itself, the OHFA considered "the Iacobucci Report to be unsound and unreliable. First, the Report both jeopardizes academic freedom and fails to consider the troubling conduct of York officials. Second, the process on which the Report is based was fundamentally unfair." The third objection to the report that the OHFA raised was the revelation that, despite the characterization of the review as impartial, the reviewer had been hired by the university as its lawyer to create the document.

In response to a request about whether submissions to the Iacobucci Review were themselves subject to the Freedom of Information Act, Iacobucci noted that

> my files in connection with my mandate are not subject to disclosure under FIPPA. I was retained in my capacity as counsel to Torys LLP and consequently my complete file is subject to solicitor and client privilege. I should add that that was my intention from the outset and an account has been established at Torys LLP for this purpose.[22]

The president of the university confirmed the understanding of Iacobucci that he was working on the file as a lawyer, with the university as his client, by saying that he "defer[red] entirely to [Iacobucci's] view of his status, his role and responsibilities, and therefore his claim of solicitor and client privilege."[23] Iacobucci was paid $25,000 to produce his report.

The OHFA[24] further faulted the Iacobucci Report on substantive grounds, noting that it "claims not to make findings of fact or fault. However, it presents a series of anonymous and unmediated assertions about the merits of the conference and its organizers."

> Mr. Iacobucci acknowledges that "relatively few of those who made submissions had been attendees at the Conference" (p. 25); and states, " ... I am cognizant of the fact that a significant element of self-selection was involved in how participants in this review came to be involved in this review" (p. 26). But he gives no serious consideration to the implications of the skewed nature of this participation. Instead, Mr. Iacobucci asserts his belief that the Report is "adequately representative" (p. 3).

In the OHFA's view,

> It is fundamentally unfair that the Report has allowed a select group of anonymous critics to impugn the conference organizers in a highly public manner. The Report repeats allegations against our colleagues, who are

> themselves easily identified, without giving them proper notice or a meaningful opportunity to reply (other than a limited opportunity to point out "factual errors" in a pre-release draft of the Report).

Ultimately, the OHFA concluded that "the Iacobucci Report is fundamentally flawed on procedural and substantive grounds and that it should be rejected in its entirety." Yet, despite the OHFA urging "the University administration to honour its commitment to academic freedom by withdrawing the Report," and despite the association's request that it be removed from the university website, where it sits as an ongoing provocation, York opted to leave the Iacobucci Report as its singular response to the concerns that I raised in July 2009 about how it had conducted itself over the course of a controversial academic event.

Public access to the website generated pressure on the administration to respond – to account for itself. Silence in the face of my "Fieldnotes" document was one thing; continued silence in the face of concerns raised by the Osgoode Hall Faculty Association was another. In response to the website being made public, the provost called a meeting with the OHFA in June 2010 to respond to their concerns in light of the FIPPA material that they had become apprised of for the first time. Although the meeting was "off the record" at the provost's insistence, I attended it and posed questions that, at least informally in light of the provost's restriction, allowed me to submit the data that I had accumulated to a personalized response.

The other leg of the theoretical triangulation facilitated by inauguration of the Iacobucci Review came from the second review that had been set in motion. *No Debate* also reviewed the Iacobucci Report and arrived at findings very similar to those of the OHFA, and Professor Thompson added a critique of the model of academic freedom that the former justice had promoted. *No Debate* generated more data for my own project, including more theoretical material from which to situate my position.

Thompson's examination of Iacobucci's work began with the structure of the report itself. Despite a clarification of his mandate – "my review does not in any way mean that I will be making findings against any individual group, or organization" – Iacobucci "included extensive criticism of the conference organizers, in the form of summaries of testimony by unnamed persons," concluded Thompson. As he observed, "the structure of Iacobucci's report was such that insufficiently attentive readers could be left with the impression that some of these criticisms [submitted by anonymous parties] were, in some sense, findings."[25] Because Iacobucci did not examine the testimony submitted against the facts but simply laid out in summary form what had been submitted to him, his lack of analysis effectively rendered these submissions into findings.

Professor Thompson provided two examples from Iacobucci's undigested "perspectives on the conference" that illustrate the problematic structure of his report. Thompson noted that Iacobucci simply said, in the passive voice, that "it was suggested that the Conference organizers were not experienced in the subject matter of the Conference."[26] Thompson was highly critical of this repetition of damaging allegations – I myself wrote a letter to Iacobucci pointing out the defamatory quality of this reiteration of unsubstantiated rumour. Thompson noted that

> this unmediated assertion had been made by several conference critics in the months immediately preceding the conference, notwithstanding the facts that the organizers had been awarded a large SSHRC conference grant on the basis of the detailed program they submitted, along with their own scholarly credentials and a detailed list of proposed speakers, and that they had the assistance of an eleven-person International Advisory Board, including very senior, internationally distinguished scholars, in developing the program. Arguably, this unmediated assertion had the effect of personally and professionally discrediting the organizers.[27]

This problematic reiteration of submissions was also illustrated in Iacobucci's unmediated repetition of an anonymous complaint that "the organizers had not consulted more broadly and had not, for example, sought the assistance of any member of York's Centre for Jewish Studies."[28] Apart from ignoring the critical consultative role of our international Advisory Committee and being inaccurate – in that Professor Ryder and I had had several meetings with members of the Centre for Jewish Studies and invited them to join our Advisory Committee – Iacobucci left the impression that it was somehow necessary or essential for the Jewish studies department to be consulted on any academic project having to do with Israel/Palestine.

The other significant finding of *No Debate* regarding Iacobucci's work related to the theory of academic freedom that drove Iacobucci's final recommendations. As Professor Thompson noted, "the other main pillar supporting Iacobucci's recommendations is a diminished – indeed reactionary – conception of academic freedom."[29]

The problematic theory begins with the opening of the Iacobucci Report, which indicates that the conference "str[uck] at the heart of deeply held religious and political beliefs."[30] This opening sets the stage for the view that an appropriate juncture for the restraint of academic freedom is when it offends the religious or political views of a particular group. As Thompson noted, "a reasonable inference [from Iacobucci's opening] is that the beliefs of some persons may trump the rights, possibly even the beliefs, of others in the academy."[31] The anxiety that this approach to academic freedom might constitute a system of prior approval and restraint of academic events, with the university as an arbitrator directing that an event be modified or cancelled on the basis of offence taken, was consolidated in Iacobucci's recommendation of a panel that would establish the basic responsibilities of academics. Iacobucci proposed that academics themselves participate in the "necessary work to instigate changes to the academic freedom policies and procedures at York" by establishing a set of "best practices." As Thompson pointed out, this proposal ignores the already extensive work that academics across the country have done in designing collective agreements that clearly lay out what is constituted by the right of academic freedom. Thompson noted that this panel of academics carrying out what Iacobucci considered their "necessary work" would embroil them in an exercise of self-censorship. To the extent that a "Best Practices" document, or a "Handbook on Academic Freedom" (both recommendations of the Iacobucci Report), were to emerge from the exercise that Iacobucci proposed, they might be considered interpretive standards for the collective agreement. As a result, and despite Iacobucci's repeated assertions that his recommendations were "not intended to be restrictive of academic freedom," Thompson found that his report "recommended a mechanism of institutional censorship."[32]

The central component of the "necessary work" that Iacobucci would assign to academics so that they might constrain the right that is currently entrenched in their collective agreements, bargained for almost universally with universities across the country, relates to "civil discourse." That this is the central worry of the Iacobucci Report is not surprising in light of the mandate of his review that was suffused with the preambulatory assertion that universities are "obliged to ensure the respectful exchange of ideas based on research." The failure of the mandate to provide a source for the supposed obligation to ensure "respectful exchange" is reproduced in the final report as well. Iacobucci asserted without foundation that "the concept of civil discourse is expressly and impliedly intended to be present in academic discussion. Likewise, mutual respect for those who are spoken with or listened to in academic settings is highlighted." If the value of "civil discourse" is "expressly" intended to be present in academic discussion, then it should have been easy for Iacobucci to cite at least one reference. As Thompson noted, "[Iacobucci] cites no significant document in support of his assertion [about the obligation of academics to be respectful in their exchanges], possibly because the history of academic freedom does not provide support."[33] The standard of civil discourse that Iacobucci imputed to academic discourse would, in fact, find a home in the setting with which he is more acquainted professionally: the judicial setting.

The proceedings that unfold in front of judges are constrained, explicitly, by requirements of judicial decorum. The *Ethical Principles for Judges*[34] laid down by the Canadian Judicial Council are clear that judges are obliged to "treat everyone before the court with appropriate courtesy." "Civil discourse," "respect," "dignity," an "obligation to be sensitive," and "responsibility" – criteria that Iacobucci imputes to the academic mission – are core requirements of the judicial enterprise. The commentaries to the *Ethical Principles* evoke deep historical roots for these obligations relating to courtroom decorum: "Socrates counseled judges to hear courteously, answer wisely, consider soberly and to decide impartially. These judicial virtues are all aspects of judicial diligence."[35]

There are further constraints on judges that underline the very different nature of the exercise in which they are engaged compared with that of scholars. Under the subheading "Principle of Impartiality," which relates to political activity, the obligation is laid out that "judges should refrain from conduct such as ... participation in public discussion which, in the mind of a reasonable, fair minded and informed person, would undermine confidence in a judge's impartiality with respect to issues that could come before the courts." This principle guiding judicial conduct explicitly counsels "the avoidance of public participation in controversial political discussions."[36] The commentary that illuminates the principles provides justification for this curtailment of a fundamental freedom – of expression – that is constitutionally secured for other citizens. The constraint derives from the office of judge and its functional demand that public confidence be maintained in a judge's independence and impartiality. As the commentary notes,

> in defining the appropriate degree of involvement of the judiciary in public debate, there are two fundamental considerations. The first is whether the judge's involvement could reasonably undermine confidence in his or her

> impartiality. The second is whether such involvement may unnecessarily expose the judge to political attack or be inconsistent with the dignity of judicial office. If either is the case the judge should avoid such involvement.[37]

It is critical to the practice of judging legal disputes that "a judge must be and be seen to be free to decide honestly and impartially on the basis of the law and the evidence, without external pressure or influence and without fear of interference from anyone."[38] And it is critical to this practice that judges manifest decorum and refrain from taking political positions on controversial matters. These features are very much part of the culture and practical morality of formal dispute resolution in a society that values impartial justice under law.

But these are not the features of the culture of academia. And it appears that former Supreme Court justice Iacobucci confounded the two and confused the task of judges with that of academics. That he conflated judicial independence and the academic mission is evident from his analysis of the 1915 document released by the American Association of University Professors (AAUP). Iacobucci claimed that the AAUP's Declaration of Principles on Academic Freedom and Academic Tenure "draws an analogy in some respects between the duties and professional self-regulation of academics and judges. I agree with," he continued, "and endorse that analogy. There is a similarity in the fulfilling of its role, particularly in the rendering of its decisions, and the academic freedom of the professoriate to pursue their teaching, research, and academic activities."[39] Thompson pointed out that Iacobucci misconstrued the AAUP declaration: "The centre (and centrepiece) of the passage [that Iacobucci] quoted ... is the following: 'So far as the university teacher's independence of thought and utterance is concerned – *though not in other regards* – the relationship of professors to trustees may be compared to that between judges of the federal courts and executive who appoints them'" (emphasis added). Thompson pointed out that "it is abundantly clear from other passages in the *Declaration* that the qualification 'though not in other regards' was of fundamental importance to the drafting committee and the new association that adopted it."[40]

The only permissible analogy between judges and academics to be drawn from the declaration is that the standards to which academics and judges should aspire be set by fellow academics and fellow judges respectively rather than by outside parties with interests not coincident with the academic or judicial mission. Judges retain both the reality and the appearance of impartiality by not handing over the project of impartial justice to the overview of masters whose special interests would warp that enterprise to their ends, and this goal is facilitated by the obligation of judges to *refrain* from cultivating political contacts and making political pronouncements. The goal of impartiality that weighs the voices of powerful parties on the same scale as the voices of the powerless – captured in the venerable legal dictum *audi alteram partem* – is *facilitated* by the obligations of decorum. But these are not the means by which the academic community protects its impartiality. And the importation of these values from the judicial context into the academic one in fact poses a potential danger to the latter.

As Professor Thompson pointed out, "professors need academic freedom as a defense against those who wish to circumscribe dissent."[41] The various declarations on academic freedom issuing from academic communities themselves, including the definition formulated by the Canadian Association of University Teachers that is commonly included in the collective agreements of faculty members across the country, are particularly circumspect about the insidious power of orthodoxy and conventional thinking to set the scope for what is considered appropriate academic work. Indeed, the very respectability of conventional thought, and the embedded power that arises from the social upsets that ensue upon offended sensibilities, comprise a common enemy of independent thought. It is particularly nefarious because respectability is such an ineffable yet hegemonic value. The demands of respectability can be insidious precisely because they go without saying – as they come without saying. The demands of decorum reinforce multiple power dynamics – some legitimate and others not – yet the foundation of their claims on us is often inscrutable. The wariness that the academic community should exercise on the often bewitching demands of convention is laid out in the 1915 declaration from which Iacobucci selectively cited. Indeed, "the dangers connected with the existence in a democracy of an overwhelming and concentrated public opinion" are precisely what render a maximally unrestrained academic freedom a force for the common good. As the declaration notes,

> the tendency of modern democracy is for men to think alike, to feel alike, and to speak alike. Any departure from the conventional standards is apt to be regarded with suspicion. Public opinion is at once the chief safeguard of a democracy, and the chief menace to the real liberty of the individual. It almost seems as if the danger of despotism cannot be wholly averted under any form of government. In a political autocracy there is no effective public

opinion, and all are subject to the tyranny of the rule; in a democracy there is political freedom, but there is likely to be a tyranny of public opinion.

The declaration goes on to assert that "an inviolable refuge from such tyranny should be found in the university."[42]

As a result of the professional obligation of academics to ensure that orthodoxy and convention do not obscure their search for the truth, rendering it banal and platitudinous, their research is often provocative and challenging. As Professor Thompson indicated, "discourse in the academy is characteristically disputatious and may often appear (and occasionally may even be) somewhat uncivil ... Contrary to what Iacobucci suggests, strong disagreement, strongly expressed, does not necessarily entail lack of professional respect."[43] Subservience to "civil discourse" and "the obligation to be sensitive" – and indeed to "collegiality" – can be a positive hindrance to the fructification of ideas that, in the words of the declaration, "though still distasteful to the community as a whole, may be allowed to ripen until finally, perchance, it may become a part of the accepted intellectual food of the nation or of the world."[44]

That there is no obligation – and that there ought not to be – on academics to couch their findings or their exchanges so as to be "sensitive" to the sensibilities of those who might take offence is strongly affirmed in *No Debate.* Any anxiety attendant upon society leaving academics to decide whether or not they prefer to come across as rude and disrespectful is largely mitigated, as Professor Thompson pointed out, by the fact that "society has expectations regarding the behavior and discourse of judges because they have the power to deprive people of their liberty or property – a power not normally possessed by academics."[45] Na'ama Carmi, for example, had no greater obstacle between her and an obligation to listen to material that she found offensive than the chairs that stood between her and the exit.

The suggestion that any analogy between judges and scholars extends to an obligation among academics to avoid "public participation in controversial political discussions" is also challenged in *No Debate.* This point is highly relevant to the events surrounding the Mapping Models conference given the repeated references to some supposed obligation of the Organizing Committee to remain "neutral" or manifest "balance." CIJA's statement conjured up this supposed obligation of neutrality: "The organizers have procured a few *balanced* speakers of high repute, but this is certainly not enough to characterize the conference as one of high academic integrity or good scholarship" (emphasis added). The dean of Osgoode referred repeatedly to the criterion of balance in his interventions with us. Examples of the consistent demand of us and our program, and indeed of our Organizing Committee, for some supposed ideal of ideologically cleansed scholarship course through this ethnography. Such demands are suspect in the first place – to wit, Piterberg's quip that "it is well known, of course, that critical works about Zionism or Israel are 'polemical' (or worse), whereas favourable ones are scholarly."[46] But, more importantly, they are fundamentally wrong-headed.

The principle of neutrality does have a place within academia. It has two edges, one that imposes an obligation of neutrality, and the other that does not. The obligation of neutrality falls on the university itself and is imposed on its administrators. This is laid out with great eloquence in one of Canada's leading and seminal statements on academic freedom, one that set the tone for the current Canadian standards for academic freedom, which are, as Professor Thompson pointed out, "better protected on a nation-wide basis than in any other country" and "more comprehensive than the conception expressed in either the 1915 *Declaration* of the AAUP or the joint 1940 *Statement* of the AAUP and the AAC (American Association of Colleges), which were both written in cautious, circumspect language, reflecting the tenor of their times."[47] The transformative moment in Canadian history for academic freedom came with the 1958 publication of the report on the dismissal of Harry Crowe by the United College in Winnipeg on the ground that "the attitude toward religion revealed by [a letter written by Professor Crowe calling religion a 'corrosive force'] is incompatible with the traditions and objectives of United College."[48] Two professors were called upon to write a report of that incident: Vernon Fowke and Bora Laskin (the Fowke-Laskin Report). They emphasized the right of professors to "utter and publish opinions in the course of teaching and research ... without liability of official censure or discipline."[49] Ten years later Laskin (then a justice of the Ontario Court of Appeal and eventually a Supreme Court justice) drafted a report for York University in his capacity as the chair of a Presidential Committee on the Rights and Responsibilities of York University. In this report, he forcefully laid out the obligation of universities to observe a principle of neutrality in their dealings with independent scholars and their academic activities:

> An essential characteristic of [the university] experience must be a capacity to tolerate unsettling opinions; and another must be the absence of

> any official doctrine or ideology. The University as a corporate community must be neutral so as to permit ... widely diverse and conflicting views, except when those views are inimical to the values and purpose of the University itself.[50]

The university, in fulfilling its mission to advance knowledge in society and to protect the values associated with that mission (most critically the value of academic freedom), has an obligation to remain neutral. Suspicions that a university has been captured by the interests of any particular group in society generate considerable risk for the reputation at its core – academic integrity.

The surest way to harm a university's reputation, then, is for its administrators to compromise on the neutrality demanded of them in their capacity to "tolerate unsettling opinions." For this reason, the several claims that Provost Monahan made in response to my requests for feedback on the harm that this work can cause need answers. His July 2011 submission to me (and his various submissions to the CAUT Inquiry) repeated a refrain submitted in his defence. He noted that he was

> stunned to learn [originally from the production of the "Fieldnotes" document] that, even prior to the conference being held, efforts were underway by Susan to create an alternative narrative of events. This alternative narrative bears little relation to my own understanding and, in my view, is clearly at odds with the contemporaneous written record taken as a whole. I was and am dismayed at the harm that this alternative narrative causes to the law school, to collegial relationships on campus, and to York University itself.[51]

The record has now been laid out a sufficient number of times and from a sufficient number of perspectives that the reader can assess whether the account in this book is at odds with all of the narratives and documentation taken as a whole. I am also unsure that it would be proper to characterize a good deal of the dean's interventions with me as "collegial." What is of greater relevance is the claim that my account will harm the law school and the university.

In light of the resounding letter from the Osgoode Hall Faculty Association, signed by almost every one of its professors, active and emeritus, in protest over the actions of the government and the Social Sciences and Humanities Research Council, and in light of the several letters of protest against the threat to academic freedom constituted by the Iacobucci Review and Report, it seems that Osgoode Hall Law School itself, through the body of its faculty (the closest thing to its constitutive body), has acquitted itself impeccably with respect to its academic integrity.

Professor Thompson also noted in *No Debate* that the Organizing Committee "went to extraordinary lengths to explain the nature of the conference to any persons and organizations, both on and off campus, that had expressed concerns about it." Thompson went on to note that

> they also went to extraordinary lengths to secure speakers/presenters who were well-informed on the conference topics, and who represented a wide range of views concerning statehood models for Israel-Palestine. They achieved substantial balance in their view represented, even though balance was not a component of their funding application to the York U50 Committee, and also was not a SSHRC requirement.[52]

In other words, our conference, carried out exactly as we had intended, did nothing to damage the reputation of York University or Osgoode Hall Law School.

Professor Thompson affirmed (and I have no reason to quibble with this finding) that the president of York University, Mamdouh Shoukri, "consistently defended the principle of academic freedom throughout the course of events, as well as the academic freedom of the conference organizers and the academic integrity of their program."[53] Similarly, Thompson found that "York University's Board of Governors conducted themselves in the best university traditions to defend academic freedom and university autonomy, and to help ensure that an appropriate academic event was held as planned and scheduled, notwithstanding the extraordinary opposition to the event."[54] In other words, the reputations of the university and the law school – which are hinged on academic integrity and thus on academic freedom – were not tarnished by the revelations of the "written record taken as a whole."

The findings of inappropriate conduct stemming from that record speak to the conduct of York's senior administration in its intervention in an independent academic work. These kinds of administrative interventions in academic freedom most perturb the academic mission of the university – and threaten its reputation.

As I noted above, the principle of neutrality has two edges in academia. While neutrality is demanded of universities as corporate communities, the academic community in Canada has endorsed a very different standard with respect to political engagement for academics. To the extent that a dominant view has emerged from a culture that is often characterized by its disputatious ethos – even on the topic of academic freedom itself – the standard for academics in terms of engagement is articulated in an article of the collective agreement of York University's faculty members (which is echoed in collective agreements for faculty members across the country): "Academic freedom does not require neutrality on the part of the individual, nor does it preclude commitment on the part of the individual. Rather, academic freedom makes such commitment possible."[55]

That scholarly work can be single-mindedly tasked to the pursuit of truth and simultaneously engaged, indeed committed, is not a simple or straightforward proposition. And it is to this complex issue of the relationship between scholarship and engagement that I turn for the concluding part of this book. Before I do so, however, I need to pull several threads together that have run through this chapter.

The thread that I need to pull through has been looping through this account of the account. I have consistently returned to the issue of triangulation and the validation of data by cross-referencing with other data and other sources beyond the world as revealed to the participant/observer. I need to make sense of that running theme, which is my next endeavour.

Objectivity

As I have indicated, the seed for this work arose from my participation in the events related to the Mapping Models conference. Early on, I became aware that the events that we were going through were pregnant with an intrigue. The intrigue began to emerge as the outlines of a story that can be told from beginning to end, one that organizes experiences. The story began to reverberate with narrative truth, what Donald Spence defines as "the criterion we use to decide when a certain experience has been captured to our satisfaction."[56] As he notes, narrative truth "depends on continuity and closure, and the extent to which the fit of the pieces take[s] on an aesthetic finality. Narrative truth is what we have in mind when we say that such and such is a good story, that a given explanation carries conviction, that one solution to a mystery must be true."[57] But the narrative that was beginning to emerge had many points of contact with a referential world. It was not simply a good story but also a story rooted in documentable experience. The narrative, in that case, needs to be more than coherent and compelling if it claims to be valid. If narrative organizes experience, this story was ignited by the interaction between organizing ideas and actual events.

The organizing rubric under which I began to pull the story out of the data was academic freedom. Going into the conference organizing, I had already absorbed an inchoate theory of academic freedom, as most academics do, and this inchoate theory about the corner of the social world in which I spend my daily life – academia – both created expectations and provoked a heightened attention to the field once they were thwarted. Provoked, I began to observe, attending both to the field in which I was immersed and to the story that I might write. Because my expectations about appropriate conduct were being thwarted, I was aware that the story that I might write was also an account that I might give.

I was not alone in this exercise of actively digesting my social world – while creating it. The Organizing Committee had many collective conversations about the significance of the events. And I had many one-on-one conversations with the other three organizers. We were working through what we were going through. The data generated by a social world are potentially unlimited and can theoretically be navigated through from a million different directions, but an intrigue sets out a trajectory through it, uncertain originally where it might lead, in part because events were still unfolding and we were not the only ones shaping the field.

Regarding the central intrigue of academic freedom – the subject of this book – it might be asked whether my role as a participant, with active demands on me to stand ground or capitulate, skewed my position as a neutral observer. Given that I was attuned early on to the story (and the account) as it was unfolding, it might seem that I generated the narrative threads from which it is constituted and that the final product thus has less "objectivity" since I was figuratively writing the story as it unfolded – and literally doing so, to the extent that I was already gathering the data in my sense-making efforts. In other words, it might be claimed that I guided my conduct according to the story that I was writing.

This issue of the role of participants in the field that they observe is not novel, not for ethnography, and indeed not for the larger social world. Despite early anthropological pretensions that the army of ethnographers examining the exotic was somehow not part of the social world being studied, it is now widely recognized that social research is never insulated from the biography of the researcher or from the social world from which the ethnographer hails. Rather, the discipline of ethnography acknowledges that social researchers are part of the world that they study. The researcher's influence on the context that he or she is scrutinizing becomes, rather, a further source of data. This is not terribly different from what social actors routinely do as they learn from the contexts in which they move about the significance of their conduct.

If I behaved differently because of my growing cognizance that there was a story to be told, that self-awareness pushed me to make my interventions regarding academic freedom more forcefully and to provide ample opportunities for others to apprehend my position and respond accordingly. I did not, however, conjure up the reactions of others out of my mind. Others in the field intervened according to the stories that they themselves were writing, as ordinary makers of social meaning do all the time. This work submits those various stories (to the extent that they can be discerned) to the scrutiny of a master narrative about academic freedom.

But the larger question of whether, and to what extent, the account that I offer is undermined since I was a participant in it is valid. I have noted the observation that those in the field, ethnographers included, are not privileged commentators on their conduct and experiences. Not only is memory corruptible, but also participants are subject to undercurrents that move them to misrecognize, misdescribe, and misinterpret what they have lived through. And interests, even if only reputational, come into play in efforts to decipher the significance of conduct. It might appear, then, that there is no secure foundation upon which definitive or valid accounts can arise in light of how knowledge is inflected by the position in the field occupied by a particular participant/observer. At various points, this was the position taken by the provost in his responses to my various submissions to him of my account to date. I have laid out the threads in this chapter to counter that position and now need to pull them together.

Epistemological charges related to ethnomethodology first arose in the meeting with the provost and president triggered by my "Fieldnotes" document. The proximity of time was invoked, with the president agreeing with the provost that I needed more time to reflect on my experiences. The suggestion of a corruption of intimacy persisted throughout my exchanges with the provost in the back and forth of the feedback process, from his July 2011 counternarrative that "support[ed] only one conclusion" to his assertion in the same document that "it is simply not possible for there to be any meaningful peer review of this evidence [that which derived from my interpretations of conversations] and, thus, the analysis and conclusions that are said to flow from it."[58] The assumption underlying these hesitations is that intimacy and proximity obscure where detachment and distance reveal. There is also a suggestion that discernible validity might not, in fact, be ultimately possible in the context of accounts in which people report on their own experiences.

Intimacy can indeed corrupt understanding; however, that form of corruption might be weighted against the corruption that derives from the illusion that there is an Archimedean point of neutrality, uninflected by a personal, social, cultural, or political point of view, that can disclose the "objective" truth about the activities in which human beings are engaged. A point of view is present in this "objective" approach to the study of human meaning; however, more perilously than accounts such as ethnography that are more conspicuously perspectival, the point of view in dispassionate and "removed" accounts is often occluded to the detriment of some of those matters being observed.

Timothy Mitchell's *Colonizing Egypt* is a brilliant study of the illusion of the dispassionate, "objective" observer and the projects to which that illusion has been hitched.[59] In his analysis, anthropology itself and the "ethnographic gaze" are implicated in the orientalism that facilitated the colonization of the Middle East. Dispassionate detachment encourages the objectification of a class or group of human beings, and this objectification in turn feeds into the surveillance and control of those subjects – a word that is susceptible to double meaning. Intimacy can corrupt the truth, but it also has the power to disclose the world in ways that a detached, putatively "objective" perspective occludes.

The administration's deployment of a former judge to scrutinize the events around the conference smacked of this kind of misrecognition and occlusion of the social world associated with that form of scrutiny. It borrowed from a story about the legal enterprise that construes the discipline of law as being primarily about the pursuit of truth, not the narration of stories. Ultimately, that story itself (the borrowed legitimacy of a former judge acting throughout as a lawyer) was transformed into data, revealed and scrutinized in the OHFA response to his terms of reference and eventual report and in the analysis of *No Debate.*

The ongoing relationship between data and intrigue – between a field and the account that emerges from it – raises questions about how one might counter the skepticism of a claim that none of it is susceptible to meaningful peer review, that there are no grounds for regarding one account as valid and another not.

Reliance on a single piece of data carries with it the risk that an inference drawn from it might be incorrect. That much I have been claiming throughout this chapter. So, for example, fieldnotes, as a preliminary culling of the intrigue in a field of potentially infinite data, if drawn solely from my interpretations of conversations, would be precarious. But it cannot be said that they are necessarily unreliable. That they might be contaminated by interest and misrecognition does not suggest that they must *logically* be regarded with suspicion. Indeed, findings of misrecognition and misdescription at some point rely on a similar base of observation of the field, from the vantage points of other, more reliable, observers. Their reliability is dependent on their familiarity with the field, which is difficult to manage without participation in it, virtually impossible without relying on the primary data – that is, views and interpretations – of at least some participants. The proposition that participant observation is necessarily unreliable eliminates the prospect of corrective interpretation.

It is conceivable that I could have presented nothing but my interpretations of various conversations between us to the provost and that we agreed about what happened. No further doubt might arise between us about the meaning of what transpired. In the busy cross-checking and confirming of data and interpretations that the conference organizers engaged in as we were going through events, there were many occasions when an account that one of us aired found confirmation in the sense-making projects of others in the field. And indeed there was a common ground of understanding between the provost and me in our various exchanges, even beyond the mundane, such as mutual reliance on a shared temporal framework and the physical location of events. For example, though built upon an interpretive base, when the provost noted as a fact in his July 2011 feedback that, "despite many challenges and difficulties, the Mapping Models conference was ultimately a success," he affirmed the possibilities for participant observation to generate credible and shared understandings of the world. As Hammersley and Atkinson note regarding the temptation to see reflexivity – the recognition that social researchers are part of the social world that they study – as undermining a commitment to accurate or true accounts, "we can work with what we currently take to be knowledge, while recognizing that it may be erroneous; and engaging in systematic inquiry where doubt seems justified."[60] At the intersection of many points of our narratives, the provost and I shared a base of unquestioned, undoubted, knowledge.

In my first "Fieldnotes" document, I supplemented my observations from the field with the data from email communications, sensing that (in light of prior conduct) the provost might not necessarily share my interpretations on first blush. And indeed the reference on July 13, 2009, to my problematic proximity to events and the administration's pursuit of a more "objective" narrator thereafter indicated that there would be a need for more systematic inquiry – as doubts had been raised.

Once those doubts had been raised, however, the original account with the inferences that it drew went through extensive cross-checking with other sources of data, other participants in the field differentially located in the setting, and other theoretical takes and positions on the same events. Furthermore, the generation of new accounts triggered by the "Fieldnotes" document allowed for the comparison of data on different points of a temporal continuum with earlier analysis consumed by subsequent interpretation, the latter itself transformed into a dense body of data and subject to further refinement and correction. From an ethnographic point of view, the intense form of respondent validation constituted by my informal and formal requests for feedback and clarification constitutes an uncommon and exceptional form of triangulation, adding to the already considerable bearings situated in the wealth of data sources from which I sought to locate my position and consolidate my account.

All of these mechanisms are the means by which ethnographers render their accounts of the world. They are the means by which valid accounts of the field are generated and by which those accounts are corrected. While the legal idiom of "evidence" was favoured by the provost in his July 2011 feedback – and implicitly in the endorsement of a former judge as an appropriate reviewer of events – the law provides but one means of generating accurate reflections of actual events, of getting at truth in the referential sense. That an ethnographic account might be erroneous does not suggest that, of necessity, it is. Just as a judge can "get it wrong" in a case, so too there are means of subjecting ethnographic accounts, generated from participation/observation and making sense of a part of the social world, to meaningful peer review.

Ethnographic accounts can be validated by the several means with which I triangulated my original "Fieldnotes" paper – which did not require corroboration to be true but which was validated by that means once doubts had been raised. In the end, the story that I told was corroborated by several other cross-references in the field, including an extensive trail of written communications fructified by the FIPPA request; including Professor Ryder, who "experienced some of [the administration] as disrespectful of our efforts and scholarly objectives" and who ultimately agreed "with all of Jon [Thompson]'s conclusions, including the conclusions he reached about inappropriate behaviour on the part of David [Dewitt] and Patrick [Monahan]"; and including the Osgoode Hall Faculty Association, which was "surprised and dismayed by the role played by several members of the

University's senior administration in relation to the Mapping Models conference" and which concluded that "senior administrators were inappropriately pressuring conference organizers to make significant changes to the conference programme and speakers, to submit to internal oversight and review, or to make other modifications of the event or its planning." Corroboration came from *No Debate* as well and is wound through Chapters 1 and 4 as data in the form of findings and in this chapter in the form of historical and theoretical analysis.

Ultimately, then, the continuity and closure of this story and its overall coherence are rooted in a form of historical account and a dense reconstruction of what we currently take to be knowledge. As such, however, and despite my claim that the story fits more or less into the ethnographic genre, it is first and foremost an accounting – an effort to hold parties to account. That the narrative borrows from the methods and tropes of ethnography (fieldnotes, participation/observation, triangulation ...) does not preclude this overarching purpose.

6

Academic Freedom and the Worthiness of Ideas

The events surrounding the Mapping Models conference constitute a potential infinitude of points on the landscape from which this ethnography has been mapped. The two years of planning for the conference and the two and a half days over which it was held at Glendon Campus provide an endless number of ways in which intrigues course through time and space, each email, conversation, and meeting, divisible into any number of perspectives and potentialities for meaning. Compound the possible number of stories that might course through the data with any number of other framing devices through which the raw data that made up the welter of moments might get construed – fiction, science, psychology, political science, performance art ... – and by the number of points of entry into the events – personal histories, world history, urban flow ... – and it soon becomes apparent that the data do not speak on their own. If they did, then an infinite number of stories could emerge from every possible point on a landscape that has no borders, no beginning, and no end. The "field" does not define itself, and an undefined field, in and of itself, is mute about how it should be navigated. It is the intrigue – the framing device – that creates the possibility for a story to find a trajectory through a landscape, the more or less loosely conceived end points of the intrigue determining its general direction.

The intrigue of this book has been academic freedom. With the same data – the emails, the reports, the conversations; the uproars, the web pages, the petitions – a wholly different intrigue could have been discerned, a completely different tale written. The very construction of these phenomena as "data" pulled from a vast and inchoate field is already shaped by my inquiry. Another researcher (e.g., from a different discipline or another walk of life) would have found (or created) salience in completely different items.

This perturbation of the observed by the frame of the observer bears some similarity to some of the things laid out in the previous chapter with respect to ethnography. A participant/observer adopts not only a partial perspective on the events to which he or she is witness and player; as participants in the field, ethnographers shape the field itself. Who they are and where and when and how they intervene in a sea of moments inflect what they report back. As much as their interests shape their queries, the queries that preoccupy them unearth data on the landscape that feed back into and transform their interests. Ethnographers construct the field as much as they report on it.

These observations have implications for knowledge – how it is both constructed and construed. And, to the extent that the advancement of knowledge is a core justification for academic freedom, these observations have relevance for the theoretical underpinnings of the doctrine. This chapter explores the quandaries that arise for academic freedom from the recognition that data are socially produced and do not speak for themselves and tell their own stories, even while research interacts with a referential world outside scholarly intrigues, one that generates the landscape against which maps are triangulated.

The first part of this chapter ("Astrologers and Holocaust Deniers") covers the communities of practice that socially produce the means by which we discern and create data and generate valid, coherent, and compelling accounts – and reject others – from the welter of possibilities. More centrally for this chapter, it looks for the justification for the doctrine of academic freedom in the sophistication and illuminative prospects arising from those communities. But that is only the first task of this chapter.

As much as the ethnographer's (or researcher's) intrigues create salience and a trajectory through the landscape, they also find themselves on landscapes not of their own creation. The accounts that scholars generate are not arbitrary and wholly internally generated. The second part of this chapter ("Engagement") starts with the recognition of reflexivity (that researchers are part of the social world that they study) and moves on to ways to think about the referential world, beyond the intersubjective practices that constitute the disciplines of the academy around which that body is also grouped. It is the ability of scholars to identify multiple landmarks and generate increasingly exact maps that allows the larger society to locate itself better, which also provides justification for the doctrine of academic freedom.

In the introduction to this monograph, I alluded to an email that a colleague sent in which he complained (early) about the content of the Mapping Models conference and its focus on the one-state model. Several months after the conference was over, he sent another email to the faculty listserv in which he assailed our credentials to hold the conference in the first place. In his opinion, we had "no credentials whatsoever to organize a true academic inter-disciplinary conference on Israel-Palestine."[1] Another York University faculty member from the Centre for Jewish Studies complained similarly to the Osgoode listserv that the conference Organizing Committee lacked the credentials even to decipher the difference between scholarly and political approaches to the Middle East. In his view, the event was a political exercise disguised as an academic conference. He opined that "a person who wants to organize a conference about Israel/Palestine, or a person who wants to express a view about whether an Israel/Palestine conference was really academic, should have training in the Middle East and should read Arabic and Hebrew."[2] This issue of expertise surfaced several times, and from several loci, over the course of the conference.

The May 13, 2009, statement put out by the Canadian Council for Israel and Jewish Advocacy also weighed in on the question of who was credentialled to speak on issues in the Middle East and who was suspect as unscholarly. In CIJA's view, "the organizers have procured a few balanced speakers of high repute, but this is certainly not enough to characterize the conference as one of high academic integrity or good scholarship as would befit a first-class institution."[3] CIJA – an advocacy organization – disabused us and our Advisory Committee and bestowed itself with the expertise to ascertain the difference between scholars worthy and unworthy of their reputations.

In our May 12, 2010, meeting with the former dean of Osgoode (self-avowedly no expert on the Middle East), he informed us that we had insufficient expertise to hold a conference on models of statehood for Israel/Palestine on our own. Unbeknownst to us, he proceeded to organize a shadow advisory committee – apparently a collection of "serious scholars" in the field – with the associate vice-president and chairman of the Board of Governors. In conjunction with these ghost advisers and a professor from York University who was leading the campaign against the conference,[4] the dean came up with an alternative list of speakers and keynotes for the event that he was prepared to push on us. Although the names of these "serious scholars" have been withheld from the material released through the Freedom of Information Act, one of them has been identified as Gerald Steinberg, a professor at Bar Ilan University in Israel, regarded as not only far right wing but also polemical to the point of dismissal by other scholars of the Middle East.

There are many things that can be said about these interventions by outsiders. Almost self-evidently (except, one assumes, to those who made or supported the interventions), many of the declarations appeared to be displays of bad faith: the real issue for our critics was that the views and materials presented happened to represent scholarship that they did not like, in large measure because it did not comport with their own political agendas and aspirations. It is not difficult to decipher the political, polemical, and activist drives of the Council for Israel and Jewish *Advocacy* or the thrust of a ghost advisory committee with Steinberg at the helm.

That we had our own Advisory Committee of internationally recognized experts on the Middle East guiding our choices was, of course, one answer to the demand for credentials, as was our own considerable collective scholarly background on the Organizing Committee in the range of conference themes; however, neither was really a necessary defence to the challenge. There are many scholarly conferences in which an advisory committee is never called together, many in which the organizing committee is not in fact expert in an issue but calls together a meeting of scholars to enrich understanding of an inchoately understood issue. Stanley Fish overstates matters when he reduces the obligations of academics to teaching the syllabus and introducing students to state-of-the-art analysis.[5] Such analyses are generated and assessed by research-related activities such as conferences and publications; academic freedom is just as, if not more, important to the research context as it is to the pedagogical one. Nevertheless, Fish's distillation of the essence of academic freedom comfortably covers the conference organizing of a complete neophyte to a topic of inquiry. As Fish notes in an otherwise controversial book, "academic freedom is the freedom of academics to *study* anything they like; the freedom, that is, to subject any body of material, however unpromising it might seem, to academic interrogation and analysis."[6] A wholly "uncredentialled" scholar should be free to transform anything into an object of academic inquiry with neither prior restraint nor orthodoxy limiting the field of legitimate intrigues.

Despite this qualification about the freedom to study, the question "who is an expert?" arises fluidly from the events surrounding the Mapping

Models conference, as do a question about the line between knowledge and politics and ultimately an epistemological question about assessing the worthiness of ideas. Recollect that, in his objection to the idea of Israel/Palestine as a single binational state, Leon Wieseltier noted that "the promotion of an idea to unthinkability says nothing about the merit of the idea; many 'unthinkable' ideas are not worthy of serious thought."[7] Although this is indubitably true, it leaves open the far more serious question about what, in fact, bestows *gravitas* on an idea. And who determines whether or not an idea, and the way in which it is floated, is indeed worthy? The answers to these questions are tied up with some of the most enduring intellectual tensions in the contemporary academy between orthodoxy and innovation and between knowledge and politics. And the doctrine of academic freedom is tied up with all of these concerns, just as it is tied up with the core mission of the university. As one of the conventional groundings of the freedom of scholars to follow their intrigues unharassed by off-campus constituencies, trustees, and administrations, expertise is a good place to segue from the concrete labour of an ethnography and its ways of constituting accounts to the theory of academic freedom.

Astrologers and Holocaust Deniers

Intellectual history is rife with examples of new ideas surpassing previous understandings of the world – understandings that were entrenched as common sense – and thus rendering them outmoded. This scenario of the seemingly haphazard progression of ideas is well illustrated with respect to the central theme of the Mapping Models conference.

Contemplation by the conference of the one-state model was hardly the first controversial idea to be floated in, or about, the Middle East. Forty years ago the idea that the model of two ethnic states, now the cornerstone of conventional wisdom, was a legitimate question for civil debate was received with withering scorn. As Yossi Sarid, a former leader of Israel's Meretz party, noted in a *Ha'aretz* article of June 19, 2009,

> for me it began in 1970. The secretariat of the Alignment party (the forerunner of Labor) convened for an initial discussion of the future of our relations with the Palestinians in the territories. Everyone was present, all the bigwigs had their say: Golda Meir and Israel Galili, Moshe Dayan and Shimon Peres – they were imbued with a messianic spirit. They raised a plethora of ideas, variations on the subject of Greater Israel, each idea more foolish than the next; history has already made a mockery of them.

> I was also given the floor, for the first time in my public life. There will be no solution without a Palestinian state, I said, trembling. For a moment there was silence, of the kind following a terror attack, even before the cries of the wounded and the sirens of the ambulances begin. They detested me.[8]

Were the now sacrosanct two-state model the theme of an academic conference in 1970, the same outcry likely would have arisen that universities hosting such debates on ideas with explosive potential have to "rigorously define the academic standards expected of all University-sponsored conferences, insist on peer review for all conference speakers, and deny its endorsement to any conference that violate[s] these academic standards."[9] The scholarly credentials of the conference organizers for a debate on the two-state model would no doubt have been called into question against the ponderous weight of "all the bigwigs" with their visions of a single Israeli state on all of the territory west of the Jordan River.

Indeed, a campaign similar to the one employed against our conference was evident when current orthodoxy was breaking new ground. In an op-ed in the *National Post* about the Mapping Models conference, Ian Lustick pointed to the historical irony of attempts by Jewish organizations to create orthodoxies by using heavy-handed tactics aimed at curtailing academic freedom:

> An episode that Bnai Brith Canada might wish to keep in mind occurred in 1983, when the ADL built a secret network of student vigilantes. They were commissioned by ADL headquarters in the United States to monitor and report on dozens of professors and graduate students at major universities who were said to be "pro-Arab sympathizers." The network of students was told that the materials they were being sent describing the blacklisted scholars "should be considered confidential ... it could easily be misconstrued." Indeed the *New York Times* did get wind of the campaign, and published an article about the ADL's blacklist. Bnai Brith immediately apologized, stressed its absolute support for academic freedom, and blamed the campaign on an "overly zealous" student intern (although the instructions quoted here were issued by Leonard Zakim, the ADL's Executive Director).
>
> What is fascinating to consider is that many of those the ADL named as dangerous enemies of Israel were in fact early supporters of the "two state solution." Although condemned at the time by so-called "Israel advocacy" organizations, advocating a two-state solution is now used as a sign of acceptability by those same organizations.[10]

That conventional wisdom is labile and often associated with entrenched power provides historical justification for not passing control of academic content to "outside groups" and "off-campus constituencies." Otherwise, good ideas can fall prey to bad contexts, and their chances of flourishing diminish.

The temptation hovers in the face of different models of statehood for Israel/Palestine and their intense repudiation in the historical context in which they are floated to root the doctrine of academic freedom in a liberal marketplace of ideas similar to the marketplace metaphors that ground freedom of expression. On this understanding of the doctrine of academic freedom, any a priori restriction on what an academic can research, publish, or teach hampers the marketplace, particularly given the vocation of scholars to float new and challenging ideas. Society is ill served when academics, like individual citizens, are restrained by political forces from populating the marketplace with as many intellectual goods as they can generate. Society is well served when ideas circulate as freely as possible and add to the overall store required for a progression from unregenerate states of ignorance to greater refinement. A constitutionally shored-up freedom of expression best protects the rights of individual citizens to contribute to this storehouse of knowledge, a fortiori credentialled scholars whose ideas have the merit of expertise. Individual academics, like individual citizens, might manifest rogue variations from one conventional epoch only to have their ideas surface in another in which their thinking is regarded as revolutionary. According to this approach to academic freedom, as a result of this familiar, though occasional, drift, there should be no constraint on what scholars, from intellectual era to era, are inclined to produce.

This understanding of academic freedom certainly supports the conclusion that the conduct of government, SSHRC, and senior administrators was inappropriate and misguided regarding the Mapping Models conference. The ability of the two-state model to thrive despite a prevailing political orthodoxy that would have stifled its emergence provides support for the view that political interference in the random flowering of ideas is misplaced; similarly, any political impediment to the flowering of the one-state idea (or any model) impoverishes the marketplace. Political impediments are easily identified as government intervention or, under the sway of a political lobby, administrative interference.

This model of academic freedom, both liberal and modernist, is based on an instrumental view of academic freedom that justifies the liberty by the ultimate service that it renders to society. Both the model and its justification have come under review from a number of quarters, troubled by postmodern epistemologies and increasingly supplanted by professional, rather than free speech, justifications for the doctrine. The connection between professional justifications and postmodern epistemologies, however, is not well worked out; the conflict in the Middle East and cases such as the Mapping Models conference provide clear challenges for contemporary ways in which the doctrine has been understood. The ways in which academic work links to a referential world (with fact, with knowledge, with truth) and the relationship between knowledge and politics remain troubled by epistemological perturbations and how they relate to the doctrine of academic freedom.

To begin with, various philosophers and legal scholars have become increasingly skeptical of the connections between freedom of expression and academic freedom. Ronald Dworkin, for example, points out the distinction between the extraordinary freedom that belongs to academics and the more tenuous rights that belong to ordinary citizens. Free speech is not violated when, for example, "a department store fires someone for denigrating its products, or when a church does not allow one of its priests to preach a rival faith from its pulpit."[11] But academic freedom is violated when an academic speaks his or her mind and is penalized when the employer imposes restrictions on speech as a condition of employment. Academic freedom requires the university to support its academic staff no matter what they write or teach or say, and as such the freedom is stronger than the more general right of free speech.[12]

Furthermore, the greater protection of our liberties as academics under the umbrella of academic freedom did not preclude our rights as ordinary citizens to be protected against unconstitutional government action. However, the effect of the Charter of Rights and Freedoms on the range of impingements endured by the conference Organizing Committee would have been slight, reserved for the point of intersection between government action and our expressive rights. The contemplated actions of the federal government and perhaps the federally funded Social Sciences and Humanities Research Council regarding the Mapping Models conference might have violated the right to free expression of the conference organizers. However, the Charter would have had dubious application to the employment relationship between York University and the Organizing Committee members because it is hard to discern government action in agents –

university administrators – who are autonomous, the autonomy of universities from government being an aspect of academic freedom as critical as the insulation of individual scholarship from administrative oversight.[13]

Rather than protecting academic freedom with the Charter (whether through freedom of expression or freedom of association), the employment relationship is increasingly regarded as a key component of the means for shoring up the doctrine. The protection of academic freedom through employment contracts, however, remains somewhat weak. Most faculties across Canada are unionized, and most collective agreements have clauses that protect academic freedom. And unionized labour contracts can indeed provide the surest protection for the freedom. However, while Osgoode's faculty began the process of certification in the winter of 2012, at the time of the conference they were not unionized. There were no explicit contractual protections for at least the two Osgoode faculty against incursions into the territory conventionally protected by the freedom, leaving little other than the dated and little used common law doctrine of tenure and the ethos of the institution and shaming as protective mechanisms. Even with collective agreements, though, the theoretical underpinnings of the doctrine require elaboration. They shore up the doctrine but do not necessarily account for it.

The idea that academic freedom has greater specificity than the constitutionally protected right to free speech, in particular a specificity that relates to the employment relationship, has been developed by Robert Post in his essay "The Structure of Academic Freedom."[14] Rooting the doctrine of academic freedom in a peculiar employment relationship resonates with his construal of the constitutional analysis as peripheral to the core of the doctrine. Although there are overlaps between academic freedom and freedom of speech, conflation of the two for Post leads to deep confusions. He looks to the seminal North American articulation of the doctrine of academic freedom, the 1915 AAUP declaration, and notes that it did not ground the doctrine in the First Amendment of the American Constitution (what would be the equivalent of section 2, relating to freedom of expression, in the Canadian Charter) but construed it as a professional freedom, the right of professional self-regulation of the professoriat.

The AAUP declaration contains an instrumental view of the freedom: the vocation of scholarship is to advance knowledge within society. But in meeting this vocation, it is the social function of the university rather than individual rights that sustains the doctrine. Knowledge is articulated by scholars, but its advancement is secured by "the free application of highly *disciplined* forms of inquiry."[15] For Post, the disciplinary nature of intellectual development is critical to justification of the liberty. The discipline of academic disciplines such as philosophy, history, political science, or law is the critical and indispensable element that adds value to scholarship.

The importance of professional self-regulation through the coterie of practices internal to the academic disciplines is what renders academic freedom distinct from freedom of speech, a constitutionally protected freedom granted to citizens as individuals. For Post, academic freedom is granted in recognition of collective rights: namely, the liberty necessary to the community of professional scholars to carry out their intrigues without the values of other normative communities, such as those of political associations, interfering with its enterprise. Academic freedom, for Post, is not the freedom of individual scholars but the freedom of the academic profession to advance its own intellectual agendas by the constraints of internal regulation. The freedom is the liberty to pursue "professional inquiry within a matrix of disciplinary norms defined and enforced by those who are competent to understand and apply such norms."[16] This is the structure that most ensures the benefit that society accrues by its recognition: namely, the social good of the advancement of knowledge. It is experts, who have received extensive and specialized training, who are best poised in society to generate this benefit, and thus they should enjoy a privilege of expertise.

The hierarchization of knowledge is a consequence that flows from this justification of the doctrine of academic freedom. As a result, marketplace metaphors are misplaced in this context. Where there is a presumed equality of status among individuals who have expressive rights, the employment of professional norms that discipline scholars in the exercise of their liberty implies that not all ideas are or should be treated equally. They need to be scrutinized for their worth according to the standards of judgment and discernment internal to the scholarly enterprise.

The professional approach to academic freedom laid out by scholars such as Post is consistent with a modernist epistemology. The instrumentalism that justifies the doctrine is consistent with a view (also promoted by the 1915 AAUP declaration) that knowledge is objective and that disinterested scholars are best poised to add cumulatively to its store. The *mechanism* by which this social good is advanced (or best advanced), according to both Post and the declaration's articulation of academic freedom, is professional self-regulation by the professoriat. Postmodern epistemologies that emerged later in the twentieth century appear to trouble that instrumental connection between scholarship and its social function in ways that scholarship on the Middle East impasse appears to exemplify. Some of those epistemologies can be squared with events surrounding the Mapping Models conference, and others are inadequate to that task.

The assumption underpinning the modernist justification for academic freedom lies in the ability of impartial scholars, guided by their disciplines, to discover objective truths about the real world. This assumption is no longer so unproblematically accepted as the goal of academic work. In the fields of ethnography and anthropology, the critique of orientalism and the *posturing* of objectivity and detachment that occludes its own perspective and interests are embedded in works such as Mitchell's *Colonizing Egypt,* referred to in the previous chapter. Similarly, the invocation of a judge to provide an authoritative account of an academic event borrows prestige from a discipline – law – that has its own style of "getting at the facts," occluding the ways in which law itself is constituted by ways of "imagining the real," to borrow Clifford Geertz's phrase.[17] Just as facts do not tell a story on their own, so too the legal representation of fact is normative from the start; or, in Geertz's more evocative formulation, "'fact-configurations' are not merely things found lying about in the world and carried bodily into the court, show-and-tell style."[18] Legal sensibilities, inflected by larger social and cultural worldviews, construct frameworks through which facts become salient. Borrowing from this normative frame by appointing a judge to dissect an academic event lends a sham objectivity to the enterprise.

In this context, questions have arisen about whether academic freedom can survive the epistemological challenges of postmodernism and, if so, on what basis. Tying this conundrum to the ethnographic account earlier provided, if it is recognized that knowledge is constructed, why would one account of the events around the conference be preferred over another? Even in the previous chapter on methodology, the lure was present in the idea that there is no basis for peer review of data emerging from participation/observation or that accounts merely accumulate one against the other in the absence of a basis for choosing among them. Historical truth appears to dissolve into narrative truth, governed by criteria such as aesthetic finality in the absence of a means to connect accounts to a referential world and assessments of validity. (And even judgments on aesthetic finality appear to be untethered to any means of improving judgment.) So, too, do a holding to account and the means of keeping political intrigues at bay in the academy.

David Rabban gives voice to this concern over the doctrine of academic freedom when it is untethered from this imagery of impartiality and expertise.[19] In his view, academic freedom needs to find new philosophical presuppositions to accommodate this epistemological revision. The old version of academic freedom deriving from the 1915 AAUP declaration that drew clear lines between politics and knowledge and praised scholars for assiduously distinguishing the two has decayed and might no longer be up to the postmodern task now demanded of it.

The fraught context of scholarship on the Middle East fuels skepticism about whether knowledge of the real world accumulates progressively – and this skepticism is part of a deeper ambivalence about whether "truth" is decipherable in general apart from what a particular group finds it advantageous to regard as given or universal.[20] In the case of the Mapping Models conference, professional norms and the concept of disciplinary constraint – and the very idea of a discipline – were used as mechanisms to shore up orthodoxy, in this case the orthodoxy of the two-state model for peace negotiations in Israel/Palestine. We were accused (falsely) of lacking expertise and engaging non-scholars to vet academic themes. The "discipline" of Middle East studies was preproscribed in such a way that "serious scholars" lined up with one particular view of outcomes and legitimate aspirations in the subject area. This cascade of contending views, histories, experts, and disciplines seems to undermine the disciplinary model that justifies academic freedom.

The conservative pull of disciplines seems to entrench incommensurabilities rather than resolve them. The claim of a Jewish studies professor that the conference organizers were not "credentialled" seems to be a transparent illustration of the marriage of a discipline (Middle East studies or Jewish studies) with a particular orthodoxy. Even interdisciplinary work, which ordinarily shakes up orthodoxies and allows new objects of inquiry to emerge, is cast as appropriate or inappropriate depending on which pull the new project shows. In a report on the conference by four Jewish studies professors at York to a university task force on student learning, the interdisciplinary aspirations of the conference were assailed on the ground that the members of the Organizing Committee, though impeccably credentialled, were all from one discipline. This qualified us (impeccably) to hold a disciplinary conference of law scholars, but

> most of the speakers were not from the field of Law and the conference itself was pitched towards goals far exceeding the bounds of the legal sphere. The organizers may not have understood the pitfalls involved in putting together a conference in Middle East Studies, and they may have lacked the

> appropriate contacts in the field of Middle East Studies to give them guidance.[21]

Interdisciplinary work, in this model, needs to be rooted in the right discipline and, the Advisory Committee aside, to draw on the right "contacts" to be credible.

Even the citation of the names of scholars (credentialled, tenured, published) immediately affiliates a project with a political agenda. For many scholars familiar with the political literature on the Middle East, the favourable citation of Gerald Steinberg as one of the "serious scholars" whose views were courted by York's administration to assess the conference program obliterates any residual claim that the administration was disinterested in its interventions. Similarly, the report on the conference from four Jewish studies members takes for granted as a stain on the intellectual dispassion of the Organizing Committee that the conference vision drew on Edward Said and Tony Judt as scholars who have written on the one-state model:

> The conference announcement and website carried a vision statement that presented the intellectual framework of the conference. The thinkers cited in it (e.g., Edward Said and Tony Judt) presented an intellectual framework that drew from only one (fairly radical) side of the discussion. Thus the vision statement already conveyed a sense of the skewed nature of the discussion that the conference would generate.[22]

In this kind of fraught intellectual climate, it is hard to perceive an uncompromised "discipline" to draw on that constrains ideas with stability and constancy. The professional norms that might guide an inquiry are virtually all contested, as is the list of eminent scholars whose work might inseminate and fructify an intrigue. Virtually every pedigree is questionable from the outset. In this context, the classic justifications for academic freedom appear to be attenuated. How do scholars "advance knowledge" in a disinterested way in this fraught field? And if they cannot establish "objectively" that they are able to do so, then what justifies the academic freedom that they enjoy?

What happened to the Mapping Models conference – a microcosm of what has happened in countless situations in which the topic of Israel/Palestine has been raised on campuses across North America – appears to trouble the doctrine of academic freedom. There seems to be no higher structure of cognitive (or political) authority that might justify the doctrine in the face of diverse contentions.

This set of quandaries has an analogue in the issues that arose regarding the validity of ethnographic accounts. There the sense was that, because of the situatedness of accounts based on participation/observation, some of which directly contradict other accounts of the same events, the delivery of validity is effectively impossible. Added to the troubles plaguing the partial perspectives of ethnographic accounts is the tendency of participants (including the ethnographer) to misdescribe or misinterpret what they have lived through. Interpretations are plagued by the lack of toehold on an agreed upon, let alone objective, world. It is tempting to conclude, with this kind of handle on reality, that the range of stories that participants tell of their experiences of events is not susceptible to peer review.

Prima facie the topic of the Middle East seems to provide *no* universal or objective purchase on which even a significant number of scholars might agree; it seems to generate a meagre harvest of universally recognized understanding. Knowledge appears to be utterly contingent on prior commitments, the common sense of one era, people, and place undermined by a different era, people, and place. Knowledge here is paradigmatically situated, local, perspectival, particular – and, most importantly, political. If scholarship is at root contingent and interested, then why not submit the process to more naked exercises of force? Why not simply allow lobbies, such as CIJA, to determine what gets vetted in academic settings?

Without clear lines between knowledge and politics, how else might the doctrine of academic freedom be justified? Academic freedom, after all, has been structured since the beginning of the past century to ensure that those with political interests (including academics) do not convert departments and disciplines into political power bases and thereby transform research and pedagogy into proselytization and the promotion of favoured pieties. Again, there are analogues to the difficulties confronting ethnographic work in which a response to the critique of naive realism – that ethnographers do not stand outside the world in order to study it – is to deny the possibilities for validity in an ethnographic account. If neither the discipline of ethnography nor that of Middle East studies is on solid ground in its generation of accounts, then why should academic freedom shore up the liberty of academics to expound from them?

Preceding Post, a string of scholars tackled the justification for the doctrine of academic freedom in light of postmodern epistemologies. Richard

Rorty wrote a 1994 article in *Academe* in which he confronted head on the idea that academic freedom requires philosophical presuppositions and concludes that the search for objective correlatives that confirm the veracity of the scholarly enterprise is wrong-headed. As he noted, "all we philosophers can do when asked for standards or methods of disinterested and objective inquiry is to describe how the people we most admire conduct their inquiries. We have no independent information about how objective truth is to be obtained." For Rorty, "objectivity is not a matter of corresponding to objects but of getting together with other subjects ... There is nothing to objectivity except intersubjectivity."[23]

Rorty's analysis seems to comport both well and problematically with scholarship on the Middle East. What happened to the Mapping Models conference – in particular the competition among experts – seems to illustrate that there is no objective world to which all proponents can turn to settle all of the broad and deep and historical disputes over the territory. In cases in which the material is fraught and contested, intersubjectivity breaks down into apparently perspectival and partial forms of life that have little more than fragile *gezerah*-like parameters to encircle their sacred truths. The analysis is problematic since intersubjectivity can swiftly descend into murky waters when it comes to distinguishing politics from scholarship and seems to be insubstantial as a means of beating back naked political interference, itself rooted in intersubjective understandings of the world, such as that of Canada's minister of science and technology. Rorty himself acknowledged that "the distinction between academic politics and the disinterested pursuit of truth is pretty fuzzy."[24]

Furthermore, reliance on intersubjectivity minimizes the large reservoir of referents that both parties to a dispute are prepared to call facts. Accounts, for their validity to be discernible, need to be drawn from and refer to this world beyond compelling and coherent narrative structures. There were a number of mundane and conspicuous points of agreement between the provost and me on the events surrounding the conference – a shared database or part of the referential world against which our accounts were triangulated. Similarly, in the Middle East, there are facts that all credible parties rely on to generate their positions. Access to the facts or data can be mediated, and they can be misinterpreted or misdescribed or represented in an overly interested manner in the case of both ethnography and the Middle East. A description of "the facts" can always be challenged, but both "the facts" and the challenge are assessed against what we currently take to be knowledge. Conservative minister Gary Goodyear's intervention in the Mapping Models conference can properly be characterized as naked and improper political interference not because it failed to stem from an intersubjective community – no doubt it did – but because the doubts that Goodyear cast on the academic integrity of the event were based not on what is currently taken to be knowledge but on misdescription, misinterpretation, and excessive interest.

Both Stanley Fish and Judith Jarvis Thomson have also problematized academic freedom by detaching its justification from the production of objective knowledge and rooting it in the more precarious intersubjectivity of academic practices.[25] Fish's article on Holocaust denial follows up on an article by Jarvis Thomson that queries the grounds on which a faculty recruitment committee might soundly deny a chaired position to an astrologist. At the heart of her paper is a concern over how orthodoxy in academic disciplines – how the scholarly enterprise itself – might be prevented from stymying the flourishing of new ideas and the grounds that might legitimately be cited for rejecting some ideas without capitulating to orthodoxy. The issue of stifling orthodoxies, of course, was central to the debates over whether the Mapping Models conference was a "legitimate" academic exercise or whether it had been captured by a non-scholarly agenda. A vein of orthodoxy in Middle East and Jewish studies (and non-academic lobbies outside the university) claimed that the one-state model was not a legitimate object of inquiry and that, if it were, there were appropriate ways to examine the object to which we were not privy in our organizing.

Jarvis Thomson raises the question of orthodoxy and the foundations of scholarly claims to authority in research in a thought experiment in which someone proposes an area of study that no university would countenance as worthy of consideration – astrology. She asks us to examine the arguments that might be floated should a hypothetical proponent argue that universities should be germinating new ideas, and astrology abounds with them. To the response that astrology does not meet the minimal standards required of a science, namely that theories explain the truth of their predictions when they are true, the astrologer, Jarvis Thomson points out, has several retorts, including allegations of fact that show the predictive standards of science are met by astrology, or a challenge to the methodological hegemony of the scientific model, or a simpler retort in the request for proof that astrology's predictions fail to meet scientific standards for prediction. Jarvis Thomson's response to this demand for proof does not recur to "objective knowledge" in order to reject the pretensions of astrology for a place in the academy:

> To begin with, could we prove that astrology fails to meet the minimal standard, and therefore is not a science? Perhaps you could, but I can't. I can't even do much in the way of formulating an argument. I believe that the motions of the heavenly bodies do not influence the everyday affairs of ordinary people, but on what ground do I believe this? My believing it is a product of a vague, loose conception of how the world works and of what causality involves and requires, picked up over the years from experience (which includes some snippets of science I have become acquainted with), and there is nothing I can produce in the way of compact, clear argument for my belief. Perhaps one of my colleagues in our physics department could do better than I can (I am, let us suppose, a member of the English department), but I say only perhaps, because demonstrating that the motions of the heavenly bodies do not influence the everyday affairs of ordinary people is not a task that the average physicist has ever thought of carrying out, and it is not obvious how he or she is to do so.[26]

Rather than eliminating the astrologist as a candidate for the hypothetical chair through recourse to putatively universal and objective criteria such as proof, Jarvis Thomson recurs to a particular historical community – the academy – with its distinctive practices and scholarly values for determining the truth. She would not deny that the various disciplines at the academy have a conservative thrust – and at times a debilitating one – in that they set the burden of proof on new fields and new ideas generally to make theoretical connections between the new and what is important to preserve of the old. However, the truths acknowledged within those disciplines enjoy a privileged status, one that imposes hurdles on those who would challenge them. Just as Post would argue that academia hierarchizes knowledge in ways that render inapt the equality of status in the field of ideas of marketplace metaphors, so too the playing field for the qualification of ideas is not level. New ideas need to earn a place that is long granted to ideas that constitute the settled background of academic knowledge. As Jarvis Thomson notes, a challenger for a new disciplinary field

> has not carried his burden of proof by virtue of saying just anything at all. (For example [in the case of the astrologer], he has not carried it if he has offered us in evidence of the powers of the stars only that they sing to him at full moon.) His carrying the burden requires his producing what we – given our past experience – can see to be reason to revise our beliefs. For what is in question is whether we would be acting responsibly in refusing to

> reverse ourselves – not whether an all-knowing God would, but whether we would. This means that our acting responsibly in refusing to reverse ourselves is entirely compatible with our being mistaken.[27]

A consequence of this practice-oriented structuring of knowledge grounded in the best available insights rather than indubitable proof is that disciplines can get dragged down by unsound orthodoxies and that placing a burden on the new might well mean that mistakes are made and sound new ideas are mistakenly rejected. Ultimately, Jarvis Thomson's point is that there is nothing other than the best practices of particular communities (academia and the scholarly values that it generates and entrenches in this case along with its cognate doctrines, such as academic freedom and the autonomy of universities from governments) that guard successfully against these errors. Similarly, the process of triangulation relates a position in a landscape of data to both other sources of data and the known maps of the area. The corrective to the mistaken rejection of ideas is similarly not to be found in a perspective outside all practices, beyond the normative standards for determining what counts as knowledge; it lies within standards generated by other fields of practice that themselves will have taken-for-granted background assumptions about the world. Jarvis Thomson is clear that this can be a fragile enterprise, the search for what is right and true. It is not *absolutely* certain – just as triangulation is done not with respect to a meta-map that corrects all cartographic enterprises but with respect to existent maps, any number of which might be adequate or inadequate to the landscapes that they represent. Again, this landscape is contained, its borders set, by the intrigue that frames a trajectory through it.

The intellectual practices that generate maps are not free-floating, however; they are engaged with landscapes – or databases – that they seek to represent. And, just as the provost and I (and the Israelis and Palestinians) agree in our different accounts about a good deal, beginning with the mundane world of time and place to which our historical accounts are tethered, so too the practices link up to undoubted landscapes and undoubted maps through which our intrigues travel. The judgment of competence or incompetence – validity or invalidity – is not made from outside the context of all practices and does not draw on some higher authority – as the concept of authority itself derives from within the practice of doing things such as ethnographic work and political and legal analysis. Even the concept of critique or error or misjudgment has meaning for those who are already full participants in the relevant community of practitioners.

There will still be means of rejecting or critiquing ideas that researchers generate, but those means will always issue from within a practice that evolves around assumptions that remain ultimately unproven (the quest for indubitable proof and meta-maps generating infinite regressions) and provide the bedrock upon which the practice is built. Like *gzerot,* these parameters of reasonable belief are contingent and revisable. Like the Torah, the practice of throwing up and modifying *gzerot* is grounded in a community of believers, the whole ultimately arbitrary to those who do not share foundational beliefs. The particular community of believers that constitutes academia, however, does not have as the goal of its activities the inculcation of god-fearing humans or advancing one or another political agenda; rather, it has the generation of knowledge as its core and paramount project, to which other goals and ends are subservient to the extent that they are coexistent. The production of knowledge is the itinerary that illuminates academia's intrigue through data of the world. This is an idea to which I will return.

Ultimately contingent as this epistemology is – though in a sense of "ultimate" that borders on empty – Jarvis Thomson is clear that, in the practice that constituted both democracy and the linked academy over the past 200 years, within our own broader society reliance on the guild-like processes of disciplines for arriving at truth generates the best standards available to us for the truth:

> It could hardly be concluded that the assessment of new ideas – for example, in deciding which to fund further research on – should be taken out of the hands of currently respected experts and turned over to people outside the field. With the best will in the world, currently respected experts may get things wrong; outsiders might be so far lucky as to get things right, but if they do then that *is* mere luck.[28]

Jarvis Thomson's rooting of the way in which to determine the validity of new ideas in practices and not in absolutely irrefutable evidence and "objective" rationality runs against the grain of the classical justification for academic freedom in the advancement of knowledge, where knowledge is taken to be the additive and objective accumulation of universal truths. But her analysis is consistent with the way in which the doctrine of academic freedom has developed in excluding off-campus constituencies and administrative overseers from substantive decisions about which ideas get vetted, funded, and sponsored in the academy.

Jarvis Thomson's analysis takes us somewhat closer to what happened with the Mapping Models conference by tackling the topic of orthodoxy and stressing the limitations (and virtues) of practices. The one-state theme that ran through the conference presented a challenge to two-state orthodoxy, a new common sense that itself used to be the pretender to the orthodoxy of Greater Israel. At almost every turn in the topic of the Middle East, there are communities of practice (in this case that unsurprisingly cleave the scholarly world as well) deeply attached to their own eminent lights, to their own methodologies, to their own historical narratives, to their own social, moral, and scholarly values. That we might be mistaken – might need to reverse ourselves in the next generation – illustrates precisely those moments in academia when there is intrasubjective strife and disagreement as a result of the precarious, ultimately ungrounded, practice-based nature of getting things right.

Fish has taken Jarvis Thomson's dissembling of modernist epistemologies and connected it more explicitly to an approach to academic freedom. His article deals with discussions of Holocaust denial and the academy and the kinds of arguments viable for refusing to engage proponents. Like Rorty and Jarvis Thomson, he notes that "the work of marking off the legitimate from the illegitimate ... [only gets done] when the content of those categories has been specified in advance, that is, when you already know (at least to your satisfaction) what is legitimate and what is not."[29] Taking on Holocaust deniers directly – as though one could enter into well-reasoned arguments rooted in a neutral, disinterested pursuit of the truth between us and them – is much like allowing a serious space at the academic table for astrologers who ask us to "prove" that the stars do not predict events in history.

Fish agrees with those scholars (Deborah Lipstadt in particular in his article) who note that one can simply refuse to debate Holocaust deniers on the ground that such a debate would confer legitimacy on a preposterous position, but he comes to this conclusion from a different place. The "irrefutable evidence," "rationality," "reasoned dialogue," and "reasonable inquiry" that scholars such as Lipstadt marshal[30] exist, for Fish, as part of a structure of belief and conviction that precedes and colours one's reception of new ideas – and Holocaust deniers do not participate in that structure of belief and conviction. Fish is clear that this structure of plausibility that derives from practices does not mean that better arguments cannot be made or that new ideas are never mistakenly rejected. Rather, better ideas "emerge and are registered as better against the background of other arguments already identified as better, arguments long since accepted and now firmly in place as cornerstones in the sedimented structure of a mind whose categories and rubrics organize the world, not after perception but in the act of perception."[31] Fish also believes that our best judgments on what counts as a legitimate argument or a sound conclusion are grounded not in absolute certainty but in our past experience, which is fragile at times; they should be squared with "the evidence provided by our best lights," which, he goes on to note, "will not be everyone's best lights."[32]

The justification for academic freedom that Fish puts forward is not as ahistorical and value-free as justifications rooted in the Enlightenment liberalism still in evidence when the AAUP formulated its first declaration on academic freedom in 1915. Fish characterizes the values subtending the modernist conception of academic freedom in the following manner:

> Those values include the disinterested search for truth, the separation of knowledge and power, the superiority of knowledge to belief, the submission of all views to the scrutiny of critical deliberation, the stigmatizing of no view in advance of its receiving a serious hearing, and the exempting of no view from the requirement that it put itself to the test of all challenges, including those that issue from sources its proponents distrust.[33]

Fish's ambitions for academic freedom are much more constrained – and based on a more empirical understanding of the way in which the concept developed and operates as part of a particular historical project. That project favours a particular set of voices, those that have earned the right to be heard. As Fish notes, "the freedom being recommended is institutionally defined and limited, is not absolute freedom but 'academic' freedom, in the sense both that it is a freedom peculiar to the academic enterprise and a freedom whose boundaries are to be determined and patrolled by academics."[34]

As much as the freedom is more constrained than the wide-open marketplace of ideas, the mechanisms that he recognizes for founding sound versus unsound ideas is more effective, more in line with the way in which the academy works (and works within society), and more intelligible. As Fish notes, the marketplace of ideas justification for academic freedom is ultimately unintelligible:

> When nothing is granted even a provisional certainty – when every fact must be tested down to its (non-available) ground – the category of the "taken-for-granted" or "what everyone knows to be true" loses its members,

> and no one can rely on truths commonly held or refute obvious falsehoods by simply declaring them to be such. The irony, as Douglas points out, is that the "evidentiary agnosticism" or "discursive neutrality" supposedly devised to safeguard truth and fact from the incursions of ideology, have instead "the effect of contributing to the erosion of the very boundary between truth and fiction it claims to police."[35]

Paraphrasing Rorty, the marketplace model of academic freedom is so open-minded that its brains have fallen out.

The alternative to this mindless open-mindedness is a rooting of our best judgment – and our defence of academic freedom – in the guild of each discipline and the traditions and practices of the academy, a foundation that Post also promotes, though with less epistemological self-consciousness. As Fish notes with respect to the exclusion of Holocaust deniers from history departments,

> standing behind the exclusion of deniers is the massive record of rigorous research undertaken by superbly credentialed men and women whose conclusions have met every reasonable test put to them. Those who have contributed to this record need not be apologetic about protecting it from the assaults of persons who would use the vocabulary and machinery of intellectual inquiry to further ends that are rarely if ever openly acknowledged, but known to everyone.[36]

Academic freedom, in this analysis, is far from absolute. It is limited by boundaries "determined and patrolled by academics,"[37] not by some invisible mind of the marketplace driven, teleologically, by society's ultimate interests, even though the long-standing practice in democracies of allowing disciplines and scholars to flourish as they move toward their goals of obtaining particular knowledge under the doctrine of academic freedom often advances society's express and unexpress need for these discrete forms of knowledge.

Characteristic of this approach to academic freedom is the justification for the doctrine in intersubjective agreement – the agreements derived from the communities of scholars that make up the academy and patrol its borders – and not in the putative view from nowhere of a marketplace of ideas. The practices of intersubjective agreement and judgment exercised in this particular type of community organize their central projects around the goal of the generation of knowledge.

This nexus of loose and often contested intersubjective agreements with an amorphous yet often settled taken-for-granted background of better judgments constitutes what Rorty calls "the ethics of the academy – the customs and practices which help to determine the attitude of students to books, faculty to students, administrators to faculty and donors, and so on."[38] Included in this culture as a taken-for-granted value that has taken shape over the past century is the doctrine of academic freedom that liberates scholars to set their own problematics and teach according to their own learned opinions without interference from administrators, off-campus constituencies, or government bodies. The culture of the academy has its own integrity, which is perturbed by attempts to insert extraneous values into its governance. This approach entails a kind of reverence for the practices and traditions of the university, a reverence that runs up against instances when the widest possible intersubjective agreement is still limited and capable of error.

This analysis, both of the academic enterprise and of academic freedom, has implications for the promotion of "balance" as a criterion of academic competence – a sham scholarly concept that surfaced repeatedly in the Mapping Models conference. Fish argues against the idea that Holocaust denial as an intellectual position should be approached as though all of our established practices are (and can be) suspected of orthodoxy and, in the alternative, can (and should) be put through the crucible of critical reason that is independent of all beliefs. Jarvis Thomson similarly argues against a kind of relativism that seeks to cast no prior judgment on belief systems such as astrology. Both Fish and Jarvis Thomson refuse this position of formal agnosticism and argue that judgment depends on a taken-for-granted set of practices and a background of prior judgments – including judgments from our brightest lights – without which judgment on particulars makes no sense. Refusing the intelligibility of these sets of practices would be akin to locating oneself in a landscape without reference to a map. In the context of Holocaust denial, Fish notes, "take the background away, and you are indeed back at ground zero with no resources to guide you and no defense at all against those willful polemicists who would substitute their history for the history you have unwisely surrendered."[39] The resources to which Fish recurs are those that emerge from the disciplines and practices of the academy. These complex, established, normative systems with judgment built upon judgment are what protect the academic project from capture by political interests. As was amply illustrated in the Mapping Models case, political interests attempted to undo the work of those established systems by appealing to external criteria such as balance that are uniquely poised for political capture. The call for balance – a judgment external to academic forms of judgment that show much greater discernment and subtlety – *is itself* a polemical call.

Robert O'Neil makes this point about the specificity of disciplinary reasoning and the forms of criteria for competence in the particular context of the Middle East. Similar to Jarvis Thomson's hypothetical chair that needs to be filled, O'Neil asks us to imagine a Department of Middle Eastern Studies that has no Zionist. As with the Mapping Models conference, intense pressure can be brought to bear on the department for the hiring of a Zionist. Any department worthy of its scholarly salt would refuse to hire someone on the basis of his or her publicly expressed Zionist viewpoint, though consideration of scholars whose expertise includes Zionism ("whatever may be his or her personal views on that volatile issue") might be a legitimate academic judgment.[40] As O'Neil notes, reflecting the kinds of decision making that go into academic judgments, "a focus on expertise is entirely appropriate, even though it may indirectly serve the viewpoint goal – that is, one whose academic competence includes Zionism may well turn out to be an advocate for that viewpoint. But there is no guarantee of such concordance, as there would be when advocacy or viewpoint is the desiderata."[41]

Reasoning from this hypothetical to our conference, the suggestion (also promoted by the former dean of the law school) that we needed to balance those whose views might incidentally be anti-Zionist (but who were selected on the basis of what they might say on the themes of the conference) with those who publicly expressed Zionist views supplants a scholarly criterion with a polemical one in which viewpoint and advocacy become the goals. While we were seeking a fruitful diversity sufficient to ferment an academic dialogue – that is, one stimulated by a range of orientations core to the academic project – theory, method, substance – the model of balance urged on us was oriented to a diversity of political positions. In other words, balance was viewed in political terms rather than academic terms. This emphasis misconstrues the central goal of the academy, which is not the achievement of a political outcome.

Although the structures put in place for decision making regarding the conference – an Advisory Committee, a call for papers on conference themes, a review of submitted abstracts based on scholarly merit and relevance to themes, et cetera – had the hallmarks of scholarly judgment, the calls for balance had the hallmarks of a particular and academically inappropriate form of political judgment. Calls for balance can appear to be a methodological tool that ensures that prior commitments, including political commitments, are banished from the academic enterprise, but ironically balance in our case advanced a political value, not an academic one. As a non-academic tool, balance is vulnerable to whichever group wishes to ensure that its agenda is promoted at junctures and in events that it finds auspicious. It is telling that those calling for balance in our program never once asked (and surely it never once occurred to them to ask) that we have a representative from Hamas to provide balance on the other end of the political spectrum.

With the understanding of knowledge and the academy presented above, the latter is guild-like, and academic freedom protects the liberty of this guild to proceed according to its own professional norms, directed as they are to the production of knowledge, and following its unique version of the integrity of the process. But if the knowledge generated is not absolute but partial and limited and ultimately predetermined by a vast network of prior judgment and interest, how prey is it to political capture? Are there neutral grounds – particularly in the context of the Middle East – to which we might turn to distinguish scholarship from activism and advocacy? Furthermore, is it necessarily a virtue for scholars to maintain that distinction in their work?

Engagement

York University has committed itself through a recent provostial paper to promoting the idea of "engaged" scholarship, the idea that there should be greater synergies between community groups and the university both in the sharing and in the development of ideas.[42] Although an extraordinarily vague and plastic term (and no doubt an expedient one for that reason), "engagement" suggests the antithesis of scholars whose central goals are the rendering of subjects into objects of inquiry and the training of students in the skills and habits of that exercise. Universities, in the engaged model, become "key drivers of economic and social innovation," collaborate with community groups "for the mutually beneficial exchange of knowledge and resources,"[43] act in a "socially responsible" manner, search for and produce "solutions to pressing social, economic, political and cultural issues,"[44] "share a vision of enhanced civic engagement, community well-being, and heightened responsiveness to pressing social issues with many external constituencies,"[45] and "prepare educated, engaged citizens and strengthen democratic values and civic responsibility."[46] If this is the mission to which the university is hinging its identity, then it is difficult to see how any conference that works with community groups and invites participation from committed actors who are actively promoting a particular vision of social justice and rehearsing their dearest ideals of civil responsibility, strengthening democratic values, responding to pressing social issues, and finding solutions to pressing political issues is doing anything other than rehearsing the very goals set by the university. By these standards, the Mapping Models conference would have met the university ideal had the Organizing Committee actively *sought* the participation of activists and advocates.[47] But also, by these standards, the line between scholarship and advocacy is less clearly demarcated, and, commensurately, the justification of academic freedom that roots the scholarly enterprise in the ability of experts to advance knowledge appears to be compromised. Scholars, in this model, advance agendas – aesthetic, social, economic, political – as much as they advance knowledge.

The postmodern epistemologies laid out above seem to move this view of the relationship between politics and knowledge forward. One feature of the approach to academic freedom noted by Rorty and others is that it localizes and historicizes the doctrine, just as knowledge itself issues from partial, historically contingent, and ultimately limited human practices. To the extent that the academic guild cannot link its advances to absolute knowledge, participants can be said to be interested from the outset in the outcomes that they seek. The proofs that they invoke and the criteria for knowledge and methodologies are already inflected by their prior commitments, beliefs, and judgments.

This is certainly the way that it often feels in the domain of Middle East studies. It appears that, between Edward Said and Benny Morris, Ali Abunimah and Gerald Steinberg, there is no objective common ground of judgment or understanding that might provide the means for resolving scholarly disagreements between them. One group of scholars chooses its objects of inquiry, the historical and narrative backgrounds that launch their intrigues, and the "facts" that are congenially assumed; these commitments – simultaneously deep political commitments – shape the research that they conduct and the conclusions that they reach. Groundless as the *gzerots* nailed down around each study on the Middle East, the intellectual tensions appear to be as nakedly political as those among actual politicians. Every intellectual position staked out seems to come down on one side or the other of a political debate, and this coincidence of conclusion and position appears to be far from coincidental. In this regard, it matters almost wholly that Said and Abunimah are Diaspora Palestinians and that Morris and Steinberg are Israeli Jews. One hardly need go further and read what they write.

Similarly, in this analysis, the preface to this book is, or should be, relevant to the reader since my personal formation has had considerable implications for my intellectual formation. The fact that I am not Jewish but am married to a Jew whose father went through the Holocaust, and the fact that I am a Montreal anglophone whose family stayed behind, leaving me culturally predisposed to binational federalism, have some bearing on the rest of the book, which is enlivened and usefully made more complex by personal revelations. These facts are far from the least relevant facts that have been presented so far in the monograph, and their presence in the preface preshadows where the book's intellectual narratives wander. My personal and political engagements have something to do with my scholarly agenda. The postmodern emphasis on the groundlessness of knowledge in anything more than familiar worlds appears to advance this thesis about the engagement of scholarship with multiple levels of being. And just as the Iacobucci Report and its putatively impartial structure of inquiry – the very heading of it by a former Supreme Court judge – renders Osgoode's former dean and former associate vice-president academic invisible and anonymous, their commitments obscure, and their actions bureaucratized, the alternative approach to texts engages the reader with the identities of authors.

The postmodern emphasis on communities of practice and the disciplinary cultures of the university might also appear to provide fodder for an erasure of clear lines between knowledge and politics (though it also suggests a means for drawing sharp lines between the two on the basis of the distinctiveness of the academy's disciplinary practices and professional norms). The return to professional norms and disciplines as the mechanisms by which to identify appropriate constraints on the production of knowledge seems to be further undermined by an awareness that disciplinary communities themselves are often fraught with hierarchies of power and self-interested orthodoxies and often manifest an inertia and power dynamic of their own. Disciplines *discipline* thought in ways that often preclude critiques of their foundational views of the world, disciplining perception and voice in ways that are often indistinguishable from the repressions of etiquette and propriety.

This disciplinary function (i.e., the conservative policing function of academic disciplines) is almost nakedly evident in the attempt to confine scholarly work on the one-state model to those within the "right" discipline and with the "right" network of contacts. Disciplinary communities can provide a more stable consensus for the special freedom of scholars from supervisory meddling; however, the structure of cognitive authority that they provide can suppress innovative thinking in the name of immutable standards. As Joan Scott points out,

> disciplinary communities are hierarchical and with a power dynamic of their own. If the community certifies the competence of its members and protects them from external meddling, it also establishes methods of inquiry ("disciplined and systematic training") and standards of judgment ("selecting and recruiting new members") as well as behavioral norms ("cooperating through mutual criticism"). Those who write the history of disciplines and those of us who have broken new ground in our fields know that discipline and disciple can be synonyms as well as antonyms and that punishment is not always the alternative to discipline, but often its regulatory tool.[48]

The very mechanisms by which disciplines purport to protect knowledge from political inflection are themselves laced with power dynamics and protective of interests. Mastery and excellence often shore up the distinct interests of the guardians of orthodoxy. The experience of Mazen Masri, a conference organizer, illustrates this point. His insights into what was happening with the conference were often just as, if not more, prescient than those of the rest of us. Yet we were encouraged to remove him from the Organizing Committee on the ground that he was only a graduate student.

It appears that this interested and committed background for academic practices should render suspect what counts as knowledge; furthermore, given the hierarchical and orthodox nature of every academic discipline and the way in which that orthodoxy becomes entrenched interstitially in the mundane and ponderous decisions about whom to hire and what to study and teach, it can appear that knowledge itself is *always* inflected with the subtleties of power. The forms of judgment requisite to the academic project can ultimately seem indistinguishable from the forms of judgment requisite to the political one – and this is a conundrum that needs to be addressed vis-à-vis the distinctive claims that the academy can make with respect to its unique liberty.

The disciplinary model of the advancement of knowledge is rendered even more fragile when the unstable nature of the way in which disciplinary norms are advanced is recognized. Robert Post himself acknowledges that it is almost the nature of professional norms that they are systematically contested: "Professional norms are also themselves forms of knowledge that are best advanced when debated with the kind of dissent that requires academic freedom. Academic freedom thus appears to be simultaneously limited by and independent of professional norms."[49] This generates what appears to be a paradox about the adequacy of professional norms, one that was implicit as a theme in this case study. The tenuous and labile nature of those scholarly standards of competence, and their vulnerability to complicity with conventional or hegemonic pieties, routinely trouble the stability of the academic mission. Although academic inquiry unsettles the established norms of inquiry and outcome, there is reassurance in the recognition that "contestation drives the conversation that constitutes ordinary scholarly life."[50] For Post, orthodoxies are challenged with sufficient vigour that only the most defensible can survive.

Judith Butler goes further than Post in unpacking the dynamic relationship between the established norms of intellectual inquiry within disciplines and the recognition that those established norms are perpetually challenged and pushed: "To limit forms of dissent in advance to those that conform to existing norms is to safeguard those very norms against dissent, not only imposing a certain censorship on the reach of dissent, but also undermining the creative power of dissenting views to initiate new fields of knowledge and new disciplinary or cross-disciplinary paradigms."[51] As much as those who justify academic freedom by the professional constraints provided by the disciplines of the academy, professional norms do not apply themselves as though they are technical tools applied to a task. Rather, professional norms "are in the process of being produced, and sometimes judgment is the very site where norms are renewed, revised, and invented. Indeed, without their contestatory character, norms would be essentially dead, frozen in time, and so too, sadly, would be the vocation of knowledge itself."[52]

To the asymmetries of power embedded in the hierarchical nature of academic disciplines and the potential for a drift toward orthodoxy within them, their very lability suggests a loosely organized and constantly evolving social foundation for the advancement of knowledge that justifies academic freedom. It is not simply discrete data that are assessed through a process of peer review but also – often and critically – the boundaries and intelligibility of the professional norms invoked. This looping can be seen in debates about the right of return or the significance of the state of Israel being Jewish: our understandings of international law and nationalism, and the disciplines specific to each topic of inquiry, are advanced by an examination of the case of Israel/Palestine just as this case is understood by reference to the disciplines of public international law and citizenship studies.

Post argues that professional competence is properly determined primarily by peers within a particular discipline. However, given the perpetual challenges to the established norms of inquiry that comprise the hallmark of innovative scholarly research, both the established body of peers and professional norms are in perpetual flux. Revelatory new work creates a new body of peers and new professional norms by which and against which intellectual work must be assessed.

These extrapolations from postmodern understandings seem to suggest that knowledge sooner or later conflates with power. It appears to be shrewd to regard what currently counts as knowledge as suspect, to hedge that no account is properly susceptible to peer review. The current structures of cognitive authority seem to be poised to reflect the ideological commitments, beliefs, and interests of those in power. If that is the case, then how can academic freedom be justified? Not only is knowledge partial and limited, but also it seems to be simultaneously groundless and biased toward whoever can capture the social capital that the academy embeds within society.

The varied accounts and conclusions of the Iacobucci Report and *No Debate* appear to be instantiations of this competition over the social capital of the academy. Yet both authors wrote as though questions about what happened and what might be said about what happened mattered and as though getting it right (about the world and vis-à-vis academic freedom), rather than spinning a tale, characterized their respective enterprises. And both the provost and I marshalled "evidence" for our accounts on the premise that bodies of data confirmed or validated them and provided means of measuring misdescription, misinterpretation, and interest.

Several things can be said about the conclusions that seem to flow naturally from the postmodern account presented by authors such as Fish and Rorty. To begin with, a simple-minded postmodernism that takes this conundrum about the relationship between knowledge and power and conflates the two would radically undermine the very work in which even the most postmodern of scholars are engaged. Said, for example, whose work on the ways in which knowledge is socially constructed and politically inflected,[53] qualifies him alongside Rorty and Fish as a leading postmodernist (in the sense of the term that I have been advancing here) could not have embarked on his examination of spurious scholarship in the Israeli/Palestinian context without making distinctions between knowledge and the ideological screens that obscure it.[54]

The most extreme conflation of knowledge and politics is difficult to get off the ground; however, finding a rebuff to the claim of conference critics that we had polemicists and activists rather than scholars presenting papers was no easy or desirable task. Is it necessarily wrong for academics to engage the political when they engage the scholarly? Is there a way of doing so that does not compromise an operational goal of academic work that justifies academic freedom? Is it possible to be politically committed and a scholar and legitimately to bring both commitments to bear on the same exercise, be it research or teaching?

This question about whether there was inappropriate politicking (activism, polemics, advocacy) in the Mapping Models conference raises several straightforward issues and some vexatious philosophical ones. The simplest issues speak to the transparent politics of groups such as CIJA and the Jewish Defence League complaining about politicking at academic events. Both groups have clear viewpoints and endpoints that they wanted to promote and protect through their interventions as well as fairly identifiable constituencies that they represented. Gary Goodyear, the Conservative minister of science and technology, who disrupted the arm's-length relationship that the government normally maintains with academic funding agencies, had a political goal and a distinct constituency in mind when he intervened.

These practical instances of the inappropriate insertion of politics into scholarship seem to be more or less clear. An agenda is being promoted; a vote is being taken; a constituency is being courted – these activities have contexts and practices readily identifiable as distinct from the academic context with its particular values. The more difficult conundrum is whether the analytical line between politics and scholarship in internal academic activities such as research or a conference such as Mapping Models can be as neatly drawn – and whether it *should* be.

In his controversial book *Save the World on Your Own Time,* Stanley Fish is emphatic that there is no place for politics in academia. This position has the virtue of maintaining the mission of academic freedom that emerged in North America with the 1915 AAUP declaration and has been honed and exemplified throughout the twentieth century and early twenty-first century. This mission hinges on the idea that scholarship is disinterested in the sense that it is primarily driven to find true answers to particular kinds of questions and that scholars need to be free to search for truth without political or other external constraints. This freedom from political constraints included, in the 1915 declaration, political values that work from inside the profession and inside the scholar/teacher and inflect the scholarship and pedagogy carried out. Academic freedom was a liberty that could be claimed only by "those who carry on their work in the temper of the scientific inquirer" and never by those who would use it "for uncritical and intemperate partisanship."[55] Fish is unequivocal that the distinction between doing scholarly work and doing political work is not only clear enough to be pragmatically useful but also critical to the integrity of the profession and the extraordinary warrant attendant upon the associated freedom.

The mechanisms by which Fish maintains this distinction derive, not surprisingly given his antecedent work, from values and practices that issue from the community of scholars, the ethos of which justifies academic freedom. The cardinal value associated with the academy is the pursuit of truth, a value that entails a deep commitment that is inconsistent with relativism as well as the metaphor of the academy as a marketplace of ideas. As Fish notes,

> by invoking the criterion of truth, I've already answered the objection that an academicized classroom – a classroom where political and moral agendas are analyzed, not embraced – would be value-free and relativistic. If anything is a value, truth is, and the implicit (and sometimes explicit) assumption in the classroom as I envision it is that truth, and the seeking of truth, must always be defended. To be sure, truth is not the only value and there are others that should be defended in the contexts to which they are central; but truth is a pre-eminent *academic* value, and adherence to it is exactly the opposite of moral relativism.[56]

The search for truth is not only the core value of the academy, but its paramountcy also overrides a great deal of the more fashionable values that many contemporary universities espouse along with those with more nefarious intentions. Respectful dialogue (espoused by the Iacobucci Report on the Mapping Models conference[57]) would be an extraneous value for Fish: if ideas are not worthy of respect because they are incoherent and unpersuasive or because they lead to false conclusions, then it would pervert the academic enterprise to respect them. Tolerance, similarly, is a value that, however vaunted outside the academy, has no place within it as a standalone virtue. Students would be ill served by a professor who tolerated intellectually intolerable arguments. And intellectual diversity and balance (goals now cynically promoted in Middle East studies by off-campus advocates such as David Horowitz as a means of ensuring that Zionists always have a say in the conversation) are not goals that a self-respecting scholar or university would promote. The only true academic requirement for a diversity of contending views is that, "no matter how many (or few) views are presented to the students, they should be offered as objects of *analysis* rather than as candidates for allegiance."[58] For Fish, the question "what is the truth?" – about a particular area of inquiry – can be answered with the kinds of things that academics typically draw on to get at the truth: the quality and quantity of evidence, the cogency of argument, the soundness of conclusions, and so on.

The method by which all academics maintain this apolitical search for the truth is, according to Fish, to transform the subject of intrigue for the scholar into an object of inquiry. Fish calls this "academicizing." There is no subject of inquiry that is incapable of being transformed into an object of inquiry, even the most politically explosive ones, such as the Israeli/Palestinian conflict. Academicizing a topic involves "detach[ing] it from the context of its real world urgency, where there is a vote to be taken or an agenda to be embraced, and insert[ing] it into a context of academic urgency, where there is an account to be offered or an analysis to be performed."[59]

This critical operation of transforming subjects into objects of inquiry entails a loosening – sometimes a radical loosening – of the scholar's prior commitments to particular outcomes or viewpoints. For Fish, to be worthy of the guild (for which the attendant freedom is justified), academics must transform objects of affection into objects of analysis. Hints of the former contaminate what enables the latter to qualify as a practice worthy of respect – both within the academy and within society at large. In this analysis, the preface to this book, to the extent that it has any scholarly merit at all, is useful as a mechanism only to enable the reader and me to detach more honestly from all of the prior commitments embedded within its narrative structure. The measure of the rest of the monograph's ability to detach thus is taken between its pages and the critical faculties honed by those participants trained to decipher truth from obfuscation in either of the book's central themes. The preface falls away almost immediately as irrelevant to this undertaking, a disposable literary snippet ultimately unrelated to the book's work.

On the surface, it might seem jarring that one of the scholars most dedicated to a postmodern epistemology of the academy and its associated liberties adopts an unusually (these days) stringent position in favour of depleting the academic mission of the interests and prior commitments that appear implicitly to structure the plausibility of the very enterprise. Knowledge in this epistemology is collectively structured by practitioners of a very specific and historically shaped form of life; it is not certified by any more transcendent truths or by an objective "real world" beyond its confines. What counts in the academy is the internal perspective of its practice – the methods of certification and validation such as peer review – rather than some external sounding board that confirms the internal perspective's validity. As a result of this historically contingent exercise, the truths generated by today's academy might be vulnerable to challenge and fraught with orthodoxies and debilitating blindspots. It is always the case that academics might get it wrong.

Fish goes on from this general theory of truth, however, to point out that this larger, ultimately fragile, epistemology does not change the particular and local intrigues with which academics are engaged. There is no logical inconsistency in Edward Said pointing to how whole disciplines such as anthropology or history have been committed through their methodologies and frameworks of knowledge to very distinctive political projects such as colonialism[60] and then debunking, with every drop of the certainty marshalled to document other historical events, claims about the departure of Palestinians from the forming state of Israel in 1948.[61]

Fish himself finesses these distinctions between general theories of truth and the criteria of truth invoked in local academic projects by noting that, "while questions of truth may be generally open, the truth of academic matters is not general but local; questions are posed and often they do have answers that can be established with certainty; and even if that certainty can theoretically be upset – one cannot rule out the future emergence of new evidence – that theoretical possibility carries with it no methodological obligation."[62] Ultimate epistemological fragility does not compel, for example, the presentation of as many pretenders to an idea as possible; nor does it require that astrologists and Holocaust deniers be given a place at the academic table. Even though the best standards available to us for arriving at the truth are only as good as those generated by our communities of practice and our best lights, those standards do generate what we mean by the truth, what we mean by certainty, and what we mean by knowledge. Our standards of proof and evidence have built up from the (usually stable) bedrock of these shared practices, which generate methods of triangulating our positions in the landscape of the referential world and criteria to determine when such an endeavour has been successful.

For Fish, this ultimately fragile epistemological base provides us with all of the certainty that we need to distinguish political from scholarly work and for a renewal of the call for administrators, the government, off-campus constituencies, *and* scholars to keep politics out of the academic mission. To the objection (cultivated by postmodernism's relentless emphasis over the past several decades on the constructed nature of knowledge) that it is not possible to hive off personal and political commitments from the work demanded by each discipline, Fish responds by noting that the difficulty of the exercise of distinguishing contexts and the behaviours appropriate to each does not equate to the impossibility of doing so. So the facts that Said (an early proponent of the binational model) was Palestinian and that Morris (a strenuous opponent of the one-state model) is Jewish Israeli do not preclude them from struggling (and largely succeeding) to academicize material when it comes to them in the context of their professional lives – just as the preface to this book is similarly irrelevant to its intellectual content. Fish notes that "we are perfectly capable of acting in accordance with the norms that belong to our present sphere of activity [academic activity in this case], even if our 'take' on those norms is inflected somewhat by norms we affirm elsewhere."[63] The forms of activity characteristic of academic life are, for Fish, relatively easy to distinguish from the forms of activity that characterize political life. Academic work should not be engaged simultaneously in advancing political causes.

Extrapolating from *Save the World on Your Own Time,* it appears that Fish would reject the entire agenda of York's "engaged" university laid out in the provost's white paper cited at the beginning of this chapter and reiterate that these values are not those of the scholarly community, which should aim at the discovery of truth, not the advancement of social, economic, or any other virtue – or at least reject an unqualified version of it. The truth might jar with each one of those agendas – yet it should always prevail for a scholar.

Even accepting Fish's stark separation of knowledge and politics in the academy, the conclusion that the line between local communities and the academy needs to be sharply drawn can be perilously overstated because much can be lost in the disengagement of the academy from its surrounding society. There should be a means by which the university remains engaged with that society that does not come at the cost of its most cherished values: that is, that courts the forms of engagement appropriate to the scholarly mission, not a civic or political or economic mission. The means of reconciling the two, while preserving the core values of the academy, might not lie in making questionable distinctions among polemicists, activists, advocates, and scholars – a schema that distinguishes types of people rather than the activities in which they engage, distinctions that often seem to be inflected by polemical and political judgments. Valorization of the scholarly impulse to transform everything into an object of inquiry – no matter how controversial and including both polemics and activism – suggests an approach with greater integrity and resilience. It also suggests that the querulous and hair-splitting banter of the academy is a better guide for what counts as scholarship than any of the other pretenders – government, on- and off-campus constituencies, and administrations.

That "academicization" – Fish's word for the transformation of subjects into objects of inquiry – is the paramount virtue that scholars provide even when they engage whole-heartedly with non-academic communities can be seen from a defence that Osgoode's former dean offered to justify his interventions in the Mapping Models conference. In his six-page "Preliminary Review" of my complaint about his conduct,[64] Patrick Monahan noted about himself that "a series of significant concerns had come to the attention of the Dean regarding the organization of the conference." To his mind, these "significant concerns" justified his involvement in the event. One of those concerns was that "the vast majority of the 40 speakers confirmed at that point appeared to be proponents of a one-state model." The dean simply assumed that this was a legitimate problem justifying his intervention. He went on, in a document meant to defend his conduct, to state unabashedly that he therefore suggested to us that, "in an effort to recruit additional internationally respected speakers at this late stage, respected proponents of a two-state model should be invited to participate as keynote speakers."

Even without this admission of intervention, the documentary record from accessed emails revealed as much, but this is not what is interesting about what he himself construed as a *defence* of his conduct. Revealingly, he assumed that there is unregenerate content that reasonable people will agree is off limits for academia. This, after all, was his justification of his conduct. It is the goes-without-saying nature of his assumption of what is beyond the pale that is intriguing. What if we had a roster of *nothing but* one-state proponents for our event – as, in fact, was not only our original intention but also the original intention that the dean supported and signed off on? Is it really so commonsensical that a dean should intervene?

Fish himself insists that there is *no* content that is too controversial to be transformed into an object of inquiry, even as he insists that academics should not be engaged in political work when they are engaged as academics (i.e., engaged in academicizing). As already argued, academicizing is not mindless detachment, which is why astrologers and Holocaust deniers are merely vacuous pretenders. It is not that scholars should exercise a constant refusal to allow prior understandings of the world to guide discovery. Indeed, quite the opposite: it is their disciplined efforts to build from the most discerning of those understandings that provide scholars with the judgment – an almost ineffable qualification – requisite to the task.

However, one way in which polemics are distinguished from scholarship is when outputs are wed to undiscerning preorganized outcomes leading the intellectual to be oblivious of essential and compelling counternarratives and data. Polemicists, it can be said by the discerning, are wed to transparently partial accounts at the expense of more robust ones.

Judith Jarvis Thomson does a beautiful job of describing the kinds of scholarly judgment that are suspect for manifesting too deep an affiliation with prior commitments, but she also points to the delicacy of assessing signs of too much commitment:

> There is such a thing as excessive love of one's own commitments, of course, even where what lies behind it is concern for the truth and not merely for status, but the signs of it are likely to be delicate. I have in mind the thinking of people who know of data that appear to conflict with their theories, but do not take seriously enough the task of confronting the data. (How seriously is seriously enough? That is hard to say. There are times when it is right simply to plow ahead, hoping that the apparent conflicts can be sorted out later.) Or the thinking of people who know of data that appear to conflict with their theories, and construct excessively ornate procedures for squaring the data with the theories. (There are epicycles in nature; which postulated epicycles are excessively ornate?)[65]

One observation worth noting about Jarvis Thomson's subtle and somewhat hesitant remarks is that we might have different things to say about people who appear to have loose relationships with data depending on where they are at in their research. It is one thing at the outset of an inquiry to put aside concerns about inconsistent material in order to make sense of a larger or proximate set of issues. There are times when it is right simply to plow ahead. In the early stages of research, nothing is yet written in stone, and a fanatical concern over incongruent details can be crippling to the overall inquiry. Indeed, as Jarvis Thomson notes, epicycles exist, and it can be untimely to foreclose an elaborate hypothesis in order to square theory with facts that can otherwise be digested. It is another thing altogether at the end of a stint of research for a scholar to knowingly occlude data that inconveniently undermine a thesis. There is less latitude at that juncture to forgive a scholar for standing back from inconvenient details and scouting around for what might improve an argument.

But before a paper is written, a presentation delivered, there is a range of research activities that does not yet demand a wholly formed and thoroughly substantiated position on which a scholar's credibility can be hinged. Academic conferences are one such activity. This takes me back to the former dean's defence that his intervention in an academic event was justified because of "significant concerns" that the majority of speakers at the Mapping Models conference were proponents of a one-state model.

Academic conferences constitute a scholarly activity different from the output that academics generate under their own names. They do not, globally, have the same kind of imprimatur (if they have one at all) that can be attributed to a scholarly author; only actual presenters at a conference are responsible for the content of their work. Conferences fall more into the domain of activities that actively transform matter into objects of inquiry. As whole events, they are characterized as much by gaze as by posture – though an active gaze, like the ethnographic one.

The purpose of academic conferences is to bring presenters and data together to subject them to the crucible of scholarly attention. There is nothing about an entire roster of one-state advocates that precludes it from this treatment. As Ian Lustick noted in the op-ed cited above, the proper measure of a valid academic exercise should come from whether or not "what will be said will contribute to the ability of members of the community to improve their arguments."[66] Whether or not a particular event achieves this ambition is not only independent of each presenter's content but also ultimately independent of the event's content – just as ethnography is capable of transforming through its gaze almost any data into evidence of cultural phenomena and is far from automatically impoverished by having dull and prosaic material as its object.

Just as an ethnographer is both participant and observer (in and of the field as much as he or she watches it), an engaged scholar, like an engaged university, can carry the academy's discreet virtue of detachment and disengagement – the methodologies or mindsets requisite to the task of transforming things into objects of inquiry – as intrepidly into any number of contexts. Precluding a priori some contexts and some content as inherently too prosaic or, more to the point, inherently imbued with political attachment makes no sense at all. Such a manoeuvre fails to apprehend the potential omnipresence of the academy's equivalent of an ethnographic gaze. And it fails to perceive how, just as certainly, the most seemingly mundane of common senses can trip a scholar up.

The ethnographer, like the conference attendee, is what completes the alchemy. Indeed, since the ability of members of the community to improve their arguments is just as reliant on the observer's capacity for discernment as the presenter's, it is theoretically possible that a roster of none but unbridled one-state *polemicists* could improve the arguments of those in attendance – just as observing the subtleties of how polemicists assail events such as academic conferences has instructive potential.

It is indeed possible for a world-class university to "sponsor" a presenter who is widely reputed to be a radical polemicist on the topic of Israel/Palestine and suffer no harm to its reputation for dedication to "rigour, reasoned discourse and a willingness to accept dissent and deal with complex issues."[67] This was certainly the case when Osgoode Hall Law School hosted Alan Dershowitz to present his views on the Middle East during Patrick Monahan's deanship. The presenter no more taints the university's or law school's character than the presence of *Mein Kampf* on the library's bookshelves aligns the institution with its content. The university becomes associated or disassociated with the content of ideas only when it weighs in – and it does so ill advisedly.

As another former dean of Osgoode and former president of York, Harry Arthurs, noted in an address on the topic of academic freedom, "if academic freedom implies the right of professors to make controversial statements, it also implies the right of other members of the community – including the president – to disagree, to condemn and or repudiate those statements."[68] This, it should be stressed, is different from determining or guiding the content of research activity.

Arthurs went on to query whether "the university's duty to abstain from punishing people also means that it has to be indifferent or silent about their behaviour." He responded to this question with a heavy note of caution:

> Generally speaking, I would say "yes." Indeed, the university should err on the side of being supportive, even when it hurts. It should defend the principle, of course, rather than the individual, and it can do this by trying to get people to see that society's long run interests are best served by allowing all opinions to be expressed, however unpalatable they may seen.[69]

When *administrators* (rather than scholars) determine that concerns over content are "significant" and reason that some content is, almost as a matter of fact, beyond the pale (or argue that some presenters are polemicists or activists or overly attached to their causes), it becomes easy to associate administrators with the content of ideas and the thrust of presenters from whom they did not dissociate themselves. At that point, the university's integrity, hinged on its ability to secure academic freedom, might already be badly tarnished. Again, the difficult work of intellectual discernment that Jarvis Thomson alludes to is best left to the noisy and querulous work of academics, not administrators or governments.

More than these fine-grained arguments being better housed within the scholarly community, the academy, with its finely honed and profoundly hierarchical judgments on what is stellar and illuminating research and what is shallow and meritless, cannot survive without making these kinds of delicate and often arcane distinctions about the quality of work to which Jarvis Thomson alludes. Indeed, this work of sifting the intellectual wheat from the chaff constitutes the bulk of the quotidian work of academics. It is the work of peer review.

By implication, it is no answer to a charge of polemics – or at least no answer worthy of the academy – that all scholarship is polemics. Polemicists, by definition, are insufficiently committed to first-class work. They first and foremost have a love of their own commitments. They are almost as much a plague on the academy as plagiarists, though they are more often tolerated on campus since their output often does not constitute an academic sin – unless banalities and blinkers are sins rather than the mundane foes of scholars. Scholarly communities need to retain the category of polemicist as much as they need to keep in sight the spectre of people who know of data that appear to conflict with their theories but do not take seriously enough the task of confronting them.

Jarvis Thomson, however (and as if we need any reminder at this juncture), points out how subtle the lines can be between polemics and scholarship and how, for that reason, vexed. As almost all interventions in the Middle East abundantly illustrate, the first line of assault against a scholar who troubles the settled world of a reviewer can be an ad hominem attack on his or her origins – a psychosocial and biographical account of motives and style of presentation rather than a confrontation of the claims with the data.

But just as commonly, and quite legitimately, the first line of assault against a polemicist can be an appraisal of the character and tone of his or her presentation – manifestations of a rant, of undue dismissiveness and irascibility, of an unseemly intolerance of conflicting positions. The cues that feed into such an account might well end up bleeding into the psychosocial and biographical background of the scholar, for that can be precisely the place from which the overweaned love of prior commitments derives. This background can be part of the data that explain the phenomenon.

And, just as worryingly for those who would like to make respectable discourse and decorum the hallmarks of the academy, those stylistic traits (ranting, irascibility, intolerance) can be the signature of a brilliant scholar who lives sufficiently outside the conventional pieties of settled accounts that he or she feels perpetually irked by imbecility – and shows it. So how exactly should the line be drawn between polemics and scholarship? And who should draw it?

The approach to ideas suggested by thinkers such as Rorty, Jarvis Thomson, and Fish suggests that the criteria for what counts as scholarship (as opposed to polemics) are best left to the "constant and indecisive quarrel"[70] that more often, and with greater integrity than decorum, is the hallmark of the academy. The judgment requisite to the scholarly endeavour is fine indeed – and often equally ineffable. If the judgment is sound (and it is more likely to be if it issues from the disciplines and rigours of the academy), then it will provide some attestation to the worthiness of an idea, for that is where some (though not all) of society's brightest lights are concentrated.

But this constant and indecisive quarrel provides no absolute warrant. The entire web of understandings on which discernment rests is partial and historically contingent, as is the web of understanding that leads to the judgment that one scholar is a bright light and the next an unregenerate apologist. And the web is paradoxically strengthened and kept glistening by being routinely shaken, torn away, and rebuilt. Yet just as consistent as the quarrel within academia is the certitude that leaving some other institution or group to build its network produces a remarkably more shoddy tissue of beliefs.

Conclusion

Epicycles and Political Work

That this text is an ethnography, albeit an unintended one, is flagged not only by its struggle to achieve a dispassionate gaze and its preoccupation with the minutiae of a particular field of human endeavour but also by one of the methodology's leading entry points into the field: participant observation. As I suggested in the last chapter, an ethnographer is in and of the field as much as he or she is outside it, taking it in. Ethnography does not allow for the neatest of separations between object and subject. The spatial (and psychological) separation of the world of the ethnographer and the world of his or her inquiry is not clean.

This blurriness between the world of ideas (generated through ethnography's kin: academicization) and the world at large has been intimated at several times in this monograph, from the idea of the "engaged" university; to Richard Rorty's affirmation that "the distinction between academic politics and the disinterested pursuit of truth is pretty fuzzy";[1] even to Stanley Fish's observation that "we are perfectly capable of acting in accordance with the norms that belong to our present sphere of activity [academic activity in this case], even if our 'take' on those norms is inflected somewhat by norms we affirm elsewhere."[2] The ghettos of the academic disciplines function in the particular ways that they do (generating Talmudic complexity, specificity, and certainty) because the connections to the surrounding society are what they are and happen to have a particular historical configuration. Practitioners within these disciplines might struggle toward autonomy, but they can never really exist and move as though they are not thoroughly ligamented to a surrounding context.

As a result, "pure" academicization – an utterly detached transformation of matters into objects of inquiry – is not only a fantasy but might actually do violence to the objects under study – and to the world and the truth. The violence stems in some measure from the sense that commitment and engagement – under the sway of a compulsion – inherently obstruct the truth. That they do not requires some epistemological unpacking. But let me begin with a methodological critique.

From a methodological point of view, participant observation is a classic form of this type of revelatory approach to the world that stems from engagement – which is not to say that intimacy with what one has lived does not present quagmires in which writing can become bogged down. Anyone who has done fieldwork can attest that finding a way into the field – connecting with it in such a way that it gets under the skin, cuts close to the bone, becomes readily available – is a daunting task that outsiders embark on with a combination of trepidation and moxy. But any ethnographer who has faced the prospect of writing up what has become second nature also knows how difficult it can be to force into the mind things that, by that point, almost go without saying. The exercise of writing up requires detaching oneself from a familiar context in order to offer an account of it. The tug of the familiar can be a distraction. Fish's observations on the academic mission jell with this aspect of ethnographic work when Fish describes academicizing as detaching a topic "from the context of its real world urgency, where there is a vote to be taken or an agenda to be embraced, and insert[ing] it into a context of academic urgency, where there is an account to be offered or an analysis to be performed." Although *Save the World on Your Own Time* is directed principally to that part of an academic's work devoted to the classroom, his view of the obligation of scholars when confronted with conflicting views from the field fits well with the other bread and butter of their daily lives: scholarship. Fish observes that the only true academic requirement with respect to a diversity of contending views is that "no matter how many (or few) views are presented ... they should be offered as objects of *analysis* rather than as candidates for allegiance."[3] The writing of a compelling ethnography also requires this difficult demand to analyze rather than resolve. If that is not the task at hand, then why not, in the idiom of anthropology, simply "go native," give up the extraordinary warrant attendant upon the freedom associated with the academy, and become an ordinary citizen, protected from the vagaries of power by the thinner rights of freedom of association and expression?

The subject of the Middle East is plagued with seemingly interminable ways in which little stays still long enough to *be* an object of inquiry, isolated from its surrounding context. Seemingly, nobody and no act are immune from the hypertrophied impulses of the Middle East to locate any intervention (including each author who has been cited in this text) on a realpolitik spectrum and treat it accordingly. There are no universally recognized authorities of the Middle East's middle ground – because there is no apparent middle ground. The biographies of many (including the literatures that they read and the news that they follow) lead them to draw often foreseeable conclusions. Just as inevitably, every author who ventures a view risks having his or her biographical life scrutinized if not impinged upon. So Benny Morris, one of the first New Historians to uncover the extent of the Palestinian catastrophe of 1948, became a *persona non grata* at a swath of academic events for his failure to condemn the ethnic cleansing that his historical research revealed.[4] And Richard Goldstone, an internationally respected authority on war crimes before he drafted his analysis of the Gaza War, found himself "in great distress and under duress"[5] and unable to attend his grandson's bar mitzvah since those who objected to his report threatened to protest at the family synagogue.[6] Movingly, Goldstone told *Ha'aretz* that, despite the attacks on him in Jewish communities, he did not regret agreeing to chair the investigative committee. "I felt that because I was Jewish, it would be hypocritical not to get involved in the Middle East," he told Akiva Eldar of *Ha'aretz,* explaining that he was a Zionist but did not intend to visit Israel any time soon because of concern over personal security. He also said that he was saddened by what he saw as recent attacks on Israel's democracy, including bills banning criticism of the Israeli defence forces.[7]

Beyond these pragmatic considerations of how work on the Middle East is digested and construed in ways that consume the middle ground, and how disciplines associated with the area are deeply contested and seemingly politicized from top to bottom, is the more subtle philosophical point that the incommensurable realpolitiks of the Middle East rest on concepts such as democracy and human rights, statehood and citizenship, that are themselves not only fraught and contested but also looped into the Middle East in such a way that our understandings of those concepts get their traction partly from the quagmire of the Middle East. The meta-concepts illuminate the particular instance just as the particular instance reconfigures our sense of the general, and this constant repositioning is not appreciable from an Archimedean point outside the endless debates that swirl around the area of inquiry.

Furthermore, there is contiguity between historical events and contemporary understandings, both political and scholarly. This is evident in the emergence of Goldstone's understanding of human rights from his understanding of the Holocaust or Morris's personal awareness of the vulnerability of the Jews informing his sense of the urgencies of war.

There is also contiguity between contemporary understandings (political and scholarly) and the rich terrain of data and meaning that gets churned up in the course of an ordinary human life. Understandings bleed into each other and transfer their associated ripples of meaning to the larger swells of individual and collective life. More to the point of this monograph, the debates on and contestations over the topic of Israel/Palestine consume at various junctures localized debates on academic freedom and change the complexion of the doctrine, presenting it with new challenges.

When we bring to bear our powers of discernment on a particular object of inquiry (in the case of this monograph, particular interventions in a conference), it is not always the case, or always beneficially the case, that these cognate forms of judgment are suspended. This is particularly so in the social sciences. Not everything counts equally as an idea worthy of thought, and deciphering the worthiness of ideas requires judgment honed by intimate familiarity with our best available insights. Some of those insights dwell in fields of inquiry cognate or proximate to academic fields. Some of them come from judgment acquired in the aesthetic or political sphere or simply in the lessons of a life well lived.

One way to decipher whether an inquiry is off kilter and problematically influenced by political commitments is to assess how many other forms of knowledge need to be revised, and with how much complexification, in order to make sense of a wide range of human understandings. That Gerald Steinberg appears to be willing to bend some of the other arrows in the quiver of human rights, for example, augurs for his commitment to academic freedom and generates a reason to suspend judgment on the authority of his other credentials without further scrutiny. Borrowing from Judith Jarvis Thomson's remarks, while epicycles do exist in nature, the need to warp a whole range of counterfactual material and accepted practices to fit into a procedure or theory tends to suggest that the latter are *excessively* ornate. What happened to the Mapping Models conference and what happened to the doctrine of academic freedom over its course illustrate this kind of building of epicycles.

Academic freedom is not universally lauded, even in universities across the world. The doctrine is not only of recent vintage but also is deeply wed to a particular political ideology. It is one of the cornerstones of democratic government. Academic freedom is just as much a political virtue as it is a tool for generating sounder foundations of knowledge, those without political or ideological taint. That said, within the communities of practice that constitute democratic governance, it is a core and (within that sphere) almost universally agreed upon value. In the parade of people who intervened in the Mapping Models conference, only one really stood out as rejecting the relative importance of the doctrine: the letter writer to the president of York University who, in all caps, under the subject heading "ANOTHER SH-T STORM COMING," screamed, "I DON'T CARE A FIG ABOUT ACADEMIC FREEDOM. I DO CARE ABOUT YORK – AND WITH OUR PROBLEMS THIS YEAR THIS IS TROUBLE WITH A CAPITAL T."[8] And even in the case of that intervenor, it is almost certain that he or she will not come forward and put a name and face to those frantic words.

Virtually every other intervenor sang the virtues of academic freedom even as they sought to undermine it. So the letter writer to the former dean who asked that the latter "do all in your power to stop this abhorrent conference from taking place" thought it important to add that he "personally feel[s] very strongly about free speech."[9] Just as disconsonantly, when the federal minister of science and technology informed SSHRC that there could be adverse consequences for its overall budget if the Mapping Models conference was not subjected to an extra level of review, he prefaced this announcement by stating that "Our government is committed to the principle [of] academic independence and the independent, arms-length, peer-review process for assessing applications for research grants."[10] Similarly, when Frank Iacobucci singled out a particular academic event for exceptional scrutiny, he did so under a banner proclaiming that "Universities are obliged to support academic debate on the pressing issues of the day."[11] Academic freedom rarely fails for a lack of eloquent supporters.

That virtually all of these intervenors (save one) never put in question the centrality of the doctrine of academic freedom itself (however they glossed it) indicates that the doctrine is now firmly in place as a cornerstone of both the academy and larger society's relationship to it. It is one of the rubrics that organizes our world "not after perception but in the act of perception."[12] This is one space, carved out of democratic society, in which popular opinion and the interests of particular constituencies have virtually no home. That is as much a statement about the academy as it is about democratic society.

Academic freedom is analogous to a Torah of the Western university, surrounded by Talmudic deliberations and a thicket of protective *gzerot.* That does not stop it, however, from being a historically contingent construct, one that can seem odd and precious to outsiders, a form of life that could have been otherwise. Nor does that stop it from being a distinctively political doctrine. As much as academic freedom creates a space in which to advance the worthiest of ideas, it also accomplishes this work by creating a *political* space in which inappropriate constituencies are kept out of the academy's form of life.

When the liberty of academics to pursue their own intrigues is impinged upon by outsiders (be they governmental outsiders or advocacy groups or administrative ones), justificatory epicycles begin. The conference critics took a looser view of the stridency with which the doctrine of academic freedom ought to have been shored up in our case. As a result, they allowed themselves to take a looser view of democratic values. Their interventions implied that the topic of Israel/Palestine is so fraught and contested that exceptions to a doctrine that has been forged and refined over the past century requires special application in order to accommodate the unique context. They spun epicycles around the Mapping Models conference and brought pressures to bear on players who, by the most conventional readings of the doctrine, ought to have declined the attempt to influence the research interests of independent scholars. And the epicycles spun have consequences for how we organize ourselves in democratic societies around a set of cherished ideals.

And so, while the central ambition of this book has been to give an account of an event and of academic freedom, it is fair to say that, if I were to write a political book on the one-state model for the Middle East, this would probably be it. In beating down a space in the political forest for academic freedom, this book enlarges the clearing for more thoughtful contemplation of an idea that aspires to coherence, compulsion, and validity, one with incidental potency.

Appendices

Correspondence and Documentation

Correspondence or documents cited in the text and obtained under the Ontario Freedom of Information and Protection of Privacy Act (FIPPA) and the Federal Access to Information Act (ATI) are listed below. The full text for each item appears at https://circle.ubc.ca/handle/2429/45061. Any misspellings or grammatical errors in the original documents have been retained when quoted in this book. Communications cited in the text that were not obtained under the FIPPA and/or ATI are in the author's possession.

Appendix 1: email from the Jewish Defence League to the president of York University, October 5, 2008.

Appendix 2: email from David Dewitt regarding Howard Adelman's satisfaction with the unchanged conference, June 8, 2009.

Appendix 3: email from the chair of York University's Board of Governors indicating that he had been cornered at a Passover seder re the Adelman memo, April 12, 2009.

Appendix 4: email to Dean Patrick Monahan complaining about the conference, April 22, 2009.

Appendix 5: emails from anonymized complainer threatening financial consequences, April 24, 2009.

Appendix 6: email with Monahan's original response to complaints about the conference, April 24, 2009.

Appendix 7: Council for Israel and Jewish Advocacy statement on the conference, May 12, 2009.

Appendix 8: email exchange between the president of York University and a donor threatening significant withdrawal of funds from the university, May 13, 2009.

Appendix 9: presidential statements on the conference.

Appendix 10: emails between Social Sciences and Humanities Research Council administrators regarding the atypical treatment of the conference, June 14, 2009.

Appendix 11: statement issued by Minister of Science and Technology Gary Goodyear, June 5, 2009.

Appendix 12: Canadian Association of University Teachers coverage of a June 5, 2009, discussion on SSHRC suffering consequences in the next budget.

Appendix 13: public statement by SSHRC re the conference being in compliance, June 15, 2009.

Appendix 14: email from anonymized party re not caring a fig about academic freedom, June 10, 2009.

Appendix 15: email from York Media re Hasbora and the JDL refusing to stand hand in hand, June 22, 2009.

Appendix 16: original draft of the conference program with the original title, March 12, 2008.

Appendix 17: email from the dean of Osgoode Hall Law School to the U50 committee re the conference, March 27, 2008.

Appendix 18: email from the dean to an anonymized complainant regarding the meaning of "sponsorship," April 24, 2009.

Appendix 19: note to Ryder and Drummond from the dean re concerns, October 3, 2008.

Appendix 20: email from the dean confirming that he asked us to take Masri off the Organizing Committee, October 10, 2008.

Appendix 21: email from the dean to Drummond and Ryder re communications from inside and outside the university re balance, April 15, 2009.

Appendix 22: email from Dewitt re scaling back the conference, April 15, 2009.

Appendix 23: email from Cohen to Shoukri/Monahan re populating the audience at the conference, April 15, 2009.

Appendix 24: email from the dean to Professor Irving Abella (copied to Supreme Court judge Rosalie Abella), April 15, 2009.

Appendix 25: email from Monahan to Shoukri/Cohen about his conversation with Abella, April 15, 2009.

Appendix 26: communications between the Office of University Events and the U50 manager of implementation, April 14, 2009.

Appendix 27: email from Cohen to Shoukri/Monahan re putting the "fear of all three gods" into the conference organizers, April 17, 2009.

Appendix 28: email from Monahan to Drummond re needing more two-state advocates, April 22, 2009.

Appendix 29: email from the dean to the president (containing Shoukri's suggestion) re strong-arming Dewitt and the conference organizers lack of flexibility, May 9, 2009.

Appendix 30: email from Monahan to Shoukri and Cohen re "a plan to try to rework the agenda," April 21, 2009.

Appendix 31: emails from Monahan to Shoukri/Cohen re Drummond's threat about speaking to CAUT, April 25, 2009.

Appendix 32: email from Monahan on securing Glendon Campus, May 10, 2009.

Appendix 33: emails between Dewitt and Monahan on Michael Bell and other matters, April 28, 2009.

Appendix 34: email from Monahan to Dewitt re "one chance to shape this in the right direction," May 2, 2009.

Appendix 35: email from Monahan to Drummond re Bob Rae, May 2, 2009.

Appendix 36: email from Monahan to Shoukri re not meeting with the organizers, May 9, 2009.

Appendix 37: Monahan and Dewitt confer, May 10, 2009.

Appendix 38: "PRIVATE & CONFIDENTIAL" email from Dewitt to Monahan, May 11, 2009.

Appendix 39: email from Dewitt to Monahan re "PLEASE DO NOT SHARE THIS," May 11, 2009.

Appendix 40: email from Dewitt to Monahan about consulting unnamed external academics for the plenary session, May 13, 2009.

Appendix 41: email from Monahan to Shoukri re postponement and finessing things, May 12, 2009.

Appendix 42: email from Monahan to Dewitt asking the latter to send the president's statement to Gerald Steinberg, May 21, 2009.

Appendix 43: email in which Dewitt forwards Steinberg's proposed article on the conference, May 22, 2009.

Appendix 44: email from Monahan to Shoukri re terms of reference, July 20, 2009.

Appendix 45: memo from Provost Monahan to staff re terms of reference and soliciting information consistent with them, September 2009.

Notes

Preface

1 For coverage of the FLQ (or October) crisis and Canada's invocation of the War Measures Act, see Dominique Clément, *Canada's Rights Revolution: Social Movements and Social Change, 1937-82* (Vancouver: UBC Press, 2008), 97-98, 105-16.

2 For an eloquent literary description of this form of curiosity and intermingling, see Sherry Simon, *Translating Montreal: Episodes in the Life of a Divided City* (Montreal: McGill-Queen's University Press, 2006).

3 In particular, Jeremy Webber was writing *Reimagining Canada: Language, Culture, Community, and the Canadian Constitution* (Montreal: McGill-Queen's University Press, 1994) at that time, and James Tully was writing *Strange Multiplicity: Constitutionalism in an Age of Diversity* (Cambridge, UK: Cambridge University Press, 1995). Both of these scholars were my mentors. Charles Taylor, Will Kymlicka, and Desmond Morton would also be considered part of this Canadian school.

4 Susan G. Drummond, *Incorporating the Familiar: An Investigation into Legal Sensibilities in Nunavik* (Montreal: McGill-Queen's University Press, 1997).

5 Susan G. Drummond, *Mapping Marriage Law in Spanish Gitano Communities* (Vancouver: UBC Press, 2006).

6 Susan G. Drummond, "Dishing Up Israel: Rethinking the Potential of Legal Mixité," *Windsor Yearbook of Access to Justice* 26, 1 (2008): 163; Susan G. Drummond, "Prolegomenon to a Pedestrian Cartography of Mixed Legal Jurisdictions: The Case of Israel/Palestine," *McGill Law Journal* 50 (2005): 899.

7 See Ian S. Lustick, "Israel and 'The Middle Eastern Muck,'" *Middle East Policy* 15, 3 (2008): 30, discussed in Part 1, Chapter 2.

8 For more on the Nationality and Entry into Israel Law (Temporary Order) 5763 (2003), see Amnesty International, *Israel and the Occupied Territories: Torn Apart:*

Families Split by Discriminatory Policies (July 2004), http://www.amnesty.org/en/library/info/MDE15/063/2004; see also the joint report of the human rights organizations B'Tselem and HaMoked, *Forbidden Families: Family Unification and Child Registration in East Jerusalem* (January 2004), http://www.btselem.org/publications/summaries/200401_forbidden_families. To learn about legal developments and petitions challenging the law, see Adalah, http://adalah.org/eng/Articles/598/Challenging-the-Citizenship-Law-Banning-Family.

9 See Martin Asser, "Lynch Mob's Brutal Attack," *BBC News,* October 13, 2000, http://news.bbc.co.uk/2/hi/middle_east/969778.stm, accessed October 31, 2009.

10 Meron Benvenisti, "The Binationalism Vogue," *Ha'aretz,* April 30, 2009.

Introduction

1 Alan K. Chen, "Bureaucracy and Distrust: Germaneness and the Paradoxes of the Academic Freedom Doctrine," *University of Colorado Law Review* 77 (2006): 958.

2 See the conference website at http://www.yorku.ca/ipconf/.

3 "Minister Goodyear's Office Threatens Federal Budget Funding for SSHRC According to Email Obtained through [Access to Information] Request," CAUT press release, Ottawa, September 28, 2009, http://www.caut.ca/news_details.asp?nid=1383&page=490.

4 Excerpt from a submission by an Osgoode professor to the Thompson Review, called by the Canadian Association of University Teachers (CAUT) on September 2, 2009, into the Mapping Models conference. My colleague's submission, dated October 12, 2009, was sent to the Osgoode faculty listserv and was preceded by emails of the same tone that were originally launched to the listserv in the fall of 2008.

5 The administration of the other sponsoring university, Queen's, refrained completely from intervening in our work.

6 Patrick Monahan left the deanship of Osgoode Hall Law School on July 1, 2009. He became the provost of York University, of which Osgoode Hall Law School is a faculty. I will refer to the former dean simply as "the dean" or "Dean Monahan" or, if the context calls for it, "Provost Monahan." The dean of Osgoode at the time of writing was Lorne Sossin, to whom I refer only once (and very obliquely) in the book. The associate vice-president of research and innovation at the time of the events described in this book was David Dewitt. I will refer to him as AVP Dewitt or "the AVP" even though he no longer occupies the post. He left York University at the end of the 2010-11 academic year and now holds a position at a private think tank in Canada, the Centre for International Governance Innovation (CIGI), founded in 2001 by Jim Balsillie, the former co-CEO of Research in Motion.

7 Excerpt from an email from the former dean of Osgoode Hall Law School to organizers of the Mapping Models conference, May 10, 2009.

8 May 12, 2009, statement by CIJA on the Mapping Models conference. The full statement can be accessed at http://www.cicweb.ca/scene/2009/05/cija-statement-on-upcoming-york-university-conference/; however, the twenty-six comments on the statement (a fair number of them critical) that also used to populate the CIJA web page were removed in the late fall of 2011.

9 Patrick Monahan, July 2011 feedback, 7.

10 Ibid.

11 CIJA, while retaining the acronym, renamed itself the Centre for Israel and Jewish Affairs in the summer of 2011.

12 See Frank Iacobucci, *The Mapping [Models] Conference and Academic Freedom: A Report to President Mamdouh Shoukri from the Honourable Frank Iacobucci,* March 2010, http://president.news.yorku.ca/2010/04/09/president-releases-iacobucci-report-on-israelpalestine-conference/.

13 Jon Thompson, *No Debate: The Israel Lobby and Free Speech at Canadian Universities* (Toronto: James Lorimer and Company, 2010).

14 Incidentally, she has also written on the topic of Sri Lanka's formal and informal banking systems.

15 For an extensive list of the literature, also see the annotated bibliography on the conference web site, http://www.yorku.ca/ipconf/annotatedbibliography.html. This bibliography extends only to the spring of 2009.

16 The assault on credentials was not isolated to the Mapping Models conference. See Martin Lockshin, "You Don't Need Credentials to Bash Israel," *National Post,* May 26, 2009.

Chapter 1: Outside Academia

1 See http://www.yorku.ca/ipconf/advisory.

2 See http://www.yorku.ca/ipconf/annotatedbibliography.html.

3 Email from Ed Morgan to Bruce Ryder and Susan Drummond, October 3, 2008.

4 Email from a colleague re change to the conference title, October 6, 2008.

5 Appendix 1: email from the Jewish Defence League to the president of York University, October 5, 2008, https://circle.ubc.ca/handle/2429/45061.

6 "ADL Applauds FBI for Arrest of JDL Leader Irv Rubin for Alleged Acts of Terrorism," Anti-Defamation League press release, 2010, http://www.adl.org/presrele/extremism_72/4016_72.asp, accessed December 15, 2010.

7 Ibid.

8 Ibid.

9 Ira Basen, "Shock Troops of the Faith," *Globe and Mail,* November 28, 1981.

10 Fern Sidman, "Jewish Defense North of the Border," *Jewish Press,* August 20, 2008.

11 See http://www.publicsafety.gc.ca/prg/ns/le/cle-eng.aspx#KACH.

12 "Rabin's Regret 'Not Enough,' Arafat Charges," *Windsor Star,* February 26, 1994.

13 Robert Stephens, "JDL Protests Kaplan's Stand on Nazis," *Globe and Mail,* April 28, 1981.

14 http://www.jdl-canada.com/.

15 Weinstein went on, in that interview, to equate the violence that he affirms as core to the JDL's principles with the martial arts. http://www.youtube.com/watch?v=oQ2MY58RunM&feature=player_embedded#at=1213.

16 Ed Morgan, "Fight Bad Speech with Good Speech," *National Post,* November 4, 2008.

17 Appendix 2: email from David Dewitt regarding Howard Adelman's satisfaction with the unchanged conference, June 8, 2009, https://circle.ubc.ca/handle/2429/45061.

18 Memo from Howard Adelman, circulated widely, March 20, 2009.

19 Ibid.
20 Appendix 3: email from the chair of York University's Board of Governors indicating that he had been cornered at a Passover seder re the Adelman memo, April 12, 2009, https://circle.ubc.ca/handle/2429/45061.
21 Ibid.
22 Appendix 4: email to Dean Patrick Monahan complaining about the conference, April 22, 2009, https://circle.ubc.ca/handle/2429/45061.
23 Appendix 5: emails from anonymized complainer threatening financial consequences, April 24, 2009, https://circle.ubc.ca/handle/2429/45061.
24 Ibid.
25 Appendix 6: email with Monahan's original response to complaints about the conference, April 24, 2009, https://circle.ubc.ca/handle/2429/45061.
26 Appendix 7: Council for Israel and Jewish Advocacy statement on the conference, May 12, 2009, https://circle.ubc.ca/handle/2429/45061.
27 Appendix 8: email exchange between the president of York University and a donor threatening significant withdrawal of funds from the university, May 13, 2009, https://circle.ubc.ca/handle/2429/45061.
28 Ibid.
29 Appendix 9: presidential statements on the conference, https://circle.ubc.ca/handle/2429/45061.
30 Appendix 10: emails between Social Sciences and Humanities Research Council administrators regarding the atypical treatment of the conference, June 14, 2009, https://circle.ubc.ca/handle/2429/45061.
31 See http://www.sshrc-crsh.gc.ca/funding-financement/using-utiliser/grant_regulations-reglement_subventions/conferences-colloques-eng.aspx#a5.
32 This communication has not been reproduced because it contains potentially defamatory content.
33 Appendix 11: statement issued by Minister of Science and Technology Gary Goodyear, June 5, 2009, https://circle.ubc.ca/handle/2429/45061.
34 Appendix 12: Canadian Association of University Teachers coverage of a June 5, 2009, discussion on SSHRC suffering consequences in the next budget, https://circle.ubc.ca/handle/2429/45061.
35 The relevant passage of the Grant Holder's Guide reads as follows: "*Program changes*: Minor changes (e.g., replacement of guest speakers, the addition of a new topic) do not require prior SSHRC approval provided the event remains essentially the same. Approval for major program changes (e.g., changing the theme or focus of the event) must be requested in writing to SSHRC. If you are unsure about what constitutes a minor or major change, consult a SSHRC program officer. *Guest speakers change*: Clearly, it is in the nature of workshops and conferences that some guest speakers may have to be replaced at the last moment. No prior SSHRC approval is required for such limited changes but they must be mentioned in the report of activities submitted at the conclusion of the grant." See http://www.sshrc-crsh.gc.ca/funding-financement/using-utiliser/grant_regulations-reglement_subventions/conferences-colloques-eng.aspx#a2.

36 Appendix 10: emails between Social Sciences and Humanities Research Council administrators regarding the atypical treatment of the conference, June 14, 2009, https://circle.ubc.ca/handle/2429/45061.
37 As cited in Jon Thompson, *No Debate: The Israel Lobby and Free Speech at Canadian Universities* (Toronto: James Lorimer and Company, 2010), 148-49.
38 Appendix 9: presidential statements on the conference, https://circle.ubc.ca/handle/2429/45061.
39 Appendix 13: public statement by SSHRC re the conference being in compliance, June 15, 2009, https://circle.ubc.ca/handle/2429/45061.
40 Thompson, *No Debate,* 283.
41 Ibid., 285.
42 Appendix 14: email from anonymized party re not caring a fig about academic freedom, June 10, 2009, https://circle.ubc.ca/handle/2429/45061.
43 Email from B'nai Brith to Professors Drummond and Aiken regarding the defamatory error in its community alert, June 12, 2009.
44 Second email from B'nai Brith to Professors Drummond and Aiken regarding the defamatory error in its community alert, June 12, 2009.
45 See the discussion above regarding Meir Weinstein, the Kach movement in Canada, and JDL Canada.
46 Appendix 7: Council for Israel and Jewish Advocacy statement on the conference, May 12, 2009, https://circle.ubc.ca/handle/2429/45061.
47 Conference feedback, June 2009. This material was received as part of an anonymous post-conference exercise.
48 Part 2 of this monograph touches on the difficulties surrounding this topic.
49 Na'ama Carmi, "Mideast Conference Anything but Academic," *Toronto Star,* June 30, 2009.
50 Ibid.
51 Ibid.
52 Frank Iacobucci, *The Mapping [Models] Conference and Academic Freedom: A Report to President Mamdouh Shoukri from the Honourable Frank Iacobucci,* March 2010, http://president.news.yorku.ca/2010/04/09/president-releases-iacobucci-report-on-israelpalestine-conference/, 25.
53 Leo Panitch, Letter to the Editor, *Toronto Star,* July 2, 2009.
54 Thompson, *No Debate,* 155; Appendix 15: email from York Media re Hasbora and the JDL refusing to stand hand in hand, June 22, 2009, https://circle.ubc.ca/handle/2429/45061.

Chapter 2: The Forbidden Question

1 Jewish Encyclopedia.com, http://www.jewishencyclopedia.com/view.jsp?artid=203&letter=G, accessed September 26, 2009.
2 Email communication, October 3, 2008.
3 Email communication, October 2, 2008.
4 It is not unusual for discussions on the one-state model to arise in Israeli universities and media. For example, just days after our conference, the Mada al-Carmel and the

Ibn Khaldoun Association co-hosted an academic conference entitled Has the Two-State Solution Collapsed? Discussions on the Idea of One State. The one-day conference was held at al-Maidan theatre in Haifa. Many of the speakers were the same as those who presented at the Mapping Models conference. For a further contrast, note that a conference on the same themes held in Cape Town, South Africa, ten days earlier than the Mapping Models conference was sponsored and funded by the government, a former minister gave a keynote address, a former deputy minister was present at all sessions, a vice-president of the university spoke, a head of the human rights commission was present, and a letter from the foreign minister was read at the beginning. See http://www.hsrc.ac.za/Event-363.phtml.

5 Email from Ed Morgan to Bruce Ryder and Susan Drummond, October 3, 2008.

6 Israel/Palestine: Mapping Models of Statehood and Paths to Peace. See the conference website for elaboration of the themes as well as the program: http://www.yorku.ca/ipconf/.

7 Memo from Hill and Knowlton and [the director of media relations] (York Media) to [the chief marketing and communications officer] (Marketing and Communications) re "Israel/Palestine: Mapping Models of Statehood and Paths to Peace," Communications Context and Strategy, May 12, 2009.

8 CIJA statement on the upcoming York University conference, May 12, 2009, http://www.cicweb.ca/scene/2009/05/cija-statement-on-upcoming-york-university-conference/, accessed October 9, 2009.

9 Stephen Scheinberg and Neil Caplan, "One State Is No Solution," *National Post,* June 23, 2009.

10 Sheri Shefa, "Jewish Link to York U 'Absolutely Essential,'" *Canadian Jewish News,* July 20, 2009.

11 The *mishnah* is the first major written redaction of the Jewish oral traditions called the "Oral Torah" and the first major work of Rabbinic Judaism. It was redacted between 70 and 200 of the Common Era, starting with the fall of the Second Temple, when the persecution of the Jews and the passage of time raised the possibility that the details of the oral traditions dating from the sixth century Before the Common Era and 70 of the Common Era would be forgotten.

12 Paul Johnson, *A History of the Jews* (London: Phoenix Press, 1987), 232 ff.

13 Celia Wasserstein Fassberg, "Language and Style in a Mixed System," *Tulane Law Review* 78 (2003): 174.

14 Amos Elon, *The Pity of It All: A Portrait of the German-Jewish Epoch, 1743-1933* (New York: Picador, 2003).

15 However, the liberal respect for freedom of speech and association is not distributed equally in Israel and can be hinged on the identity of the speaker or journalist (Jewish or non-Jewish Israeli). This can be seen in the response of the state to demonstrations by Palestinian Israelis against the 2006 Lebanon War, and the 2008-9 Gaza War was greeted with heavy-handed repression. See http://www.adalah.org/eng/pressreleases/pr.php?file=09_09_22. Furthermore, the Mapping Models conference was unable to secure the participation of the only Palestinian scholar from Gaza because he was not permitted by Israel to leave Gaza to attend the conference.

16 Nathan Jeffay, "Ben-Gurion U. Debates Cost of Academic Freedom," *Jewish Daily Forward,* September 2, 2009.

17 Rivka Carmi, "Neve Gordon's Divisive Op-Ed," *Los Angeles Times,* September 1 2009. Clearly, this commitment to Enlightenment values, however, is just as fragile in Israel as it is elsewhere. The fall 2011 report of an international committee entrusted with evaluating the political science departments of Israeli universities appeared to have engaged in a political assessment of scholarly work in recommending that the department in which Gordon teaches be shut down; the department was accused of having an "anti-Zionist" bias. The report was endorsed by Israel's Council of Higher Education (CHE), which had solicited the report, and this endorsement provoked a petition of more than 150 Israeli and international academics asking for the CHE to ignore the call. See Talila Nesher, "International Academics Seek to Keep 'Biased' Department at Israeli University Open; Ben-Gurion University's Politics and Government Department Ha[ve] Been Accused of Having an 'Anti-Zionist' Bias," December 20, 2011, http://www.haaretz.com/print-edition/news/international-academics-seek-to-keep-biased-department-at-israeli-university-open-1.402450.

18 See, for example, Nehemia Shtrasler, "The Haredi Takeover Must Be Prevented," *Ha'aretz,* August 4, 2009; also see a Canadian summary of the tensions in Patrick Martin, "A Hostile Takeover of Zionism: Israel Is Teetering toward Theocracy, with the Rise of the Haredim," *Globe and Mail,* September 26, 2009.

19 See, for example, the Clinton Parameters and the Geneva Initiative. See also the Beilin Abu Mazen Agreement reported in Ze'ev Schiff, "The Teams Held 20 Meetings in Israel and Europe," *Ha'aretz,* 22 February 1996, reprinted in "Documents and Source Material," *Journal of Palestine Studies* 26, 1 (1996): 148. See also http://www.washingtonpost.com/wp-dyn/content/article/2006/05/04/AR2006050400940.html; http://www.haaretz.com/hasen/spages/1069195.html.

20 Arafat and Barak discussed the issue of Palestinian refugees at the Camp David negotiations, but no details were made public. See Akram Hanieh, "The Camp David Papers," *Journal of Palestine Studies* 30, 2 (2001): 75; Interview of Salim Tamari by Thomas Abowd (July 23, 1999), *Journal of Palestine Studies* 24, 1 (1999): 81. See also the Moratinos non-paper published in "The Taba Negotiations (January 2001)," *Journal of Palestine Studies* 31, 3 (2002): 79.

21 See Yehuda Ben Meir and Olena Bagno-Moldavsky, *Vox Populi: Trends in Israeli Public Opinion on National Security, 2004-09* (Tel Aviv: Institute for National Security Studies, 2010), 80, citing approval ratings for the acceptance of "a limited number of refugees [being] permitted to return to Israel" in the range of 11 percent to 20 percent, with 11 percent being the most recent statistic, http://www.inss.org.il/upload/(FILE)1291193491.pdf. See also the statistics from Professor Ephraim Ya'ar (Tel Aviv University) and Professor Tamar Hermann (Israel Democracy Institute and the Open University of Israel) gathered in their ongoing public opinion survey called the Peace Index. In a 2000 Peace Index survey, the following question was asked of Israelis: "To what extent do you support or oppose the following conditions if they lead to achieving a peace agreement with the Palestinians – To allow 100,000

refugees to return to the places they lived in inside the Green Line, i.e., inside Israel?" In a second Peace Index survey in 2000, the question was this: "Would you, in return for declaring an end to the conflict with the signing of the peace agreement, and Palestinians declaring that they have no claims from Israel after the implementation of the agreement, support or oppose the Clinton parameters (which says that return will be the West Bank and Gaza Strip)?" The results were definitely opposed: 52.7 percent; opposed: 17.3 percent; in favour: 17.7 percent; definitely in favour: 6.4 percent; don't know: 6 percent. http://www.peaceindex.org/innerEng.aspx?page=5.

22 Ehud Barak, with Benny Morris, "Camp David and After – Continued," *New York Review of Books,* June 27, 2002, http://www.nybooks.com/articles/archives/2002/jun/27/camp-david-and-aftercontinued/?pagination=false.

23 Hasan Abu-Libdeh, "Statistical Data on Palestinian Refugees: Prospects for Contribution to Final Settlement," paper presented at the International Development Research Centre Stocktaking II Conference on Palestinian Refugee Research, Ottawa, June 17-20, 2003, http://www.idrc.ca/uploads/user-S/10575995470Session_1-_Abu-Libdeh-paper-_abstractdoc.doc. Here Palestinians of refugee and non-refugee status and living in the OPT were surveyed. More than 72 percent preferred the right of return of refugees in the OPT to their original homes and villages, and more than 74 percent felt the same way about the right of return of refugees currently living outside the OPT.

24 Hussein Agha and Robert Malley, "Camp David and After: An Exchange (2. A Reply to Ehud Barak)," *New York Review of Books,* June 13, 2002, http://www.nybooks.com/articles/archives/2002/jun/13/camp-david-and-after-an-exchange-2-a-reply-to-ehud/?pagination=false.

25 Section 2(II) Arab Peace Initiative; endorsed by the Palestinian Authority. The PLO took the unprecedented step of advertising its endorsement of the initiative in four Hebrew-language newspapers in Israel. See "Arab Peace Plan Ads in Israeli Papers," *Brunei Times,* November 21, 2008, http://www.bt.com.bn/.

26 Naseer Aruri, ed., *Palestinian Refugees: The Right of Return* (London: Pluto Press, 2001); Abbas Shiblak and Uri Davis, *Civil and Citizenship Rights of Palestinian Refugees* (Jerusalem: SHAML, 1996); Salim Tamari, *Palestinian Refugee Negotiations: From Madrid to Oslo II* (Washington, DC: Institute for Palestine Studies, 1996); John Quigley, "International Law and the Palestine Refugees," *Hastings International and Comparative Law Review* 28 (2005): 405.

27 For readings on both sides of this issue, see W. Mallison and S. Mallison, *An International Law Analysis of the Major United Nations Resolutions Concerning the Palestinian Question* (New York: United Nations, 1979); J. Quigley, "Displaced Palestinians and a Right of Return," *Harvard International Law Journal* 39 (1998): 171; S. Akram and T. Rempel, "Recommendations for Durable Solutions for Palestinian Refugees: A Challenge to the Oslo Framework," *Palestinian Yearbook of International Law* 11 (2000-1): 1; L. Takkenberg, *The Status of Palestinian Refugees in International Law* (Oxford: Clarendon Press, 1998); Victor Kattan, "The Nationality of Denationalized Palestinians," *Nordic Journal of International Law* 74 (2005): 67; Kathleen Lawand, "The Right of Return of Palestinians in International Law," *International Journal of Refugee Law* 8, 4 (1996): 532; Gail Bowling, *The 1948*

Palestinian Refugees and the Individual Right of Return: An International Law Analysis, 2nd ed. (Bethlehem: Badil Resource Center, 2007); Ruth Lapidoth, "Israel and the Palestinians: Some Legal Issues," *Die Friedens-Warte (Journal of International Peace and Organization)* 76, 2-3 (2001): 211; Ruth Lapidoth, "The Right to Return in International Law, with Special Reference to Palestinian Refugees," *Israel Yearbook on Human Rights,* 16 (1986): 103; E. Benvenisti and E. Zamir, "Private Claims to Property Rights in the Future Israeli-Palestinian Settlement," *American Journal of International Law* 89 (1995): 295; J. Weiner, "The Palestinian Refugees Right to Return and the Peace Process," *Boston College International and Comparative Law Review* 20 (1997): 1; Yoav Tadmor, "Comment: The Palestinian Refugees of 1948: The Right to Compensation and Return," *Temple International and Comparative Law Journal* 8 (1994): 403; Lewis Saideman, "Do Palestinian Refugees Have a Right of Return to Israel? An Examination of the Scope of and Limitations on the Right of Return," *Virginia Journal of International Law* 44 (2004): 829.

28 Bill to Amend the Penal Law (Prohibition of Publicizing Incitement Negating the Existence of Israel as a Jewish and Democratic State), 2009: "Any person who publicizes a call to negate the existence of the State of Israel as a Jewish and Democratic State, and according to the content of the publication there is a reasonable probability that the publication will lead to committing an act of hatred, contempt or disloyalty to the State or the authorities of the governance or law that were created according to the law – he shall be liable for imprisonment for one year of prison." The bill was passed in its initial hearing on May 27, 2009. It was then transferred to the Knesset Committee, and on June 8, 2009, this committee decided that the Constitution, Law, and Justice Committee would discuss it.

29 See Nadav Shragai, "Knesset Okays Initial Bill to Outlaw Denial of 'Jewish State,'" *Ha'aretz,* May 27, 2009.

30 A.B. Yehoshua, "Why Do We Insist on a 'Jewish' State?," *Ha'aretz,* June 10, 2009.

31 Ibid.

32 See Netanyahu's June 14, 2009, speech at Bar Ilan University, http://www.haaretz.com/hasen/spages/1092810.html.

33 See "Speech by PM Sharon at the Herzliya Conference – 4-Dec-2002," posted by the Israeli Ministry of Foreign Affairs, http://www.mfa.gov.il/MFA/Government/Speeches+by+Israeli+leaders/2002/Speech%20by%20PM%20Sharon%20at%20the%20Herzliya%20Conference%20-%204, accessed October 2, 2009.

34 "Palestinians Harden Refusal to Accept a 'Jewish State,'" *Jerusalem Post,* November 15, 2007.

35 Ian S. Lustick, "Abandoning the Iron Wall: Israel and 'The Middle Eastern Muck,'" *Middle East Policy* 15, 3 (2008): 33.

36 See Yonatan Touval, "A Recognition Israel Doesn't Need," *New York Times,* May 12, 2009.

37 Natasha Mozgovaya, "Netanyahu: No Peace until Palestinians Accept Israel as Jewish State," *Ha'aretz,* September 24, 2009.

38 This is not the only model of the relationship between citizenship and nationality. Canada, as a leading example, houses multiple national identities among its citizens in the Québécois population as well as in the multiple Aboriginal nations that have

been recognized and dealt with in distinctive manners, particularly in the Constitution.

39 Gideon Levy, "Word Games," *Ha'aretz,* April 27, 2009.

40 Cited in "Palestinians Harden Refusal to Accept a 'Jewish State,'" *Jerusalem Post,* November 15, 2007.

41 Levy, "Word Games."

42 See Ruth Gavison, *Israel: A Jewish and Democratic State* (in Hebrew) (Jerusalem: VanLeer and Hakibutz Hameuhad, 1999); Amnon Rubinstein and Alexander Yakobson, *Israel and the Family of Nations: A Jewish Nation State and Human Rights* (London: Routledge, 2008) (originally published in Hebrew in 2003); Ruth Gavison, "The Jewish State: The Principle Justification and the Desirable Character" (in Hebrew), *Tkhelet* 13 (2002): 50; Ruth Gavison, "Jewish and Democratic? A Rejoinder to the 'Ethnic Democracy' Debate," *Israel Studies* 4, 1 (1999): 44; Azmi Bishara, *From the Jewish State to Sharon: A Study in the Contradictions of the Israeli Democracy* (in Arabic) (Ramallah: MUWATIN – Palestinian Institute for the Study of Democracy, 2005); Oren Yiftachel, "Democracy or Ethnocracy: Territory and Settler Politics in Israel/Palestine," *Middle East Report* 207 (1998): 9; Joseph E. David, ed., *The State of Israel: Between Judaism and Democracy* (Jerusalem: Israeli Democracy Institute, 2003); Alan Dowty, "Is Israel Democratic? Substance and Semantics in the 'Ethnic Democracy' Debate," *Israel Studies* 4, 2 (1999): 1; Oren Yiftachel, *Ethnocracy* (Philadelphia: University of Pennsylvania Press, 2006); Sammy Smooha, "The Model of Ethnic Democracy: Israel as a Jewish and Democratic State," *Nations and Nationalism* 8, 4 (2002): 475; Sammy Smooha, "Ethnic Democracy: Israel as an Archetype," *Israel Studies* 2, 2 (1997): 198; As'ad Ghanem, Nadim Rouhana, and Oren Yiftachel, "Questioning 'Ethnic Democracy': A Response to Sammy Smooha," *Israel Studies* 3, 2 (1998): 253; Nadim Rouhana, "'Jewish and Democratic'? The Price of a National Self-Deception," *Journal of Palestine Studies* 35 (2006): 64.

43 See, for example, Himani Bannerji, *The Dark Side of the Nation: Essays on Multiculturalism, Nationalism, and Gender* (Toronto: Canadian Scholars' Press, 2000); John Comaroff and Jean Comaroff, *Of Revelation and Revolution: The Dialectics of Modernity on a South African Frontier* (Chicago: University of Chicago Press, 1997); Stuart Hall, David Held, Don Hubert, and Kenneth Thompson, eds., *Modernity: An Introduction to Modern Societies* (Cambridge, MA: Blackwell, 1996); Ronald Beiner, *Liberalism, Nationalism, Citizenship: Essays on the Problem of Political Community* (Vancouver: UBC Press, 2003); Jeff Spinner Halev, *The Boundaries of Citizenship: Race, Ethnicity, and Nationality in Liberal States* (Baltimore: Johns Hopkins University Press, 1994); Iris Marion Young, *Inclusion and Democracy* (Oxford: Oxford University Press, 2000).

44 Shabtai Rosenne, *Practice and Methods of International Law* (New York: Oceana Publications, 1984), 55; see also Martin S. Flaherty, Chibli Mallat, Karl-Heinz Ziegler, and Reuven S. Avi-Yonah, "International Law," in *The Oxford International Encyclopedia of Legal History,* ed. Stanley N. Katz (New York: Oxford University Press, 2009): "First, a rule of customary international law must reflect the 'general practice' of nations for a significant period of time ... [and] second, state practice must result not from a simple policy choice but out of a sense of legal obligation, a requirement

usually rendered as *opinio juris sive necessitatis* (an opinion of law or necessity). Note also that art. 38 (1)(b) of the Statute of the International Court of Justice states that the Court shall apply, among other things, 'international custom, as evidence of a general practice accepted as law.'"

45 Tony Judt, "Israel: The Alternative," *New York Review of Books,* October 23, 2003, http://www.nybooks.com/articles/archives/2003/oct/23/israel-the-alternative/.

46 Leon Wieseltier, "Israel, Palestine, and the Return of the Bi-National Fantasy: What Is Not to Be Done," *New Republic,* October 27, 2003, http://www.newrepublic.com/.

47 See Tony Karon, "Did Netanyahu Best Obama in Mideast-Peace Tussle?," *Time Online,* September 23, 2009, http://www.time.com/time/magazine. See also Ali Abunimah's analysis of the Obama initiative in "Obama's Peace Effort Has Failed but Our Struggle Continues," *Electronic Intifada,* September 24, 2009, http://electronicintifada.net/.

48 For a sense and a summary of how bleak the situation has become, see Michael Bell, "Why the Israeli-Palestinian Conundrum Is Playing to Pessimists," *Globe and Mail,* November 16, 2009.

49 The PLO recognized Israel on September 9, 1993, in a letter from Arafat to Rabin in which Arafat said that "the PLO recognizes the right of the State of Israel to exist in peace and security." See http://www.mfa.gov.il/MFA/Peace%20Process/Guide%20to%20the%20Peace%20Process/Israel-PLO%20Recognition%20-%20Exchange%20of%20Letters%20betwe. The Arab League has also flagged its preparedness to recognize Israel's right to exist. This recognition is a component of the Arab peace initiative of 2002, re-endorsed at the Riyadh Summit in 2007. See "Arab League Extends 'Hand of Peace' to Israel in Historic Visit," *Mail Online,* July 25, 2007, www.dailymail.co.uk. See *The Arab Peace Initiative,* accessible at the Jordanian Embassy's US website, http://www.jordanembassyus.org/arab_initiative.htm. Note also that the Arab Peace Initiative (API) is based on United Nations Security Resolution 242, which uses the language of "acknowledgment of the sovereignty, territorial integrity and political independence of every State in the area and their right to live in peace within secure and recognized boundaries free from threats or acts of force" and "guaranteeing the territorial inviolability and political independence of every State in the area"; therefore, adoption of the API is implicit de facto (as opposed to de jure) recognition of Israel. The API further proposes normal relations (beyond recognition). Acceptance of the API will lead to full normalization of relations. The text of the API is available at http://www.jordanembassyus.org/arab_initiative.htm.

50 See Article 5 of the Declaration of Principles on the Interim Self-Government Arrangements of 13 September 1993 – the official name of the Oslo Accords – and Article 31(5) of the Palestinian-Israeli Interim Agreement on the West Bank and the Gaza Strip, Washington, DC, September 28, 1995.

51 "Netanyahu Offers Settlement Freeze in Return for Recognition as Jewish State, Palestinians Say No," *Ha'aretz,* October 11, 2010.

52 For a response to Olmert's position on the preconditional recognition of Israel as a Jewish state, see http://www.jpost.com/servlet/Satellite?cid=1195036610009&pagename=JPost%2FJPArticle%2FShowFull; for a response to Netanyahu's position on the preconditional recognition of Israel as a Jewish state, see Mel Frykberg,

"Netanyahu Offer a 'Big Zero,'" *Inter Press Service (IPS) News Agency Online,* June 15, 2009, http://www.ipsnews.net.

53 Fadi Eyadat, "Survey Finds Nearly Half of Israeli Arabs Deny Holocaust," *Ha'aretz,* May 19, 2009. The author of this survey, a Jewish Israeli scholar at the University of Haifa and a confirmed Zionist and two-state proponent, was on the Advisory Committee of the Mapping Models conference and presented a paper with the results of his sociological work as it related to models of statehood.

54 For survey results from a Palestinian Israeli scholar working on the same set of questions about the degree to which Israeli Palestinians see Israel as just, accept its Jewish character, and so on, see Nadim Rouhana, "Relations between Arab Minority and the Israeli State," Chapter 3 of the *Mada al-Carmel Survey Research Unit Report,* http://www.mada-research.org/UserFiles/file/ch3.pdf.

55 Eyadat, "Survey Finds Nearly Half of Israeli Arabs Deny Holocaust."

56 The most prominent of the New Historians are Simha Flapan, Benny Morris, Ilan Pappé, Tom Segev, and Avi Shlaim. See Simha Flapan, *The Birth of Israel: Myths and Realities* (New York: Pantheon Books, 1987); Benny Morris, *Righteous Victims: A History of the Zionist-Arab Conflict, 1881-1999* (New York: Knopf, 1999), and *The Birth of the Palestinian Refugee Problem Revisited* (Cambridge, UK: Cambridge University Press, 2004); Ilan Pappé, *Britain and the Arab-Israeli Conflict, 1947-51* (Basingstoke: Macmillan, in association with St. Antony's College, Oxford, 1988), and *The Ethnic Cleansing of Palestine* (Oxford: Oneworld, 2006); Tom Segev, *One Palestine, Complete: Jews and Arabs under the British Mandate* (New York: H. Holt, 2001); and Avi Shlaim, *Collusion across the Jordan: King Abdullah, the Zionist Movement, and the Partition of Palestine* (New York: Columbia University Press, 1988), and *The Iron Wall: Israel and the Arab World* (London: W.W. Norton, 2001).

57 See, for example, Yoav Gelber, *Palestine, 1948: War, Escape, and the Emergence of the Palestinian Refugee Problem* (Portland: Sussex Academic Press, 2001); Itamar Rabinovich, *The Road Not Taken: Early Arab-Israeli Negotiations* (New York: Oxford University Press, 1991); Anita Shapira, *Land and Power: The Zionist Resort to Force, 1881-1948,* trans. William Templer (New York: Oxford University Press, 1992); and Shabtai Teveth, *Ben-Gurion and the Palestinian Arabs: From Peace to War* (Oxford: Oxford University Press, 1985).

58 See Morris, *The Birth of the Palestinian Refugee Problem Revisited;* Pappé, *The Ethnic Cleansing of Palestine;* and Shlaim, *The Iron Wall,* 28-53.

59 Some say 18 percent since East Jerusalemites should not be counted as a Palestinian minority since they are without Israeli citizenship. Furthermore, use of the 18 percent statistic is a refutation of Israel's claim that East Jerusalem is part of Israel and signifies that it is occupied.

60 There are 4.7 million refugees registered with the United Nations Relief Works Agency (UNRWA) (of these, approximately 1.3 million live in one of the fifty-eight camps); over 1.7 million refugees are not registered with UNRWA. Internally displaced persons (therefore not technically "refugees," living in Israel or the Occupied Palestinian Territory) number at 455,000. The total Palestinian population is 10.6 million worldwide. Therefore, 67 percent of the Palestinian population is comprised

of forcibly displaced persons (i.e., refugees or internally displaced persons). See http://www.un.org/unrwa/publications/index.html, http://www.badil.org/en/documents/category/23-population?download=442%3A2008-survey-summary-of-statistical-findings-number-distribution-of-displaced-palestinians.

61 See Adalah, "Introduction," in *The Democratic Constitution,* 2007, http://www.adalah.org/eng/Articles/1483/The-Democratic-Constitution; Mada al-Carmel, *The Haifa Declaration,* 2007, http://mada-research.org/en/2007/09/12/the-haifa-declaration-arabic-english-hebrew-2007/; High Followup Committee for the Arabs in Israel and National Committee for the Heads of the Arab Local Authorities in Israel, *The Future Vision of the Palestinian Arabs in Israel,* 2006, http://onlinebooks.library.upenn.edu/webbin/book/lookupname?key=National%20Committee%20for%20the%20Heads%20of%20the%20Arab%20Local%20Authorities%20in%20Israel; Ibrahim Tarek, *On the Margins: Annual Review of Human Rights Violations of the Arab Palestinian Minority in Israel 2006* (Nazareth: Arab Association for Human Rights, 2007), http://www.iataskforce.org/node/884.

62 The narrative and experience of refugeehood and exile have been prominent in all aspects of Palestinian life since 1948. They can be seen clearly in Palestinian literature, in which refugeehood and exile are dominant themes. See, for example, Ghassan Kanfani's *Men in the Sun, The Land of Sad Oranges, All That's Left to You, On Men and Rifles, Umm Sa'd,* and *Return to Haifa.* The theme of exile emerges in a strong way from Mahmoud Darwish's poetry and prose; see, for example, *Mahmoud Darwish, Exile's Poet: Critical Essays,* ed. Hala Nassar and Najat Rahman (Northampton, MA: Olive Branch Press, 2008). Thanks to Mazen Masri for this source of further reading.

63 Matti Friedman, "Israel Cuts Al-Naqba, Palestinian Tragedy, from Textbooks," *Huffington Post,* July 22, 2009.

64 "Israel Bans Use of Palestinian Term 'Nakba' in Textbooks," *Ha'aretz,* July 22, 2009.

65 For a summary of the proposed legislation, see Mada's online political monitoring report, April-May 2009, http://www.mada-research.org/?LanguageId=1&System=Item&MenuId=4&PMenuId=4&MenuTemplateId=&CategoryId=13&ItemId=286&ItemTemplateId=1, accessed September 30, 2009.

66 "Lieberman's Party Proposes Ban on Arab Nakba," *Ha'aretz,* May 15, 2009.

67 See http://www.knesset.gov.il/mk/eng/mk_eng.asp?mk_individual_id_t=214.

68 See Shaul Arieli, Doubi Schwartz, with the participation of Hadas Tagari, "Injustice and Folly: The Proposals to Cede Arab Localities from Israel to Palestine," Floersheimer Institute for Policy Studies, July 2006. For commentary on the Lieberman plan, see Uri Dromi, "Israeli Arabs and the Vote," *New York Times,* March 23, 2006; and Akiva Eldar, "Let's Hear It for the Haiders," *Ha'aretz,* October 30, 2006.

69 There are two "loyalty oath" bills aimed at Palestinian Israelis turning citizenship from a right into a conditional privilege: Bill to Amend the Citizenship Law, 1952 (Bill 102/18) and Bill to Amend the Population Registration Law, 1965 (Bill 811/18). See Adalah and the Arab Association for Human Rights, "New Legal Developments: The New Israeli Government Launches ... Legislation in Violation of the Rights of Palestinian Arab Citizens of Israel," June 4, 2009, http://www.old-adalah.org/newsletter/eng/jun09/Adalah_HRA_Briefing_note_FINAL_4.6.09.pdf.

70 Rachel Shabi, "Israel Should Remember Nakba Day: Trying to Erase Palestinian History by Banning Nakba Day Would Not Strengthen Israel but Undermine It," *Guardian Online,* May 28, 2009, http://www.guardian.co.uk/.

71 Stephen E. Ambrose and Douglas G. Brinkley, *Rise to Globalism: American Foreign Policy since 1938* (London: Penguin, 1997); John Mearsheimer and Stephen Walt, *The Israel Lobby and US Foreign Policy* (New York: Farrar, Straus and Giroux, 2007); Jeremy Bowen, *Six Days: How the 1967 War Shaped the Middle East* (London: Simon and Schuster UK, 2003).

72 See Paul Heinbecker, "Tilting toward Israel," *Globe and Mail,* July 25, 2006.

73 Richard J. Goldstone, "Ceremonial Address of Justice Richard J. Goldstone at John Shattuck Inauguration," Central European University, March 11, 2009, http://www.ceu.hu/news/2009-11-03/transcript-ceremonial-address-of-justice-richard-j-goldstone-at-john-shattuck-inaugu.

74 United Nations, "Richard J. Goldstone Appointed to Lead Human Rights Council Fact-Finding Mission on Gaza Conflict," press release, April 3, 2009, http://www.unhchr.ch/huricane/huricane.nsf/0/2796E2CA43CA4D94C125758D002F8D25?opendocument, accessed October 4, 2009.

75 United Nations, "United Nations Fact Finding Mission on the Gaza Conflict," UN Doc. A/HRC/12/48 (hereinafter the Goldstone Report), September 25, 2009, para. 1. The Goldstone Report was the latest in a series of reports documenting violations of international law in the Gaza conflict. Other reports include those produced by Amnesty International, *Israel/Gaza: Operation "Cast Lead": 22 Days of Death and Destruction,* July 2, 2009, http://www.amnesty.org/en/library/info/MDE15/015/2009; Human Rights Watch, *Deprived and Endangered: Humanitarian Crisis in the Gaza Strip,* January 13, 2009, http://www.hrw.org/news/2009/01/12/deprived-and-endangered-humanitarian-crisis-gaza-strip; Human Rights Watch, *White Flag Deaths: Killings of Palestinian Civilians during Operation Cast Lead,* August 13, 2009, www.hrw.org/sites/default/files/reports/ioptwf0809webwcover_1.pdf. The Goldstone Report echoed the findings of these earlier reports, each of which had been dismissed by the Israeli establishment as biased. See Human Rights Watch, "False Allegations about Human Rights Watch's Latest Gaza Report," August 14, 2009, http://www.hrw.org/en/news/2009/08/14/false-allegations-about-human-rights-watch-s-latest-gaza-report; Amira Hass, "Israel: Amnesty Report on Gaza Ignores Fact Hamas Are Terrorists," *Ha'aretz,* February 23, 2009; Kenneth Roth, "Right of Reply: Don't Smear the Messenger," *Jerusalem Post Online,* August 25, 2009, http://www.jpost.com/.

76 Goldstone Report, paras. 30-31. See also Amnesty International, *Israel/Gaza,* Introduction.

77 "UN Appoints Gaza War-Crimes Team," *BBC Online,* April 3, 2009, http://www.bbc.com/.

78 Anshel Pfeffer, "Goldstone: Holocaust Shaped View on War Crimes," *Ha'aretz,* September 19, 2009.

79 Cited in Haroon Siddiqi, "Israel Keeps Shooting the Messenger," *Toronto Star,* September 27, 2009. Falk goes on to note that, "if [Goldstone] can be attacked as biased against Israel, then anyone on the planet is susceptible to that attack."

80 Goldstone Report, paras. 75, 77.

81 Ibid., para. 79.
82 Ibid., para. 103.
83 Ibid., para. 108.
84 Ibid., para. 109.
85 Israel was invited to participate in the Goldstone fact-finding mission and chose not to do so; if there are lacunas in the report, then the Israeli government bears considerable responsibility for them.
86 Goldstone Report, para. 27.
87 Ibid., para. 311.
88 Ibid., para. 326.
89 Ibid., para. 1877.
90 Ibid.
91 Indeed, the isolation and collective punishment of Gaza go much deeper than the electoral victory of Hamas in 2006. Gaza has long been described as an isolated open-air prison as a result of a long-standing siege and enclosure of the densely populated strip of land. See Amira Hass, *Drinking the Sea at Gaza: Days and Nights in a Land under Siege* (New York: Holt Paperbacks, 2000). For a contemporary picture of life in Gaza, see Lawrence Wright, "Captives: What Really Happened during the Israeli Attacks," *New Yorker,* November 9, 2009, http://www.newyorker.com/reporting/2009/11/09/091109fa_fact_wright?currentPage=all.
92 Barak Ravid, "Netanyahu Didn't Mean He Backed Israel Probe of Gaza War," *Ha'aretz,* October 24, 2009.
93 Barak Ravid and Amos Harel, "Livni: Goldstone Probe Based on 'Perverted System of Values,'" *Ha'aretz,* October 25, 2009.
94 Goldstone Report, para. 1879.
95 Ibid., Chapter 7.
96 Ibid., Chapter 13.
97 Ibid., Chapter 9.
98 Ibid., para. 516.
99 Ibid., Chapter 11.
100 Ibid., para. 46.
101 Ibid., para. 1969, subsections a-c.
102 See, for example, Barry Rubin, "The Gaza Report Is a Disaster for Human Rights and Peace: How Could Goldstone's Commission Rely on Such Questionable Testimony?," *Globe and Mail,* September 24, 2009; and Daniel Friedmann, "Exclusive: 'Goldstone Report – the Terrorists' Magna Carta,'" *Jerusalem Post Online,* October 29, 2009, www.jpost.com/.
103 Barak Ravid, "Netanyahu Nixes Call for Israeli Inquiry into Gaza War," *Ha'aretz,* October 1, 2009. The American government has apparently taken up this charge and, with apparent success, pressured the Palestinians to drop further action on the report. See Barak Ravid and Natasha Mozgavaya, "Source: Palestinians Drop Endorsement of Goldstone Report," *Ha'aretz,* October 2, 2009.
104 Erna Paris, "Israel and Hamas Both Get a Fair Shot in the Goldstone Report on Gaza: In the Fractured Middle East, Only the Long View Matters," *Globe and Mail,* September 25, 2009.

105 Gideon Levy, "Disgrace in the Hague," *Ha'aretz,* September 17, 2009.

106 Lustick, "Abandoning the Iron Wall," 33. Lustick was both on the Advisory Committee of the Mapping Models conference and one of the event's keynote speakers.

107 Mainstream Zionists, however, were originally convinced that Palestinians would accept the creation of a Jewish state in their midst. It was only in the early 1930s that awareness took hold that the Palestinians actually perceived the Zionists as colonizers. Jabotinsky, writing in 1923, did not reflect the perceptions of the leadership. See Teveth, *Ben-Gurion and the Palestinian Arabs.*

108 Lustick, "Abandoning the Iron Wall," 30.

109 Ibid., 34.

110 Efraim Inbar and Ian Lustick, "Israel's Future: The Time Factor," *Israel Studies Forum* 23, 1 (2008): 8.

111 Lustick, "Abandoning the Iron Wall," 43, 42.

112 Ibid., 47.

113 Ibid.

114 For the interim Winograd Commission report, see Israel Ministry of Foreign Affairs, "Winograd Commission Submits Interim Report," April 30, 2007, http://www.mfa.gov.il/MFA/Government/Communiques/2007/Winograd+Inquiry+Commission+submits+Interim+Report+30-Apr-2007.htm; for the full rport, see "Judge Winograd Reveals War Committee's Findings: Full Text of Judge Eliyahu Winograd's Press Conference on Inquiry into 2006 Lebanon War," *Yedioth Ahronoth Online,* January 30, 2008, http://www.ynetnews.com/articles/0,7340,L-3500810,00.html.

115 Gideon Levy, "Disgrace in the Hague," *Ha'aretz,* September 17, 2009.

116 Lustick, "Abandoning the Iron Wall," 48.

117 Ibid., 51.

118 Jimmy Carter, "The Elders' View of the Middle East," *Washington Post,* September 6, 2009.

119 See Brenda Goodman, "Carter Center Advisers Quit to Protest Book," *New York Times,* January 12, 2007; James Traub, "Does Abe Foxman Have an Anti-Anti-Semite Problem?," *New York Times,* January 14, 2007; Ethan Bronner, "Jews, Arabs, and Jimmy Carter," *New York Times,* January 7, 2007; and Jeffrey Goldberg, "What Would Jimmy Do? A Former President Puts the Onus for Resolving the Mideast Conflict on the Israelis," *Washington Post,* December 10, 2006.

120 Jimmy Carter, *Palestine Peace Not Apartheid* (New York: Simon and Schuster, 2007), 216.

121 United Nations, Security Council, Resolution 242: The Situation in the Middle East [hereinafter UN Resolution 242], UN Doc. S/RES/242 (1967), http://daccess-dds-ny.un.org/doc/RESOLUTION/GEN/NR0/240/94/IMG/NR024094.pdf?OpenElement.

122 Ibid., sec. 1 (ii).

123 Ibid., sec. 2 (b).

124 See Michael Lynk, "Conceived in Law: The Legal Foundations of Resolution 242," *Journal of Palestine Studies* 37, 1 (2007): 7.

125 UN Resolution 242, Preamble, sec. 1 (i), stating that the resolution emphasizes that "all Members states in their acceptance of the Charter of the United Nations have undertaken a commitment to act in accordance with Article 2 of the Charter."

126 See Lynk, "Conceived in Law."

127 See Thomas W. Mallison and Sally V. Mallison, "The Role of International Law in Achieving Justice and Peace in Palestine-Israel," *Journal of Palestine Studies* 3, 3 (1974): 77; and Richard Falk and David Kretzmer, *The Occupation of Justice: The Supreme Court of Israel and the Occupied Territories* (Albany: SUNY Press, 2002).

128 See United Nations, Security Council, Resolution 446, UN Doc. S/RES/446 (1979); Resolution 452, UN Doc. S/RES/452 (1979); Resolution 465, UN Doc. S/RES/465 (1980); http://domino.un.org/UNISPAL.NSF/db942872b9eae454852560f6005a76fb/5aa254a1c8f8b1cb852560e50075d7d5; Resolution 471, UN Doc. S/RES/471 (1980); and Resolution 476, UN Doc. S/RES/476 (1980).

129 See Conference of High Contracting Parties to the Fourth Geneva Convention at International Review of the Red Cross, "Implementation of the Fourth Geneva Convention in the Occupied Palestinian Territories: History of a Multilateral Process (1997-2001)," December 5, 2001, No. 847; see also the Mitchell Report, named after US senator George Mitchell, currently leading peace negotiations in the Middle East on behalf of the United States as a special envoy, also known as the "Report of the Sharm el-Sheikh Fact-Finding Committee," April 30, 2001, in particular 65: "Security Council Resolution 1322, consideration of which forms part of this Committee's mandate, makes explicit reference to several other Security Council resolutions, all of which emphasize the *de jure* applicability of the Fourth Geneva Convention ('Convention') to the Occupied Palestinian Territories, the illegality of Israel's unilateral annexation of Jerusalem and of the steps Israel has taken to change the city's character. The international community, including the five permanent members of the UN Security Council, has repeatedly affirmed that the Convention applies *de jure* to the Occupied Palestinian Territories and the International Court of Justice has noted that the Geneva Conventions are customary international law as well. Israel itself originally recognised the Convention's *de jure* applicability but subsequently reversed itself. The Committee's recommendations are in line with the Convention, and appear directly linked to the Convention's application. Israel's settlement policy, for example, is 'illegal under international law' precisely because of the application of Article 49 of the Convention which prohibits the transfer of an Occupying Power's civilian population into the territory it occupies."

130 International Committee of the Red Cross, Geneva Convention (IV), Relative to the Protection of Civilian Persons in Time of War, adopted on August 12, 1949, 75 UNTS 287.

131 *Legal Consequences of the Construction of a Wall in the Occupied Palestinian Territory, Advisory Opinion,* I.C.J. Reports, 2004.

132 Ibid., paras. 95-101.

133 Ibid., para. 120.

134 Carter, *Palestine Peace Not Apartheid,* 151-52.

135 Jonathan Marcus, "The 2009 Israeli Election: A Bump in the Road to Peace?," *Washington Quarterly* 32, 3 (2009): 62.

136 Etgar Lefkovits, "Netanyahu: Jerusalem Will Never Be Divided," *Jerusalem Post,* May 21, 2009.

137 Mark Landler and Isabel Kershner, "Israeli Settlement Growth Must Stop, Clinton Says," *New York Times,* May 27, 2009; see also Jonathan Lis, "Israel: Won't Accept 'Complete Freeze' on Settlement Building," *Ha'aretz,* September 14, 2009.

138 "France Urges Israel to Reconsider East Jerusalem Building Plans," *Ha'aretz,* October 16, 2010.

139 Mahmoud Abbas was still committed to negotiations; he saw the bid at the United Nations as a way of improving the position of the Palestinians in negotiations. See his May 16, 2011, op ed, for example, in the *New York Times,* http://www.nytimes.com/2011/05/17/opinion/17abbas.html.

140 "Palestinian UN Bid Goes to Security Council", *CBC News,* http://www.cbc.ca/news/world/story/2011/11/11/palestinian-un-membership-security-council.html.

141 Jennifer Steinhauer and Steven Lee Myers, "House G.O.P. Tightens Its Bond with Netanyahu," *New York Times,* September 20, 2011, http://www.nytimes.com/2011/09/21/world/middleeast/house-gop-finds-a-growing-bond-with-netanyahu.html?pagewanted=2.

142 Benjamin Netanyahu, "40 Signatures Speech," November 23, 2011, http://www.pmo.gov.il/English/MediaCenter/Speeches/Pages/speech40sign150611.aspx.

143 Carter, *Palestine Peace Not Apartheid,* 214.

144 Article 49 of the Fourth Geneva Convention, which, as noted above, applies to Israel both with respect to its general commitment as a signatory (with reservations) and with respect to the occupied territories, speaks not only to settlement activity but also to the scenario of transfer: "Individual or mass forcible transfers, as well as deportations of protected persons from occupied territory to the territory of the Occupying Power or to that of any other country, occupied or not, are prohibited, regardless of their motive." International Committee of the Red Cross, Geneva Convention (IV), Relative to the Protection of Civilian Persons in Time of War, adopted on August 12, 1949, 75 UNTS 287.

145 Carter, *Palestine Peace Not Apartheid,* 215.

146 See Alan Dershowitz, "The World According to Jimmy Carter," *Huffington Post,* November 22, 2006; Brenda Goodman, "Carter Center Advisers Quit to Protest Book," *New York Times,* January 12, 2007; James Traub, "Does Abe Foxman Have an Anti-Anti-Semite Problem?," *New York Times,* January 14, 2007; Ethan Bronner, "Jews, Arabs, and Jimmy Carter," *New York Times,* January 7, 2007; Jeffrey Goldberg, "What Would Jimmy Do? A Former President Puts the Onus for Resolving the Mideast Conflict on the Israelis," *Washington Post,* December 10, 2006.

147 Carter, *Palestine Peace Not Apartheid,* 215. Carter is not alone in troubling the connection between Israel and apartheid states. See, for example, "Occupation, Colonialism, Apartheid? A Re-Assessment of Israel's Practices in the Occupied Palestinian Territories under International Law," a study coordinated by the Middle East Project of the Democracy and Governance Programme, Human Sciences Research Council of South Africa, May 2009.

148 Carter, *Palestine Peace Not Apartheid,* 216.

149 Ibid., 48.

150 Carter, "The Elders' View of the Middle East."

151 See Ian Lustick, "The Evolution of Gush Emunim," in *For the Land and the Lord: Jewish Fundamentalism in Israel* (New York: Council on Foreign Relations, 1988), reproduced at http://www.sas.upenn.edu/penncip/lustick/lustick13.html.

152 Carter, "The Elders' View of the Middle East."

153 Ibid.

154 Scheinberg and Caplan, "One State Is No Solution."

155 See references at note 147.

156 Scheinberg and Caplan, "One State Is No Solution."

157 Richard Goldstone, "Reconsidering the Goldstone Report on Israel and War Crimes," *Washington Post,* 1 April 2011, http://www.washingtonpost.com/opinions/reconsidering-the-goldstone-report-on-israel-and-war-crimes/2011/04/01/AFg111JC_story.html.

158 Human Rights Council, Sixteenth Session, March 18, 2011, Report of the Committee of Independent Experts in International Humanitarian and Human Rights Law Established Pursuant to Council Resolution 13/9 (a.k.a. McGowan Davis Report), http://www2.ohchr.org/english/bodies/hrcouncil/docs/16session/A.HRC.16.24_AUV.pdf.

159 John Dugard, "Where Now for the Goldstone Report?," *New Statesman,* April 6, 2011; see also Roger Cohen, "The Goldstone Chronicles," *New York Times,* April 7, 2011.

160 Thomas Friedman, "One Wall, One Person, One Vote," *New York Times,* September 14, 2003.

161 Irene L. Gendzier, "Palestine and Israel: The Binational Idea," *Journal of Palestine Studies* 4, 2 (1975): 30.

162 Ibid.; see also Tamar Hermann, "The Bi-National Idea in Israel/Palestine: Past and Present," *Nations and Nationalism* 11, 3 (2005): 384.

163 Hermann, "The Bi-National Idea in Israel/Palestine," 385.

164 Lustick, "Abandoning the Iron Wall," 30.

165 That these pronouncements by Ben-Gurion and Weizman were strategic and part of an effort to ensure that the Arabs and the British would not undermine their more gradualist agenda indicates at least an awareness of the fundamental injustice of the aspiration to Judaize Palestine at the expense of the Palestinians. Ben-Gurion's hidden gradualist agenda has been made clear by a number of Israel's New Historians. Simha Flapan notes that Ben-Gurion told the Zionist Executive in 1937 that, "after the formation of a large army in the wake of the establishment of the state, we will abolish partition and expand to the whole of Palestine." Flapan, *The Birth of Israel,* 22. Avi Shlaim notes that he told his son in the same year, "erect a Jewish State at once, even if it is not in the whole land. The rest will come in the course of time. It must come." Shlaim, *The Iron Wall,* 21.

166 Gendzier, "Palestine and Israel," 31.

167 Ibid.

168 Helena Cobban, "Ends and Means," *Boston Review* 26, 6 (2001-2): 4, http://bostonreview.net/BR26.6/cobban.html.

169 Carter, *Palestine Peace Not Apartheid,* 151-52.

170 Hermann, "The Bi-National Idea in Israel/Palestine," 386.

171 See Leonard Fein, "A Response to 'The Case for Binationalism,'" *Boston Review* 26, 6 (2001-2): 1, http://bostonreview.net/BR26.6/fein.html.

172 George E. Bisharat, "Maximizing Rights: The One State Solution to the Palestinian-Israeli Conflict," *Global Jurist* 8, 2 (2008): 3. Bisharat was one of the three keynote speakers at the Mapping Models conference.

173 Uri Avnery and Ilan Pappé, "Two States or One State," debate sponsored by Gush Shalom, Tel Aviv, May 8, 2007, 5; for the full transcript, see http://www.countercurrents.org/pappe110607.htm, accessed October 18, 2009.
174 Yossi Klein-Halevi, "Only the Naïve or the Malicious Would Urge a Binational Israel," *Los Angeles Times,* October 10, 2003.
175 Benvenisti was a member of the conference Advisory Committee and a presenter at the conference.
176 Ari Shavit, "Cry the Beloved Two-State Solution," *Ha'aretz,* August 6, 2003.
177 Ibid.
178 Ibid.
179 Judt, "Israel."
180 Graham Usher, "Bantustanisation or Bi-Nationalism? An Interview with Azmi Bishara," *Race and Class* 37, 2 (1995): 43.
181 Ibid., 47.
182 Ari Shavit, "Top PM Aide: Gaza Plan Aims to Freeze the Peace Process," *Ha'aretz,* October 6, 2004, http://www.haaretz.com.
183 Efraim Inbar and Ian Lustick, "Israel's Future: The Time Factor," *Israel Studies Forum* 23, 1 (2008): 3-11; also see Stephen M. Walt, "The Treason of the Hawks," *Foreign Policy,* April 28, 2009; and Judt, "Israel."
184 See, for example, Nehemia Shtrasler, "The Haredi Takeover Must Be Prevented," *Ha'aretz,* August 4, 2009; also see a Canadian summary of the tensions in Patrick Martin, "A Hostile Takeover of Zionism: Israel Is Teetering toward Theocracy, with the Rise of the Haredim," *Globe and Mail,* September 26, 2009.
185 Inbar and Lustick, "Israel's Future," 5.
186 See David Landau, "Maximum Jews, Minimum Palestinians," *Ha'aretz,* November 13, 2003; Aluf Benn, David Landau, Barak Ravid, and Shmuel Rosner, "Olmert to Haaretz: Two-State Solution, or Israel Is Done For," *Ha'aretz,* November 29, 2007; Barak Ravid, "PM at Final Cabinet Meeting: Greater Israel Is No More," *Ha'aretz,* September 16, 2008.
187 Barak Ravid, "PM at Final Cabinet Meeting: Greater Israel Is No More," *Ha'aretz,* September 16, 2008.
188 David Landau, "Maximum Jews, Minimum Palestinians," *Ha'aretz,* November 13, 2003.
189 Lama Abu-Odeh, "The Case for Binationalism: Why One State – Liberal and Constitutionalist – May Be the Key to Peace in the Middle East," *Boston Review* 26, 6 (2001-2), http://bostonreview.net/BR26.6/abu-odeh.html.
190 Ibid., 6.
191 Ibid., 4.
192 Ibid.
193 See Jonathan Spyer, "Forward to the Past: The Fall and Rise of the One-State Solution," *Middle East Review of International Affairs* 12, 3 (2008): 102.
194 Ibid.
195 Ibid., 105; see also Joseph Massad, "The Binational State and the Reunification of the Palestinian People," *Global Dialogue* 4, 3 (2002), http://bostonreview.net/BR26.6/abu-odeh.html.
196 Abu-Odeh, "The Case for Binationalism."

197 Ibid., 14.

198 Salim Tamari, "The Binationalist Lure," *Boston Review* 26, 6 (2001-2), http://bostonreview.net/BR26.6/tamari.html.

199 This growing literature is considerable. For an annotated bibliography of some of the leading articles, books, and chapters on the one-state model, see the conference website, http://www.yorku.ca/ipconf/annotatedbibliography.html.

200 Meron Benvenisti, "Which Kind of Binational State?," *Ha'aretz,* November 20, 2003.

201 Ibid.

202 Her article generated a cluster of responses from a range of perspectives from Helena Cobban, Leonard Fein, Efraim Karsh, Ian Lustick, Ebrahim Moosa, Jerome Segal, Louis Michael Seidman, and Salim Tamari. Each can be found in *Boston Review* 26, 6 (2001-2).

203 Ian Lustick, "The Cunning of History," *Boston Review* 26, 6 (2001-2), http://bostonreview.net/BR26.6/lustick.html.

204 See, for example, Brian Barry, "The Consociational Model and Its Dangers," *European Journal of Political Research* 3 (1975): 393; Ian Lustick, "Stability in Deeply Divided Societies: Consociationalism versus Control," *World Politics* 31, 3 (1979): 325; and Ian Lustick, "Lijphart, Lakatos, and Consociationalism," *World Politics* 50, 1 (1997): 88.

205 See Will Kymlicka, "Minority Rights and the New International Politics of Diversity," paper presented at the Legal Theory Workshop Series 2006-7, Faculty of Law, University of Toronto, January 5, 2007, 1; see also Iris Marion Young, "Self-Determination as Non-Domination: Ideals Applied to Israel/Palestine," *Ethnicities* 5, 2 (2005): 139; Chaim Gans, *The Limits of Nationalism* (Cambridge, UK: Cambridge University Press, 2003); and Karen Knop, *Diversity and Self-Determination in International Law* (Cambridge, UK: Cambridge University Press, 2002).

206 Daniel J. Elazar, "Federal/Confederal Solutions to the Israeli-Palestinian-Jordanian Conflict: Concepts and Feasibility," 1998, http://www.jcpa.org/dje/articles/fedconfed-sol.htm.

207 Meron Benvenisti, "The Binationalism Vogue," *Ha'aretz,* April 30, 2009.

208 See http://www.yorku.ca/ipconf/videoaudio.html.

Chapter 3: Mixing Jurisdictions

1 This is a paraphrase of Alistair McIntyre, *After Virtue: A Study in Moral Theory,* 2nd ed. (Indiana: University of Notre Dame Press, 1984).

2 President Lorna Marsden, "On the Autonomy of Universities," http://www.yorku.ca/yfile/archive/index.asp?Article=8670.

3 John J. Mearsheimer and Stephen M. Walt, *The Israel Lobby and US Foreign Policy* (Toronto: Penguin Canada, 2007), 112 ff.

4 Sheri Shefa, "'Israel Lobby' Stifles Campus Speech: Report," *Canadian Jewish News,* October 10, 2011.

5 Ibid.

6 Jewish Canada (B'nai Brith), email communication to supporters, June 8, 2009.

7 Mearsheimer and Walt, *The Israel Lobby and US Foreign Policy,* 113-14.

8 Ibid., 114.

9 Meron Benvenisti, "The Binationalism Vogue," *Ha'aretz,* April 30, 2009.
10 Mearsheimer and Walt, *The Israel Lobby and US Foreign Policy,* 336.
11 Paul Heinbecker, "Tilting toward Israel," *Globe and Mail,* July 25, 2006.
12 See "PM's Rhetoric Hurts Canada's Peacemaking Chances: Opposition," *CBC News,* July 18, 2006, http://www.cbc.ca/.
13 "Harper Says Comparison of Hezbollah, Nazis Is Fair: Prime Minister Stephen Harper Said Tuesday It's Not Unfair to Liken Hezbollah to the Nazis, Who Once Ruled Germany, Because Both Stand for the Destruction of the 'Jewish Nation,'" *National Post,* August 23, 2006, http://www.nationalpost.com.
14 Irwin Cotler, "Being Even-Handed Not Part of Mideast Policy – Canada Was Right in Rejecting Threats to Annihilate Israel," *Toronto Star,* August 19, 2006.
15 Paul Heinbecker, "Tilting toward Israel," *Globe and Mail,* July 25, 2006; see also Paul Heinbecker and Bessma Momani, *Canada and the Middle East: In Theory and Practice* (Waterloo: Wilfrid Laurier University Press, 2007).
16 Former American president Jimmy Carter, who assisted in monitoring the 2006 Palestinian Authority elections, referred to them as "orderly and peaceful," "honest, fair and safe," and exhibiting "conduct of exemplary democratic elections." Jimmy Carter, *Palestine Peace Not Apartheid* (New York: Simon and Schuster, 2007), 182-83. Carter's assessment was shared by Edward McMillan-Scott, the British Conservative head of the European Parliament's monitoring team, who described the polls as "extremely professional, in line with international standards, free, transparent and without violence." His colleague, Italian Communist MEP Luisa Morgantini, said that there was "a very professional attitude, competence and respect for the rules." See Edward McMillan-Scott, "Delegation to Observe Legislative Elections in Palestine," February 2006, http://www.europarl.europa.eu/intcoop/election_observation/missions/2004-2009/20060119_palestine.pdf; and Luisa Morgantini, "Hamas, una vittoria annunciate," *Liberazione,* January 31, 2006, http://luisamorgantini.net/node/152.
17 In this use of funding for political ends, Canada was preceded only by Israel, which refused to transfer the tax money that it collects on behalf of the Palestinian Authority.
18 Conal Urquhart, "Gaza on Brink of Implosion as Aid Cut-Off Starts to Bite: The End of Western Funding and Israel's Crossing Closure Sharpen Palestinian Divisions," *The Observer,* April 16, 2006; see also Lawrence Wright, "Captives: What Really Happened during the Israeli Attacks," *The New Yorker,* November 9, 2009.
19 Conal Urquhart, "Gaza on Brink of Implosion as Aid Cut-Off Starts to Bite: The End of Western Funding and Israel's Crossing Closure Sharpen Palestinian Divisions," *The Observer,* April 16, 2006.
20 Goldstone Report, para. 1877.
21 "Harper Says Hostage-Takers Could Stop the Conflict," *CTV News,* July 13, 2006.
22 Etgar Lefkovits, "Canadian Government Forming Pro-Israel Lobby," *Jerusalem Post,* February 4, 2007. This report is flawed in that Parliament does not establish lobbies; it registers and regulates them. It is common, however, for non-partisan caucuses to form around special interest issues. These caucuses are different from parliamentary groups such as the Canada-Israel Inter-Parliamentary Group and other government

committees, which receive government funding and are involved in the passage of legislation. Members of Parliament sit on both caucuses and committees but not on lobbies.

23 See http://www.iiacf.org/index.php/site/member_nations/. Lunney can also be seen on the video of the meeting of the presidents of the International Israel Allies Caucus at the following link: http://www.iiacf.org/index.php/site/media_gallery/.

24 Established in 1981, the C-IIG aims "to work for a greater friendship and goodwill between parliamentarians of Canada and Israel and thereby serve to further cooperation between national parliaments of both countries and between both countries." See http://www2.parl.gc.ca/iia/Association.aspx?Lang=E&DCId=4&DTId=6&P=over view&ORGId=10793.

25 Conal Urquhart, "Gaza on Brink of Implosion as Aid Cut-Off Starts to Bite: The End of Western Funding and Israel's Crossing Closure Sharpen Palestinian Divisions," *The Observer,* April 16, 2006.

26 "Declaration of Purpose and Solidarity with the People and State of Israel," presented to the Knesset Christian Allies Caucus, February 19, 2008, ratified by the International Israel Allies Caucus Chairmen, May 22, 2008, http://www.iiacf.org/index.php/site/about/, accessed October 27, 2009.

27 Ibid.

28 Ibid., Article 4.

29 See http://www.iiacf.org/index.php/site/news/.

30 Mearsheimer and Walt, *The Israel Lobby and US Foreign Policy,* 132-39.

31 January 4, 2009, statement by Lawrence Cannon on the issue of Israel and the peace process, cited in Nidal al-Mughrabi, Reuters, "Israelis Storm into Gaza as Tanks Counter Rockets," *Windsor Star,* January 5, 2009, http://www.windsorstar.com/index.html.

32 "Ignatieff Backs Israel's Offensive: Liberal Leader Echoes Tory Government, Blames Hamas for 'Organizing, Instigating Rocket Attacks,'" *Toronto Star,* January 9, 2009.

33 Stephen Thorne, "Besieged Canadians Await Evacuation from Gaza Fighting," *Toronto Star,* January 6, 2009.

34 Goldstone Report, paras. 475-78.

35 Ibid., Executive Summary, para. 55.

36 See http://www.cjpac.ca/people/view/164.

37 "Ignatieff Admits Gaffe over Mideast Conflict," *CTV News,* August 10, 2006, www.ctv.ca.

38 "Ignatieff Backs Israel's Offensive: Liberal Leader Echoes Tory Government, Blames Hamas for 'Organizing, Instigating Rocket Attacks,'" *Toronto Star,* January 9, 2009.

39 In light of the recent controversy over Conservative mail-outs to ridings with large Jewish communities in which voters were asked to choose which federal leader "is on the right track to represent and defend the values of Canada's Jewish community," it is fair to say that both the Liberals and the Conservatives compete over which party supports Israel more. See Richard J. Brennen, "PM's Jewish Pitch Hits a New Low: Critics Say Tory Flyer Suggests Liberals Are Anti-Semitic," *Toronto Star,* November 19, 2009.

40 "Prime Minister Harper Receives Saul Hayes Human Rights Award," press release, Office of the Prime Minister, May 31, 2009.
41 See, for example, Mary Ellen Turpel, "Aboriginal Peoples and the Canadian Charter: Interpretive Monopolies, Cultural Differences," *Canadian Human Rights Yearbook* 4, 3 (1989-90): 3.
42 "Remarks by PM Harper Accepting B'nai Brith International's Presidential Gold Medallion for Humanitarianism Award," June 27, 2008, http://www.bnaibrith.ca/prdisplay.php?id=1349.
43 Laura Payton, "Tories' Israel Policy Damaging: UN Rapporteur: Siding with Israel Hurts Canada's Role as a 'Fair and Balanced Interpreter' of Events: Falk," *Embassy,* September 30, 2009.
44 Paul Heinbecker, "Tilting toward Israel," *Globe and Mail,* July 25, 2006.
45 Mearsheimer and Walt, *The Israel Lobby and US Foreign Policy,* 185.
46 Ibid., 168 ff.
47 *Tikkun* is a publication that borrows its name from the Hebrew expression *tikkun olam* – "social justice and repair of the world" – and that focuses "on social theory, religion/spirituality, social change, contemporary American and global politics and economics, ecology, culture, psychology, and Israel/Palestine." See "About the Magazine," http://www.tikkun.org/index.php?topic=about, accessed November 2, 2009.
48 David Theo Goldberg and Saree Makdisi, "The Trial of Israel's Campus Critics," *Tikkun,* September-October 2009, http://www.tikkun.org/article.php/sept_oct_09_goldberg_makdisi. See also Matthew Abraham, *Out of Bounds: Academic Freedom and the Question of Palestine* (London: Pluto Press, 2008).
49 "About Us," Israel on Campus Coalition, http://www.israelcc.org/home/about-us.
50 Goldberg and Makdisi, "The Trial of Israel's Campus Critics."
51 Ibid.
52 Israel on Campus Coalition, Maryland, "Academic Rights, Academic Responsibilities: A New Approach," 2007.
53 Ibid., 1.
54 Ibid., 6.
55 Ibid., 19.
56 Goldberg and Makdisi, "The Trial of Israel's Campus Critics."
57 Marci McDonald, "The Heather and Gerry Show," *Toronto Life,* June 2009, 39, 6, 54.
58 Ibid., 64.
59 Ibid., 65.
60 Paul Lungen, "CIJA Officials Look Back on First Year," *Canadian Jewish News,* August 23, 2004.
61 Ibid.
62 McDonald, "The Heather and Gerry Show."
63 According to Ibbitson, instruction for the change in policy came directly from the Prime Minister's Office, where Martin was "under intense pressure" from CIJA co-founder Schwartz. John Ibbitson, "In Case You Missed It, Our Mideast Policy Has Shifted," *Globe and Mail,* December 3, 2004. See also Diane Koven, "PM Reaffirms Support of Israel," *Canadian Jewish News,* November 5, 2004.

64 See, for example, Daniel Freeman-Maloy, "Organizing the Canada-Israel Alliance," *Canadian Dimension,* October 29, 2006, http://canadiandimension.com/articles/1819: "In May of that year, according to the *Canadian Jewish News,* AIPAC's annual conference in Washington, D.C., 'included a one-day event ... aimed at helping Canadian and European communities develop the kind of grassroots organizational strength that AIPAC has shown over the years.' As early as 2004, CIJA officials had already said that the 'ultimate goal' of the Canadian PAC should be 'to act as a partisan entity that would support candidates.' Some months after the May 2005 AIPAC tutorial, just in time for the Canadian federal election, CIJA-PAC was disbanded to make way for an organization more suited to this work."
65 "About Us," Israel on Campus Coalition, http://www.israelcc.org/home/about-us.
66 "President's Statement on Academic Freedom and the Role of the University," York University Media Relations, May 21, 2009, http://www.yorku.ca/mediar/archive/Release.php?Release=1678, accessed November 4, 2009.
67 ICC, "Academic Rights, Academic Responsibilities," 6.
68 See President Lorna Marsden, "On the Autonomy of Universities," http://www.yorku.ca/yfile/archive/index.asp?Article=8670.

Chapter 4: Inside Academia

1 Appendix 9: presidential statements on the conference, https://circle.ubc.ca/handle/2429/45061.
2 See http://www.caut.ca/pages.asp?lang=1&page=247.
3 See http://www.yorku.ca/ipconf/advisory.html.
4 See Appendix 16: original draft of the conference program with the original title, March 12, 2008, https://circle.ubc.ca/handle/2429/45061.
5 See Desmond Tutu, "Israel: Time to Divest," *New Internationalist* 353 (2003), http://www.newint.org/columns/viewfrom/2003/01/01/israel/; see also http://www.bdsmovement.net/call.
6 Email to Organizing Committee from Daniel Dewitt, April 2, 2008.
7 Email to Organizing Committee from Dean Patrick Monahan, March 12, 2008.
8 Appendix 17: email from the dean of Osgoode Hall Law School to the U50 committee re the conference, March 27, 2008, https://circle.ubc.ca/handle/2429/45061.
9 "Preliminary Review" of the original synopsis by Drummond of administrative interventions, July 2009.
10 Appendix 18: email from the dean to an anonymized complainant regarding the meaning of "sponsorship," April 24, 2009, https://circle.ubc.ca/handle/2429/45061.
11 Jon Thompson, *No Debate: The Israel Lobby and Free Speech at Canadian Universities* (Toronto: James Lorimer and Company, 2010), 245 ff.
12 Ibid., 251.
13 This email is discussed in Chapter 1.
14 Complaint by a colleague re the Bil'in seminar, email, October 5, 2008.
15 See http://www.torontolife.com/features/yorks-middle-east-war/.
16 Appendix 19: note to Ryder and Drummond from the dean re concerns, October 3, 2008, https://circle.ubc.ca/handle/2429/45061.

17 Email from the dean with the *Toronto Life* article attached, October 8, 2008.
18 Appendix 20: email from the dean confirming that he asked us to take Masri off the Organizing Committee, October 10, 2008, https://circle.ubc.ca/handle/2429/45061.
19 Patrick Monahan, July 2011 feedback, 7.
20 Email communication, October 2, 2008.
21 See the beginning of Chapter 1.
22 Email from associate dean of research and graduate studies (ADRGS) to Masri re the politically heated nature of the topic, October 6, 2008.
23 Email from ADRGS to Masri re "postponement" of the Bil'in seminar, October 14, 2008.
24 Email from Masri to ADRGS re how cancelling the Bil'in seminar would look, October 19, 2008.
25 Appendix 3: email from the chair of York University's Board of Governors indicating that he had been cornered at a Passover seder re the Adelman memo, April 12, 2009, https://circle.ubc.ca/handle/2429/45061.
26 Ibid.
27 Appendix 21: email from the dean to Drummond and Ryder re communications from inside and outside the university re balance, April 15, 2009, https://circle.ubc.ca/handle/2429/45061.
28 Appendix 22: email from Dewitt re scaling back the conference, April 15, 2009, https://circle.ubc.ca/handle/2429/45061.
29 Thompson, *No Debate,* 231.
30 Appendix 22: email from Dewitt re scaling back the conference, April 15, 2009, https://circle.ubc.ca/handle/2429/45061.
31 Thompson, *No Debate,* 230.
32 See Appendix 6: email with Monahan's original response to complaints about the conference, April 24, 2009, https://circle.ubc.ca/handle/2429/45061.
33 Appendix 23: email from Cohen to Shoukri/Monahan re populating the audience at the conference, April 15, 2009, https://circle.ubc.ca/handle/2429/45061.
34 Appendix 24: email from the dean to Professor Irving Abella (copied to Supreme Court judge Rosalie Abella), April 15, 2009, https://circle.ubc.ca/handle/2429/45061.
35 Appendix 25: email from Monahan to Shoukri/Cohen about his conversation with Abella, April 15, 2009, https://circle.ubc.ca/handle/2429/45061.
36 Thompson, *No Debate,* 240.
37 Appendix 26: communications between the Office of University Events and the U50 manager of implementation, April 14, 2009, https://circle.ubc.ca/handle/2429/45061.
38 Appendix 23: email from Cohen to Shoukri/Monahan re populating the audience at the conference, April 15, 2009, https://circle.ubc.ca/handle/2429/45061.
39 Appendix 27: email from Cohen to Shoukri/Monahan re putting the "fear of all three gods" into the conference organizers, April 17, 2009, https://circle.ubc.ca/handle/2429/45061.
40 Ibid.
41 Appendix 28: email from Monahan to Drummond re needing more two-state advocates, April 22, 2009, https://circle.ubc.ca/handle/2429/45061.

42 Appendix 29: email from the dean to the president (containing Shoukri's suggestion) re strong-arming Dewitt and the conference organizers' lack of flexibility, May 9, 2009, https://circle.ubc.ca/handle/2429/45061.
43 Ibid.
44 Thompson, *No Debate,* 239.
45 Appendix 22: email from Dewitt re scaling back the conference, April 15, 2009, https://circle.ubc.ca/handle/2429/45061.
46 Appendix 30: email from Monahan to Shoukri and Cohen re "a plan to try to rework the agenda," April 21, 2009, https://circle.ubc.ca/handle/2429/45061.
47 Emails between Drummond and the dean re Dewitt's participation in the conference, April 27, 2009.
48 Ibid.
49 Ibid.
50 On several occasions, beginning in July of 2009, I sought feedback and clarification from Patrick Monahan regarding his interventions in the Mapping Models conference. The feedback was solicited on the basis of statements of fact laid out in earlier drafts of this book. In July of 2011, Patrick Monahan submitted a lengthy response to these factual claims. This July 2011 feedback document is herein cited.
51 "Preliminary Review" of the original synopsis by Drummond of administrative interventions, July 2009.
52 Appendix 31: emails from Monahan to Shoukri/Cohen re Drummond's threat about speaking to CAUT, April 25, 2009, https://circle.ubc.ca/handle/2429/45061.
53 Ibid.
54 Ibid.
55 Appendix 22: email from Dewitt re scaling back the conference, April 15, 2009, https://circle.ubc.ca/handle/2429/45061.
56 Appendix 32: email from Monahan on securing Glendon Campus, May 10, 2009, https://circle.ubc.ca/handle/2429/45061; emphasis added.
57 Thompson, *No Debate,* 75.
58 Appendix 33: emails between Dewitt and Monahan on Michael Bell and other matters, April 28, 2009, https://circle.ubc.ca/handle/2429/45061.
59 Ibid.
60 Appendix 31: emails from Monahan to Shoukri/Cohen re Drummond's threat about speaking to CAUT, April 25, 2009, https://circle.ubc.ca/handle/2429/45061.
61 Appendix 34: email from Monahan to Dewitt re "one chance to shape this in the right direction," May 2, 2009, https://circle.ubc.ca/handle/2429/45061.
62 Thompson, *No Debate,* 95.
63 Appendix 35: email from Monahan to Drummond re Bob Rae, May 2, 2009, https://circle.ubc.ca/handle/2429/45061.
64 Appendix 32: email from Monahan on securing Glendon Campus, May 10, 2009, https://circle.ubc.ca/handle/2429/45061.
65 Appendix 36: email from Monahan to Shoukri re not meeting with the organizers, May 9, 2009. https://circle.ubc.ca/handle/2429/45061.
66 Appendix 32: email from Monahan on securing Glendon Campus, May 10, 2009, https://circle.ubc.ca/handle/2429/45061.

67 Thompson, *No Debate*, 263.
68 Ibid.
69 Ibid., 265.
70 Appendix 32: email from Monahan on securing Glendon Campus, May 10, 2009, https://circle.ubc.ca/handle/2429/45061.
71 Ibid.
72 Feedback document from Monahan, July 2011.
73 Personal communication, December 20, 2011.
74 Email from Ryder to Monahan (forwarded in December 2011), May 9, 2009.
75 Email from Provost Monahan to Professor Drummond, January 3, 2012.
76 Frank Iacobucci, *The Mapping [Models] Conference and Academic Freedom: A Report to President Mamdouh Shoukri from the Honourable Frank Iacobucci*, March 2010, 10-11, http://president.news.yorku.ca/2010/04/09/president-releases-iacobucci-report-on-israelpalestine-conference/.
77 Email from Ryder to Monahan (forwarded in December 2011), May 9, 2009.
78 See Thompson, *No Debate*, 127-28.
79 Ibid., 251-52.
80 Appendix 37: Monahan and Dewitt confer, May 10, 2009, https://circle.ubc.ca/handle/2429/45061.
81 Appendix 38: "PRIVATE & CONFIDENTIAL" email from Dewitt to Monahan, May 11, 2009, https://circle.ubc.ca/handle/2429/45061.
82 See http://www.ngo-monitor.org/articles/staff.
83 Appendix 38: "PRIVATE & CONFIDENTIAL" email from Dewitt to Monahan, May 11, 2009, https://circle.ubc.ca/handle/2429/45061.
84 Thompson, *No Debate*, 233. He went on to qualify his observation by noting that, "more precisely, the parts of the email message made available to CAUT by York University did not contain this additional information. It is not known to this Inquiry whether the dean learned of these endeavours of Steinberg from Dewitt or from some other source, or whether the dean already knew about NGO Monitor and its president."
85 Appendix 38: "PRIVATE & CONFIDENTIAL" email from Dewitt to Monahan, May 11, 2009, https://circle.ubc.ca/handle/2429/45061.
86 Appendix 39: email from Dewitt to Monahan re "PLEASE DO NOT SHARE THIS," May 11, 2009, https://circle.ubc.ca/handle/2429/45061.
87 Ibid.
88 Thompson, *No Debate*, 233.
89 Email from Dewitt to Drummond, December 20, 2011.
90 Thompson, *No Debate*, 233.
91 Ibid., 235.
92 Ibid., 235-36.
93 Appendix 39: email from Dewitt to Monahan re "PLEASE DO NOT SHARE THIS," May 11, 2009. https://circle.ubc.ca/handle/2429/45061.
94 Appendix 40: email from Dewitt to Monahan about consulting unnamed external academics for the plenary session, May 13, 2009, https://circle.ubc.ca/handle/2429/45061.

95 Thompson, *No Debate,* 257-59.

96 Appendix 39: email from Dewitt to Monahan re "PLEASE DO NOT SHARE THIS," May 11, 2009, https://circle.ubc.ca/handle/2429/45061.

97 Ibid.

98 In a February 2011 submission to the CAUT Inquiry, Provost Monahan noted that "it is difficult to recall the precise comments that were made during this meeting, which took place almost two years ago"; Thompson, *No Debate,* 270. However, I took extensive and detailed notes at the meeting and am considerably less challenged in my recall of it.

99 It is interesting to contrast these concerns with the May 17, 2009, comments of another colleague at Osgoode Hall Law School (who has subsequently moved to the Faculty of Law at Queen's University, where he teaches in conjunction with his position as an Oxford professor in the philosophy of law). In a comment to the CIJA statement on its website – a comment that has subsequently been removed by CIJA – Professor Les Green noted in response to CIJA's call for the removal of the university's sanction for the event, "[CIJA CEO] Mr Ezrin seriously misunderstands the relationship between a university and the events that occur in it. The organization of a conference, or for that matter the reading of a book, are not actions 'sanctioned' in any relevant sense (i.e., approved, endorsed, etc.) by a university. They are actions 'permitted' by the university. Subject to the usual criminal and civil laws, universities must be places where controversial and, to some, misguided and pernicious ideas may be thoroughly explored and debated. The CIJA should be ashamed of itself for calling for the shut-down of an academic conference of this kind."

100 http://www.cija.ca/campus/cija-statement-on-upcoming-york-university-conference/.

101 Thompson, *No Debate,* 177.

102 Appendix 41: email from Monahan to Shoukri re postponement and finessing things, May 12, 2009, https://circle.ubc.ca/handle/2429/45061.

103 Appendix 42: email from Monahan to Dewitt asking the latter to send the president's statement to Gerald Steinberg, May 21, 2009, https://circle.ubc.ca/handle/2429/45061.

104 Appendix 43: email in which Dewitt forwards Steinberg's proposed article on the conference, May 22, 2009, https://circle.ubc.ca/handle/2429/45061.

105 Ibid.

106 Ibid.

107 Email to Drummond from Shoukri, April 20, 2009.

108 Email from Dewitt to Drummond, December 20, 2011.

109 Thompson, *No Debate,* 236.

110 Ibid., 114.

111 Harry Arthurs, "Academic Freedom: When and Where?," Notes for Panel Discussion, Annual Conference of AUCC, Halifax, October 5, 1995.

112 The other context was the submission by four of my colleagues from York's Centre for Jewish Studies to a March 2009 York University Task Force on Student Life, Learning, and Community in which the Mapping Models conference was critiqued as a component of student life, learning, and community. I do not cover the Task Force in this book; further coverage of it can be found on page 163 and following

of *No Debate;* the briefs by my Jewish studies colleagues and my former Osgoode colleague can be found on page 167 and following.

113 See http://www.hillandknowlton.ca/index.php/about_us.html.

114 Hill and Knowlton Communications Context and Strategy, May 12, 2009.

115 See http://www.jewishtribune.ca/uncategorized/2009/06/24/is-media-barred-from-anti-israel-conference-at-york-university.

116 In his July 2011 feedback to me, Provost Monahan took issue with my characterization of this phone call. He noted that "it is stated [in the factual summary that I provided of what the manuscript would cover] that during the conference call on June 11, 2009 I urged the organizers to 'simply meet what you [Monahan] perceived to be the reasonable request of SSHRC for a report about major or minor changes to the conference program.' The claim that I described the SSHRC request as 'reasonable' is incorrect. In fact, Susan's email written immediately after the conference call states precisely the opposite, namely that Stan Shapson and I expressed the view 'that the matter of the Minister's statement and phone call to SSHRC requesting that our grant application be subject to a second peer review process raises serious concerns ... '" Despite Provost Monahan's recollection of the phone call, I remain faithful to what I recount since I took detailed notes of that conversation.

117 "SSHRC Upholds Funding for York Conference," *Yfile,* June 18, 2009, http://www.yorku.ca/yfile/archive/index.asp?Article=12798.

118 Thompson, *No Debate,* 106-7.

119 Ibid.

120 Ibid., 116-17.

121 Ibid., 143-44.

122 Patrick Martin, "Has the Two-State Ship Sailed?," *Globe and Mail,* June 5, 2009.

123 For two articulate arguments about whether or not the rubric of apartheid is appropriate for Israel/Palestine, see Richard Goldstone, "Israel and the Apartheid Slander," *New York Times,* October 31, 2011; and Richard Falk, "Is Israel Guilty of the Crime of Apartheid?," *Aljazeera,* December 5, 2011.

124 Thompson, *No Debate,* 142-43.

125 Ibid., 256.

Chapter 5: Accountability and Validity

1 Martyn Hammersley and Paul Atkinson, *Ethnography: Principles in Practice,* 3rd ed. (London: Routledge, 2007), 182.

2 Ibid., 182-83.

3 Patrick Monahan, July 2011 feedback, 34.

4 Hammersley and Atkinson, *Ethnography,* 182.

5 Ibid. 183.

6 Ibid.

7 Monahan's "Preliminary Review" was his first response to the concerns that I raised when I presented the dean of Osgoode and the president of York with an earlier version of Chapter 4 of this monograph (aside from a response to the Osgoode Hall Faculty Association that he insisted was "off the record"). He passed this document to me in our meeting of July 13, 2009, in the president's office. The review was "prelim-

inary" to the Iacobucci Review, intended to be the "official" response to the concerns that I raised. The "Preliminary Review" was followed up by a thirty-four-page response in July 2011.

8 Email from Shoukri to Drummond, July 16, 2009.
9 Ann Kavoukian, *Practices No. 16: Maintaining the Confidentiality of Requesters and Privacy Complainants,* Tip Sheet for Government Organizations on Handling Information Number 16, Information and Privacy Commissioner, Ontario, September 1998.
10 Monahan, July 2011 feedback, 32.
11 Kavoukian, *Practices No. 16*.
12 Appendix 44: email from Monahan to Shoukri re terms of reference, July 20, 2009, https://circle.ubc.ca/handle/2429/45061.
13 Appendix 45: memo from Provost Monahan to staff re terms of reference and soliciting information consistent with them, September 2009, https://circle.ubc.ca/handle/2429/45061.
14 See terms of reference for Iacobucci Review, http://www.yorku.ca/yfile/archive/index.asp?Article=13025.
15 Robert C. Post and Matthew W. Finkin, *For the Common Good* (New Haven: Yale University Press, 2009), 154-55.
16 Irving Abella and Harold Tooper, *None Is Too Many: Canada and the Jews of Europe, 1933-1948* (Toronto: Lester and Orpen Dennys, 1986).
17 See http://www.yorku.ca/yfile/archive/index.asp?Article=13025.
18 Email from Drummond to Iacobucci re FIPPA material, March 23, 2010.
19 Email from Iacobucci to Drummond re FIPPA material, March 25, 2010.
20 Email from Professor Ryder to Professor Drummond, December 19, 2011.
21 Letter from the Osgoode Hall Faculty Association, April 26, 2010.
22 Email from Iacobucci to Drummond re the solicitor-client relationship with York University, January 27, 2010.
23 Email from Shoukri confirming that Iacobucci was the university's counsel, February 3, 2010.
24 Letter from the Osgoode Hall Faculty Association, April 26, 2010
25 Thompson, *No Debate,* 286.
26 Iacobucci Report, 30.
27 Thompson, *No Debate,* 287.
28 Iacobucci Report, 32.
29 Thompson, *No Debate,* 288.
30 Iacobucci Report, 1, cited in ibid., 289.
31 Ibid., 289.
32 Ibid.
33 Ibid., 293.
34 Canadian Judicial Council, *Ethical Principles for Judges,* published in 1994 and renewed by endorsement in 2004 by Chief Justice of Canada Beverley McLachlin.
35 Ibid., 1.8.
36 Ibid., 4.1.
37 Ibid.

38 Ibid.
39 Iacobucci Report, 38-40, cited in Thompson, *No Debate,* 292.
40 Ibid., 290 ff.
41 Ibid., 293.
42 Cited in ibid., 185.
43 Ibid., 293-94.
44 Cited in ibid., 186.
45 Ibid., 293.
46 Ibid., 230.
47 Ibid., 207, 213.
48 Ibid., 204.
49 Ibid., 211.
50 Cited in ibid., 221.
51 Patrick Monahan, July 2011 submission, 2.
52 Thompson, *No Debate,* 223.
53 Ibid., 225.
54 Ibid., 226.
55 Cited in ibid., 220.
56 Cited in Ruth Buchanan and Rebecca Johnson, "Getting the Insider's Story Out: What Popular Film Can Tell Us about Legal Method's Dirty Secrets," *Windsor Yearbook of Access to Justice* 20 (2001): 97.
57 Ibid.
58 Footnote to July 2011 feedback.
59 Timothy Mitchell, *Colonizing Egypt* (Berkeley: University of California Press, 1991).
60 Hammersley and Atkinson, *Ethnography,* 16.

Chapter 6: Academic Freedom and the Worthiness of Ideas

1 Excerpt from a submission by an Osgoode professor to the Thompson Review, sent to the Osgoode faculty listserv, October 12, 2009.
2 Email to Osgoode faculty listserv, July 1, 2009. I have discussed some of the ironies of this requirement in the preface.
3 See http://www.cicweb.ca/scene/2009/05/cija-statement-on-upcoming-york-university-conference/.
4 Namely Professor Irving Abella; AVP Dewitt told me and Professor Ryder about Abella's campaign against the conference in a spring 2009 meeting, and the FIPPA record confirms the key role that Abella played behind the scenes with administrators Monahan and Dewitt; see "Abella" in the index to Jon Thompson, *No Debate: The Israel Lobby and Free Speech at Canadian Universities* (Toronto: James Lorimer and Company, 2010).
5 Stanley Fish, *Save the World on Your Own Time* (New York: Oxford University Press, 2008), 97.
6 Ibid., 87. Fish echoes a long-standing view of the essential nature of academic freedom. The 1915 statement on academic freedom by the American Association of University Professors (AAUP) noted that, "in all ... domains of knowledge, the first condition of progress is complete and unlimited freedom to pursue inquiry and

publish its results. Such freedom is the breath in the nostrils of all scientific activity." Cited in Joan W. Scott, "Knowledge, Power, and Academic Freedom," *Social Research* 76, 2 (2009): 458.

7 Leon Wieseltier, "Israel, Palestine, and the Return of the Bi-National Fantasy: What Is Not to Be Done," *New Republic Online,* October 27, 2003.

8 Yossi Sarid, "Netanyahu's Acceptance of My Ideas Only Made Me Angrier," *Ha'aretz,* June 19, 2009.

9 UJA Federation of Greater Toronto, "Submission to the York University Task Force on Student Life, Learning, and Community," July 28, 2009, cited on the Canada-Israel Committee website, http://www.cicweb.ca/scene/2009/07/submission-to-the-york-u-task-force-on-student-life-learning-and-community/.

10 Ian Lustick, "The Conference Must Go On," *National Post,* June 12, 2009. Ironically, it was also a student intern to blame for B'nai Brith's defamatory allegation that we were hosting Holocaust deniers.

11 Ronald Dworkin, "We Need a New Interpretation of Academic Freedom," in *The Future of Academic Freedom,* ed. Louis Menand (Chicago: University of Chicago Press, 1999), 184.

12 Ibid.

13 Ibid., 183. This view of the autonomy of universities from government was also emphatically voiced by former president Marsden of York University in her statement cited in Chapter 3 of this monograph, "On the Autonomy of Universities," http://www.yorku.ca/yfile/archive/index.asp?Article=8670.

14 Robert Post, "The Structure of Academic Freedom," in *Academic Freedom after September 11,* ed. Beshara Douamani (New York: Zone Books, 2006), 61.

15 Ibid., 69; emphasis added.

16 Ibid., 72.

17 Clifford Geertz, *Local Knowledge: Further Essays in Interpretive Anthropology* (New York: Basic Books, 1985), 173.

18 Ibid.

19 David Rabban, "Can Academic Freedom Survive Postmodernism?," *California Law Review* 86, 6 (1998): 1377.

20 See the essays in Louis Menand, *The Future of Academic Freedom* (Chicago: University of Chicago Press, 1999).

21 Carl Ehrlich, Sara Horowitz, Eric Lawee, and Martin Lockshin, "Comments on the Report of the Organizing Committee for the Conference 'Israel/Palestine: Mapping Models of Statehood and Paths to Peace,'" submitted to the Task Force on Student Life and Community, York University, July 2009, 2-3.

22 Ibid., 3.

23 Richard Rorty, "Does Academic Freedom Have Philosophical Presuppositions?," *Academe* 80, 6 (1994): 55.

24 Ibid., 56.

25 Stanley Fish, "Holocaust Denial and Academic Freedom," *Valparaiso University Law Review* 35 (2000-1): 499; Judith Jarvis Thomson, "Ideology and Faculty Selection," *Law and Contemporary Problems* 53, 3 (1990): 155.

26 Jarvis Thomson, "Ideology and Faculty Selection," 159.

27 Ibid., 160.
28 Ibid., 162.
29 Fish, "Holocaust Denial and Academic Freedom," 528.
30 Cited in ibid., 500.
31 Ibid., 502.
32 Ibid., 503.
33 Ibid., 499.
34 Ibid.
35 Ibid., 505.
36 Ibid., 512.
37 Ibid., 518.
38 Rorty, "Does Academic Freedom Have Philosophical Presuppositions?," 58.
39 Fish, "Holocaust Denial and Academic Freedom," 506.
40 Robert M. O'Neil, "Bias, 'Balance,' and Beyond: New Threats to Academic Freedom," *University of Colorado Law Review* 77, 4 (2006): 985.
41 Ibid., 1012-13.
42 Patrick Monahan, Vice-President Academic and Provost, York University, "Building a More Engaged University: Strategic Directions for York University, 2010-2020," April 2010, http://vpap.info.yorku.ca/white-paper/.
43 Ibid., 8.
44 Ibid., 7.
45 Ibid., 57.
46 Patrick Monahan, Vice-President Academic and Provost, York University, White Paper Companion, 3, http://vpap.info.yorku.ca/white-paper/.
47 It is hard to resist the conclusion that what the Mapping Models conference appeared to do was seek the wrong kind of activists and advocates: that is, those whose political visions were not consonant with those of a more powerful and noisy "community group." We engaged local communities in our scholarship – just the wrong ones.
48 Scott, "Knowledge, Power, and Academic Freedom," 461.
49 Post, "The Structure of Academic Freedom," 75.
50 Ibid., 76.
51 Judith Butler, "Academic Norms, Contemporary Challenges: A Reply to Robert Post on Academic Freedom," in *Academic Freedom after September 11,* ed. Beshara Doumani (New York: Zone Books, 2006), 114.
52 Ibid., 123.
53 Edward Said, *Orientalism* (New York: Vintage, 1979); Edward Said, *Culture and Imperialism* (New York: Vintage, 1994).
54 Edward Said and Christopher Hitchens, *Blaming the Victims* (London: Verso, 1986).
55 Fish, *Save the World on Your Own Time,* 80.
56 Ibid., 39.
57 See http://www.yorku.ca/yfile/archive/index.asp?Article=13025.
58 Fish, *Save the World on Your Own Time,* 87 (emphasis added).
59 Ibid., 27.
60 Said, *Orientalism;* Said, *Culture and Imperialism.*

61 Said and Hitchens, *Blaming the Victims.*
62 Fish, *Save the World on Your Own Time,* 120.
63 Ibid., 23.
64 Monahan's "Preliminary Review" was his first response to the concerns that I raised when I presented the dean of Osgoode and the president of York with an earlier version of Chapter 4 of this monograph (aside from a response to the Osgoode Hall Faculty Association that he insisted was "off the record"). He passed this document to me in our meeting of July 13, 2009, in the president's office. The review was "preliminary" to the Iacobucci Review, intended to be the "official" response to the concerns that I raised. The "Preliminary Review" was followed up by a thirty-four-page response in July 2011.
65 Jarvis Thomson, "Ideology and Faculty Selection," 163.
66 Ian Lustick, "The Conference Must Go On," *National Post,* June 12, 2009.
67 This is the language of President Shoukri in his statement on academic freedom in response to the furor regarding the Mapping Models conference. See "President's Statement on Academic Freedom and the Role of the University," York University Media Relations, May 21, 2009, http://www.yorku.ca/mediar/archive/Release.php?Release=1678.
68 Harry Arthurs, "Academic Freedom: When and Where?," Notes for Panel Discussion, Annual Conference of AUCC, Halifax, October 5, 1995.
69 Ibid.
70 Rorty, "Does Academic Freedom Have Philosophical Presuppositions?," 56.

Conclusion

1 Richard Rorty, "Does Academic Freedom Have Philosophical Presuppositions?," *Academe* 80, 6 (1994): 56.
2 Stanley Fish, *Save the World on Your Own Time* (New York: Oxford University Press, 2008), 23.
3 Ibid., 27.
4 See Ari Shavit, "Survival of the Fittest: An Interview with Benny Morris," *Ha'aretz,* January 9, 2004.
5 Natasha Mozgovaya, "Judge Goldstone Defends Role, but Feels Distressed: Former Judge Complains that Close Friends Kept Away from Him and Some Family Members Even Had Reservations about His Cooperation with the UN Human Rights Council," *Ha'aretz,* April 4, 2011.
6 See http://www.guardian.co.uk/world/2010/apr/30/richard-goldstone-south-africa-jews.
7 Natasha Mozgovaya, "Judge Goldstone Defends Role, but Feels Distressed: Former Judge Complains that Close Friends Kept Away from Him and Some Family Members Even Had Reservations about His Cooperation with the UN Human Rights Council," *Ha'aretz,* April 4, 2011.
8 Appendix 14: email from anonymized party re not caring a fig about academic freedom, June 10, 2009, https://circle.ubc.ca/handle/2429/45061.
9 Appendix 4: email to Dean Patrick Monahan complaining about the conference, April 22, 2009, https://circle.ubc.ca/handle/2429/45061.

10 See Appendix 11.

11 See terms of reference for Iacobucci Review, http://www.yorku.ca/yfile/archive/index.asp?Article=13025.

12 Stanley Fish, "Holocaust Denial and Academic Freedom," *Valparaiso University Law Review* 35 (2000-1): 502.

Selected Bibliography

Abowd, Thomas. "Palestinian Refugees and the Palestinian-Israeli Negotiations: An Interview with Salim Tamari" [July 23, 1999]. *Journal of Palestine Studies* 29, 1 (1999): 81.

Abu-Odeh, Lama. "The Case for Binationalism: Why One State – Liberal and Constitutionalist – May Be the Key to Peace in the Middle East." *Boston Review* 26, 6 (2001-2), http://bostonreview.net/BR26.6/abu-odeh.html.

Agha, Hussein, and Robert Malley. "Camp David and After: An Exchange (2. A Reply to Ehud Barak)." *New York Review of Books*, June 13, 2002, http://www.nybooks.com/articles/archives/2002/jun/13/camp-david-and-after-an-exchange-1-an-interview-wi/?pagination=false.

Akram, Susan, and T. Rempel. "Recommendations for Durable Solutions for Palestinian Refugees: A Challenge to the Oslo Framework." *Palestinian Yearbook of International Law* 11 (2000-1): 1.

Arieli, Shaul, Doubi Schwartz, with the participation of Hadas Tagari. *Injustice and Folly: On the Proposals to Cede Arab Localities from Israel to Palestine*. Jerusalem: Floersheimer Institute for Policy Studies, 2006.

Arthurs, Harry. "Academic Freedom: When and Where?" Notes for Panel Discussion, Annual Conference of AUCC, Halifax, October 5, 1995.

Aruri, Naseer, ed. *Palestinian Refugees: The Right of Return*. London: Pluto Press, 2001.

Barry, Brian. "The Consociational Model and Its Dangers." *European Journal of Political Research* 3, 4 (1975): 393.

Benvenisti, Eyal, and E. Zamir. "Private Claims to Property Rights in the Future Israeli-Palestinian Settlement." *American Journal of International Law* 89 (1995): 295.

Bisharat, George E. "Maximizing Rights: The One State Solution to the Palestinian-Israeli Conflict." *Global Jurist* 8, 2 (2008): 1.

Bowen, Jeremy. *Six Days: How the 1967 War Shaped the Middle East.* London: Simon and Schuster, 2003.

Bowling, Gail. *The 1948 Palestinian Refugees and the Individual Right of Return: An International Law Analysis.* 2nd ed. Bethlehem: Badil Resource Center, 2007.

Butler, Judith. "Academic Norms, Contemporary Challenges: A Reply to Robert Post on Academic Freedom." In *Academic Freedom after September 11,* ed. Beshara Doumani. New York: Zone Books, 2006.

David, Joseph E., ed. *The State of Israel: Between Judaism and Democracy.* Jerusalem: Israeli Democracy Institute, 2003.

Dowty, Alan. "Is Israel Democratic? Substance and Semantics in the 'Ethnic Democracy' Debate." *Israel Studies* 4, 2 (1999): 1.

Dworkin, Ronald. "We Need a New Interpretation of Academic Freedom." In *The Future of Academic Freedom,* ed. Louis Menand Chicago: University of Chicago Press, 1999.

Falk, Richard, and David Kretzmer. *The Occupation of Justice: The Supreme Court of Israel and the Occupied Territories.* Albany: SUNY Press, 2002.

Fish, Stanley. "Holocaust Denial and Academic Freedom." *Valparaiso University Law Review* 35 (2000-1): 499.

–. *Save the World on Your Own Time.* New York: Oxford University Press, 2008.

Flapan, Simha. *The Birth of Israel: Myths and Realities.* New York: Pantheon Books, 1987.

Gans, Chaim. *The Limits of Nationalism.* Cambridge, UK: Cambridge University Press, 2003.

Gavison, Ruth. *Israel: A Jewish and Democratic State* [in Hebrew]. Jerusalem: VanLeer and Hakibutz Hameuhad, 1999.

–. "Jewish and Democratic? A Rejoinder to the 'Ethnic Democracy' Debate." *Israel Studies* 4, 1 (1999): 44.

–. "The Jewish State: The Principle Justification and the Desirable Character" [in Hebrew]. *Tkhelet* 13 (2002): 50.

Gelber, Yoav. *Palestine, 1948: War, Escape, and the Emergence of the Palestinian Refugee Problem.* Portland: Sussex Academic Press, 2001.

Ghanem, As'ad, Nadim Rouhana, and Oren Yiftachel. "Questioning 'Ethnic Democracy': A Response to Sammy Smooha." *Israel Studies* 3, 2 (1998): 253.

Hammersley, Martyn, and Paul Atkinson. *Ethnography: Principles in Practice.* 3rd ed. London: Routledge, 2007.

Hanieh, Akram. "The Camp David Papers." *Journal of Palestine Studies* 30, 2 (2001): 75.

Inbar, Efraim, and Ian Lustick. "Israel's Future: The Time Factor." *Israel Studies Forum* 23, 1 (2008): 3.

Jarvis Thomson, Judith. "Ideology and Faculty Selection." *Law and Contemporary Problems* 53, 3 (1990): 155.

Judt, Tony. "Israel: The Alternative." *New York Review of Books,* October 23, 2003, http://www.nybooks.com/articles/archives/2003/oct/23/israel-the-alternative/.

Kattan, Victor. "The Nationality of Denationalized Palestinians." *Nordic Journal of International Law* 74 (2005): 67.

Lakkenberg, Lex. *The Status of Palestinian Refugees in International Law.* Oxford: Clarendon Press, 1998.

Lapidoth, Ruth. "Israel and the Palestinians: Some Legal Issues." *Die Friedens-Warte* [Journal of International Peace and Organization] 76 (2003).

–. "The Right to Return in International Law, with Special Reference to Palestinian Refugees." *Israel Yearbook of Human Rights* 16 (1986): 103.

Lawand, Kathleen. "The Right of Return of Palestinians in International Law." *International Journal of Refugee Law* 8, 4 (1996): 532.

Lustick, Ian. "Abandoning the Iron Wall: Israel and 'the Middle Eastern Muck.'" *Middle East Policy* 15, 3 (2008): 30.

–. "The Cunning of History." *Boston Review* 26, 6 (2001-2), http://bostonreview.net/BR26.6/lustick.html.

–. "Lijphart, Lakatos, and Consociationalism." *World Politics* 50, 1 (1997): 88.

–. "Stability in Deeply Divided Societies: Consociationalism versus Control." *World Politics* 31, 3 (1979): 325.

Lynk, Michael. "Conceived in Law: The Legal Foundations of Resolution 242." *Journal of Palestine Studies* 37, 1 (2007): 7.

Mallison, Thomas W., and Sally V. Mallison. *An International Law Analysis of the Major United Nations Resolutions Concerning the Palestinian Question.* New York: United Nations, 1979.

–. "The Role of International Law in Achieving Justice and Peace in Palestine-Israel." *Journal of Palestine Studies* 3, 3 (1974): 77.

Massad, Joseph. "The Binational State and the Reunification of the Palestinian People." *Global Dialogue* 4, 3 (2002), http://www.worlddialogue.org/content.php?id=240.

Mearsheimer, John, and Stephen Walt. *The Israel Lobby.* New York: Farrar, Straus and Giroux, 2007.

Menand, Louis. *The Future of Academic Freedom.* Chicago: University of Chicago Press, 1999.

Morris, Benny. *The Birth of the Palestinian Refugee Problem Revisited.* Cambridge, UK: Cambridge University Press, 2004.

–. *Righteous Victims: A History of the Zionist-Arab Conflict, 1881-1999.* New York: Knopf, 1999.

Morris, Benny, and Ehud Barak. "Camp David and After – Continued." *New York Review of Books*, June 27, 2002, http://www.nybooks.com/articles/archives/2002/jun/27/camp-david-and-aftercontinued/?pagination=false.

Pappé, Ilan. *Britain and the Arab-Israeli Conflict, 1947-51.* Basingstoke: Macmillan, in association with St. Antony's College, Oxford University, 1988.

–. *The Ethnic Cleansing of Palestine.* Oxford: Oneworld, 2006.

Post, Robert. "The Structure of Academic Freedom." In *Academic Freedom after September 11,* ed. Beshara Douamani. New York: Zone Books, 2006.

Quigley, John. "Displaced Palestinians and a Right of Return." *Harvard International Law Journal* 39 (1998): 171.

–. "International Law and the Palestine Refugees." *Hastings International and Comparative Law Review* 28 (2005): 405.

Rabban, David. "Can Academic Freedom Survive Postmodernism?" *California Law Review* 86, 6 (1998): 1377.

Rabinovich, Itamar. *The Road Not Taken: Early Arab-Israeli Negotiations.* New York: Oxford University Press, 1991.

Rorty, Richard. "Does Academic Freedom Have Philosophical Presuppositions?" *Academe* 80, 6 (1994): 52.

Rouhana, Nadim. "'Jewish and Democratic'? The Price of a National Self-Deception." *Journal of Palestine Studies* 35 (2006): 64.

Rubinstein, Amnon, and Alexander Yakobson. *Israel and the Family of Nations: A Jewish Nation State and Human Rights.* London: Routledge, 2008.

Saideman, Lewis. "Do Palestinian Refugees Have a Right of Return to Israel? An Examination of the Scope of and Limitations on the Right of Return." *Virginia Journal of International Law* 44 (2004): 829.

Scott, Joan. "Knowledge, Power, and Academic Freedom." *Social Research* 76, 2 (2009): 451.

Segev, Tom. *One Palestine, Complete: Jews and Arabs under the British Mandate.* New York: H. Holt, 2001.

Shapira, Anita. *Land and Power: The Zionist Resort to Force, 1881-1948.* Trans. William Templer. New York: Oxford University Press, 1992.

Shiblak, Abbas, and Uri Davis. *Civil and Citizenship Rights of Palestinian Refugees.* Jerusalem: SHAML, 1996.

Shlaim, Avi. *Collusion across the Jordan: King Abdullah, the Zionist Movement, and the Partition of Palestine.* New York: Columbia University Press, 1988.

–. *The Iron Wall: Israel and the Arab World.* London: W.W. Norton, 2001.

Smooha, Sammy. "Ethnic Democracy: Israel as an Archetype." *Israel Studies* 2, 2 (1997): 198.

–. "The Model of Ethnic Democracy: Israel as a Jewish and Democratic State." *Nations and Nationalism* 8, 4 (2002): 475.

Spyer, Jonathan. "Forward to the Past: The Fall and Rise of the One-State Solution." *Middle East Review of International Affairs* 12, 3 (2008): 102.

Tadmor, Yoav. "Comment: The Palestinian Refugees of 1948: The Right to Compensation and Return." *Temple International and Comparative Law Journal* 8 (1994): 403.

Tamari, Salim. "The Binationalist Lure." *Boston Review* 26, 6 (2001-2), http://bostonreview.net/BR26.6/tamari.html.

–. *Palestinian Refugee Negotiations: From Madrid to Oslo II.* (Washington, DC: Institute for Palestine Studies, 1996.

Teveth, Shabtai. *Ben-Gurion and the Palestinian Arabs: From Peace to War.* Oxford: Oxford University Press, 1985.

Usher, Graham. "Bantustanisation or Bi-Nationalism? An Interview with Azmi Bishara." *Race and Class* 37, 2 (1995): 43.

Weiner, Justin. "The Palestinian Refugees' Right to Return and the Peace Process. *Boston College International and Comparative Law Review* 20 (1997): 1.

Wieseltier, Leon. "Israel, Palestine, and the Return of the Bi-National Fantasy: What Is Not to Be Done." *New Republic Online,* October 27, 2003.

Yiftachel, Oren. "Democracy or Ethnocracy: Territory and Settler Politics in Israel/Palestine." *Middle East Report* 207 (1998): 8.

–. *Ethnocracy.* Philadelphia: University of Pennsylvania Press, 2006.

Index

Printed and bound in Canada by Friesens

Set in Futura Condensed and Warnock
by Artegraphica Design Co. Ltd.

Copy editor: Dallas Harrison